MIKE LOWERY

The Illustrator 9 WOW! Book

Sharon Steuer
Steven Gordon
Sandra Alves
with Sandee Cohen

The Illustrator 9 Wow! Book

Sharon Steuer, Steven Gordon, Sandra Alves

Peachpit Press
1249 Eighth Street
Berkeley, CA 94710
510/524-2178
510/524-2221 (fax)

Peachpit Press is a division of Addison Wesley Longman.

Book design: Barbara Sudick
Cover design: Andrew Faulkner, afstudio, with Mimi Heft; Illustration: Nancy Stahl

ISBN 0-201-70453-6
0 9 8 7 6 5 4 3 2

Printed and bound in the United States of America.

Revision Production Credits

Managing Author: Sharon Steuer

Step-by-Step & Gallery Co-author: Steven H. Gordon

Preface, Chapter 1, and Intros Co-author: Sandra Alves

Contributing Writers: Diane Hinze Kanzler, Sandee Cohen, Victor Gavenda

Updating of Lessons and Galleries: Diane Hinze Kanzler

Illustrator 9 Creative Consultant and Kibbitzer: Sandee Cohen

Illustrator 9 Technical Consultants: Jean-Claude Tremblay, Sandee Cohen

Wow! CD-ROM Coordinator: Diane Hinze Kanzler

Wow! CD-ROM Mastering: Victor Gavenda

Wow! Testers: Adam Z Lein, Lisa Jackmore, Ivan Torres, Diane Hinze Kanzler, Linnea Dayton, Victor Gavenda, Jean-Claude Tremblay

Assistant to the Author: Diane Hinze Kanzler

Revisions Copyeditors: Linnea Dayton, Cynthia Baron, Mindi Englart, Victor Gavenda, Whitney Walker

Index: Rosemary Michelle Simpson

Cover Design: Andrew Faulkner, afstudio, with Mimi Heft

Front Cover Illustration: Nancy Stahl

Back Cover Illustrations: Sharon Steuer, Ellen Papciak-Rose with Sandee Cohen

Contents

3

4

Brushes

5

Layers

7

8   **Transparency, Styles & Effects**

9

10

11 Web, Multimedia & Animation

Important: **Read me first!**

Critical print resolution issues

Illustrator's new features require that you manually set the proper resolution for output of images that include transparency or live effects! For details, see the *Transparency* chapter introduction.

What's new in Illustrator 9?

If you're upgrading from a previous version of Adobe Illustrator, take a few minutes to look over the "What's new in Illustrator 9?" Preface (following the "How to Use this Book" section). This summary of new features will direct you to specific sections of this book where you'll find more details on each new feature.

Additional Illustrator training

You can find more than thirty examples of artwork to analyze and experiment with in the Artists folder on the *Wow!* disk. You'll also find detailed lessons in the Training folder, including the *Zen Lessons* (which supplement the *Zen* chapter). These lessons walk you through some basics of working with the Pen tool, Bézier curves, layers and stacking order. If you're new to Illustrator, you may want to begin with a class. Find additional suggested reading in the *Publications* appendix.

This book has been entirely redesigned to help beginning, as well as seasoned, Illustrator users to master the exciting (and sometimes perplexing) new features of Adobe Illustrator 9. You'll find hundreds of new pages of essential production techniques, timesaving tips and beautiful art generously shared by *Illustrator Wow!* artists worldwide. All lessons are deliberately kept short to allow you to squeeze in a lesson or two between clients, and to encourage the use of this book within the confines of a supervised classroom.

In order to keep the content in this book tantalizing to everyone—from novice to expert—I've assumed a reasonable level of competence with basic Mac and Windows concepts, such as opening and saving files, launching applications, copying objects to the clipboard and doing mouse operations. I've also assumed that you've read through "An Overview of Adobe Illustrator" in the beginning of the *User Guide*, and understand the basic functionality of the tools.

I'd love to tell you that you can learn Adobe Illustrator by flipping through the pages of this book, but the reality is that there is no substitute for practice. The good news is, the more you work with Illustrator, the more techniques you'll be able to integrate into your creative process.

Use this book as a reference, a guide for specific techniques or just a source of inspiration. After you've read this book, read it again, and you'll undoubtedly learn something you missed the first time. As I hope you'll discover, the more experienced you become with Adobe Illustrator, the easier it will be to assimilate all the new information and inspiration you'll find in this book.

Happy Illustrating!

Sharon Steuer

How to use this book...

Before you do anything else, read the *Wow! Glossary* on the pull-out quick reference card at the back of the book. The *Glossary* provides definitions for the terms used throughout *The Illustrator 9 Wow! Book* (for example, ⌘ is the Command key for Mac).

WELCOME TO *WOW!* FOR WINDOWS AND MAC

If you already use Adobe Photoshop, you'll see many interface similarities to Illustrator 9. Adobe intends this version of Illustrator to create, in part, a common look and feel across Photoshop, InDesign and Illustrator. The change should make the time you spend learning each program much shorter (especially if you're a newcomer to all three products). Your productivity should also increase across the board once you adjust to the new shortcuts and methodologies (see "Shortcuts and keystrokes" following, and the *Illustrator Basics* chapter).

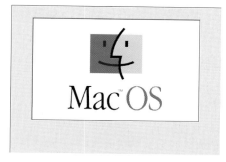

Shortcuts and keystrokes

Because you can now customize keyboard shortcuts, we're eliminating most of the keystrokes references in the book. We will keep keystroke references when it's so standard that we assume you'll keep the default, or when there is no other way to achieve that function (such as Lock All Unselected objects). We'll always give you Macintosh shortcuts first, then the Windows equivalent (⌘-Z/ Ctrl-Z). For help with customizing keyboard shortcuts, and tool and menu navigation (such as single key tool access and Tab to hide palettes), see the *Basics* chapter.

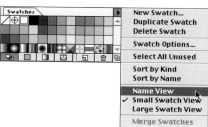

With the All Swatches icon selected and the Option/Alt key pressed, choosing "Name" from the Swatches pop-up

Setting up your palettes

In terms of following along with the lessons in this book, you'll probably want to disable the "Type Area Select" option (see Tip "One option you may not want" in the *Type* chapter). Next, if you want your palettes to look like our palettes, you'll need to set swatches to be sorted by

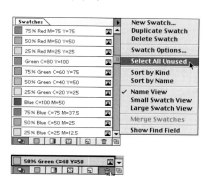

Choosing Select All Unused from the Swatches pop-up; then immediately clicking the Trash icon to safely remove unused swatches

1

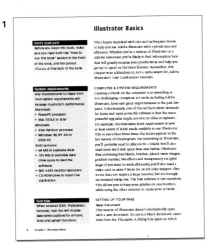

2 *The CD icon indicates that related artwork can be found on the Wow! disk*

Tip boxes

Look for these gray boxes to find Tips about Adobe Illustrator.

Red Tip boxes

The red Tip boxes contain warnings or other essential information.

3

Creating a Simple Object Using the Basic Tools

name: hold down Option (Mac) or Alt (Win) and choose "Name" from the Swatches pop-up menu to list all Swatch views by name (see figures on previous page).

By default, Illustrator sometimes has the habit of filling palettes with excess styles; in order to customize the default settings loaded into new documents, see the Tip "Using Startup documents" in the *Basics* chapter. To clear out an existing Swatches palette of unwanted, unused swatches, first click on the All Swatches icon, then choose "Select All Unused" from the Swatches pop-up, and immediately click the Trash icon to remove these unwanted extras.

HOW THIS BOOK IS ORGANIZED…

You'll find six kinds of information woven throughout this book—all of it up-to-date for Illustrator 9: **Basics**, **Tips**, **Exercises**, **Techniques**, **Galleries** and **References**.

1 Basics. *Illustrator Basics* and *The Zen of Illustrator* qualify as full-blown chapters on basics and are packed with information that distills and supplements your Adobe Illustrator manual and disk. Every chapter starts with a general overview of the basics. Although these sections have been designed so that advanced users of Illustrator can move quickly through them, I strongly suggest that the rest of you read them very carefully. Please keep in mind that this book serves as a supplement to, not a substitute for, your Adobe Illustrator *User Guide*.

2 Tips. When you see this icon ⊙, you'll find related artwork in the Artists folder on the Wow! disk. Look to the information in the gray and red boxes for hands-on Tips that can help you work more efficiently. Usually you can find tips alongside related textual information, but if you're in an impatient mood, you might just want to flip through, looking for interesting or relevant tips. The red arrows ⟶, red outlines and red text found in tips (and sometimes with artwork) have been added to emphasize or further explain a concept or technique.

3 Exercises. (Not for the faint of heart.) I have included step-by-step exercises to help you make the transition to Illustrator technician extraordinaire. *The Zen of Illustrator* chapter and the *Zen Lessons* on the *Wow!* disk are dedicated to helping you master the mechanics (and the soul) of Illustrator. Take these lessons in small doses, in order, and at a relaxed pace. All of the Finger Dances are now customized for Mac and Windows.

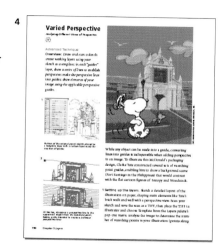

4 Techniques. In these sections, you'll find step-by-step techniques gathered from almost a hundred *Illustrator Wow!* artists. Most *Wow!* techniques focus on one aspect of how an image was created, though I'll often refer you to different *Wow!* chapters (or to a specific step-by-step technique, Tip or Gallery where a technique is introduced) to give you the opportunity to explore a briefly-covered feature more thoroughly. Feel free to start with almost any chapter, but, since each technique builds on those previously explained, try to follow the techniques within each chapter sequentially. Some chapters conclude with **Advanced Technique** lessons, which assume that you have assimilated all of the techniques found throughout the chapter. *Advanced Techniques* is an entire chapter dedicated to advanced tips, tricks and techniques.

5 Galleries. The Gallery pages consist of images related to techniques demonstrated nearby. Each Gallery piece is accompanied by a description of how the artist created that image, and may include steps showing the progression of a technique detailed elsewhere. *Illustrator & Other Programs* consists almost entirely of Gallery pages to give you a sense of Illustrator's flexibility.

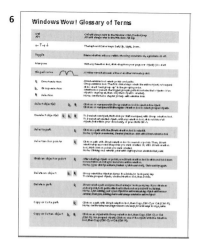

6 References. *Technical Notes, Resources, Publications* and *Artists* appendixes, *Glossaries* and *General Index* can be found in the back of this book. In addition, we'll occasionally direct you to the *User Guide* when referring to specific information already well-documented in the *Adobe Illustrator User Guide*.

What's New in Illustrator 9?

by Sandra Alves

Top 5 new features!

Apply transparency attributes
- Opacity slider
- Blending modes
- Opacity masks
- Advanced knockout controls

Create effects
- Transformations
- Pathfinders & Shapes
- Filter type operations

Save and apply styles
- Save graphic appearance attributes as a style (Styles palette)
- Apply a style to an object, group of objects or layer
- Replace styles to efficiently update applied appearances

(For more see the *Transparency, Styles & Effects* chapter)

Use Layers more efficiently
- Content-generated thumbnails
- Hierarchical view of individual objects on a layer
- Nested sublayers
- Target and selection indicators
- Move appearances from one object, group or layer to another object, group or layer

(For more see the *Layers* chapter)

Save for web optimizations
- Experiment with different optimization settings and compare them 2-up or 4-up before saving your final file
- Manage the number of colors

(For more see the *Web* chapter)

The extensive list of new features in Adobe Illustrator 9 means that we have a lot to cover in this edition of *The Illustrator Wow! Book*. To orient you, we'll begin with an overview, followed by more in-depth descriptions of each feature. As always, this book is full of great tips on how to become more productive and work more efficiently with Illustrator.

ADOBE UNDERSTANDS

Adobe has been responding to requests and suggestions from designers. With every version of Illustrator, tasks become easier to perform and the program becomes more tightly integrated with, and focused on, what designers need and want to accomplish.

Whether you are upgrading to a newer version, or using Illustrator for the first time, spend some time with Tool Tips enabled. They not only provide short tool descriptions, they help you learn shortcuts. Tool Tips, on by default, can be *disabled* in Edit: Preferences: General.

NEW DOCUMENT DIALOG

Right away, you'll notice something different about Illustrator 9. It doesn't automatically open with a blank document. In the New Document dialog (File: New) you need to decide what color mode (or *color space*) to work in, and what size you want the document to be. When you select a color mode, you are also specifying which Startup page will be used when you open your document. There are two Startup documents (application folder: Plug-ins), one for RGB and one for CMYK. The Startup page tells the application what types of filters, swatches, gradients, patterns, styles or brushes will be loaded and available. Once open, the document's color mode is always displayed in the title bar along with the view mode (see the *Illustrator Basics* chapter for more information on setting up new documents).

KEYBOARD SHORTCUTS

Adobe appears to be committed to making their applications easier to use. The shortcuts for this release, for the most part, are the same as the last version. If you are comfortable with Illustrator 8's keyboard shortcuts, or have been reluctant to upgrade from an older version because you haven't wanted to learn new shortcuts, you don't have to worry. With the introduction of the Keyboard Shortcut editor (Edit: Keyboard Shortcuts) you can remain as efficient as ever. Simply customize Illustrator's shortcuts by assigning the command of your choice to a task (tool or menu item), or load a file that contains the desired predefined set of shortcuts (see the *Basics* chapter). Illustrator ships with an Adobe Illustrator 6 set of shortcuts (application folder: Keyboard Shortcuts). Also see the *Wow!* disk for more custom sets.

COLOR MANAGEMENT AND SOFT-PROOFING

Have you ever been surprised to find that the on-screen colors in your Illustrator file look completely different when they're printed or viewed on other monitors? Every monitor display is slightly different, as is each platform. Colors will always appear somewhat darker on a PC and lighter on a Mac. Color fidelity also depends on how well the monitors are calibrated and/or how old they are.

Color management and soft-proofing have gotten a great deal of consideration in this release (see the Basics chapter). Define your RGB and CMYK working spaces (see Tip "Enable color management" to the left) and save ICC Color Profiles with your documents. If you give your settings file to your co-workers as well, your files will basically look the same on any computer.

Illustrator can simulate on-screen (soft-proof) what the final printed piece will look like, but it's still not possible to emulate the separation printer (offset press) on the composite printer (desktop printer). You can find the soft-proofing commands in the View menu. First, enable your color settings (Edit: Color Settings), then select your soft-proofing conditions (View: Proof Setup). Once you

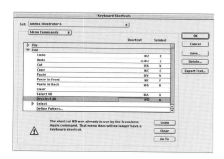

Calibrate your monitor!

To optimally color manage your files in Illustrator, you must:

- Calibrate your monitor.
- Create a monitor profile.
- Assign the monitor profile at the OS level.

Adobe Gamma and Apple Color-Sync are examples of software-based monitor calibration. Use one or the other, but not both. You will obtain better results from a system for measuring color temperatures that uses a suction puck attached to the screen.

Enable color management

By default, Illustrator's color management is disabled. To start color managing your files and to enable soft-proofing, select Edit: Color Settings and select a predefined settings file, or make your choices from the pop-up menus (see the *User Guide* for more info). After enabling color management, select a soft-proofing setup by choosing an alternate color mode or a specific device from View: Proof Setup, then enable soft-proofing select View: Proof Colors.

Document's color profile

To display the document's current color profile, select Document Color Profile from the pop-up menu in the lower left corner of the document window, next to the zoom level.

Pixel Preview: Off

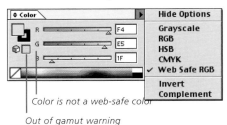

Pixel Preview: On

Web Safe RGB Color palette

Color is not a web-safe color

Out of gamut warning

RGB Color palette

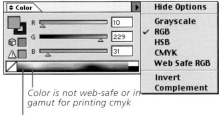

Color is not web-safe or in gamut for printing cmyk

Out of gamut warnings

have defined the proof setup, enable or disable soft-proofing by toggling Proof Colors on or off. This feature only enables a *preview* of what the colors would look like if they were converted to the profile selected in the Proof Setup dialog. The colors in your file are never automatically converted. You can change your proof setup at any time without damaging or permanently converting the colors in your file. By enabling Proof Colors, you are only changing how those colors are displayed on the monitor.

With the use of the ICC Color Profiles and Proof Setup, you can experiment with how colors will look when they're converted from one space to another, or if they're printed under different press conditions. If you do decide you need to change the assigned profile of a file (retag the document), select Edit: Assign Profile. You can retag a document or assign a new profile only within the same color space. Retagging the color information does not convert the document colors. To view the document's current color profile, see Tip "Document's color profile" to the right.

When you change your document from one color space to another (File: Document Color Mode), you *are* converting the colors using the working spaces you chose in Color Settings.

WEB SUPPORT

For those of you designing graphics for the web, this release offers some really great web features. These new web features have been tightly integrated with other applications that support web file formats. For example, there is now vector-based support for web formats such as Flash (SWF), and SVG (Scalable Vector Graphics). Other enhanced formats include optimized GIF and JPEG (supported in the File: Save for Web dialog). If you are familiar with Adobe ImageReady or Photoshop, you will feel right at home with the new Save for Web dialog, where you can compare different optimization settings before saving an image. Other web features include a Pixel Preview, which is a raster preview of your vector artwork, web-safe color swatches, a web-safe color picker and polygonal image map areas. A new item, Release to Layers (Layers palette pop-up menu) is a quick and simple way to create an animation (see the *Web* chapter).

Preparing for scalable web art

SVG is a file format that allows you to view scalable vector graphics in your web browser. You must know JavaScript syntax to use this palette. Similar to the Flash plug-in that is required to view Flash files, the SVG plug-in or SVG Viewer must be installed on your computer to view SVG graphics. (See the *Web, Multimedia & Animation* chapter for a full description of this feature.)

TRANSPARENCY AT LAST!

It's hard to believe it has taken Adobe this long to give us transparency. However, it appears they took this long because they wanted to do it right. They didn't *just* give us the ability to alter the opacity of an object or blend modes, they gave us a mini Photoshop, right inside Illustrator. This feature is so robust, we've devoted an entire chapter to discuss how objects, groups and layers interact with transparency. We really can't do justice to this feature in the overview, so we're only going to mention the highlights. (See the *Transparency* chapter for details.)

The simplest way to apply transparency is to select an object and adjust the opacity slider in the Transparency palette. Move the object on top of another object and you'll see the transparent interaction between the two objects.

Next, just as you can in Photoshop, select an object and change the way it blends with other objects by choosing a blend mode other than Normal. Blending modes behave a little differently depending on the color space (see Tip "Blending modes" on this page).

If you really want to explore the more powerful aspects of transparency, expand the palette to show more options via the palette pop-up menu, or click on the double arrows located on the palette tab. In the expanded

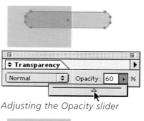

Adjusting the Opacity slider

Adjusting Blending Mode & Opacity slider

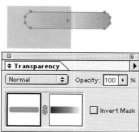

Using an Opacity Mask to fine tune amounts of transparency

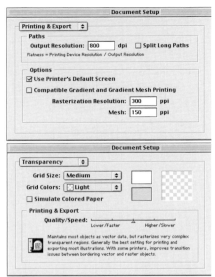

Settings in both the Printing & Export and Transparency panels of File: Document Setup will affect how your document will print if it contains any transparency attributes or effects

Align with Use Preview Bounds "On" or checked

Transparency Attributes of Focal stroke

Focus of appearance is on the stroke

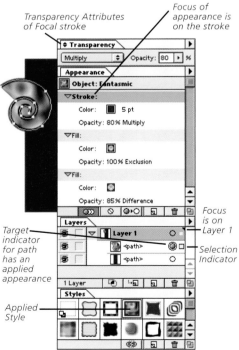

Focus is on Layer 1

Target indicator for path has an applied appearance

Selection Indicator

Applied Style

palette, you can create opacity masks, isolate blending, create knockout groups and/or use some combination of all of these options to create transparency.

IMPORTANT: *When you're using transparency (Transparency palette or Effects), you are creating resolution* dependent *artwork! Do not take this matter lightly. Depending on how overlaying objects and neighboring objects (including text) interact with transparent areas, they too might become resolution* dependent. *There is a chance these objects will be rasterized when the file is printed. Rasterization depends on your settings in the Document Setup dialog (see the* Transparency *chapter).*

PALETTES WORK TOGETHER

The Layers, Appearance, Transparency and Styles palettes work best as companions to one another. You can examine how an applied style was constructed by looking at its specific components in the Appearance palette. You can view the Layers palette to see which objects, groups of objects or whole layers have appearances applied to them (a gradient-filled appearance icon is next to the items). Between the Appearance and Layers palettes, there are quite a few new icons to learn.

Layers palette

The most noticeable change to the Layers palette is the ability to view the layer contents in a thumbnail similar to Photoshop's. In previous versions, you could show or hide the contents of a single layer, but there wasn't a quick way to visually scan each layer's contents. Select Palette Options from the palette pop-up menu to change the size of the thumbnails, or to hide them.

The second change to the Layers palette is the ability to view the hierarchy (stacking order) of individual objects, groups of objects, and images contained on a single layer. By default, the contents of a layer are not fully disclosed. To view the contents within a layer, you need to click on the disclosure triangle located to the left of the layer thumbnail. Once the arrow is pointing down, all the container layer contents are visible. How you view the contents is also determined in the Palette Options.

Anyone creating inserts will like the new Sublayer feature. Create sublayers within a layer by clicking on the Create New Sublayer button at the bottom of the palette. (For more information, see the *Layers* chapter.)

Appearance palette

All objects or images have physical characteristics associated with them. The combination of these characteristics gives the objects, group of objects or layers an appearance. The appearance consists of strokes, fills, transparency values and effects. For help with the Appearance palette, see the *Transparency, Styles & Effects* chapter.

Styles palette

A style is a collection of appearance attributes, defined within the Appearance palette, that can be saved and applied to an object, group of objects or a layer. Styles can contain multiple effects, color fills, strokes and transparency values. The styles are *live*, in that they can be altered and replaced. (You'll find Replace "*Style Name*" in the Appearance palette pop-up menu, not in the Styles palette pop-up menu.) As a result, all artwork using a style will be dynamically updated. The ability to save and apply a style can greatly increase your productivity (see the *Transparency, Styles & Effects* chapter).

THERE IS NEVER A SHORTAGE OF PALETTES
Align palette

A new addition to the Align palette is the ability to select the key object. All selected objects are then aligned or distributed based on the position of this object. Clicking (not Shift-clicking) on an object after all the objects have been selected makes that object the key object. Other enhancements to this palette are a specified distribution space (Show Options from the palette pop-up menu) and Use Preview Bounds (palette pop-up menu). With Use Preview Bounds on or checked, the alignments and

Show Color palette

When the Color palette isn't showing, an alternative to selecting Show Color from the Window menu is to simply click on either the Fill or Stroke proxy in the Toolbox to open the palette.

ALVES

Using a grayscale image as an opacity mask; then applying a style or appearance attributes to the background object

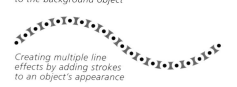

Creating multiple line effects by adding strokes to an object's appearance

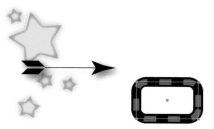

Using the effects found in the submenu Stylize to create inner and outer glows, along with drop shadows and soft feathered edges; adding different arrowheads to the start and end of a path; adding rounded corners to a rectangle

Choosing Polygon for an Image Map area

Convert to Shape text buttons

Using Simplify path to distort the text characters on type that has been converted to outlines

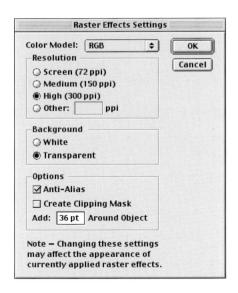

Raster Effects Settings affect the entire document; therefore, changing any of the settings will affect all objects that currently have applied effects. If you want some effects to have different rasterization settings, you'll have to flatten the artwork at one setting before making any changes to this dialog.

 Lasso tool

 Direct-Select Lasso tool

distributions will factor in the stroke values and/or effects applied to an object. If it is off or unchecked, your alignment or distribution is calculated using only the path.

SIMPLIFY PATH

The new Simplify command (Object: Path: Simplify) is a more automated and global version of the Smooth tool. It reduces the number of anchor points on one or more selected paths. In addition, you can make curved line segments into straight lines by checking the Straight Lines option. Best of all, you can view the original unaffected selection at the same time you're viewing the changes by checking Show Original (see *Lines, Fills & Colors* chapter).

EFFECTS

Not to be confused with the Filter menu, the items under Effects are *dynamic* versions of some of the filters (including the pathfinder filters) along with quite a few new items. Effects are non-destructive and can be applied, changed or removed from an object, group of objects or a layer at any time. Because the effects are dynamic, they can always be edited, adjusted (Effects: Rasterize: Raster Effects Setting) or removed, even after the file has been saved. (For more on effects, see the *Transparency, Styles & Effects* chapter.)

Converting Shapes

Shapes are considered *dynamic* because they too can be altered at any time. If you have made a rectangle and then decide you need an ellipse, all you have to do is convert the object to the new shape (Effect: Convert to Shape). Buttons can be made effortlessly from any path, including text, and changed at any time. (For more on Convert to Shape, see the *Transparency, Styles & Effects* chapter.)

LASSO TOOL

The Lasso tools in Illustrator function a bit differently from other Lasso tools you may have encountered. You still make selections by clicking and dragging around an area. However, while the Lasso tool in Photoshop creates a freeform selection of pixels, the Lasso tools in Illustrator select individual anchor points or objects.

The Direct-select Lasso tool (with the open arrow) in Illustrator selects anchor points by dragging around them without selecting unwanted points or objects. In past versions of Illustrator you could marquee around anchor points to select them, but when you had Use Area Select checked in Preferences you could accidentally select entire objects and move them as you clicked and dragged. Now, with the Lasso tool, you only select the specific points you encircle. This tool is an excellent choice for selecting nodes of a gradient mesh.

If you want to completely select an object or multiple objects, use the Lasso tool (with the solid arrow). Again, you click and drag around anchor points with the tool, but entire objects are selected instead of individual anchor points. Clicking and dragging across an object with the Lasso tool will also select the entire object. These tools are great for selecting text as well.

EDITABLE TEXT

You can now export your Illustrator file in PSD format and open it in Photoshop. As long as you have Editable Text checked, any *Point*-type created in Illustrator will now be treated as editable text when the file is opened in Photoshop. This feature does have limitations. You cannot *round trip* the file back to Illustrator and continue to edit the text. Once the file has been saved within Photoshop, the text is converted to a rasterized image and is no longer an editable vector object (see the *Type* chapter).

TOOL OPTIONS

The Eyedropper tool can now copy the formatting of a graphic style, and the Paint-bucket tool can be used to apply the graphic style to an object. To predetermine what appearance attributes the Eyedropper samples and the Paint-bucket applies, double-click either tool to open the Options dialog (see the *Lines, Fills & Colors* chapter).

If you are missing fonts when you open a document, click the Obtain Fonts button in the Font Problems dialog. This will launch your Browser and take you directly to the Adobe website where you can purchase the font. Once you have purchased and installed the font, reopen your file.

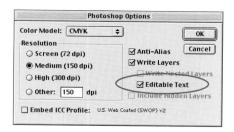

To continue to edit your point-text in Photoshop, make sure you check Editable Text

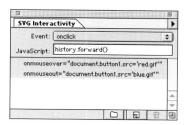

Selecting an object, assigning JavaScript event handlers and then exporting to SVG file format

Illustrator Basics

1

Illustrator Basics

Don't start yet!

Before you begin this book, make sure you read both the "How to Use This Book" section in the front of the book, and the pullout *Glossary* at the back of the book.

System requirements

Any improvements to these minimum system requirements will increase Illustrator's performance.

Macintosh:
- PowerPC processor
- Mac OS 8.5 or later

Windows:
- Intel Pentium processor
- Windows 98, NT 4.0 or 2000 OS

Both systems:
- 64 MB of available RAM
- 105 MB of available hard drive space to load the software
- 800 x 600 monitor resolution
- CD-ROM drive to install the application.

Tool tips

When enabled (Edit: Preferences: General), tool tips will display descriptive captions for all icons, tools and certain functions.

This chapter is packed with tips and techniques chosen to help you use Adobe Illustrator with optimal ease and efficiency. Whether you're a veteran of Illustrator or a relative newcomer, you're likely to find information here that will greatly increase your productivity and help you get up to speed on the latest features. Remember, this chapter is an addendum to, not a replacement for, Adobe Illustrator's *User Guide*.

COMPUTER & SYSTEM REQUIREMENTS

Creating artwork on the computer is as rewarding as it is challenging. Computer art tools, including Adobe Illustrator, have seen great improvements in the past few years. Unfortunately, one of the sad facts about demands for faster and more powerful software is that the more powerful upgrades might not run on older computers. For example, the minimum RAM requirement is now at least 64MB of RAM made available to run Illustrator. This is more than three times the RAM required in the last version of the program. For rasterizing in Illustrator, you'll probably need to allocate 90–120MB. You'll also need more hard disk space than ever before: Illustrator files containing live blends, brushes, placed raster images, gradient meshes, live effects and transparency are quite large! If you want to work efficiently, you'll also need a video card or extra VRAM for 24-bit color support. Illustrator does not require a large monitor, but we strongly recommend using one. The best solution is two monitors. This allows you to keep your palettes on one monitor, while using the other monitor to create your artwork.

SETTING UP YOUR PAGE
New Document

This version of Illustrator doesn't automatically open with a new document. To create a blank document, select New from the File menu. A dialog box opens in which you will select the document color space (CMYK or RGB) and the Artboard Size (the document dimensions). The default page size is 612 pts x 792 pts, which is equivalent to 8.5 x 11 inches. Illustrator will no longer allow you to create new art that uses both CMYK and RGB colors in the same document.

The Artboard

A box with a solid black outline defines the artboard dimensions and the final document size. The dotted line indicates the page margins, which represent the printable area of the current selected printer. Double-click the Hand tool to fit your image to the current window. Use View: Hide Page Tiling to hide the dotted lines. Use the Page tool to click-drag the dotted-line page parameters around the Artboard; only objects within the dotted line will print to your printer.

Document Setup

Once you have created your new document you should make a habit of opening the Document Setup dialog box (File: Document Setup). Here you change the size, orientation and view of the artboard. You also determine the output, rasterization and mesh resolution settings, as well as adjusting the print quality of a document containing transparency, (see the *Transparency, Styles & Effects* chapter).

To match the artboard to your current printer, make sure Use Page Setup is enabled (default is on) and choose from one of the pop-up presets, or set the size. This will switch your paper size to "Custom." The maximum size can be as large as 227" x 227".

Page Setup

Use Page Setup if you want to change the paper size and page orientation for the currently selected printer. Select your desired page size from the Paper Size pop-up menu, and choose portrait or landscape orientation. Only the paper sizes your target printer can support will display in the Paper Size pop-up.

A zoomed-out view of the Artboard

Using startup documents

In your Plug-ins folder (in the Adobe Illustrator folder) are two files called "Adobe Illustrator Startup_CMYK" and "Adobe Illustrator Startup_RGB"; these files automatically load information into the application—such as colors, patterns, brushes and gradients—when you open a new document. To create a *custom* Startup file, make a duplicate of the original and move the original to a safe place (out of the plug-ins folder). Open the copy from within Illustrator, add or subtract styles from this document, then save— the next time you launch Illustrator, this Startup file will determine the set of styles available to new files. (For more details see the *User Guide.*)

Hint: *You can make different Startup files for each project!*

If you double-click the Scale tool, you can resize your selection with or without altering line weights:

- To scale a selection, while also scaling line weights, make sure to enable the Scale Strokes & Effects checkbox.
- To scale a selection while maintaining your line weights, disable Scale Strokes & Effects.
- To decrease line weights (50%) without scaling objects, first scale the selection (200%) with Scale Strokes & Effects disabled. Then scale (50%) with it enabled. Reverse to increase line weights.

STEUER

Changing keyboard shortcuts

To assign a shortcut to a menu item or tool, select Edit: Keyboard Shortcuts. Making any changes will rename the set "Custom." If you choose a shortcut already in use, you will get a warning that it is currently being used and that reassigning it will remove it from the item it is currently assigned to. When you exit the dialog you will be asked to save your *custom* set. You can't overwrite a *preset*.

There are times when you want to change the size of your artboard. Commonly, you might be creating a large image that you'll eventually print to an imagesetter, but which first needs to be proofed on your local laser printer. For Mac only, you have the option to scale your image in relation to the Page Setup by reducing the image size to fit your current printer's paper size. Alternatively, you can enlarge your Page Setup to tile your image onto smaller pages. Then you can paste the sheets together to simulate the larger page size. This is a terrific way to scale something quickly to see how it looks when printed smaller or larger. A 4" line of a 4-pt weight, printed at 25% reduction (the maximum you can reduce), will print as a 1", 1-pt line. In addition, Page Setup only scales your image in relation to the current printing setup. It won't affect the size of the image when placed into another program or document.

Note: *The Document Setup can be different from the Page Setup. If you change one, you should update the other.*

MAKING YOUR MOVES EASIER

Look over this section to make sure you're aware of the many ways to select tools and access features. Learning these simple techniques will free you from mousing to the toolbox or using the pull-down menus.

Single key tool-selection and navigation

Need to access a tool? Press a key. Press "T" to choose the Type tool, "P" for the Pen tool, and so on. Choose any tool in the toolbox by pressing its single-key equivalent. To learn the default single-key equivalent for your tools, with Show Tool Tips enabled (by default this is on), hold the cursor over any tool in the toolbox, and its single-key shortcut will appear in parentheses next to the tool name (toggle the Tool Tip option in Edit: Preferences: General).

In older versions of Illustrator, you could access hidden tools that are part of the same tool set by pressing the Shift key before pressing the single key until the desired tool appeared. For example, to access the Star tool, you would have pressed Shift-L until the Star tool was selected. With the introduction of Keyboard Shortcuts (Edit menu) this no longer works, but now you can assign your tools to any key or combination that you like.

Note: *Single-key navigation won't work inside a text block.*

Keyboard shortcuts

To change a shortcut for a tool or menu item, open the Keyboard Shortcut dialog (Edit: Keyboard Shortcuts). Making a change to a shortcut will change the *Set* name to "Custom." When you're finished making changes and want to exit the dialog box, you will be asked to save your shortcuts to a new file. This file will be saved in the Illustrator application folder and will end in ".kys". As long as these file types are located in the application folder they will be available as a choice in the *Set* pop-up menu. In addition, every time you make any changes to a saved set (not a default preset) you'll be asked if you want to overwrite that set. You can also use the Save button to create a new keyboard shortcut file. Click the Export Text button if you need a text file as a reference for a specific set of shortcuts or need to print them.

Note: *You cannot customize any palette items such as the Pathfinder filters or palette pop-up menu items.*

Context-sensitive menus

If you're not already familiar with context-sensitive menus, you might find them a great timesaver. Windows users merely click the right mouse button. If you're on a Mac, press the Control key while you click and hold the mouse button. In both cases a menu pops up (specific to the tool or item you are working with) providing you with an alternative to the regular pull-down menus.

Tear-off palettes

The Illustrator toolbox lets you *tear off* subsets of tools so you can move the entire set to another location. Click on a tool with a pop-up menu, drag the cursor to the arrow end of the pop-up and release the mouse.

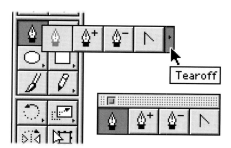

Tear-off tool palettes

Changing measurement units

To set units of measurement for rulers, palettes and some dialog boxes or filters, choose File: Document Setup. To set units for *new* documents, change units in General Preferences.

Note: *Control-click (Mac), or right mouse-click (Win) the rulers to select alternate units.*

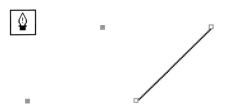

Clicking with the Pen tool to create anchor points for straight lines

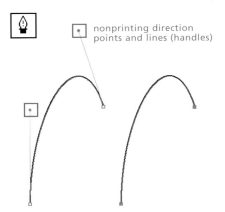

nonprinting direction points and lines (handles)

Click-dragging with the Pen tool to create anchor points and pulling out direction lines for curves

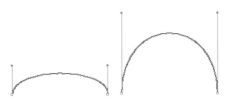

When direction handles are short, curves are shallow; when handles are long, curves are deep

The length and angle of the handles determine the gesture of the curves

WORKING WITH POSTSCRIPT OBJECTS
Anchor points, lines and Bézier* curves

Adobe uses its own language, PostScript, to mathematically describe each of the objects you create in Illustrator. Instead of using pixels to draw shapes, Illustrator creates objects made up of points, called "anchor points." They are connected by curved or straight outlines called "paths," and are visible if you work in Outline (formerly Artwork) mode (View: Outline). The PostScript language describes information about the location and size of each path, as well as its dozen or so attributes, such as its fill color, and its stroke weight and color. Because you are creating objects, you'll be able to change the order in which they stack. You'll also be able to group objects together so you can select them as if they were one object, and even ungroup them later, if you wish.

If you took geometry, you probably remember that the shortest distance between two points is a straight line. In Illustrator, this rule translates into each line being defined by two anchor points you create by clicking with the Pen tool.

In mathematically describing rectangles and ellipses, Illustrator computes the center, length of the sides or the radius, based on the total width and height you specify. For more complex shapes involving freeform curves, Adobe Illustrator allows you to use the Pen tool to create Bézier curves, defined by nonprinting anchor points (which literally anchor the path at that point), and direction points (which define the angle and depth of the curve). To make these direction points easier to see and manipulate, Illustrator connects each direction point to its anchor point with a nonprinting direction line, also called a "handle." The direction points and handles are visible when you're creating a path with the Pen tool or editing the path with the Direct-selection tool. While all of this might sound complicated, manipulating Bézier curves can prove quite intuitive. Mastering these curves, though initially awkward, is the heart and soul of using Illustrator.

* Named after the software engineer who pioneered its use, Pierre Bézier

More about Bézier curves

If you're new to Bézier curves, you should go through the Adobe training materials. The *Wow!* disk includes several "Zen" practice lessons that will help you fine-tune your Bézier capabilities (in the Training folder).

Many graphics programs include Béziers, so learning to master the Pen tool, though challenging at first, is very important. Friskets in Corel Painter, paths in Photoshop, and the outline and extrusion curves of many 3D programs all use the Bézier curve.

The key to learning Béziers is to take your initial lessons in short doses and stop if you get frustrated. Designer Kathleen Tinkel describes Bézier direction lines as "following the gesture of the curve." This artistic view should help you to create fluid Bézier curves.

Some final rules about Bézier curves

- The length and angle of the handles "anticipate" the curves that will follow.
- The length of the handles is equal to approximately one-third the length of the curve, if it were straightened.
- To ensure that the curve is smooth, place anchor points on either side of an arc, not in between.
- The fewer the anchor points, the smoother the curve will look and the faster it will print.
- Adjust a curve's height and angle by dragging the direction points, or grab the curve itself to adjust its height.

WATCH YOUR CURSOR!

Illustrator's cursors change to indicate not only what tool you have selected, but also which function you are about to perform. If you watch your cursor, you will avoid the most common Illustrator mistakes.

If you choose the Pen tool:

- **Before you start,** your cursor displays as the Pen tool with "×" indicating that you're starting a new object.

- **Once you've begun your object,** your cursor changes to

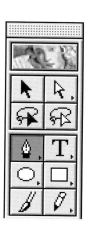

Starting an object

Adding a point

Removing a point

Creating a corner (when over an existing point)

Continuing from an anchor point

Joining two line segments

Closing an object

Basic cursor feedback for the Pen tool, (P)

Illustrator paths on your screen

Edit: Preferences: General: Anti-aliased Artwork, helps paths (including type) appear more accurately drawn to the screen. By default it is on, however it may slow down screen redraws on large files. If you are experiencing problems, try switching it off. Anti-alias Artwork *on* is great for doing screen shots but not so great for thin line weights.

Anti-alias Artwork - Off

Anti-alias Artwork - On

Pen tool (P)

Add-anchor-point tool (+)

Delete-anchor-point tool (-)

Convert-anchor-point tool (Shift C)

a regular Pen. This indicates that you're about to add to an existing object.

- **If your cursor gets close to an existing anchor point,** it will change to a Pen with "–" indicating that you're about to delete the last anchor point! If you click-drag on top of that anchor point, you'll redraw that curve. If you hold the Option (Mac)/Alt (Win) key while you click-drag on top of the point, you'll pull out a new direction line, creating a corner (like the petals of a flower). If you click on top of the point, you'll collapse the outgoing direction line, allowing you to attach a straight line to the curve.

- **If your cursor gets close to an end anchor point of an object,** it will change to a Pen with "o" to indicate that you're about to "close" the path. If you do close the path, then your cursor will change back to a Pen with "×" to indicate that you're beginning a new object.

- **If you use the Direct-selection tool to adjust the object as you go,** make sure that you look at your cursor when you're ready to continue your object. If it's still a regular Pen, then continue to place the next point, adding to your object. If the Pen tool has "×" (indicating that you are about to start a new object), then you must redraw your last point. As you approach this last anchor point, your cursor will change to a Pen with "/"; click and drag over this last point to redraw the last curve. To form a corner on the point as you draw, hold down your Option (Mac)/Alt (Win) key to click-drag out a new direction line.

BÉZIER-EDITING TOOLS

The group of tools you can use to edit Illustrator paths are called Bézier-editing tools. To access them, click and hold the Pen, Pencil or Scissors tool and drag to select one of the other tools. You can also tear off this palette. (To learn about *filters* that edit, see details on Pathfinder filters in the *Lines* chapter.)

- **The Pen tool and Auto Add/Delete** can perform many functions. Auto Add/Delete, when enabled (General Preferences), allows the Pen tool to change automatically to the Add-anchor-point tool when the tool is over a selected path segment, or to the Delete-anchor-point tool when over an anchor point. To temporarily disable the Auto Add/Delete function of the Pen tool, hold down the Shift key. If you don't want the path to constrain to an angle, release the Shift key prior to releasing the mouse.

- **The Convert-anchor-point tool,** found hidden within the Pen tool (default is Shift-C), lets you convert an anchor point on a path from a smooth curve to a corner point by clicking on the anchor point. To convert it from a corner point to a smooth curve, click-drag on the anchor point counterclockwise to pull out a new direction handle (or twirl the point until it straightens out the curve). To convert from a smooth curve to a hinged curve (two curves hinged at a point), grab the direction point and Option (Mac)/Alt (Win)-drag it to the new position. With the Pen tool selected, you can temporarily access the Convert-anchor-point tool by pressing the Opt/Alt key.

- **The Add-anchor-point tool,** accessible from the Pen pop-up menu or by pressing +, adds an anchor point to a path at the location where you click.

- **The Delete-anchor-point tool,** accessible from the Pen pop-up menu or by pressing –, deletes an anchor point when you click *directly* on the point.
  Note: *If you select the Add/Delete-anchor-point tools by pressing + or –, you must press P to get the Pen tool.*

- **The Pencil tool** reshapes a path when Edit selected paths is checked in the tools preferences. Select a path and draw on or close to the path to reshape it.

- **The Smooth tool** merely smoothes points on a path, keeping the original shape of the path intact.

Tool tolerance options

Drawing freehand while holding a mouse or even a digital pen can be less than elegant. The Pencil, Smooth and Brush tools contain options that can help you to create more types of paths, ranging from very realistic to more shapely and graceful ones, without the constant need to adjust anchor points. Double-click on the tool to view the options.

- **Fidelity:** Increases or decreases the distance between anchor points on the path created or edited. The smaller the number, the more points that will make up the path and vice versa.

- **Smoothness:** The smoothness option varies the percentage of smoothness you'll see as you create and edit paths. Use a lower percentage of smoothness for more realistic lines and brush strokes, and a higher percentage for less realistic but more elegant lines.

Note: *Closing Pencil and Brush tool paths is a bit awkward. If you hold down the Option (Mac)/Alt (Win) key when you are ready to close a path, a straight line segment will be drawn between the first and last anchor points. If you hold down the Opt/Alt key and extend slightly past the first anchor point, the path will close automatically. Set the tool preferences to low numbers to make closing easier. — Sandee Cohen*

Serious fun with shapes

The Ellipse (or oval select by typing "L"), Polygon, Star and Spiral are simple but powerful tools. Used in conjunction with the following key combinations, they are likely to become indispensable:

- **Spacebar-drag** allows you to reposition your object.
- **Shift** constrains the object's proportions.
- **Up-arrow** (↑) increases points on a star, sides on a polygon and coils on a spiral.
- **Down-arrow** (↓) removes points from a star, sides from a polygon, and coils from a spiral.
- **Option (Mac)/Alt (Win)** increases the angle of the star's points.
- **Command-drag** changes the inside and outside radius of a star, or increases or decreases the decay in a spiral.
- **Option (Mac)/Alt (Win)-click** to create the object numerically.
- **Various combinations of the above:** Try experimenting with all the keys separately and in combination with the other keys. Actually, playing with the modifier keys as you draw is the only way to fully understand these fun and powerful tools.
- For full details, see "GeoTools by Scott McCollom.pdf" on the *Wow!* disk ("Plug-ins" folder).

- **The Erase tool** removes sections of a selected path. By dragging along the path you can erase or remove portions of it. You must drag along the path—drawing perpendicular to the path will result in unexpected effects. This tool adds a pair of anchor points to the remaining path, on either side of the erased section of the path.

- **The Scissors tool** cuts a path where you click by adding two disconnected, selected anchor points exactly on top of each other. To select just one of the points, deselect the object, then click with the Direct-selection tool on the spot where you cut in order to select the upper anchor point, and drag it to the side to see the two points better.

- **The Knife tool** slices through all unlocked visible objects and closed paths. Simply drag the Knife tool across the object you want to slice, then select the object(s) you want to move or delete (see Tip "A more precise slice" on page 12).

GEOMETRIC OBJECTS

The Ellipse, Rectangle, Polygon, Spiral and Star tools create objects called "geometric primitives." These objects are mathematically-described symmetrical paths grouped with a nonprinting anchor point, which indicates the center. Use the centers of the geometric objects to snap-align them with each other, or with other objects and guides. You can create these geometric objects numerically or manually. Access the Polygon, Star and Spiral tools in the pop-up palette from the Ellipse tool in the Toolbox. Access the Rounded Rectangle tool hidden within the Rectangle tool. (See the *Zen* chapter for exercises in creating and manipulating geometric objects, and Tip at left.)

- **To create a geometric shape manually,** select the desired geometric tool, and click-drag to form the object from one corner to the other. To create the object from the center, hold down the Option (Mac)/Alt (Win) key and drag from the center outward (keep the Option/Alt key down until you release the mouse button to ensure that it draws from the center). Once you have drawn the geometric objects, you can edit them exactly as you do other paths.

- **To create a geometric object with numeric input,** select the desired geometric tool and click on the artboard to establish the upper left corner of your object. Enter the desired dimensions in the dialog box and click OK. To create the object numerically from the object's center, Option (Mac)/Alt (Win)-click the artboard.

SELECTING & GROUPING OBJECTS
Selections
There are several ways to make selections with this version of Illustrator. You can use the Selection tools to select individual or multiple objects. You can use the target indicators in the Layers palette to select and target objects, groups and layers. Targeting a group or layer selects everything contained within it. (For more on this, see the *Layers* chapter.)

Use the Lasso tool to select an entire path or multiple paths by encircling them with the tool. Option (Mac)/Alt (Win) + the Lasso tool subtracts entire paths from a selection. Shift + Lasso tool adds entire paths to a selection.

Use the Direct-select Lasso tool to select individual anchor points or path segments by encircling them with the tool. Option (Mac)/Alt (Win) + Direct-select Lasso tool subtracts anchor points from a selection. Shift + Direct-select Lasso tool adds anchor points to a selection.

Grouping and selections
Many object-oriented programs (programs that create objects, such as Illustrator and CorelDraw) provide you with a grouping function so you can act upon multiple objects as one unit. In Illustrator, grouping objects places all the objects on the same layer and creates a group container in the Layers palette with a triangle next to it. You don't want to group objects unless you actually need to. (For more on layers and objects, see the *Layers* chapter.)

Selection tool

Direct-selection tool

Group-selection tool

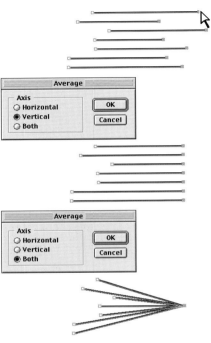

Using the Average command to align selected endpoints vertically, then choosing Both

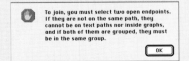
So, when do you want to group objects? Group objects when you need to select them *repeatedly* as a unit or want to apply an appearance to the entire group. Take an illustration of a bicycle as an example. Use the Group function to group the spokes of a wheel. Next, group the two wheels of the bicycle, then group the wheels with the frame. We will continue to refer to this bicycle below.

- **With the Direct-selection tool.** Click on a point or path with the Direct-selection tool to select that point or portion of the path. If you click on a spoke of a wheel, you'll select the portion of the spoke's path you clicked on.

- **With the Selection tool.** Click on an object with the Selection tool to select the largest group containing that object. In our example, it would be the entire bicycle.

- **With the Group-selection tool.** Use the Group-selection tool to select sub-groupings progressively. The first click with the Group-selection tool will select a single object. The next click will select the entire spoke path. The third click selects the entire wheel, the fourth selects both wheels, and the fifth, the entire bicycle.
  Note: *Once you've selected objects with the Group-selection tool, if you want to grab and move them you must change to one of the other selection tools, or during a selection, you click and drag without releasing the mouse. When you continually click with the Group-selection tool, you're always selecting the next group up.*

- **See the "Finger Dance" lessons in the *Zen* chapter.** This section includes a variety of selection exercises.

JOINING & AVERAGING

Two of Illustrator's most useful functions are Average and Join (both found under the Object: Path menu or in the context-sensitive menu). Use the Average function to place two endpoints at a single location, averaged between them. Use the Join function to join two endpoints. The

Join function will operate differently depending on the objects.

Averaging also allows you to align selected *points*. (To align objects, use the Align palette.) To average, use the Direct-selection tool or Direct-select Lasso tool to marquee-select or Shift-select any number of points belonging to any number of objects. Then use the Context-sensitive menu (Control key for Mac/right mouse button for Win) to average, aligning the selected points horizontally, vertically or along both axes.

- **If the two open endpoints are exactly on top of each other,** then Join opens a dialog box asking if the join should be smooth (a curved Bézier anchor with direction handles) or a corner (an anchor point with no handles). Both points will fuse into one point.

- **If the two open endpoints are *not* exactly on top of each other,** then Join will create a straight line joining the two points. If you attempt to join two points to fuse as one but you don't get the dialog box, then you have merely added an adjoining straight line! Undo (⌘-Z/ Ctrl-Z) and see "Averaging & Joining" below.

- **If you select an open path** (in this case, you don't need to select the endpoints), then Join closes the path.

- **If the two open endpoints are on different objects,** then Join connects the two paths into one.

Averaging & Joining in one step. Hold down Option (Mac)/Alt (Win) and choose Object: Path: Join. The join forms a corner if joining to a line, or a hinged curve if joining to a curve.

WORKING WITH PALETTES

Most of Illustrator's palettes are accessible via the Window menu. Each palette is unique, but many share common features:

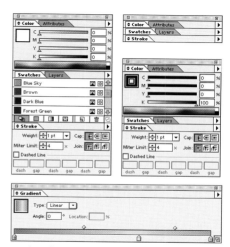

Modes of expansion for docked palettes; lower figure is Gradient palette, alone and expanded

Palette be gone!

Press Tab to hide the palettes and toolbox, then Tab to toggle them into view again. If you'd rather keep the toolbox and hide the other palettes, just use Shift-Tab.

If you can't see the appearance

If you are trying to alter an appearance but nothing seems to change on the screen, make sure:

- your objects are selected
- you are in Preview mode

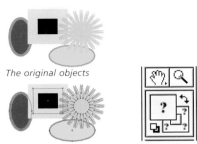

The original objects

Objects selected (the bottom of the toolbox indicates different stokes and fills are selected)

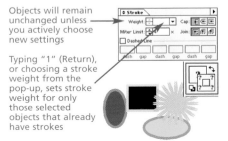

Objects will remain unchanged unless you actively choose new settings

Typing "1" (Return), or choosing a stroke weight from the pop-up, sets stroke weight for only those selected objects that already have strokes

The objects after setting a stroke weight of 1

Easy default styling

Select an object with the appearance you want your next object to have. Illustrator automatically resets the appearance, so the next drawn object will be identical to the last one selected.

Note: *This does not work for type.*

- **Regrouping tabbed palettes to save desktop space.** Reduce the space that palettes require by nesting the palettes together into smaller groups. Grab the palette tab and drag it to another palette group to nest it. You can also drag a tab to the *bottom* of a palette to dock the palettes one on top of another.

- **You can make most palettes smaller or larger.** If there's a sizing icon in the lower right corner, click and drag it to shrink or expand the palette. Palettes also have a pop-up menu offering additional options. If a palette contains more options, it will have a double set of triangles just to the left of the palette name on the tab. Click on the arrows to cycle through the various options. Click the square (minimize box), on the top right side of the title bar to shrink all palettes docked or nested together down to just title bars and tabs. Click the right square again, and the palettes will re-expand. Double-click the title bar to cycle through the states from maximum to collapsed.

- **You must select your object(s) first if you want to make changes.** With your objects selected, you can click on the label or right inside any edit box in the palette containing text and type. If you're typing something that has limited choices (such as a font or type style), Illustrator will attempt to complete your word; just keep typing until your choice is visible. If you're typing into a text field, use the Tab key to move to other text fields within the palette. IMPORTANT: *When you're finished typing into palette text fields, you must press Return (or Enter). This action signals the application that you are ready to enter text somewhere else or resume manipulating your artwork.*

- **You can edit selective characteristics on multiple objects.** With palettes, you can set one specific style for all selected objects without affecting any other characteristics. For example, your selection might contain multiple objects: one with no stroke, and the rest with outlines of different colors and weights. If, in the Stroke palette, you set the stroke weight to 1 (point) and leave the other choices unchanged, this will set the stroke weight of all objects that have strokes to 1 (point), but it won't add strokes to unstroked objects and won't affect the colors of any strokes. You can use the same technique to change assorted text blocks to the same typeface while maintaining differences in type sizes and other formatting.

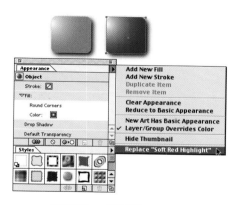

- **The many ways to fill or stroke an object**
Focus on a selected object's fill or stroke by clicking on the Fill or Stroke icon near the bottom of the Toolbox, or toggle between them by pressing the "X" key (if you want to set the stroke or fill to None, use the "/" key). Set the color you want by: 1) adjusting the sliders or sampling a color from the color ramp in the Color palette, 2) clicking on a swatch in the Swatches palette, 3) sampling colors from the color picker, or 4) using the Eyedropper tool to sample from other objects in your file. In addition, you can drag color swatches from palettes to selected objects or to the Fill/Stroke icon in the Toolbox.

- **Objects, a group of objects or a layer can have an appearance associated with it.** Not only can objects have fill and stroke characteristics, they can also have transparency and effects as part of their appearance. Not all objects, groups or layers have styles applied to them, but most will have an appearance, even if that appearance is only a stroke and a fill (basic appearance).

To update or replace a style throughout the entire document, select an object and apply the style you want to modify and update. With the object selected, make changes to it's appearance and choose Replace from the Appearance palette menu. The name of the style will display next to the replace command. This will globally update all objects using this named style. To change the name of the style, double-click on the proxy in the Styles palette and rename it.

- **Apply a Style to an object, group of objects, or a layer.** Also new to this version of Illustrator is the Styles palette. The total sum of applied characteristics can be saved as a style in the Styles palette. Styles in this version of Illustrator are "live" (updatable) combinations of fills, strokes, blending modes, opacity and effects. For details about working with the Styles palette, see the *Transparency, Styles & Effects* chapter, especially the chapter introduction and the "Scratchboard Style" lesson.

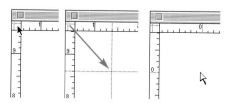

Grabbing and dragging the ruler corner to re-center the ruler origin (zero point)

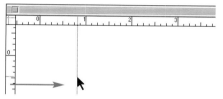

Clicking inside the ruler and dragging into your image to create a vertical or horizontal guide

If you want to continue to work with your graph numerically, *don't*, under any circumstances, ungroup your graph; it will make numerical data changes impossible. To avoid losing the special graph formatting, follow these special precautions:

- Use the Selection tool to select the entire graph for changes in style. Once your graph is selected, 1) Double-click the Graph tool to change the graph style; 2) Choose Object: Graphs: Data to change numeric data; or 3) To apply shaped design elements, see "Customizing graph designs" in this section.
- Use the Group-selection tool to select a category of data, then restyle or recolor as desired.
- Use the Type tool or Direct-selection tool to select and change individual text elements.
- Use the Direct-selection tool to select individual elements to change their styling.

Once you're *completely* finished numerically adjusting a graph, you may wish to delete some objects. Select the graph (with the Selection tool) and Ungroup (⌘-U /Ctrl-U). Once ungrouped, the objects are no longer part of a graph, and can be deleted.

GRAPHING & CHARTING

Through the Graph tool, Illustrator allows you to create charts and graphs in nine different styles. If you are new to charts or graphs, I suggest you thoroughly read the graph chapter in the *User Guide*. Please keep in mind that the purpose of a chart or graph is clear communication of numeric information as a visual aid. A properly selected chart design will accomplish this. If you create a lot of charts or graphs, you can look into a specialty graphic application, such as DeltaGraph Pro.

Before you begin, set a default chart or graph style by double-clicking on the Graph tool and choosing the style you want. To produce your graph, use the Graph tool as you would use the Rectangle tool: either click-drag to create a rectangular object from corner to corner, or hold down the Option key and click with the tool to numerically specify the dimensions of your graph.

After you establish the dimensions, the Graph dialog box opens, awaiting input of numeric data. Enter labels and numbers by highlighting the desired cell and typing into the entry line along the top. Tab to enter text in the next horizontal cell. You must look carefully in the *User Guide* to determine how you should enter data for the specific graph style you want.

Note: *It's very easy to enter text into the wrong field by mistake; so be meticulous. Mistakes are difficult to correct.*

Alternatively, you can import data that's been saved in *Tab-delineated* text format. Most word processing, spreadsheet or charting programs let you save or export data and labels as text, separated by Tabs and Returns.

To change the style of an existing graph, select the entire graph with the Selection tool and double-click on the Graph tool in the Toolbox. Choose another style and click OK. Be aware that each type of chart cannot necessarily be translated to all other formats.

To re-access a graph's numeric data, save your graph, then use the Selection tool to select your graph and choose Object: Graphs: Data. There is no Cancel command in data entry, but you can always use Undo (⌘-Z/Ctrl-Z).

Customizing graph designs

Being able to insert design elements into a graph is a snazzy—but much overused—aspect of the graphing feature. Illustrator allows you to define graph designs, which can be used as substitutes for rectangular column bars and line markers. For instance, using the "scaling" option, you can take a heart-shaped design and incorporate it into a graph by stretching (vertically scaling) or enlarging (uniformly scaling) the heart to the correct height. A variant of this technique allows you to define a portion of the heart to be scaled (called the "Sliding" Design). By using the "repeating" option, you can get the hearts to stack on top of each other until they reach the correct height.

Defining a graph design element works much the same way as defining a pattern design (see the *Lines, Fills & Colors* chapter). After creating the object(s) you wish to use as a design element, place a rectangle to enclose your design (with no fill or stroke) behind that element (choose Arrange: Send To Back), select the rectangle with its design and choose Object: Graphs: Design. In the dialog box, click New and name your design. To apply the design, use the Selection tool to select the graph, choose Object: Graphs: Columns and select the desired method of fitting your design to the column size. You can also use design elements to serve as "markers" (indicating plotted points) for line and scatter graph styles. Follow the above procedure, but choose Object: Graphs: Marker.

In speaking with the art departments at some of the nation's busiest newspapers and periodicals, I discovered that even though they often finish their charts and graphs in Illustrator, most use other programs to translate numbers into graphics. Included on the *Wow!* disk, however, is the shareware premiere of Chronchart, created by Eric Jungerman for the *San Francisco Chronicle*. Chronchart works with Microsoft's spreadsheet Excel to take any subset of your information (including stipulations such as "the 30 most recent sales over $1000") and transform it into graphs and charts editable by Illustrator.

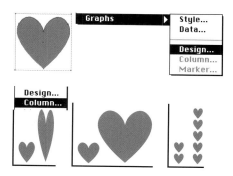

Defining a design; using the heart to create columns vertically scaled; uniformly scaled; forming a repeating design

Using graphs as templates

Many designers use the Graph tool to plot points and generate the scale and legend. They can create an illustration that uses the placement of the graph as a guide (see *Chapter 4* for help in locking the graph for use as a template).

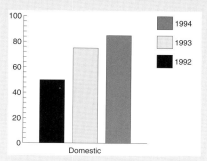

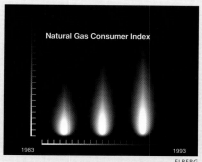

Eve Elberg used this bar graph as a template to plot the basic points in this illustration. For the glowing effect, she used blends and gradients (see the Blends chapter).

Transform again

Illustrator remembers the last transformation you performed—from simple moves to rotating a *copy* of an object. Use the context-sensitive menu to repeat the effect (Transform Again).

Moving complex images

If the Transform palette fails, create a proxy rectangle closely surrounding the objects you wish to move. Move the proxy in one motion to the desired location, and delete. To apply the move, select your objects, double-click the Selection arrow and click OK.

Free Transform variations

With the Free Transform tool you can apply the following transformations to selected objects:

- **Rotate**–click outside the bounding box and drag.
- **Scale**–click on a corner of the bounding box and drag. Option-drag / Alt-drag to scale from the center and Shift-drag to scale proportionally.
- **Distort**–click on a corner handle of the bounding box and ⌘ / Ctrl-drag.
- **Shear**–click on a side handle of the bounding box and ⌘ / Ctrl-drag the handle.
- **Perspective**–click on a corner handle of the bounding box and ⌘-Option-drag/Ctrl-Alt-Shift-drag.

TRANSFORMATIONS

Moving, scaling, rotating, reflecting and shearing are all operations that transform selected objects. Always begin by selecting what you wish to transform. If you're not happy with the transformation you've just applied, use Undo before applying a new transformation—or you'll end up applying the new transformation on top of the previous one.

In Illustrator, you can perform most transformations manually (see the *Zen* chapter for exercises), through a dialog box for numeric accuracy, with the Free Transform tool, as an effect, or with the Transform palette. In addition, you can also select more than one object and choose Object: Transform: Transform Each.

Illustrator remembers the last transformation you performed, storing those numbers in the appropriate dialog box until you enter a new transform value or restart the program. For example, if you previously scaled an image numerically and chose not to scale the line weights, the next time you scale, manually or numerically, your line weights will not scale.

The Bounding Box

The Bounding Box should not be confused with the Free Transform tool (which allows you to perform additional functions; see discussion of the Free Transform tool below). The Bounding Box appears around selected objects when you are using the Selection tool (solid arrow), and can be useful for quick moving, scaling, rotating or duplicating objects. With the Bounding Box, you can easily scale several objects at once. Select the objects, click on a corner of the Bounding Box and drag. To constrain proportionally while scaling, hold down the Shift key and drag a corner. By default, the Bounding Box is on. Toggle it on/off via the View: Hide/Show Bounding Box, or switch to the Direct-selection tool to hide the Bounding Box. To reset the Bounding Box after performing a transformation so it's once again square to the page, choose Object: Transform: Reset Bounding Box.

Moving

In addition to grabbing and dragging objects manually, you can specify a new location numerically: Double-click the Selection arrow in the Toolbox or use the Context-sensitive menu to bring up the Move dialog box (select the Preview option). For help determining the distance you wish to move, click-drag with the Measure tool the distance you wish to calculate. Then *immediately* open the Move dialog box to see the measured distance loaded automatically, and click OK (or press Return).

The Free Transform tool

The Free Transform tool (E) can be an all-in-one way to transform objects if you learn the numerous keyboard combinations to take advantage of its functions. In addition to performing transformations such as rotate, scale and shear, you can also create perspective and distortions (see Tip "Free Transform variations" opposite, and the Distort Dynamics" lesson in the *Lines, Fills & Colors* chapter). Keep in mind that the Free Transform tool bases its transformations on a fixed center point. You can't change this fixed point, from which your transformations are based, using the Free Transform tool; if you need to use this point, use the individual transformation tools, Transformation palette or the Transform Each command.

The Transform palette

From this palette, you can determine numeric transformations that specify an object's width, height and location on the document and how much to rotate or shear it. You can also access a palette pop-up menu which offers options to Flip Horizontal and Vertical, Transform Object, Pattern or Both, as well as to enable Scale Strokes & Effects. The current Transform palette is a bit odd: you can Transform Again once you've applied a transformation, but the information in the text fields is not always retained. To maintain your numeric input, apply transformations through the transform tool's dialog box, discussed on the next page.

Transform palette modifiers

To modify your transformations when you press Return, hold down Option (Mac)/Alt (Win) to transform and make a copy. Click a point in the Transform palette to select a reference point.

An exception to the rule!

Usually, you should scale an image before placing it in a page layout program. However, if your file contains brushes, patterns, gradients and gradient meshes, you may want to scale the final image after you have placed it, (see Tip "Printing speed" in this chapter).

Scaling objects to an exact size

- *The transformation palette way:* Type the new width or height in the palette and press Return.
- *The proxy way:* Create a proxy rectangle the size of your image, then from the upper left corner of the proxy, Option /Alt-click to create another rectangle in the target dimensions. Then with your proxy selected, click with the Scale tool in the upper left and grab-drag the lower right to match the target. (Hold down Shift to scale in only one dimension.) Delete these rectangles, select your objects, double-click the Scale tool and apply the settings.

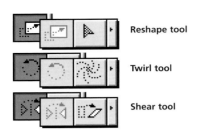

Reshape tool

Twirl tool

Shear tool

The selected area indicated in red

Direct-selected and dragged wing objects

HESS

For Eric Hess's "Soaring Hearts Futons" logo, he roughly Direct-selected, then with Reshape he marqueed as indicated above, and dragged

Individual transformation tools

For scaling, rotation, reflection and shearing of objects with adjustable center points, you can click (to manually specify the center about which the transformation will occur), then grab your object to transform it. For practice with manual transformations see the *Zen* chapter.

From the dialog box you can specify distance, degree of rotation, number of steps or scale percentage. You can also decide whether to scale lines, make a copy of the object, or transform patterns that fill the objects. (For more about transforming patterns see the *Lines* chapter). Here's how the transformation will affect the selected objects:

- **Double-click on a transformation tool** to access the dialog box. This allows you to transform the objects numerically, originating from an object's center.

- **Option (Mac)/Alt (Win)-click on your image with a transformation tool** to access the dialog box that allows you to transform your objects numerically, originating from where you clicked.

- **Click-drag on your image with a transformation tool** to transform the selected objects, originating from the center of the group of selected objects.

Reshape, Twirl & Shear

The Reshape tool is quite different from the other transformation tools. Start by Direct-selecting the paths you wish to reshape. If you use the Selection tool by mistake, the entire path will move, and if you haven't made any selection you won't be able to use the tool. Next, choose the Reshape tool from the Scale tool pop-up. With this tool, marquee or Shift-select all points you wish to affect, then drag the points to reshape the path. The selected points move as a group.

Using the Twirl tool (found within the Rotate tool), click-drag or Option (Mac)/Alt (Win)-click to transform selected objects (for details, see "GeoTools by Scott

McCollom.pdf" in the Plug-ins folder on the *Wow!* disk.

You will find the Shear tool hidden within the Reflect tool. It is used to slant objects.

Transform Each

To perform multiple transformations at once, open the Transform Each dialog box (Object: Transform: Transform Each). You can perform the transformations on several objects or on a single one. Additions to this dialog include the ability to reflect objects over the X and Y axis, and to change the point of origin. If you want to apply a transformation, but you think you might want to change it later, try a Transformation Effect (see the *Transparency* chapter).

WORKING SMART
Saving strategies

Probably the most important advice you'll ever get is to save every few minutes. Whenever you make a substantial change to your image, use File: Save As and give your image a new name.

It's much more time-efficient to save incremental versions of your image than it is to reconstruct an earlier version. Back up your work at least once a day before you shut down. Just think to yourself, "If this computer never starts up again, what will I need?" Develop a backup system using disks, Zip or Jaz drives, DATs (digital audio tapes), opticals or CDs so you can archive all of your work. Use a program such as Dantz's Retrospect to automatically add new and changed files to your archives.

Get in the habit of archiving virtually everything, and develop a file-naming system that actually helps you keep track of your work-in-progress—simplifying your recovery of a working version if necessary. A good system involves three components. First, start with a meaningful description of your current image ("hearts compound") and second, add a numerical notation of the version ("1.0"). Keep your numbering system consecutive, regardless of the label, throughout the entire project. Keep the number in a decimal sequence when you make

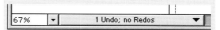

To make changes to a path, click on the path with the Direct-selection tool. Then make adjustments by selecting and dragging anchor points, direction points or the curve itself. If you select an object but don't see direction handles:

- Deselect it, then try again.
- If you're in Preview mode, be sure to click on the *path itself* or switch to Outline mode.
- Uncheck Use Area Select in the General Preferences.
- Enable View: Show Edges.

Note: *Only* curves *have handles!*

Interrupting Preview

You don't have to wait for Illustrator to finish redrawing the Preview before you pull down the next menu or perform another task. You can interrupt redrawing the preview and go to Outline mode by typing ⌘ (Mac)/Ctrl (Win)-. *period,* or the Esc key for Windows.

Two new views

Overprint and Pixel Preview are two new view modes now available in Illustrator. Use Pixel Preview when creating web graphics.

Zoom shortcuts while typing

Press ⌘/Ctrl+spacebar to zoom in or ⌘-Option/Ctrl-Alt+spacebar to zoom out even while typing.

an incremental change to your image ("1.1, 1.2, 1.3…"). Change to the next numeric sequence when you make a substantive change ("2.0"). Don't start numbers at 1.0 for each phase of the project or you'll be unable to figure out which came first: "Sky 1.0" or "Heart 1.0." Instead, if labels are "Sky 1.0" and "Heart 4.0," then the creation order is self-explanatory. Lastly, add a suffix to indicate its file type (.ai for Illustrator, .psd for Photoshop, .eps for Encapsulated PostScript file). Also, make sure that you keep all files in a named and dated folder that distinguishes them from other projects. (For saving in other formats see "Image Formats" later in this chapter.)

Multiple Undos

Most programs give you one chance to undo your last move. Illustrator allows up to 200 levels of undo, but will only hold the user-specified number of undos if there is enough memory. When it needs to purge levels of undo to regain memory, Illustrator will remove all levels beyond what you've specified as your minimum. In File: Preferences: Units & Undo you can set the number of levels of undo to a number less than 200. Usually 20 to 30 levels is adequate and keeps you aware that you should still save frequently.

Even after you save a file, your Undos (and Redos) are still available, making it possible to save the current version, undo it to a previous stage and then save it, or continue working from an earlier state. Having 20 to 30 undos available in each of multiple documents should come close to the experience of having infinite undos! **Note:** *Not all operations, such as Preferences, are undoable.*

CHANGING YOUR VIEWS
Preview and Outline

To control the speed of your screen redraw, learn to make use of the various Preview and Outline (formerly Artwork) modes (View menu). In Preview mode, the document is viewed in full color; in Outline mode you only see the wire frames of the objects.

New View

New View (View: New View) allows you to save your current window viewpoint, remembering also your zoom level and which layers are hidden, locked or in Preview mode. Custom views are added to the bottom of the View menu to easily recall a saved view (see the *Layers* chapter for more details on views). You can rename a view, but the views themselves are not editable—if you need to make a change to a view, you'll have to make a New View.

New Window

Illustrator gives you the ability to display different aspects of your current image simultaneously. This allows you to separately view different Proof Setups, Overprint or Pixel Previews and zoom levels. You can resize them, have edges hidden or visible, or hide or lock different *layers* in Preview or Outline (see the *Layers* chapter and "Hide/ Show Edges" below). Most window configurations are saved with the file.

Window controls

As in Photoshop, you'll see three small icons at the very bottom of the toolbox. One is always selected; this is the default in which Illustrator will display your file window. Starting at the far left, choose from Standard Screen Mode (desktop showing around the edges of your file), Full Screen Mode with Menu Bar (file window visible, but confined to the center of the screen with no desktop showing; you can access your menu bar) and Full Screen Mode (same as above, but you cannot access your menu bar). Toggle among the views by pressing the "F" key.

ZOOMING IN & OUT

Illustrator provides many ways to zoom in and out.

- **From the View menu.** Choose Zoom In/Out, Actual Size, or Fit in Window.

- **With the Zoom tool.** Click to zoom *in* one level of

Where did the window go?

If you have many file windows open, simply select the file you want to bring to the front from the list of files at the bottom of the Window menu.

The Navigator palette & views

The Navigator palette (always in Preview mode) offers many ways to zoom in and out of documents:

- Double-click the mountain icons along the bottom edge of the palette window to increase or decrease the amount of zoom in 200% increments.

- Hold the ⌘ (Mac)/Ctrl (Win)-key and drag to marquee the area in the palette thumbnail that you want to zoom into or out from.

- Enable View Artboard Only to keep your view limited to the artboard area. This is helpful if you are working on a large document with objects on the pasteboard that are distracting your focus.

Change the color of the border around the thumbnail in the View Options dialog (found in the Navigator palette pop-up menu.)

Note: *Navigator might slow down large files. If Illustrator is running sluggishly, quit Illustrator, move the Navigator file out of the Plug-ins folder and relaunch Illustrator.*

Zippy zooming

Current magnification is displayed in the bottom left corner of your document. Access a list of percentages (3.13% to 6400%) or Fit on Screen from the pop-up, or simply select the text and enter any percentage within the limit.

Glorious grids

Customize your grids in Illustrator. Select a grid style and color.

- View: Show Grid, use the context-sensitive menu or ⌘ (Mac)/Ctrl (Win)-' *apostrophe.*
- Toggle Snap To Grid on and off from the View menu or use the shortcut ⌘ (Mac)/Ctrl (Win)-Shift-' *apostrophe*
- Set the division and subdivision for your grid in Preferences: Guides & Grid and choose either dotted divisions or lines and the color of those lines.
- To toggle the grid display in front or in back of your artwork, check or uncheck the Grids In Back checkbox (Preferences: Guides & Grid).
- Tilt the grid on an angle by choosing File: Preferences: General, and in Tool Behavior change the Constrain angle. **Note:** *The Constrain angle affects the angle at which objects are drawn and moved. (See the* Lines, Fills & Colors *chapter on how to adjust it for creating isometrics.)*

magnification; hold down the Option (Mac)/Alt (Win) key and click to zoom *out* one level. You can also click-drag to define an area, and Illustrator will attempt to fill the current window with the area that you defined.

- **Use the shortcut ⌘ (Mac)/Ctrl (Win) for Zoom.** With any tool selected, use ⌘-hyphen (Mac)/Ctrl-hyphen (Win)—think "minus to zoom out"—and ⌘+ (Mac)/ Ctrl+ (Win)—think "plus to zoom in".

- **Use context-sensitive menus.** With nothing selected, Control-click (Mac) or use the right mouse button (Windows) to access a pop-up menu so you can zoom in and out, change views, undo, and show or hide guides, rulers and grids.

- **Navigator palette.** With the Navigator palette, you can quickly zoom in or out and change the viewing area with the help of the palette thumbnail (see Tip "The Navigator palette & views" in this chapter).

SHOW/HIDE CHOICES

From the View menu, you can show and hide several combinations of items, such as grids, guides, smart guides, transparency grid, edges, artboard and page tilings.

Rulers, Guides, Smart Guides and Grids

Toggle Illustrator's Show/Hide Rulers, or use the Context-sensitive menu (as long as nothing in your document is selected). The per-document ruler units are set in Document Setup. If you want all new documents to use a specific unit of measurement, you should change your preferences for Units (Edit: Preferences: Units & Undos).

In some previous versions of Illustrator, the ruler origin (where 0,0 is) was in the lower right corner of the image. Now, the ruler origin is in the lower left corner. To change the ruler origin, grab the upper left corner (where the vertical and horizontal rulers meet) and drag the crosshair to the desired location. The zeros of the rulers will reset to the point where you release your mouse (to reset the rulers to the default location, double-click the upper left corner). But beware—resetting your ruler origin will realign all new patterns and affect alignment of Paste In Front / Back between documents (see the *Layers* chapter for more on Paste In Front / Back).

To create simple vertical or horizontal ruler guides, click-drag from one of the rulers into your image. A guide appears where you release your mouse. You can define guide color and style in General Preferences. Guides automatically lock after you create them. To release a guide quickly, ⌘ / Ctrl-Shift-double-click on it. You can lock and unlock guides with the context-sensitive menu in Preview mode. You should note that locking or unlocking guides affects every open document. If you have too many guides visible in your document, simply choose View: Guides: Clear Guides. This only works on guides that are on visible, unlocked layers. Hiding or locking layers retains any guides you have created (see the *Layers* chapter). To learn how to create custom guides from objects or paths, see the "Varied Perspective" lesson in the Layers chapter.

Smart Guides can be somewhat unnerving when you see them flash on and off as you work. However, with practice and understanding of each option, you'll be able to refine how to incorporate them into your workflow.

Illustrator also has automatic grids. To view grids, select View: Show Grid, or use the Context-sensitive menu. You can adjust the color, style of line (dots or solid), and size of the grid's subdivisions from File: Preferences: Guides & Grid.

As with guides, you can also enable a snap-to grid function. Toggle Snap To Grid on and off by choosing View: Snap To Grid (see Tip "Glorious grids" opposite). IMPORTANT: *If you adjust the x and y axes in File: Preferences: General: Constrain Angle, it will affect the drawn objects and transformations of your grid, as they will follow the adjusted angle when you create a new object. This is great, however, if you're doing a complicated layout requiring alignment of objects at an angle.*

Understanding Smart Guides

There are a multitude of Smart Guide preferences. Here's what each one does:

- **Text Label Hints** provide information about an object when the cursor passes over it—helpful for identifying a specific object within complicated artwork.
- **Construction Guides** are the temporary guidelines that help you align between objects and anchor points.
- **Transform Tools** help with transformations.
- **Object Highlighting** enables the anchor point, center point and path of a deselected object to appear as your cursor passes within a specified tolerance from the object. This can be very useful for aligning objects. For best alignment results, select an object's anchor point or center point.

Note: *Smart Guides will slow you down when working on very large files. Also, you can't align using Smart Guides if View: Snap To Grid is enabled.*

Edges and the bounding box

When you toggle to Hide Edges and have Show Bounding Box enabled (both in the View menu), the bounding box will remain visible while the anchor points and paths of objects will be hidden.

Tools: Ellipse, Polygon, Star, Spiral, Rectangle, Rotate, Scale, Shear and Reflect.

File menu: New, Open, Close, Save, Save As, Save a Copy, Revert, Place and Export.

Edit: Cut, Copy, Paste, Paste In Front, Paste In Back, Clear, Select All, Deselect All and the Select pop-up menu items.

Object: Transform Again, Move, Scale, Rotate, Shear, Reflect, Transform Each, Arrange pop-up items, Group, Ungroup, Lock, Unlock All, Hide Selection, Show All, Expand, Rasterize, Blends, Mask, Compound Path and Crop Marks.

Type: Character, Paragraph, MM Design, Tab Ruler, Block, Wrap, Fit Headline, Create Outlines, Find/Change, Find Font, Change Case, Rows & Columns, Type Orientation and Glyph Options.

Filters: Colors, Create, Distort and Stylize.

Guide-related views.

Window: Transform, Align, Pathfinder, Color, Gradient, Stroke, Swatches, Brushes, Styles, Layers, Attributes and Actions.

Bounding Box transformations.

Selecting objects in an action

When recording an action, use the Attributes palette (Show Note) to name an object, and Select Object (Action pop-up) to type in the object's name (note) to select it.

Transparency Grid & Simulate Color Paper

Now that Illustrator can use transparency, you might want to change the background of the artboard to the transparency grid, or better yet, to a color. Both the transparency grid and simulated color paper are non-printable attributes.

To view the transparency grid, select View: Show Transparency Grid. Change the grid colors in the Transparency panel of the Document Setup dialog. If you change both grid colors to the same color, you can change the white background to a color (see the *Transparency* chapter).

Hide / Show Edges

If looking at all those anchor points and colored paths distracts you from figuring out what to do with selected objects in your current window, choose View: Hide/Show Edges to toggle them on or off. Once you hide the edges, all subsequent path edges will be hidden until you show them again. Hide/Show Edges is saved with your file.

ACTIONS

Actions are a set of commands or a series of events that you can record and save as a set in the Action palette. Once a set is recorded, you can play back an action in the same order in which you recorded it, to automate a job you do repeatedly (a production task or special effect).

Select the action in the Action palette and activate it by clicking the Play icon at the bottom of the palette, choosing Play from the pop-up menu, or assigning the action to a keyboard F-key (function key) so you can play the action with a keystroke. You can select an action set, a single action, or a command within an action to play. To exclude a command from playing within an action, click the checkbox to the left of the command.

In order to play some types of actions, you may have to first select an object or some text. Load action sets using the pop-up menu. (Find sets of actions on the Adobe Illustrator Application CD in the Illustrator Extras folder, as well as in *Wow! Actions* on the *Wow!* disk.)

Since you must record actions and save within an action set, begin a new action by clicking the Create New Set icon, or by choosing New Set from the pop-up. Name the action set and click OK. With the new set selected, click the Create New Action icon, name the action, and click Record. Illustrator records your commands and steps until you click Stop. To resume recording, click on the last step, choose Begin, and continue adding to the action. When you've finished recording, you'll need to save the action file by selecting the action set and choosing Save Actions from the pop-up menu.

When you are recording, keep in mind that not all commands or tools are recordable. For example, the Pen tool itself is not recordable, but you can add the paths the Pen tool creates to an action by selecting a path and choosing Insert Selected Paths again from the pop-up menu. For a more complete list of what is recordable, see Tip "Action—what's recordable" in this chapter. Recording actions takes some practice, so don't get discouraged, always save a backup file, and refer to the *User Guide* for more details on Actions.

COLOR IN ILLUSTRATOR

Consumer-level monitors, which display color in red, green and blue lights (RGB), cannot yet match four-color CMYK (cyan, magenta, yellow, black) inks printed onto paper. Therefore, you must retrofit the current technology with partial solutions, starting with calibrating your monitor.

Some programs (such as the Adobe Gamma utility installed with Photoshop) provide some degree of control over the way your monitor displays colors. ColorSync (Mac) and Kodak Digital Science Color Management (Windows) are the two main systems. The CMS (Color Management System) that ships with this version of Illustrator has been greatly improved. The colors displayed on the screen will be closer to the color you output if you follow a few key steps (see the *User Guide* for more information on using color management).

CMY Color Model   RGB Color Model

CMY (Cyan, Magenta, Yellow) **subtractive** *colors get darker when mixed; RGB (Red, Green, Blue)* **additive** *colors combine to make white*

Whiter whites / blacker blacks

If your whites or blacks seem to be taking on an undesirable color cast, look to your color management system as the possible source of the problem. (See the *User Guide* for more details on color management in this version of Illustrator.) Also, check your Proof Setup or preview modes.

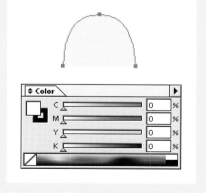

Converting RGB to CMYK

Although Illustrator can make conversions from RGB to CMYK (and vice versa), File: Document Color Mode: CMYK/RGB, such conversions may result in undesirable color shifts. Consult the *User Guide*, your service bureau and/or printer for detailed directions based on your job specifications.

Continuous-tone, anti-aliased bitmapped images naturally form "traps" to hide misregistration of CMYK inks, but hard, crisp Post-Script edges are a registration nightmare. Some products can globally trap pages. If you know the exact size and resolution of your final image, you can rasterize Illustrator files (or specific objects) into raster images by using Object: Rasterize and Flatten Transparency or rasterize in Photoshop (see the *Other Programs* chapter).

If your image is not rasterized:

- Construct your images so that overlapping shapes having common inks form natural traps (see the *Lines* chapter*)*.
- Set individual colors to Over-print in the Attributes palette.
- Globally set blacks to overprint (Filter: Colors: Overprint Black).
- See the *User Guide* for details on setting traps in *solid* objects using Pathfinder palette: Trap.
- For trapping patterns and gra-dients (see Tip "Manual Trap-ping..." in the *Lines* chapter).

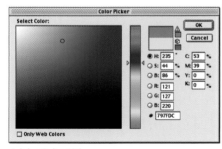

Adobe Color Picker

In addition to software calibration, methods of hard-ware calibration are available that actually adjust the beams of the cathode-ray tube emitting the RGB lights. Generally, the larger the monitor, the more likely the colors will vary in different areas of the screen. Monitor color is also affected by the length of time your monitor is on and the ambient light in your workroom.

In order to produce an accurate proof (if a printing press is your target), Illustrator needs to support printing profiles for both composite (your printer) and separation (the final printing device) ICC(M) printers. Illustrator now supports ICC(M) profiles for both types of printing, although it is still not possible to emulate the separation printer on the composite printer. It is, however, possible to use Illustrator for proofing directly on your screen and for printing a more accurate proof to your printer when you are not soft proofing to the screen. If you are creating art for placement into QuarkXPress or PageMaker, there is no application-level color management module cur-rently supporting the EPS file format. Always consult with your prepress house and run a proof prior to print-ing an entire job.

Working in RGB or CMYK

Illustrator offers you the flexibility of working and printing in either RGB or CMYK color. This is a mixed blessing, because the printing environment cannot accurately capture vibrant RGB colors. As a result, the RGB colors are usually muddy or muted when printed. If your final artwork is going to be printed, work in CMYK!

Working in an RGB color space is great for creating artwork that will be displayed on-screen and for identify-ing particular spot colors (such as day-glo colors) to your printer. (For more on working in RGB, see the *Web, Multimedia & Animation* chapter.)

Single color space

When you open a new document, you select a color model (or color space). Illustrator no longer allows you to work in multiple color spaces at the same time. If you work in print, always check your files to make certain they are in the appropriate color model before you output. The document's color model is always displayed next to the file name, on the title bar.

Opening legacy documents (documents created with older versions of Illustrator) with objects containing mixed color spaces will invoke a warning asking you to decide which color space (RGB or CMYK) the document should open in. Currently, linked images are not converted to the document's color space. If you open the Document Info palette and select Linked Images, the "Type" info is misleading. For example, if you have a CMYK document with a linked RGB image, the linked image type is Transparent CMYK. The linked image has not been converted, but the image preview has been converted to CMYK.

Enabling color management

The default color setting for Illustrator is "Emulate Adobe Illustrator 6.0", which is all color management *off*. To start color managing your documents, select Edit: Color Settings. Choose a setting from the pop-up menu, or customize your own setting. Depending on how you set up color management, you might get several warnings about colors, such as when you open documents or paste colors between documents. The *User Guide* offers detailed explanations about these warnings and what to do.

Color systems and libraries

Besides creating colors in RGB, HSB or CMYK, you can also select colors from other color matching systems, such as the 216-color "web-safe" color palette or the color picker. You can access Focoltone, Diccolor, Toyo, Trumatch and Pantone libraries or the web palette by choosing Window: Swatch Libraries, then selecting it from the menu. Keep in mind that color libraries open as separate uneditable palettes, but once you use a color swatch, it will automatically load into *your* Swatches palette, where you can then edit it. The default for the Swatches palette

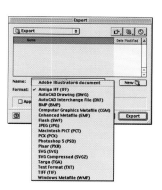

is to open with swatches—*not* view by name. Use the palette menu to change to Name View if you prefer. Holding down Option/Alt while you choose a view will set that view for each of the types of swatches.

To access styles, brushes or swatches in other documents, choose Window: Style, Brush or Swatch Libraries: Other Library. Then select the file that contains the item you want. This opens a new palette with that document's components. To store a component from an open library in your current document, just use the style, brush or swatch—or drag the swatch from its library palette to the document's palette.

IMAGE FORMATS

You might need to open a document created in an earlier version of Illustrator (FreeHand, Canvas, CorelDraw, and a number of 3D programs allow you to save images in older Illustrator formats). To open any file saved in an earlier version, drag it onto an Illustrator alias, or open the older formatted file from within Illustrator by choosing File: Open and selecting the document you want to open. If it's a file you plan to work on or open again, use Save As to save a copy in the current Illustrator format.

EPS (Encapsulated PostScript)

EPS is a universal format, meaning that a wide variety of programs support importing and exporting EPS images for printing to PostScript printers. As in most programs, when saving an image in EPS format you can choose to include a Preview. This preview is an on-screen PICT or TIFF representation of your image. When an EPS image is placed in another program without a preview, it will print properly, but can't be viewed. To import an EPS image into Illustrator, choose File: Place (see the *Layers* and *Other Programs* chapters for more about EPS).

Other image formats

Illustrator supports a wealth of file formats (such as SWF, SVG, GIF, JPEG, TIFF, PICT, PCX, Pixar and Photoshop).

You can also open and edit PDF (Acrobat format) documents, and even "raw" PostScript files, directly from within Illustrator. If you place images into your document, you can choose whether these files will remain *linked* (see Tip "Links are manageable" in this chapter) or will become *embedded* image objects (see the *Other Programs* chapter for specifics on embedding, and the *Web* chapter for details on web-related formats). If you choose Open, most images become embedded. (See the Adobe *User Guide* and *Read Me* files for lists of supported formats that shipped with this version.) Check Adobe's website (www.adobe.com) for the latest information on supported formats, as well as additional file format plug-ins. (For more on file format issues, see the *Other Programs* chapter.*)

POSTSCRIPT PRINTING & EXPORTING

When you're ready to print your image (to a laser or inkjet printer, imagesetter or film recorder), you should use a PostScript printing device. Adobe owns and licenses the PostScript language, making PostScript printers somewhat more expensive than non-PostScript printers. Some companies produce PostScript-compatible printers or provide PostScript emulation. Although Illustrator images often print just fine to these printers, sometimes you can run into problems. In general, the newer the PostScript device, the faster and less problematic your printing will be. PostScript Level 2 and Level 3 printers provide better printing clarity and even some special effects, such as Illustrator's integration of PostScript Level 3's "smooth shading" technology (which should greatly enhance gradients and reduce banding problems). Lastly, the more memory you install in your printer, the quicker your text and images will print. For crucial jobs, develop good relations with your service bureau, and get into the habit of running test prints to identify possible problems. (Also see Tip "Proofing your prints," in this chapter.)

Correcting and avoiding printing problems

If you have trouble printing, first make sure your placed

Saving time and space

Note: *Before you attempt to minimize the size of your file, make certain that you're working on a copy.* To minimize the size of your file, first remove all your unused colors, patterns and brushes. Open the Swatches palette, click the All Swatches icon, choose Select All Unused from the Swatches pop-up menu, then click the Trash icon to delete. (You may have to repeat the select and delete process to remove *all* the excess colors.) Next open the Brushes palette, choose Select All Unused from the Brushes pop-up menu. Then click the Trash icon. You should minimize the time it takes to print an Illustrator file, even if it's been placed into another program, such as QuarkX-Press or PageMaker (see the *Other Programs* chapter for details on exporting). If you've scaled or rotated an Illustrator image once it's been placed into another program, note the numeric percentages of scaling and the degrees of rotation. Next, reopen the file in Illustrator, perform the identical scale or rotation, then place this pretransformed version back into the other program, make sure you reset scaling and rotation to zero. **Note:** *Be certain to scale line weight, objects and pattern tiles when you perform these transformations in Illustrator.*

Hand tool while typing

First press ⌘/Ctrl+spacebar, then release the ⌘/Ctrl key to access the Hand tool even while typing.

Cleanup

Select Object: Path: Cleanup and check the items you want to delete from your document. Choose Stray Points, Unpainted Objects and/or Empty Text Paths. Click OK and all of those items are removed.

In a jam? There's help available

Adobe provides many ways to help you learn Illustrator

and troubleshoot problems. Find help under the Help menu (Mac or Windows), along with instant access to Adobe Online. Adobe Online is also accessed by pressing the Venus icon on top of the toolbox.

When to use the Lasso tools?

- Use the Direct-select Lasso tool to select hard-to-select individual anchor points or gradient mesh nodes.
- Use the Lasso tool for selecting type and hard-to-select objects without having to use the Layers palette to target an object.

images are linked properly and the fonts needed to print the document are loaded. Second, check for any complex objects in the document. Use Save a Copy (to retain the original file), remove the complex object(s), and try to print. If that doesn't work, make sure File: Document Setup and Separation Setup have the correct settings for your output device. (See the *Blends & Gradients* chapter for issues regarding printing gradient mesh objects.) If you are using transparency, or effects that contain transparency, you might want to output a sample file saved with different quality settings. Printing results will vary depending on these settings (see the *Transparency* chapter for printing and transparency issues).

More about controlling the size of your files

The major factors that can increase your file size are the inclusion of image objects, path pattern, brushes and ink pen objects, complex patterns, a large number of blends and gradients (especially gradient mesh objects and gradient-to-gradient blends), linked bitmapped images and now transparency. Although linked bitmaps can be large, the same image embedded as an image object is significantly larger. If your Illustrator file contains linked images, and you need to save the entire file in EPS (for placement and printing in other programs), you have the option Include Linked Files. Most service bureaus highly recommend this option, as it will embed placed images in your Illustrator file and make printing from page layout programs and film recorders much more predictable (be sure to see Tip "Proofing your prints," in this chapter). However, since including placed images will further increase the file size, wait until you've completed an image and are ready to place it into another program before you save a copy with placed images embedded. Whether or not you choose to embed linked images, you must collect all of the files that have been linked into your Illustrator documents and transport them along with your Illustrator file. Illustrator makes your task easier if you choose File: Document Info: Linked Images, which outputs a text file of all images in your document. Press Save to create a text file that you can file for future reference or give to your service bureau as a record of the images included in your files.

Printing speed

A related, but even more crucial, factor to consider when creating an image is knowing what elements make an image take longer to print. Special effects such as transforming or masking placed images, using complex patterns or a slew of patterns, gradients, live blends, brushes, path pattern, ink pen effects or transparency are the worst culprits for increasing file size, and thus printing time. If your image contains transparency or Effects, the file becomes dependent on a series of resolution settings that will affect both how your printed image looks and how long it takes to print (see the *Transparency* chapter introduction for more on these issues).

In most cases you'll want to perform any scaling of your final image in Illustrator before placing it into a page layout program (make certain to enable the Scale Strokes & Effects option of the Scale tool). However, images containing brushes or Effects may not scale properly within Illustrator; instead, you'll need to scale these images within your page layout program. If you intend to scale an image in a page layout program, and the image contains transparency, gradient mesh, or Effects, you'll need to adjust the resolution settings for that file before placing and scaling it in another program.

If you're going to place raster images into your Adobe Illustrator file, you'll greatly reduce your printing time and ensure the optimal printing resolution if you perform all scaling and transformations of the images before placing them in Illustrator (see Tip "Resolution of placed images" at the end of the *Other Programs* chapter introduction for specific information). Talk to your service bureau and print house for advice about your specific job before you make decisions about what resolution your raster images should be.

Transparency and file size

Adding transparency to an image will increase the file size, and will change it from being resolution independent to being dependent on resolution settings (see "Printing speed" at left and Tips below).

Transparency & speed!

If your image includes transparency, mesh or Effects, for optimal printing results you should set the "Transparency slider" (Document Setup: Transparency: Quality/Speed) to the extreme right (vector setting). However, if your image won't print at that setting, test to see if moving the slider to the extreme left (raster setting) yields acceptable results. See the *Transparency* chapter and *Tech Notes* appendix for more on transparency and resolution issues.

Shortcuts setting resolution

If you're saving a batch of documents, and want all to have the same resolution settings (see Tip above), set all settings in the first document and Save your file. Then copy and paste the next image into that document, and Save As with a new name. Repeat for the other images that require that setting. You can also create "stationery" documents for each resolution setting you require, and start new images with these preset resolution documents.

The Zen of Illustrator

2

The Zen of Illustrator

Zen: *"Seeking enlightenment through introspection and intuition rather than scripture."**

You're comfortable with the basic operations of your computer. You've read through "An Overview of Adobe Illustrator" in the *User Guide*. You've logged enough hours in Illustrator to be familiar with how each tool (theoretically) functions. You even understand how to make Bézier curves. Now what? How do you take all this knowledge and turn it into a mastery of the medium?

As with learning any new artistic medium (such as engraving, watercolor or airbrush), learning to manipulate the tools is just the beginning. Thinking and seeing in that medium is what really makes those tools part of your creative arsenal. Before you can determine the best way to construct an image, you have to be able to envision at least some of the possibilities. The first key to mastering Illustrator is to understand that Illustrator's greatest strength comes not from its many tools and functions, but from its extreme flexibility in terms of how you construct images. The first part of this chapter, therefore, introduces you to a variety of approaches and techniques for creating and transforming objects.

Once you've got yourself "thinking in Illustrator," you can begin to *visualize* how to achieve the final results. What is the simplest and most elegant way to construct an image? Which tools will you use? Then, once you've begun, allow yourself the flexibility to change course and try something else. Be willing to say to yourself: How else can I get the results that I want?

* Adapted from *Webster's New World Dictionary of the English Language*

The second key to mastering Illustrator (or any new medium) is perfecting your hand/eye coordination. In Illustrator, this translates into being proficient enough with the "power-keys" to gain instant access to tools and functions by using the keyboard. With both eyes on the monitor, one hand on the mouse, and the other hand on the keyboard, an experienced Illustrator user can create and manipulate objects in a fraction of the time required otherwise. The second part of this chapter helps you to learn the "finger dance" necessary to become a truly adept power-user.

The ability to harness the full power of Illustrator's basic tools and functions will ultimately make you a true master of Adobe Illustrator. Treat this chapter like meditation. Take it in small doses if necessary. Be mindful that the purpose of these exercises is to open up your mind to possibilities, not to force memorization. When you can conceptualize a number of different ways to create an image, then the hundreds of hints, tips, tricks, and techniques found elsewhere in this book can serve as a jumping-off point for further exploration. If you take the time to explore and absorb this chapter, you should begin to experience what I call the "Zen of Illustrator." This magical program, at first cryptic and counterintuitive, can help you achieve creative results not possible in any other medium.

Building Houses

Sequential Object Construction Exercises

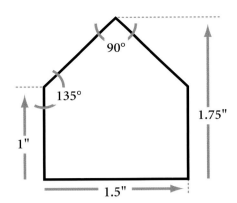

Overview: *Explore different approaches to constructing the same object with Illustrator's basic construction tools.*

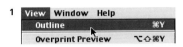

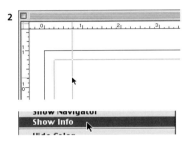

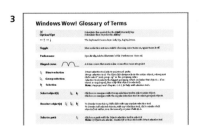

Dragging out a guide from the Ruler, and choosing Window: Show Info to open the Info palette if it's not open before you begin

This sequence of exercises explores different ways to construct the same simple object, a house. The purpose of these exercises is to introduce you to the flexibility of Illustrator's object construction, so don't worry if some exercises seem less efficient than others. In Edit: Preferences: Units & Undo, set Units: General for Inches (so you can use the numbers provided and the measurements above). Read through the recommendations below for preparing your working environment.

1 Work in Outline mode. Doing so keeps you from being distracted by fills or line weights, and lets you see the centers of geometric objects (marked by "×").

2 Use Show Rulers and Show Info. Choose Show Rulers (View menu) so you can "pull out" guides. Use the Info palette to view numeric data as you work, or ignore the numeric data and just draw the houses by eye.

3 Read through the *Wow! Glossary*. Please be sure to read *How to use this book* and the *Glossary* pull-out card.

4 Use "modifier" keys. These exercises use Shift and Option (Opt) or Alt keys, which you must hold down until *after* you release your mouse button. If you make a mistake, choose Undo and try again. Some functions are also accessible from the Context-sensitive menu. Try keyboard shortcuts for frequently-used menu commands.

Hint: Hold down the Shift key to constrain movement to horizontal/vertical direction. For more modifier key help, see the end of this chapter for the "Finger Dance" lesson.

Exercise #1:

Use Add-anchor-point tool

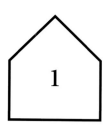

1 Create a rectangle and a vertical guide. Create a wide rectangle (1.5" x 1") and drag out a vertical guide that snaps to the center.

2 Add an anchor point on the top. Use the Add-anchor-point tool to add a point on the top segment over the center guide.

3 Drag the new point up. Use the Direct-selection tool to grab the new point and drag it up into position (.75" for a total height of 1.75").

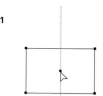

1

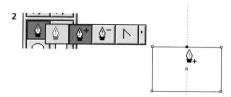

2

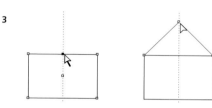

3

Exercise #2:

Make an extra point

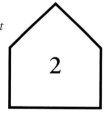

1 Create a rectangle, delete the top path and place a center point. Create a wide rectangle (1.5" x 1"). With the Direct-selection tool, select the top path segment and delete it. With the Pen tool, place a point on top of the rectangle center point.

2 Move the point up. Double-click on the Selection tool in the Toolbox to open the Move dialog box, and enter a 1.25" vertical distance to move the point up.

3 Select and join the point to each side. Use the Direct-selection tool to select the left two points and Join (Object : Path: Join) them to the top point. Repeat with the right two points.

1

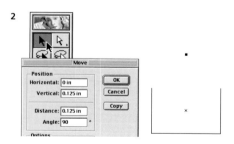

2

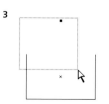
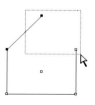

3

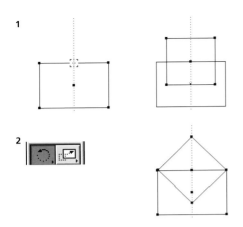

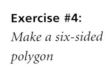

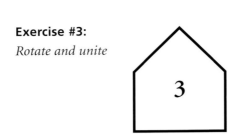

Exercise #3:
Rotate and unite

1 Create two rectangles, one centered on the other. Create a wide rectangle (1.5" x 1") and drag out a vertical guide, snapping it to the center. Hold down Opt/Alt and click with the Rectangle tool (Opt/Alt-click) on the center guide (on the top segment). Enter 1.05" x 1.05".

2 Rotate one rectangle. Double-click the Rotate tool to rotate the new rectangle around its center and enter 45°.

3 Select and unite the rectangles. Marquee-select both objects, show the Pathfinder palette (Window menu) and click on the Unite icon.

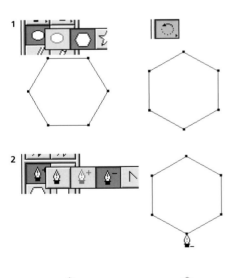

Exercise #4:
Make a six-sided polygon

1 Create a six-sided polygon. With the Polygon tool selected, click once and enter 6 sides and a .866" Radius. Then double-click the Rotate tool and enter 30°.

2 Delete the bottom point. With the Delete-anchor-point tool, click on the bottom point to delete it.

3 Move the two bottom points down, then the two middle points. Use the Direct-selection tool to select the bottom two points. Then grab one of the points and Shift-drag in a vertical line (down .423"). Lastly, Direct-select, grab and Shift-drag the middle two points down vertically into position (down .275").

Exercise #5:

Use Add Anchor Points filter in a three-sided polygon

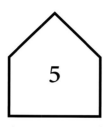

1 Create a three-sided polygon. With the Polygon tool selected, click once and enter 3 sides and a 1.299" Radius.

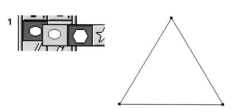

2 Use the Add Anchor Points filter. With the polygon still selected, choose Object: Path: Add Anchor Points (use the default keyboard shortcut, or create your own).

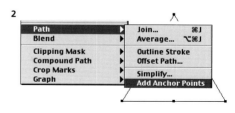

3 Average the two left points, then Average the two right points. Direct-select the two left points and Average them along the vertical axis (Context-sensitive: Average, or Object: Path: Average), then repeat for the two right points.

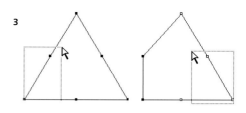

4 Delete the bottom point. With the Delete-anchor-point tool, click on the bottom center point to delete it.

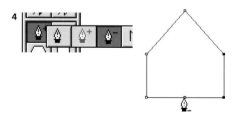

5 Move the top point down. Use the Direct-selection tool to select the top point, then double-click on the Selection tool itself in the Toolbox to open the Move dialog box and enter a −.186" vertical distance.

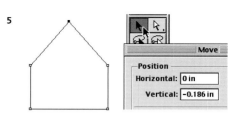

6 Slide in the sides towards the center. Use the Direct-selection tool to click on the right side of the house and drag it towards the center until the roofline looks smooth (hold down your Shift key to constrain the drag horizontally). Repeat for the left side of the house. Alternatively, select the right side and use the ← key on your keyboard to nudge the right side towards the center until the roofline looks smooth. Then, click on the left side to select it, and use the → key to nudge it towards the center. (If necessary, change your Cursor-key setting in Edit: Preferences: Keyboard Increments.)

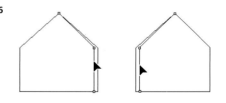

Exercise #6:
*Cut a path and
Paste In Front*

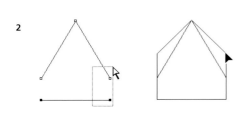

1 Cut, paste, then move the bottom of a triangle. With the Polygon tool selected, click once and enter 3 sides and a .866" Radius. With the Direct-selection tool, select and Cut the bottom path to the Clipboard, Choose Edit: Paste In Front, then grab the bottom path and drag it into position (down .423").

2 Create the sides and move middle points into place. Direct-select the two right points and Join them, then repeat for the two left points. Finally, select the two middle points, and grab one to drag *both* up (.275").

Exercise #7:
Join two objects

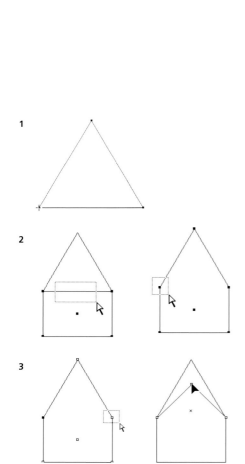

1 Make two objects. Click once with the Polygon tool, enter 3 sides and a .866" Radius. Zoom in on the lower left corner and, with the Rectangle tool, click exactly on the lower left anchor point. Set the rectangle to 1.5" x 1".

2 Delete the middle lines and join the corners. Direct-select marquee the middle bisecting lines and delete. Select the upper-left corner points and Average-Join by either Averaging and then Joining the points (see Exercises #5 and #6 above), or by pressing ⌘-Shift-Option-J/ Ctrl-Shift-Alt-J to average and join simultaneously. Select and Average-Join the upper right points.

3 Drag the top point down. Grab the top point, hold the Shift key and drag it into position (down .55").

Exercise #8:

Use Add Anchor Points filter, then Average-Join

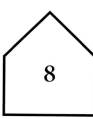

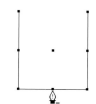

1. **Make a tall rectangle, delete top path, add anchor points, remove bottom point.** Create a tall rectangle (1.5" x 1.75") and delete the top path. Choose Add Anchor Points (Object: Path) and use the Delete-anchor-point tool to remove the bottom point.

2. **Select and Average-Join the top points and move middles into position.** Direct-select the top two points and Average-Join (see Exercise #7, step 2). Then Direct-select the middle points, grab one, and with the Shift key, drag them both into position (up .125").

Exercise #9:

Reflect a Pen profile

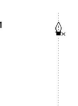

1. **Create a house profile.** Drag out a vertical guide, then reset the ruler origin on the guide. To draw the profile, use the Pen tool to click on the guide at the ruler zero point, hold down Shift (to constrain your lines to 45° angles) and click to place the corner (.75" down and .75" to the left) and the bottom (1" down).

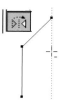

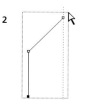

2. **Reflect a copy of the profile.** Select all three points of the house profile. With the Reflect tool, Option/Alt-click on the guide line. Enter an angle of 90° and click Copy.

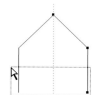

3. **Join the two profiles.** Direct-select and Join the bottom two points. Then Direct-select the top two points and Average-Join (see Exercise #7, step 2).

A Classic Icon

Five Ways to Re-create Simple Shapes

Overview: *Finding different ways to construct the same iconic image.*

McSHANE, ADIGARD / M.A.D.

1

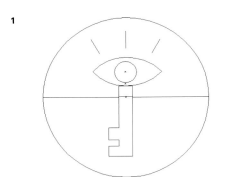

The Outline view of the original logo

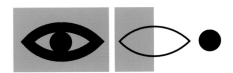

The original logo, constructed from a stroked line and a solid circle

You can construct even the simplest of iconic images in many ways. Patricia McShane and Erik Adigard of the M.A.D. graphics firm designed this classic logo for the *Computers Freedom & Privacy* annual conference. This conference addresses the effects of computer and telecommunications technologies on societal and personal freedom and privacy. This simple iconic representation of an eye is a perfect example of how you can explore different ways to solve the same graphics problem.

1 First, construct your logo in the way that seems most logical to you. Everybody's mind works differently, and the most obvious solutions to you might seem innovative to the next person. Follow your instincts as to how to construct each image. But if design changes require you to rethink your approach (for instance, what if the client wanted a radial fill instead of the black fill?), then try something slightly, or even completely, different.

Viewed in Outline mode, the original *Computers Freedom & Privacy* logo is clean and elegant with a minimum number of anchor points and lines. The M.A.D. team constructed the eye from a stroked line (made with the Pen tool) and a filled, black circle.

2 Make the outer eye shape. Create the solid black, almond-shaped object in any way you wish: Try drawing it with the Pen tool like M.A.D. did, or convert an oval into the correct shape by clicking on the middle points with the Convert-anchor-point tool in the Pen tool pop-up.

3 Try using solid objects. Starting with your base object, construct the eye with overlapping solid objects. Scale a version of the outline for the green inset and place a black circle on the top.

4 Try making a compound object. Use the objects that you created in the previous version to make a compound object that allows the inner part of the eye to be cut out. Select the outer black outline and the inner green inset and choose Object: Compound Path: Make.

5 Try making the eye from a symbol font. Included on the *Wow!* disk is a sample international symbols font from Image Club called "Mini Pics International." The character "W" is an eye very close to our icon. First, load your Mini Pics font (see your operating system manual for loading fonts). Choose the Mini Pics font from the Character palette, then click with the Type tool and type the character "W". Next, click on a Selection tool (this selects your type as an object) and choose Type: Create Outlines. This command converts the letter into a compound object different from the one you made in version 4 (above), with three objects cut out of the outline. Since the eye you're trying to make doesn't have a dark solid center, use the Direct-selection tool to select and delete the center compound object. Then try to match the original eye by adjusting the remaining compound paths with the Direct-selection and Scale tools.

Converting and transforming this symbol font may be a convoluted way to create such a simple shape, but the technique may come in handy.

2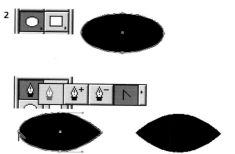

One way to create the back of the eye

3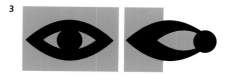

Constructing the logo with three solid objects

4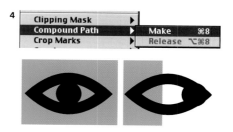

Constructing the logo from an outer compound object and an inner solid circle

5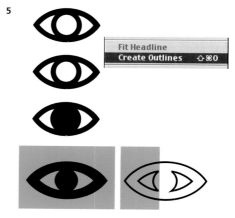

The same logo constructed from a text object converted to an outline, then scaled

Zen Scaling

Note: *Use the Shift key to constrain proportions.* ***Zen Scaling*** *practice is also on the* ***Wow!*** *disk.*

1 Scaling proportionally towards the top Click at the top, grab lower-right (LR), drag up

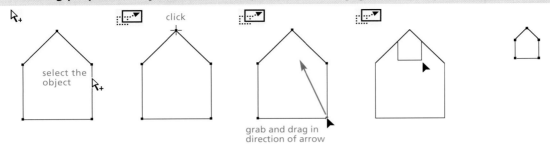

select the object

click

grab and drag in direction of arrow

2 Scaling horizontally towards the center Click at the top, grab LR, drag inward

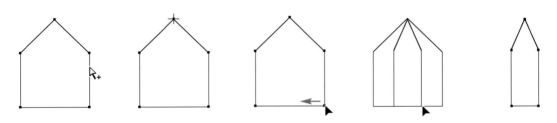

3 Scaling vertically towards the top Click at the top, grab LR, drag straight up

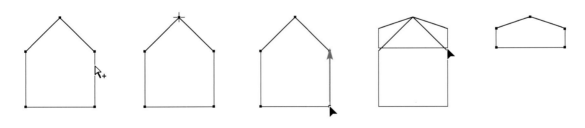

4 Scaling vertically and flipping the object Click at the top, grab LR, drag straight up

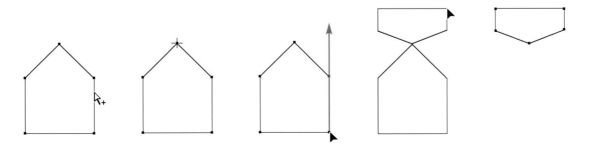

Zen Scaling *(continued)*

Note: *Use the Shift key to constrain proportions. **Zen Scaling** practice is also on the **Wow!** disk.*

---

5 Scaling proportionally towards lower-left (LL) Click LL, grab upper-right, drag to LL

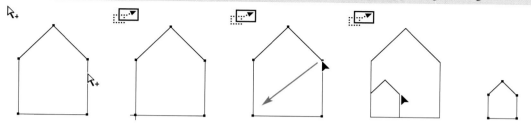

---

6 Scaling horizontally to the left side Click LL, grab lower-right (LR), drag to left

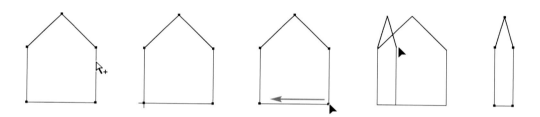

---

7 Scaling vertically towards the bottom Click center bottom, grab top, drag down

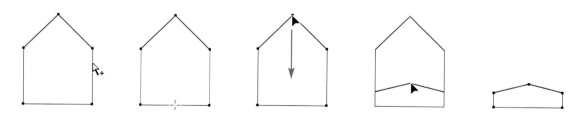

---

8 Scaling proportionally towards the center Click the center, grab corner, drag to center

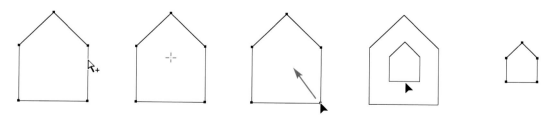

Or, to scale about the center, use the Scale tool to click-drag outside the object towards the center

Zen Rotation

Note: *Use the Shift key to constrain movement.* ***Zen Rotation*** *practice is also on the* ***Wow!*** *disk.*

1 Rotating around the center Click in the center, then grab lower-right (LR) and drag

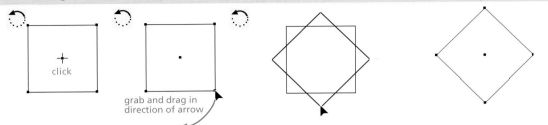

Or, to rotate about the center, use the Rotate tool to click-drag outside the object towards the center

2 Rotating from a corner Click in the upper left corner, then grab LR and drag

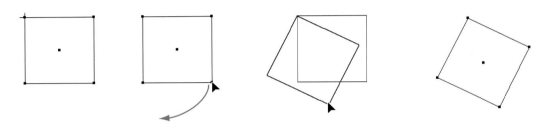

3 Rotating from outside Click above the left corner, then grab LR and drag

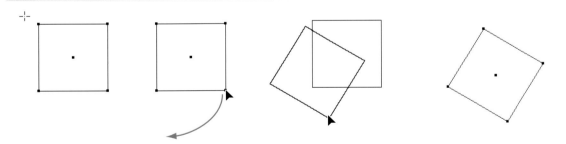

4 Rotating part of a path Marquee points with the Direct-selection tool, then use Rotate tool

Marquee the forearm with Direct-selection tool   *With the Rotate tool, click on the elbow, grab the fingers and drag them around*

Creating a Simple Object Using the Basic Tools

Key: *Click where you see a* RED *cross, grab with the* GRAY *arrow and drag towards* BLACK *arrow.*

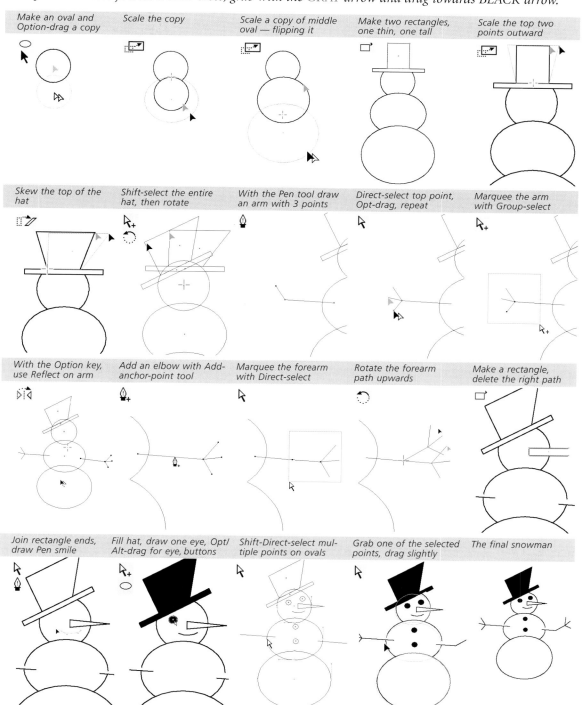

Make an oval and Option-drag a copy

Scale the copy

Scale a copy of middle oval — flipping it

Make two rectangles, one thin, one tall

Scale the top two points outward

Skew the top of the hat

Shift-select the entire hat, then rotate

With the Pen tool draw an arm with 3 points

Direct-select top point, Opt-drag, repeat

Marquee the arm with Group-select

With the Option key, use Reflect on arm

Add an elbow with Add-anchor-point tool

Marquee the forearm with Direct-select

Rotate the forearm path upwards

Make a rectangle, delete the right path

Join rectangle ends, draw Pen smile

Fill hat, draw one eye, Opt/Alt-drag for eye, buttons

Shift-Direct-select multiple points on ovals

Grab one of the selected points, drag slightly

The final snowman

A Finger Dance

Turbo-charge with Illustrator's Power-keys

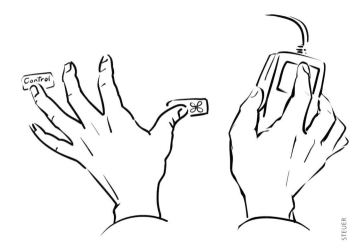

Overview: *Save hours of production time by mastering the finger dance of Illustrator's power-keys.*

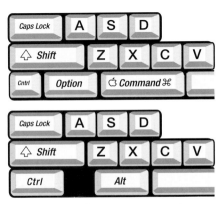

Find a summary of Finger Dance power-keys on the pull-out quick reference card

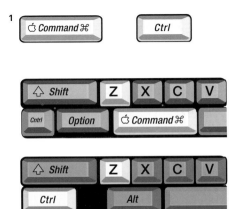

If you are using the mouse to choose your selection tools from the Toolbox, then you need this lesson. With some time and patience, you'll be able to free up your mouse so that practically the only thing you do with it is draw. Your other hand will learn to dance around the keyboard accessing all of your selection tools, modifying your creation and transformation tools, using your Zoom and Hand tools, and last but not least, providing instant Undo and Redo.

This "Finger Dance" is probably the most difficult aspect of Illustrator to master. Go through these lessons in order, but don't expect to get through them in one or even two sittings. When you make a mistake, use Undo (⌘/Ctrl-Z). Try a couple of exercises, then go back to your own work, incorporating what you've just learned. When you begin to get frustrated, take a break. Later—hours, days or weeks later—try another lesson. And don't forget to breathe.

Rule #1: Always keep one finger on the ⌘ key (CTRL for Windows). Whether you are using a mouse or a pressure-sensitive tablet, the hand you are not drawing with should be resting on the keyboard, with one finger (or thumb) on the ⌘ key. This position will make that all-important Undo (⌘/Ctrl-Z) instantly accessible.

Rule #2: Undo if you make a mistake. This is so crucial an aspect of working in the computer environment that I am willing to be redundant. If there is only one key combination that you memorize, make it Undo (⌘/Ctrl-Z).

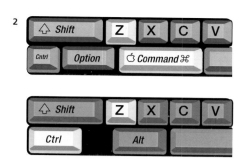

Rule #3: The ⌘ (Ctrl) key turns your cursor into a selection tool. In Illustrator, the ⌘/Ctrl key does a lot more than merely provide you with easy access to Undo. The ⌘/Ctrl key will convert any tool into the selection arrow that you last used. In the exercises that follow, you'll soon discover that the most flexible selection arrow is the Direct-selection tool.

Rule #4: Watch your cursor. If you learn to watch your cursor, you'll be able to prevent most errors before they happen. And if you don't (for instance, if you drag a copy of an object by mistake), then use Undo and try again.

Rule #5: Pay careful attention to *when* you hold down each key. Most of the modifier keys operate differently depending on *when* you hold each key down. If you obey Rule #4 and watch your cursor, then you'll notice what the key you are holding does.

Rule #6: Hold down the key(s) until after you let go of your mouse button. In order for your modifier key to actually modify your action, you *must* keep your key down until *after* you let go of your mouse button.

Rule #7: Work in Outline mode. When you are constructing or manipulating objects, get into the habit of working in Outline mode. Of course, if you are designing the colors in your image, you'll need to work in Preview, but while you're learning how to use the power-keys, you'll generally find it much quicker and easier if you are in Outline mode.

Remove "Easy Access"! (Mac)

When you're using Illustrator, you must take the Apple program called *Easy Access* out of the Extensions folder (in the System folder). Although *Easy Access* was developed as an aid to mouse movements for people with limited manual mobility, it interferes with Illustrator's normal functioning. If you have limited manual dexterity, try using QuicKeys to simplify menu selection, keystrokes and object creation.

MACINTOSH FINGERDANCES

Before you begin this sequence of exercises, choose the Direct-selection tool, then select the Rectangle tool and drag to create a rectangle.

1 Finger Dance (⌘) Grabbing a selected object and moving it

2 Finger Dance (⌘) Deselecting an object, selecting a path and moving it

3 Finger Dance (⌘-Shift) Moving a selected object horizontally

4 Finger Dance (⌘-Shift) Deselecting an object, selecting a path and moving it horizontally

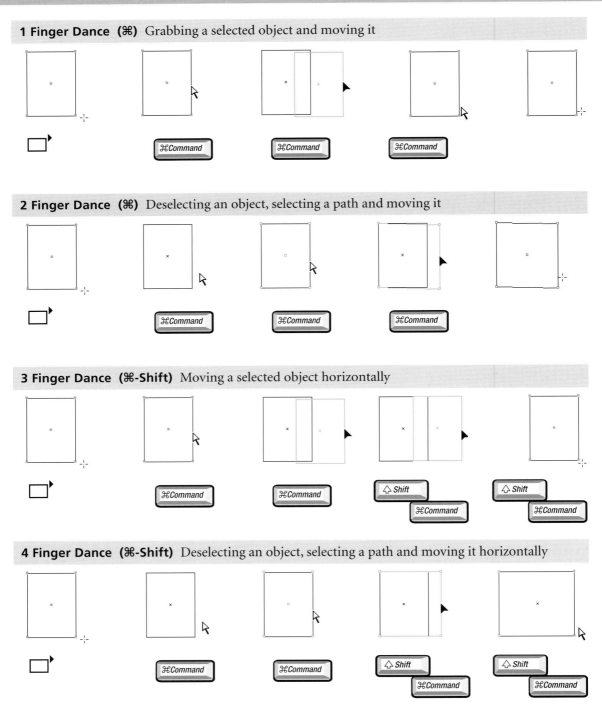

Before you begin this sequence of exercises, choose the Direct-selection tool, then select the Rectangle tool and drag to create a rectangle.

1 Finger Dance (Ctrl) Grabbing a selected object and moving it

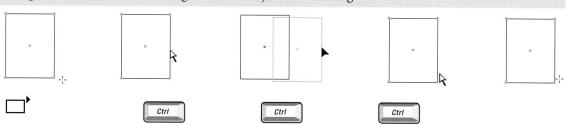

2 Finger Dance (Ctrl) Deselecting an object, selecting a path and moving it

3 Finger Dance (Ctrl-Shift) Moving a selected object horizontally

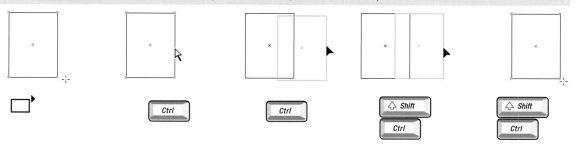

4 Finger Dance (Ctrl-Shift) Deselecting an object, selecting a path and moving it horizontally

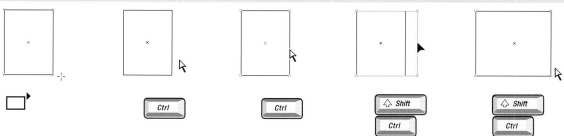

Before you begin this sequence of exercises, choose the Direct-selection tool,
then select the Rectangle tool and drag to create a rectangle.

5 Finger Dance (⌘, then ⌘-Option) Moving a copy of a selected object

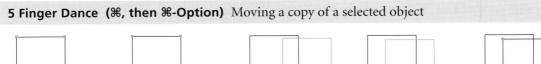

6 Finger Dance (⌘, then ⌘-Option) Deselecting an object, moving a copy of a path

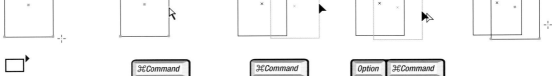

7 Finger Dance (⌘, then ⌘-Shift-Option) Moving a copy of a selected object horizontally

8 Finger Dance (⌘, then ⌘-Shift-Option) Deselecting, moving a copy of the path horizontally

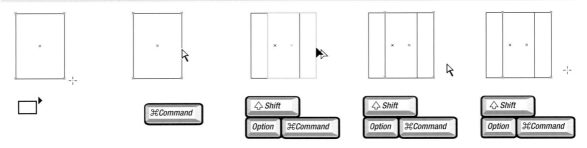

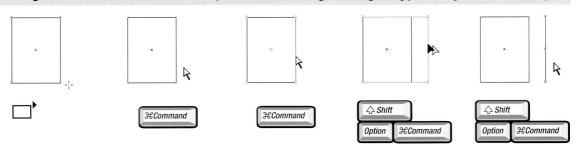

Before you begin this sequence of exercises, choose the Direct-selection tool,
then select the Rectangle tool and drag to create a rectangle.

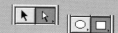

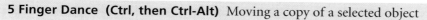

5 Finger Dance (Ctrl, then Ctrl-Alt) Moving a copy of a selected object

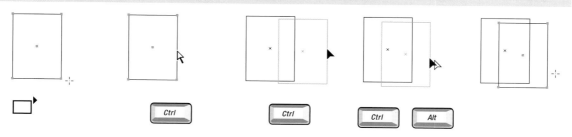

6 Finger Dance (Ctrl, then Ctrl-Alt) Deselecting an object, moving a copy of a path

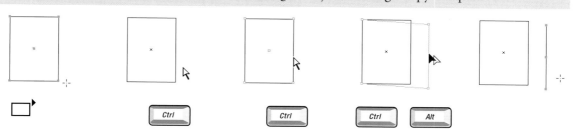

7 Finger Dance (Ctrl, then Ctrl-Shift-Alt) Moving a copy of a selected object horizontally

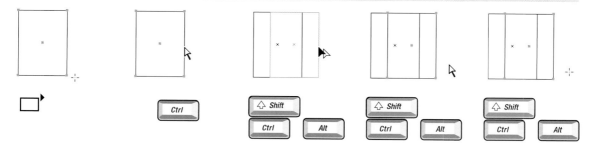

8 Finger Dance (Ctrl, then Ctrl-Shift-Alt) Deselecting, moving a copy of the path

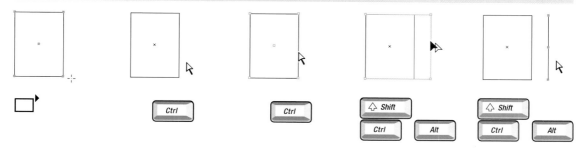

MACINTOSH FINGERDANCES

Before you begin this sequence of exercises, choose the Direct-selection tool,
then select the Rectangle tool and drag to create a rectangle.

9 Finger Dance (⌘-Option, then ⌘-Option) Deselecting, Group-selecting, moving a copy

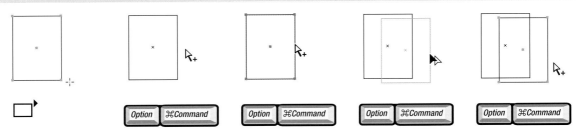

10 Finger Dance (⌘-Option, ⌘-Shift) Group-selecting, moving an object horizontally

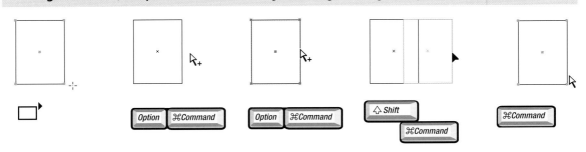

11 Finger Dance (⌘-Option, ⌘-Option-Shift) Moving copies horizontally, adding selections

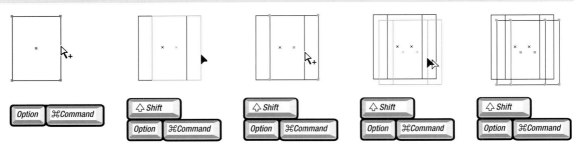

12 Finger Dance (⌘-Option, ⌘-Option-Shift, ⌘) Moving a copy, adding a selection, moving

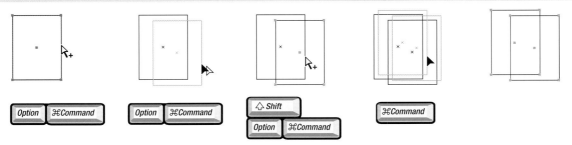

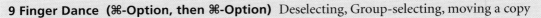

WINDOWS FINGERDANCES

Before you begin this sequence of exercises, choose the Direct-selection tool, then select the Rectangle tool and drag to create a rectangle.

9 Finger Dance (Ctrl-Alt, then Ctrl-Alt) Deselecting, Group-selecting, moving a copy

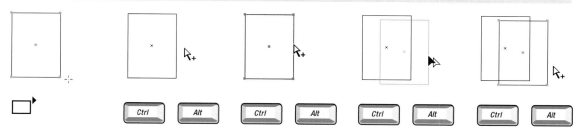

10 Finger Dance (Ctrl-Alt, Ctrl-Shift) Group-selecting, moving an object horizontally

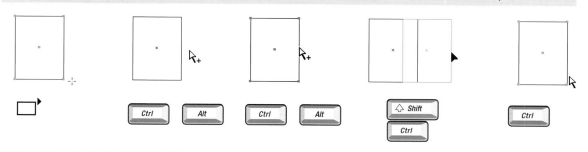

11 Finger Dance (Ctrl-Alt, Ctrl-Alt-Shift) Moving copies horizontally, adding selections

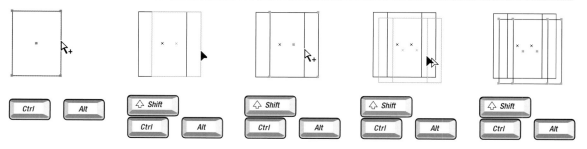

12 Finger Dance (Ctrl-Alt, Ctrl-Alt-Shift, Ctrl) Moving a copy, adding a selection, moving

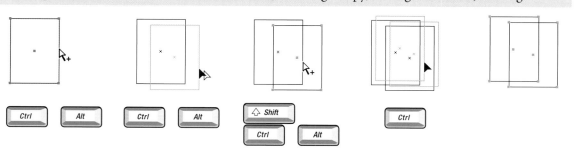

Lines, Fills & Colors

3

Lines, Fills & Colors

Core palettes

- **The Color palette** lets you mix colors by adjusting the color space sliders or sample colors from the color ramp. (See the *Web* chapter for warnings and Tips for working in RGB.)
- **The Stroke palette** lets you set the weight, cap, join method, miter limit and dash style of a stroke (see more in this chapter).
- **The Gradient palette** is used to create gradient fills (see the *Blends & Gradients* chapter).
- **The Swatches palette** contains a default set of color swatches, gradients and patterns, along with any colors you want to save with the document. Using and/or pasting a color from a Library adds that color to your Swatches palette.
- **The Styles palette** also contains a default set of styles, and can store any style you want saved. Using and/or pasting a style from a Library adds that style to the Styles palette (see the *Transparency* chapter).

Preference: Use Preview Bounds

When this is checked, the calculated size (width and height) of stroked objects displayed in the Info, Transform and Align palettes includes the stroke weight.

Lines, fills and colors are the core elements for creating with Illustrator. Once you've mastered them, this version of Illustrator offers unlimited possibilities for creating quick, simple and elegant images without the fuss of complex steps or special effects. All the basic techniques in this chapter are used in combination with some of the more advanced techniques found in the chapters that follow.

CREATING WITH LINES, FILLS AND COLORS

Illustrator has separate palettes for Color, Stroke, Gradient, Swatches and Styles. To set an object's fill or stroke, select the appropriate fill or stroke proxy from the Toolbox and then use one of the palettes to alter the object's appearance. To open the Adobe Color Picker, double-click the fill or stroke icons in the Toolbox or the Color palette. To insure that your colors are web safe, check Only Web Colors, (see the *Web* chapter for more on creating web graphics).

Use the Color palette to create a color. This palette has a fill of None and a Last Color proxy. which retains the color in use when you change to either a pattern or gradient fill. Palette menu options include Invert and Complement. Complement locates the color complement of a selected color (though the complements don't seem to correlate to art school color wheels). New to this version is a menu choice for Web Safe RGB colors. When selected, the slider edit box displays the color's hexadecimal values. If a non-web safe color is selected in RGB mode, an out of web color warning displays in the Color palette above the CMYK out of gamut warning.

You can drag and drop colors between palettes. To save colors within your document, drag them to the Swatches palette from either the Color or Gradient palette, or from the Toolbox. Whenever you copy and paste objects that contain custom swatches or styles from one document to another, you'll be pasting those elements into the new document's palettes.

Double-click a swatch to open the Swatch Options. If you select (check) the Global checkbox (default *off*), adjust the sliders, or change the process color definition, you will update all objects filled with the original color to the new color.

Color modification filters

The Adjust Colors filter lets you adjust the tint of Global colors in selections or convert them to Grayscale. Illustrator no longer allows multiple color spaces in a single document, so some color spaces might be unavailable. The Saturate filter (which integrates Saturate, Saturate More, Desaturate and Desaturate More filters) lets you adjust the saturation of objects and image objects via sliders or numerically. (See index for examples using these filters.)

More tools

Two easily overlooked Illustrator tools are the Eyedropper (which *picks up* stroke, fill, color and text formatting) and the Paint-bucket (which *deposits* stroke, fill, color and text formatting). These two tools offer some useful shortcuts for copying and applying appearances from one object to another. To set the default appearance for your next object, click on an object with the Eyedropper tool. To apply the current appearance to an object, click on it with the Paint-bucket tool. With one tool selected, access the other by holding down the Option (Mac)/Alt (Win) key. Use the Eyedropper tool to sample colors from an object or hold down the Shift key to sample from a raster image.

You can also use the Eyedropper tool to copy a style from one object to another. Select the object you would like to change, and with the Eyedropper tool click an object that has the style you like. *Voilà!* Your selected object now has the appearance of the one you clicked on. By default, both the Eyedropper and Paint-bucket tools copy the appearance of an object, but double-clicking either of these tools in the Toolbox allows you to customize the settings for both.

Creating patterns

To create a pattern from an object, just drag the object to the Swatches palette!

When deleting swatches

When you click the Trash icon in the Swatches palette to delete selected swatches, Illustrator does *not* warn you that you might be deleting colors used in the document. Instead Illustrator will convert global colors and spot colors used to fill objects to non-global process colors. To be safe, choose Select All Unused and then click the Trash.

Note: *You are also not warned when you are deleting styles that might be used in the document.*

Pencil tool paths disappearing?

If paths disappear when you draw them close together, check the options for the Pencil and Smooth tools. Disabling the Keep Selected option deselects each path as you create it, so you won't accidentally reshape or lose it while you draw.

"K" Paint-bucket tool
"I" Eyedropper tool

Filling open objects

Illustrator allows you to fill both closed *and* open objects.

Outline   **Preview**

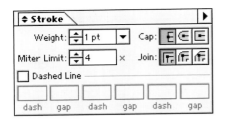

The Stroke palette

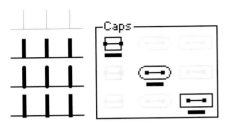

The same lines shown first in Outline, then in Preview with Butt-cap, Round-cap and Projecting-cap

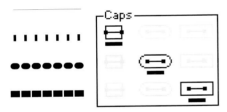

A 5-pt dashed line with a 2-pt dash and 6-pt gap shown first in Outline, then Preview with a Butt-cap, Round-cap and Projecting-cap

A path shown first in Outline, then in Preview with a Miter-join, Round-join and Bevel-join

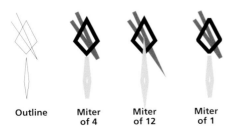

| Outline | Miter of 4 | Miter of 12 | Miter of 1 |

Objects with 6-pt strokes and various Miter-limits, demonstrating that the angles of lines, as well as their weight, affect Miter-limits

To copy type attributes using the Eyedropper tool, select the text block or portions of the text you want to affect with the Type tool. Then using the Eyedropper, click on the type that has attributes you wish to copy. To apply sampled *type* attributes, use the Paint-bucket tool to select a text string or a single word.

The end of the (path) line

An aspect of Illustrator that often mystifies newcomers is the way endpoints of lines are drawn. There are many times when it's easier and more efficient to work in Outline mode, but you quickly discover that although a set of lines seem to match up perfectly when viewed in Outline mode, they visibly overlap when previewed. Solve this by changing the end caps in the Stroke palette. Access the palette by choosing Window: Show Stroke.

Select one of the three end cap styles to determine how the endpoints of your selected paths will look when previewed. The first (and default) choice is called a Butt-cap; it causes your path to stop at the end anchor point. Butt-caps are essential for creating exact placement of one path against another. The middle choice is the Round-cap, which rounds the endpoint in a more natural manner. Round-caps are especially good for softening the effect of single lines or curves, making them appear slightly less harsh. The final type is the Projecting-cap, which can extend lines and dashes at half the stroke weight beyond the end anchor point. In addition to determining the appearance of path endpoints, cap styles also affect the shape of dashed lines.

You can also adjust the corners in an angled path if they appear too flat or stick out too far behind the anchor points. The default Miter-join with a limit of 4 usually looks just fine, but if you want to round or bevel your corners, simply choose the Round-join or Bevel-join. Each line weight has a particular Miter-limit at which the joins switch from blunt to pointy; the thicker the line, the higher the limit will be. Miter-limits can range from 1 (which is always blunt) to 500.

SIMPLIFY FILTER

More is not better when it comes to the number of anchor points you use to define a path. The more anchor points, the more complicated the path, which makes the file size larger and harder to process when printing. The Simplify filter (Object: Path: Simplify) removes excessive anchor points from one or more selected paths without making major changes to the path's original shape. You might want to apply this filter after using the Auto Trace tool, opening a clip art file, or using Adobe Streamline.

Two sliders control the amount and type of simplification. Adjust the Curve Precision slider to determine how accurately the new path should match the original path. The higher the percentage, the more anchor points will remain, and the closer the new path will be to the original. The endpoints of an open path are never altered. The Angle Threshold determines when corner points should become smooth. The higher the threshold, the more likely a corner point will remain sharp. As you adjust the sliders, a static display will appear comparing the original number of points to the current number. Check Show Original and Preview to visually compare your proposed changes to the original path.

PATHFINDER PALETTE

Pathfinders (Window: Show Pathfinder) allow you to combine or separate objects with a single command. Holding your cursor over an icon displays a tooltip that describes the operation that will be performed if selected. The charts on pages 86-87 demonstrate the effects of the Pathfinder filters applied to simple geometric objects. For more examples of practical applications of the various Pathfinder commands (filters), see *Wow!* artists' work later in the chapter. The filters can irrevocably change your objects, so either work on copies of your objects or use the Pathfinder Effects. Unlike the filters, the Pathfinder Effects are non-destructive because they don't actually perform the operation (see the *Transparency, Styles & Effects* chapter for more on Pathfinder Effects).

Using the libraries

The Swatch Library palettes (Window: Swatch Libraries) let you open swatch palettes for specific color systems. Or choose Other Library to access saved colors from any *unopened* document. **Note:** *You can't access saved swatches from documents that are open.*

RGB and CMYK color sliders

Switching back and forth between open RGB and CMYK files does not switch the color mode of the sliders in the Color palette. The colors you mix will be in the document's correct color space because Illustrator automatically converts them.

Pathfinder palette options

Use the palette pop-up menu to view all options which include Hard Mix, Soft Mix and Trap.

Simplify filter options

Use the options to create straight lines or view the original path with Preview checked. You won't see the original path otherwise, and it will be hard to determine what effect checking Straight Lines will have on your path if you can't see it.

Pathfinder actions

Import *Wow! Actions* (located on the *Wow!* disk) to apply Pathfinder filters by name.

Avoiding compound drop-out

When you create a compound path of multiple objects (see "Make compound paths" in this chapter), the back object will "drop out" to white where it overlaps other objects.
To avoid this, temporarily add another object and choose Object: Arrange: Send To Back. After compounding all the objects, Direct-select and delete this extra object and proceed.
Note: *The newly created compound path will take on the appearance of the "extra" object.*

Outline dashed strokes

- Create a dashed line.
- Set the opacity of the stroke to 99.999% (Transparency palette).
- Choose Object: Flatten Transparency and select the Higher/Slower setting for the slider.
—*Ted Alspach & Sandee Cohen*

Helpful filters

Uniformly Add Anchor Points to your path or object (Object: Path: Add Anchor Points). Having trouble selecting an object? Select the ones you don't want, and choose Edit: Select: Inverse. Two other useful filters are Edit: Select: Stray Points, which selects lone points, and Object: Path: Cleanup, which can delete stray points, unpainted objects and empty text paths.

Working with Pathfinder filters

Here are a few tips for working with Pathfinder filters:

- **Pathfinder Operations** Divide and Trim leaves filled styles intact.

- **With most Pathfinder filters, the top color will be maintained.** With the notable exception of the Minus Front filter, which subtracts the front object from the back (keeping the back object's color), most Pathfinder filters that combine objects will result in an object the color of the topmost object. Be aware that some filters (such as Trim, Merge and Crop) delete the path strokes of your objects (another reason to keep originals and work with a copy).

- **Make compound paths to run Pathfinder filters on multiple separate objects.** Some filters, such as Minus Front (or Minus Back), result in a single object which is affected by the other objects. If you wish to maintain multiple separate objects that are affected by a single object, copy the group of objects you want to behave as a unit and choose Object: Compound Paths: Make. All objects will now be styled as the backmost object and will operate as a unit when you apply the filter. (If your objects overlap, see the Tip "Avoiding compound drop-out" on this page.) Then, use the Direct-selection tool to edit individual objects.

DISTORTION FILTERS

The Distort filters (Filter menu) Scribble and Tweak, Punk and Bloat, Zig Zag and Roughen all distort paths based on the paths' anchor points. They either move, randomly distort, or add anchor points to create distortions. Preview lets you see and modify the results as you're experimenting with the filters. Much of the Free Distort functions can be performed with the Free Transform tool (for a lesson with the Free Transform tool, see "Distort Dynamics" later in this chapter).

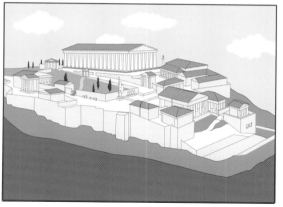

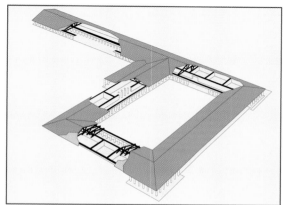

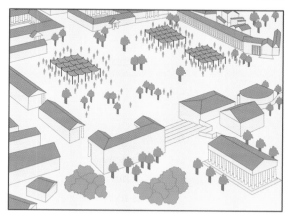

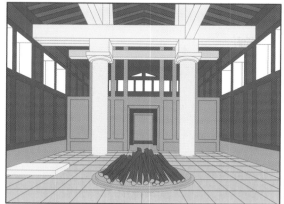

FERSTER

Gary Ferster

Using only simple filled and stroked objects, Gary Ferster was able to create this series of illustrations on Roman life for a children's educational CD-ROM titled "Ancient 2000." For help making perspective guidelines, see "Varied Perspective" in the *Layers* chapter.

Simply Realistic

Realism from Geometry and Observation

Overview: *Re-create a mechanical object using and altering the Rectangle or Elipse tools; place all inner enclosed objects while finding the right values; add selected highlights and offset shadows and reflections.*

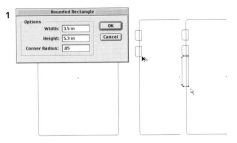

Creating and adjusting rounded rectangles to construct the basic forms

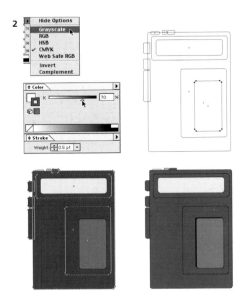

After choosing Grayscale from the Color pop-up menu, filling objects with tints of black, stroked with a .5-pt, 100% black line

Many people believe the only way to achieve realism in Illustrator is with elaborate gradients and blends, but this illustration by Patrick Lynch proves that artistic observation is the real secret. For his *Manual of Ornithology* (with Noble S. Proctor, for Yale University Press), Lynch needed equipment illustrations to aid in birdwatching.

1 Re-creating a mechanical object with repeating geometric shapes, by altering copies of objects. Most artists find that close observation, not complex perspective, is the most crucial aspect to rendering illustrations. To focus your attention on the power of basic shapes, select a simple mechanical device to render in grayscale, and choose Grayscale from the Color palette pop-up menu. Experiment with the Ellipse, Rectangle and Rounded Rectangle tools to place the basic elements. Especially with mechanical devices, components often tend to be similar; thus, make sure to adjust a *copy* of an object, rather than create one that might not align perfectly. For his personal stereo/radio knobs, Lynch dragged a copy of one knob (holding Option/Alt-Shift), stretched it by selecting one end with the Direct-selection tool and dragged it down (with the Shift key), creating a line of knobs with the same width, but different lengths.

2 Using tints to fill the objects. Select all your objects and choose a .5-pt black stroke from the Stroke and Color palettes. Then select an object (or set of objects), set the Fill to Black and Option/Alt-click on the New Swatch icon to name it "Black," and set the Color Mode to Spot Color. Click OK and create a tint using the Tint slider in the Colors palette. Continue to fill and adjust the tints for individual objects until you are happy with the basic value structure. Lynch used percentages from 10–80%, with most of the objects being 80% black.

3

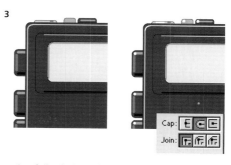

Carefully placing a few lighter-tinted, filled circles and lines with Round-caps for highlights

3 Creating a few carefully placed highlights. Look closely at your object and decide where to place selected highlights. Start with a couple of thin, lighter-tinted lines, making sure to choose Round-caps for the lines (in the expanded Stroke palette). In a couple of instances, place shorter and slightly heavier lines of an even lighter tint on top of the first lines. For lines that follow the contour of your object, select part of your object's path with the Direct-selection tool and copy and Paste In Front that part of the path. Use your cursor-keys to offset the contour and use the Eyedropper tool to double-click on one of your highlight lines to set the contour with the highlight line style. If you need to trim contours, use the Scissors tool and delete the unwanted portion of the path. Lastly, using a light tint as a fill, with no stroke, create a small circle at the confluence of two lines (try leaving a small gap between the lines and the circle). Option/Alt-drag the circle if you'd like to place it in other locations. For his highlights, Lynch used lines varying in weight from .5 to 2 points, in tints from 0 (white) to 50%, and five carefully placed white circles.

4

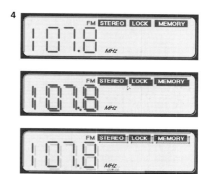

Creating text and LED numbers, then offsetting objects and giving offsets a darker gray tint

Making subtle changes in value to create the illusion of transparency

4 Creating shadows and transparencies. Follow the same procedure as above, but this time use darker tints to create shadows and transparencies. Make sure to offset shadows behind the object, especially if the shadows have solid fills.

The Outline view of the final illustration

Combining Circles

Cutting and Joining Overlapping Objects

LINO BOY'S MOTTO: "I AM HIGHLY RESOLVED!"

Overview: *Design an illustration using overlapping objects; cut and remove overlaps and join objects.*

1

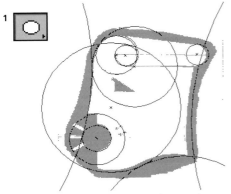

Using the Ellipse tool to trace circles over the PICT template

2

Selecting an object and locking everything else, then using the Scissors tool to cut overlaps

The first cut section, selecting pairs of anchors after moving the excess paths out of the way, then Average-Joining the pair

Illustrator is flexible enough to accommodate many different illustration styles. Mark Fox has always designed using a compass to draw perfect circles, an unusual drawing style that translates easily to computer illustration. Use the technique in this lesson to join any two objects, but also look at Pathfinder filters (later in this chapter).

1 Placing your objects. Fox scanned a sketch he made with his compass, saved it as a PICT, and opened it as a template. Chose File: Open, locate the image you wish to use as a template and enable the "Template" option (see lessons in the *Layers* chapter for more template help). Create your objects without worrying about how they overlap. Holding down the Shift key, Fox traced circles with the Ellipse tool.

2 Cropping the objects, removing the excess and joining the objects. To lock all *unselected* objects, select one object and press ⌘-Shift-Option-2/Ctrl-Shift-Alt-2. With the Scissors tool, click on the path where this object will overlap and join with others. Then choose Arrange: Unlock All and repeat the above procedure for other objects to be joined. After selecting and deleting excess paths, Direct-select each pair of points you want to join (one pair at a time), and Average-Join them in one step by pressing ⌘-Shift-Option-J/Ctrl-Shift-Alt-J.

Mark Fox / BlackDog

Mark Fox's whimsical design style hasn't visibly changed since his transition from ink and compass to Adobe Illustrator. The sketch to the right, for "Horse of a Different Color," shows Fox's notations for compass centers, as well as the circles. Although most people rely primarily on the Pen tool when drawing in Illustrator, Fox creates all his logos by cutting and joining rectangles and circles—occasionally using the Pen tool (for straight lines) and the Rotate tool.

Isometric Systems

Cursor Keys, Constrain-angles & Formulas

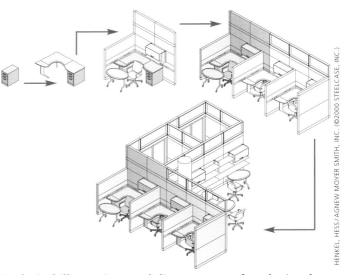

HENKEL, HESS/AGNEW MOYER SMITH, INC. (©2000 STEELCASE, INC.)

Overview: *Create detailed views of an object from front, top and side; use an isometric formula to transform the objects; set "Constrain-angle" and "Cursor key" distance; use Lasso and cursor keys with snap-to-point to adjust and assemble objects.*

Stubborn snapping-to-point

Sometimes if you try to move an object just slightly, it will annoyingly "snap" to the wrong place. If this happens, move it away from the area and release. Then grab the object again at the point you'd like to align and move it so that it snaps into the correct position. If you still have trouble, zoom in. As a last resort, you can disable "Snap to point" in Edit: Preferences: General.

1

Top, front and side faces with more than one component are grouped

2

Scaling, skewing and rotating

Technical illustrations and diagrams are often depicted in isometrics, and Adobe Illustrator can be the ideal program both for creating your initial illustrations, and for transforming them into this projection. The artists at Agnew Moyer Smith (AMS) created and transformed the diagrams on these pages using their three-step iso projection. For both the initial creation and manipulation of the isometric objects in space, AMS custom-set "Cursor key distance" and "Constrain angle" (in Edit: Preferences: General) and made sure that View: Snap to point was enabled.

1 **Creating detailed renderings of the front, side and top views of your object to scale.** Before you begin a technical illustration, you should choose a drawing scale, then coordinate the settings Preferences: General to match. For instance, to create a file drawer in the scale of 1 mm = 2", set the ruler units to millimeters and "Cursor key" distance to .5 mm, and make sure that the "Snap to point" option is enabled. With these features enabled and matching your drawing scale, it's easy to create detailed views of your object. To easily keep track of your object sizing as you work, choose Window: Show Info. If a portion of the real object is inset 1" to the left, you can use the ← cursor-key to move the path one increment (.5 mm) farther left. Finally, Snap-to-point will help you

align and assemble your various components. Select and group all the components of the front view. Separately group the top and side so you'll be able to easily isolate each of the views for transformation and assembly. AMS renders every internal detail, which allows them to view "cut-a-ways" or adjust individual elements, or groups of elements—for instance, when a drawer is opened.

2 Using an isometric formula to transform your objects, then assembling the elements. The artists at AMS created and transformed the diagrams on these pages using their three-step process, which is fully demonstrated on the *Wow!* disk. To transform your objects, double-click on the various tools to specify the correct percentages numerically. First, select all three views and scale them 100% horizontally and 86.6% vertically. Next, select the top and side, shear them at a −30° angle, and then shear the front 30°. Rotate the top and front 30° and the side −30°. The movement chart shows angles and directions.

To assemble the top, front and side, use the Selection tool to grab a specific anchor-point from the side view that will contact the front view, and drag it until it snaps into the correct position (the arrow turns hollow). Next, select and drag to snap the top into position. Finally, select and group the entire object for easy reselection.

3 Using selection, Constrain-angle and cursor keys to adjust objects and assemble multiple components. Try using the Direct-selection Lasso tool to select a portion of an object (Shift-Lasso adds points to a selection; Option-Lasso /Alt-Lasso deletes points from a selection), setting the Constrain-angle to 30°, then slide your selection along the isometric axes using alternating cursor keys. Select entire objects and snap them into position against other objects. Also, look at the movement chart (top of the page) to determine the direction in which to move, then double-click the Selection tool in the toolbox to specify a numeric movement for selections or objects.

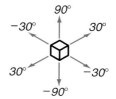

A cursor movement chart based on a Constrain Angle of 30°; a fully transformed and assembled object is then grouped for easy selection; setting Constrain Angle in Edit: Preferences: General

3

You can use the Direct-selection Lasso to select the points you want to move.

To lengthen the cart, select the points indicated and move in the direction of the arrow (−30°)

To widen the cart, select the points indicated, and either double-click on the Selection tool in the Toolbox to specify a Move numerically, or use your cursor keys

Transforming one object into the next, by Direct-selecting the appropriate anchor points and using the Move command, or by setting and using a custom Constrain-angle and cursor keys

Automated Isometric Actions!
Rick Henkel of AMS created *Wow! Actions* that automate formulas for isometrics (on the *Wow!* disk).

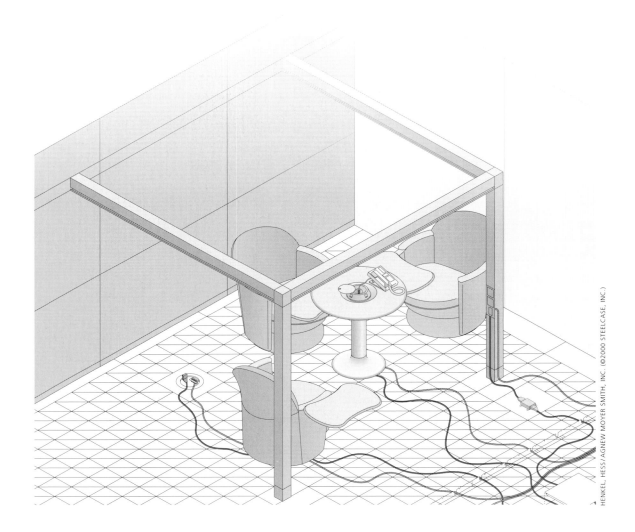

Gallery: Rick Henkel, Kurt Hess / Agnew Moyer Smith, Inc.

Agnew Moyer Smith's artists use Illustrator not only to create discrete elements, but also because it provides so much flexibility in composing an environment with those elements. Objects can be saved in separate files by category and used as "libraries" when constructing different scenes.

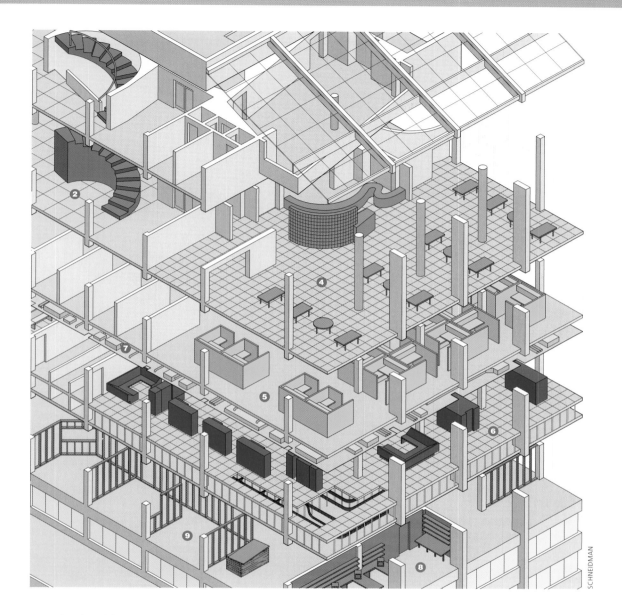

SCHNEIDMAN

Jared Schneidman

Jared Schneidman illustrated this building for a capabilities brochure for Structure Tone, an interior construction company. Schneidman traced a scan of an architectural drawing of the building, rendered originally in an isometric view. While drawing, Schneidman set the Constrain Angle (Edit: Preferences: General) to 30°, so he could edit objects by dragging selected points or lines along the same angles as the isometric view (he held down the Shift key while dragging to constrain movement to the set angles).

Objective Colors
Custom Labels for Making Quick Changes

Overview: *Define custom spot colors, naming colors by the type of object; repeat the procedure for each type of object; use Select filters to select types of objects by spot color name to edit colors or objects.*

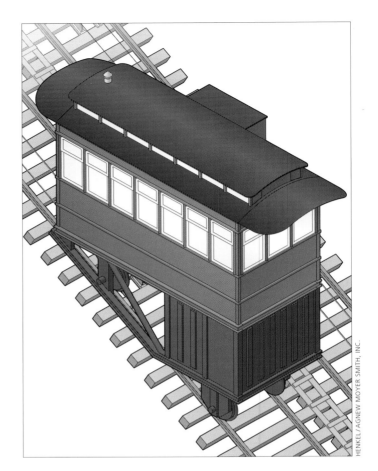

HENKEL / AGNEW MOYER SMITH, INC.

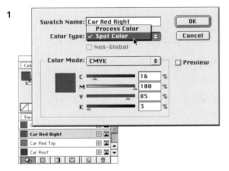

1

Option-clicking on the New Swatch icon to directly access Swatch Options; naming the color, then setting the color to be a Spot Color, which allows global changes and tinting

A spot color swatch with its custom label

When you need to frequently adjust the colors of an illustration, it's essential to find a way of organizing your colors. This illustration by Rick Henkel demonstrates how his firm, Agnew Moyer Smith (AMS), uses colors to label different categories of objects, making it simple to isolate and update colors. This method also makes it easy to find all objects in a category in order to apply any other global changes, such as changing the stroke weight or scaling, or adding transparency or effects.

1 Creating custom spot colors. AMS uses spot colors, even for process color jobs, to allow easy access to tints. (You can also use Process colors by checking the Global option in the Swatches palette.) In the Swatches palette,

Opt/Alt-click on the New Swatch icon. If you have pre-mixed a color in the Colors palette, this color will be loaded in the color mixer. If you are not pleased with the color, then edit it accordingly. Now give your color a name that conveys the kind of object you plan to fill with the color and choose Spot Color from the Color Type pop-up. Rick Henkel used labels such as "CamRight" and "DriveLeft" to label the colors he would use in his illustration of the Duquesne Incline. To help his selection of reliably reproducible colors, Henkel used the Agfa PostScript Process Color Guide to look up the color he actually wanted and then entered the CMYK percentages.

2 Repeating the procedure for all colors and labels, and changing color definitions as necessary. Create colors for each type of object to be styled differently, naming each color for the objects it will fill (to speed creation, see the Tip at the right). Henkel created spot colors, properly labeled, for each type of object included in this incline railroad illustration.

The spot color system makes it easy to change definitions of colors. From the Swatches palette, double-click on the color you want to change in order to open Swatch Options, where you can change the color recipe. Click OK to apply the changes to all objects containing that color.

3 Using the labels to find all like objects. To select all like objects—for example, those colored with "CamRight"—click on that color name in your Swatches palette list and choose Edit: Select: Same Fill Color. Once selected, you can edit other attributes besides color (like stroke width, layer position and alignment).

Creating custom spot color swatches for each category of object to be styled differently

With a color swatch label selected, choosing Edit: Select: Same Fill Color to find the objects filled with that color

After selecting the next color swatch, using the Select Again command to select all objects colored with that swatch

Spot colors for four-color-process jobs

Illustrator's process colors don't update globally by default (as Spot colors do). If you choose to define all swatches as spot colors, be sure to enable "Convert to Process" options in the File: Separation Setup dialog when generating separations.

From one swatch to another

When defining swatches with custom parameters in Swatch Options, such as Spot colors or Global process colors, instead of having to continually set similar parameters, simply select a swatch that is close to the color you want, then Opt/Alt-click the New Swatch icon to redefine and name the Swatch.

Organizing Color
Arranging an Artist's Palette of Colors

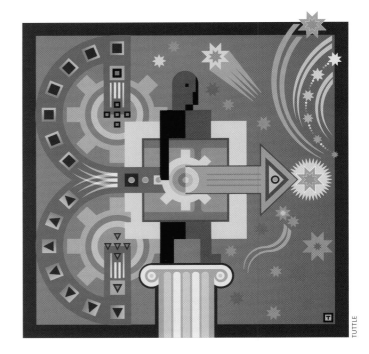

Overview: *Work with color swatches to choose initial colors; make adjustments to, and rename, custom colors; save a palette of your custom colors.*

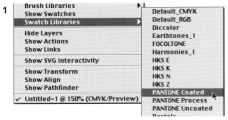

Opening one of the Pantone spot color palettes

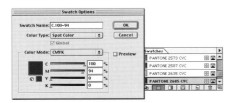

Respecifying and renaming custom spot colors to form an orderly, accessible palette

Moving multiple sliders

With the Shift key down, grabbing one color slider moves all colors together. Grabbing the right-most slider gives the greatest control. Drag to the right to 100% to saturate the color fully. Drag left to desaturate.

As any colorist knows, a well-organized palette can go beyond providing you with mere colors; it can facilitate the creative process. Progress Software Company's product signature color is the deep Pantone Violet #2685. When art director Deborah Hurst commissioned artist Jean Tuttle to create a series of illustrations for a "family" of Progress sales literature, they worked closely to develop a limited palette that would feel related to the signature color. Tuttle developed a method to organize the colors so she could work with them in an intuitive manner.

1 Using swatches of printed colors to choose ranges of colors to work with. As mentioned in *Chapter 1*, color on the screen is not a reliable predictor of the color you will get in print. Therefore, start with one of the computer-to-print color matching systems to choose your initial colors. Since Hurst was in Boston and Tuttle was in upstate New York, the two used the Pantone spot color system as a reference in choosing swatches of color to consider for the palette. Once they had agreed upon the general color scheme, Tuttle could open the Pantone

Coated color palette (Window: Swatch Libraries) and gain access to the computer version of the colors from within Illustrator. For each color she was considering, Tuttle put a square filled with that color into the document. After using the basic colors she wanted, she could close the Pantone palette—leaving her with just the color swatches she had chosen for her palette in the document.

Tuttle renamed each color in her palette based on five color groupings: Blues, Purples, Blue Violets, Red Violets and Accents. Because Illustrator, by default, lists custom colors alphabetically, Tuttle preceded each color grouping by a letter that would automate how Illustrator grouped the colors. Using a process color matching book as a guide, Tuttle then rounded off the CMYK percentages for each individual color, incorporating the color formulas in the name (B.50-50, for example, would be Purples: 50% Cyan/50% Magenta), and created variants on each of the colors as well, saving each color swatch into her palette. To visually separate the color groupings as they list in the Swatches palette, she created a series of white swatches to use purely as name placeholders—for example, one white was named "B. Purples" (the space before the "P" makes it list ahead of the numbered purples in the list)—while making sure that each of these white custom colors used as a label was placed into a square in the palette as well. To develop your custom set of swatches, select each palette object, Option-click on the New Swatches icon to specify the name, and choose "Spot" from Color Mode (see the previous lesson for more on making spot colors).

2 Accessing and tinting colors with your palette.

Another benefit to using spot colors in your palette is that you can easily specify tint percentages for any color. Just select the color and adjust the Tint slider in the Colors palette or type in a percentage in the text box. For each illustration Tuttle produced for this series, she had access to her entire set of colors and their tints. With this palette, Tuttle was able to create a "smoky blue" color environment to use for the entire family of illustrations.

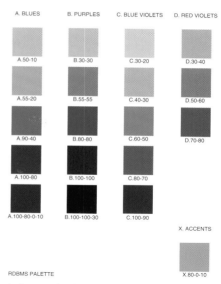

A chart made of the custom colors for future access to the full palette, including a rectangle for each white made as a name placeholder

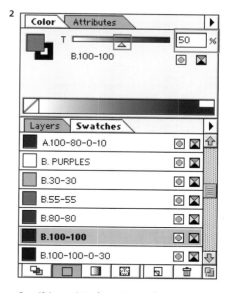

Specifying a tint of a custom color

Tints will "stick" until changed
The tint percentages of your last selected object will set the tint of your next fill and stroke color, unless you manually change them.

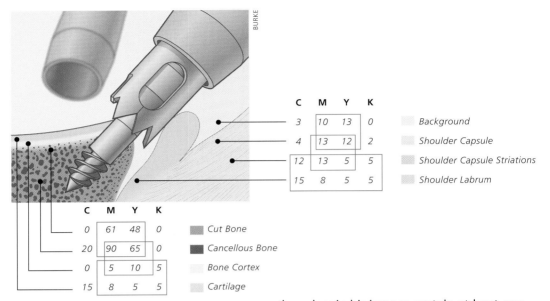

C	M	Y	K	
3	10	13	0	Background
4	13	12	2	Shoulder Capsule
12	13	5	5	Shoulder Capsule Striations
15	8	5	5	Shoulder Labrum

C	M	Y	K	
0	61	48	0	Cut Bone
20	90	65	0	Cancellous Bone
0	5	10	5	Bone Cortex
15	8	5	5	Cartilage

Christopher Burke

When printed in CMYK, Illustrator's smooth, crisp edges can be a registration nightmare. Even the slightest misregistration of inks can create visually disturbing white gaps between colors. So, although you shouldn't have to worry about what happens to your illustration once it's completed, the reality is that in this phase of computer graphics evolution, you still have to help your printer along. "Trapping" is a technique of printing one color over the edge of another—usually achieved by creating over-printing strokes that overlap adjacent objects. Christopher Burke uses a work-around where the colors in his images contain at least one (preferably two) of the color plates in every region of his image. As long as adjacent objects share at least 5% of at least one color, no white gaps can form, and trapping will natu-rally occur. This technique ensures "continuous coverage" of ink and maintains a full spectrum palette while keeping just enough in common between adjacent colors. (Also see Tip below and Tip "Trapping Issues" in the *Basics* chapter) The background image is a rasterized Illustrator drawing with an applied blur effect; raster images are free of trapping problems (see the *Illustrator & Other Programs* chapter for more on rasterizing Illustrator images).

Manual trapping of gradients and pattern fills

Since you can't style strokes with gradients or patterns, you can't trap using the Pathfinder Trap filter either. To trap gradients and patterns manually, first duplicate your object and stroke it in the weight you'd like for a trap. Then use Object: Path: Outline Stroke to convert the stroke to a filled object, which you should fill in the same style as the object you'd like to trap. Lastly, en-able the Overprint Fill box in the Attributes palette. If necessary, use the Gradient tool to unify gradients across objects (see page 200), and manually replicate pattern transformations.

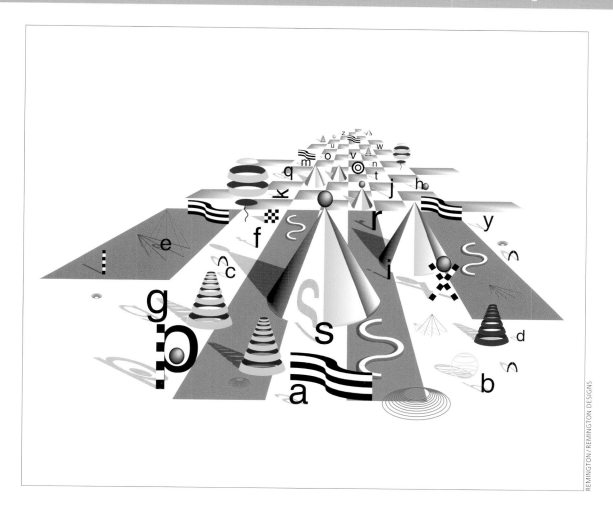

REMINGTON / REMINGTON DESIGNS

Dorothy Remington / Remington Designs

Color printers are notoriously unpredictable in terms of color consistency, so Dorothy Remington developed a method to increase consistency from proof to final output. When Remington constructs an image, she freely chooses colors from any of the CMYK process color models (such as Pantone Process, TruMatch, Focoltone, Toyo, etc.) that come with Illustrator, provided that she has the matching color swatchbooks. When she sends the computer file to the service bureau for proofing, as well as for final output, she also sends along the color swatches representing colors used in the image. Remington asks the service bureau to calibrate the printer to match her swatches as closely as possible. Although requesting such special attention might result in a small surcharge, it can save you an immense amount of time with the service bureau, and expense in reprinting the image because colors did not turn out as expected.

TATE (©1999 UNITED FEATURE SYNDICATE, INC.)

Clarke Tate

Setting the familiar characters, Woodstock and Snoopy, in famous locations, Clarke Tate illustrated this scene for a McDonald's Happy Meal box designed for Asian markets. Tate produced a palette of custom colors with descriptive names. You can view color names by selecting Name View from the Swatches palette pop-up menu.

▦	Bamboo Or Tan 2	☒
▢	Bamboo Y Hlite 1	☒
▦	Bamboo Shadow	☒

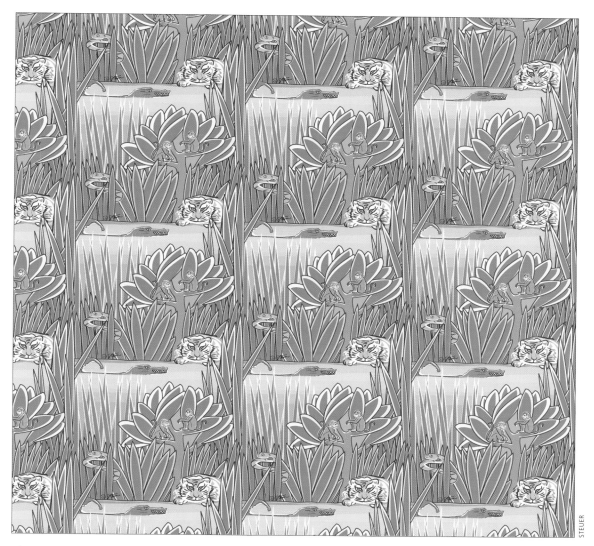

Sharon Steuer

Sharon Steuer drew the primary elements in this pattern tile using the Calligraphic Brush tool (see "Brush Strokes" in the *Brushes* chapter). She created the color transitions in the sky and leaves with blends (see the *Blends & Gradients* chapter) and then expanded the blends (Object: Expand) so they could be used within a pattern. To create the overlapping pattern elements, she dragged copies of

objects along with their "registration" marks, and then defined the pattern as described in the next lesson "Intricate Patterns."

Intricate Patterns

Designing Complex Repeating Patterns

Advanced Technique

Overview: *Design a rough composition; define a pattern boundary and place behind everything; use the box to generate trim marks, copy and position elements using trim marks for alignment; define and use the pattern.*

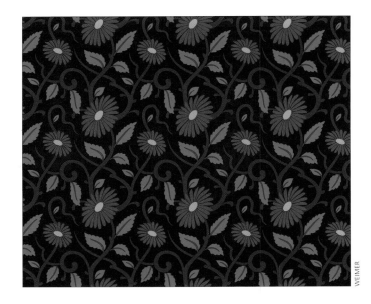

WEIMER

Arranging pattern elements into a basic design on the left; on the right, adding the pattern tile rectangle behind the pattern elements

Creating trim marks based on selection of the pattern tile rectangle

Included with Illustrator are many wonderful patterns for you to use and customize, and the *User Guide* does a good job of explaining pattern-making basics. But what if you want to create a more complex pattern?

A simple trick with trim marks can help to simplify a tedious process of trial and error. With some help from author and consultant Sandee Cohen, Alan James Weimer used the following technique to experimentally design an intricate tile that prints seamlessly as a repeating pattern.

1 Designing your basic pattern, drawing a confining rectangle, then creating trim marks for registration.
Create a design that will allow for some rearrangement of artwork elements. **Hint:** *you can't make a pattern tile that contains rasterized or placed images, or unexpanded and unmasked patterns, gradients, blends or brushes.* Use the Rectangle tool to draw a box around the part of the image you would like to repeat. This rectangle defines the boundary of the pattern tile. Send the rectangle to the bottom of the Layers palette or to the bottom of your drawing layer (Object: Arrange: Send to Back). This boundary rectangle, which controls how your pattern repeats, must be an unstroked, unfilled, nonrotated,

nonskewed object. Next, make sure that the rectangle is still selected and select Filter: Create: Trim Marks. Lastly, Ungroup these marks (in the next step, you'll use the trim marks to align elements that extend past the pattern tile).

2 Developing the repeating elements. If your pattern has an element that extends beyond the edge of the pattern tile, you must copy that element and place it on the opposite side of the tile. For example, if a flower blossom extends below the tile, you must place a copy of the remainder of the blossom at the top of the tile, ensuring that the whole flower is visible when the pattern repeats. To do this, select an element that overlaps above or below the tile and then Shift-select the nearest horizontal trim mark (position the cursor on an endpoint of the trim mark). While pressing Shift-Opt/Alt keys (the Option key copies the selections and the Shift key constrains dragging to vertical and horizontal directions), drag the element and trim mark upward until the cursor snaps to the endpoint of the upper horizontal trim mark. (For any element that overlaps the left or right side of the tile, select the element and the vertical trim mark and Shift-Opt/Alt drag them into position.)

3 Testing and optimizing your pattern. To test your pattern, select your pattern elements (including the bounding rectangle), and either choose Edit: Define Pattern to name your pattern, or drag your selection to the Swatches palette (double-click the swatch later to customize its name). Then create a new rectangle and select the pattern as your fill from the Swatches palette. Illustrator will fill the rectangle with your repeating pattern. If you redesign the pattern tile and then wish to update the pattern swatch, select your pattern elements again, but this time Option-drag the elements onto the pattern swatch you made before.

Optimize your pattern for printing by deleting excess anchor points. Select pattern elements and use the Simplify command (Object: Paths: Simplify).

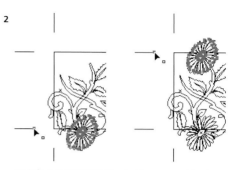
2

At left, selecting the flower blossom and horizontal trim mark; at right, after dragging a copy of the flower blossom and trim mark into position at the top of the pattern tile artwork

Finished artwork for the pattern tile, before turning into a pattern swatch in the Swatches palette

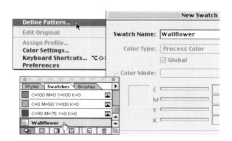

Speeding redraw with patterns
After filling an object with a pattern, speed up screen redraw by setting View to Outline mode, or by rasterizing a copy of the object (keep the original object unfilled in case you need to use it later).

Distort Dynamics

Adding Character Dynamics with Distort

Overview: *Create characters and group them; use the Free Distort tool to drag one corner to exaggerate the character; draw a sun and use the Free Distort tool to add dynamics to geometrics.*

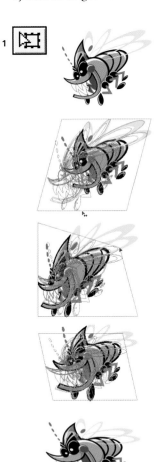

The original bug (top); then with the Free Transform tool the jaw is enlarged, the back is squashed and the entire character is skewed forward

After John Kanzler creates the cast of characters in his scenes, he often uses the Free Transform tool on each of the characters one at a time in order to add energy, movement, dynamics and action.

1 Creating and grouping a character, then applying the Free Transform tool. After building his bug one object at a time, Kanzler thought it needed a more menacing look, and wanted the bug to appear as if it was charging forward. By grabbing and moving various handles, he was able to enlarge the jaws while squashing the body. Then he skewed the bug to the left to give a sense of forward motion and more energy than the original. Select your objects and choose the Free Transform tool (E-key). Now, this is essential throughout this lesson: grab a handle and *then* hold down ⌘ (Mac)/Ctrl (Win) to pull only that selected handle to distort the image.

Look carefully at what results from movement of each of the Free Distort handles. For his hovering wasp, Kanzler used the Free Transform tool to give the wasp a little more "personality" by pulling a corner out to one side. Notice that as you pull a *corner* sideways to expand in one direction, the opposite side distorts and compresses—if you pull a *center* handle, you will merely skew the objects, elongating them toward the pulled side.

The effect of Free Distort on the hovering wasp

2 Applying the Free Transform tool to regularly shaped objects to add perspective and dynamics. In creating an "action line" for his illustration, Kanzler used the Free Transform tool to make an arc of dots skew out of uniformity, while constraining the arc of the skewed path to that of the original, unskewed path. First, he applied a custom dotted Pattern Brush to a curved path (see the *Brushes* chapter for help). Then he chose Object: Expand Appearance to turn the brushed path into a group of oval objects. By carefully tucking and pulling with the Free Transform tool, Kanzler was able to add flair to the arc while keeping the same general size.

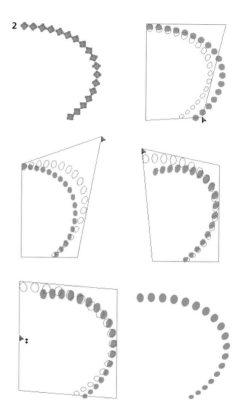

Using the Free Transform tool, pull different handles to create action and perspective effects

3 Making a sun, then creating extreme perspective using the Free Transform tool. To make the sun object, draw a circle (hold Shift as you draw with the Ellipse tool). In Outline mode (View menu), place your cursor over the circle centerpoint, hold Opt/Alt *and* Shift keys while drawing a second, larger concentric circle and make it into a Guide (View: Guides: Make Guides). With the Pen tool, draw a wedge-shaped "ray" that touches the outer-circle guide. Select the wedge, and with the Rotate tool, Opt/Alt-click on the circle's center point. Decide how many rays you want, divide 360 (the degrees in a circle) by the number of rays to find the angle to enter in the dialog box and click Copy. To create the remaining rays, keep repeating Transform Again, ⌘-D (Mac) or Ctrl-D (Win). Select all sun objects and choose Object: Group. Then choose the Free Transform tool and grab one single corner handle to skew the sun's perspective.

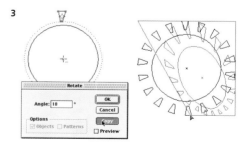

The sun object shown in Outline mode, before the process of Transform Again; and while pulling a Free Transform handle

The default settings for *were used unless otherwise noted. Artists' work may use custom settings.*

Unite

Before and after Unite

MARQUARDT

Intersect

Two objects, then overlapping and selected, then after choosing Intersect

Copies of intersection

SHIELDS DESIGN

Exclude

Two objects

Both objects selected

YOU'RE IN BUSINESS
PRODUCTS FOR LEASE

WHYTE

Minus Front

Before Minus Front

After Minus Front

The object rendered in Dimensions (see **Chapter 9** *for info)*

ELBERG

Minus Back

Green objects selected and made compound paths

After Minus Back, objects can then be filled separately

KINGSLAND

WHYTE

Divide

(Objects moved to show results)

Four objects

Objects divided

Each newly divided object filled

GROSSMAN

The default settings for *were used unless otherwise noted. Artists' work may use custom settings.*

Outline

(Objects moved and line weights increased to .5-pt to show results)

Before Outline

After Outline, and resetting line weight

STEUER

Trim

(Objects moved to show results)

Before Trim; in Preview and Artwork

After Trim; overlaps are reduced, BUT strokes are lost

SHIELDS DESIGN

Merge

(Objects moved to show results)

Before Merge in Artwork

After Merge; like fills are united, BUT strokes are lost

STAHL

Crop

A copy of the fish in front to use for Crop

After Crop; objects are now separated

DROBLAS GREENBERG

Hard Mix

Same color objects don't mix, so overlapping objects were colored differently

After Hard filter; Each overlap is now a separate object

After using the Eyedropper to switch the colors in the front objects

MARGOLIS PINEO (digitized by Steuer)

Soft Mix

Before Soft filter; the blue wave overlaps the detail along the bottom of the rocks

After Soft filter (see "SandeeC's Mix Soft Chart" in the Plug-ins folder on the Wow! disk)

FERSTER

Practical Path-cuts

Preparing for Blends with Pathfinder Filters

Overview: *Use a bisecting path with Intersect; combine drawn elements and copies using Unite; create see-through details using Exclude.*

1

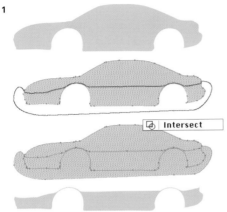

An object; drawing a bisecting path; selecting and intersecting

2

Drawing a fender-well; selecting it with copies of tires to unite; the final path united

3

The outer portion of the wiper and drawing the inner objects; selecting them both to exclude

Pathfinder filters can be astounding time-savers. To form the basic shapes used for photorealistic blends, Thomas Neal (of Thomas•Bradley Illustration & Design) used to painstakingly cut and join paths using the Scissors tool with Average and Join (for cutting and joining help, see "Combining circles," earlier in this chapter). Pathfinder filters practically automate Neal's tasks for preparing objects to use for blending. (See the *Layers* chapter for help hiding, locking and reordering objects, and the other Thomas • Bradley techniques in this book.)

1 Using Intersect to create a subsection of your car. Copy your car-body object, Lock it (Object menu) and use Paste In Front (Edit menu) to paste a copy exactly on top. Using the Pen tool, draw a path bisecting the car, then loop the path around to create a closed path surrounding the car so that the car can only be divided along your bisecting path. Select both objects and choose Pathfinder: Intersect, which deletes the paths that lie outside of the car subsection.

2 Using Unite to create the undercarriage. Using the Pen tool, draw a path that defines the shadow in the fender-wells. Copy and Paste In Front the four wheels, and Group them. With the Shift key, select the fender-wells with the grouped wheels and choose Pathfinder: Unite.

3 Creating see-through details. Create an object that forms the outline of your wiper. Using filled black objects, draw the areas you want to cut out of the outline. Select the outer and inner objects and choose Pathfinder: Exclude.

KLINE / ACME DESIGN

Michael Kline / Acme Design

When Michael Kline uses the Pathfinder
palette, he always uses a copy of the object in
case he needs that object again for something
else. With this illustration for *Kids Discover*
magazine, Kline kept an earlier version of the
house handy so that, if he needed to, he could
quickly copy the original and use Paste In Front
to place it into the working version. For the
lines in the roof, Kline used the Calligraphic
Brush tool, set at 2.5 points, 130° calligraphic
angle, and 60% black. Once all the lines were
drawn, he used Crop in the Pathfinder palette
to "cookie-cut" the basic shape of the roof, and

for most of the siding. Kline also used the Soft
Mix Pathfinder filter at varying percentages to
create the detail in the shadows—again, using
a copy of all his objects to retain the integrity
of originals in case he needed to reuse them.

Cubist Constructs

Creative experimentation with Pathfinders

Overview: *Create objects as the basis for Pathfinder commands; use commands on different sets of objects; make color and object adjustments.*

1

The scanned sketch placed as a template

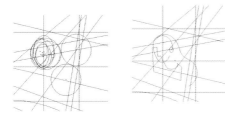

Before and after circles are cut and joined

2

On the left, three objects (shown with different stroke colors); on the right, the objects with colored fills (no stroke) prior to running the Soft Mix command

Soft Mix applied, then objects recolored

To build his geometrically complex style, Ron Chan depends on Illustrator's drawing tools and the Pathfinder palette commands. Many different ways exist to achieve similar effects. Here are some that Chan has perfected.

1 Preparing the basic objects you will work from.

Create the objects that will form the basis for your filtering. Chan used methods discussed elsewhere in the book to prepare the initial objects, including scanning a sketch to use as a template (*Layers* chapter), creating a custom drawing grid (*Type* chapter) in its own layer and making a masking layer (*Advanced Techniques* chapter). He cut and joined circles to form elements such as the head (shown at left). For cutting and joining help, see "Combining circles," earlier in this chapter.

2 Selecting overlapping objects and applying Soft Mix.

After creating a few overlapping objects, you might choose to see how those objects "cut into" each other. First, select the objects with any selection tool. Then use the Pathfinder commands (Window: Show Pathfinder). Although you can use the Divide Pathfinder to create separate objects for each area in which the objects intersect, Chan prefers to use the Soft Mix Pathfinder. Soft Mix creates new colors where objects overlap, making the intersections easy to see. (If you don't see the Soft Mix icon at the bottom of the Pathfinder palette, choose Show Options from the palette's pop-out menu.) Chan can then use the Direct-selection tool on particular divided objects for recoloring individually. He can also recolor like-colored objects as a unit by Direct-selecting one color and using Edit: Select: Same Fill Color, which selects all objects of that color.

3 Outlining and offsetting paths. Turning paths into outlined shapes gives you flexibility in styling and aligning lines. Chan stroked the jaw path and then outlined it using Object: Path: Outline Stroke. This allowed him to align the bottom edge of the line to the chin object. If you outline a path, you can fill it with gradients (see the *Blends & Gradients* chapter) or patterns (see the *Lines, Fills & Colors* chapter). Another way to turn a path into a fillable shape is to offset a copy of a selected path (Object: Path: Offset) and then join the endpoints of the copy and the original.

4 Cropping copies for an inset look. To create the look of an inset or lens of your image, first select and copy all the objects that will be affected, and then use Paste In Front and Group on the copy you just made. Using any method you wish, create a closed object to define the inset area. With the object still selected, press the Shift key and use the Selection tool to select the grouped copy. Choose Crop from the Pathfinder palette and then Ungroup the cropped objects. Select different objects and change color or opacity, or apply effects from the Effect menu. Also, try experimenting with the Colors: Adjust Colors filter (Filter menu) until you achieve a color cast you like.

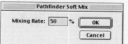

Soft Mix converts spot colors
Be aware that the Soft Mix filter automatically converts colors from spot to process (even where the original color remains!).

3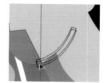

Selecting a path and then applying Object: Path: Outline Stroke

The outlined path was moved up (Smart Guides are turned on), then recolored

4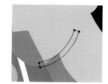

Artwork copied and pasted in front, then circle drawn for inset shape

After Pathfinder: Crop, then recolored

Brushes

4

Brushes

This chapter focuses on creating and applying brushes. These lessons and Galleries, as well as the special supplement by Sandee Cohen at the end of this chapter, are certain to broaden your possibilities for drawing and painting in Illustrator. For instance, did you know that you can actually create brushes that let you paint with leaves, or chain links, or even entire fields of grass? Did you know that using the Calligraphic tool allows you to paint marks that look like they were drawn with ink, but are much more easily adjusted and edited than similar marks made traditionally, or even in Corel Painter or Photoshop? Did you know that mapmakers can use brushes to create symbols that can be easily replaced and updated?

In this chapter you'll find lessons and galleries that explore these and other exciting ways to use Illustrator brushes. In addition to the brushes examples in this chapter, you'll also find Galleries that include brushes in almost every chapter, and additional step-by-step lessons involving brushes in the *Type* and *Transparency, Styles & Effects* chapters (in the *Type* chapter, see the "Brushed Type" lesson, as well as the Galleries that follow, and in the *Transparency, Styles & Effects* see the "Scratch-board Art" lesson).

Unleash your creativity with brushes

Double-click the Paintbrush tool to set application-level preferences for all brushes. With Fidelity and Smoothness, lower numbers are more accurate, and higher numbers are smoother. Uncheck Fill new brush strokes if the brush path shouldn't take on the fill color in addition to the stroke color. When Keep Selected is enabled, the last path drawn stays selected, and drawing a new path close to the selected path will redraw that path. Disabling Keep Selected deselects the last-drawn path, allowing you to draw paths near each other, instead of redrawing the

---

Constraining a brush

You can't use the Shift key to constrain the Brush tool to draw a straight path, so draw the path first with the Pen tool, *then* select the desired brush in the Brushes palette.— *Robin AF Olson*

Scaling brushes

To scale artwork that contains paths with applied brushes:

- Expand the brushed path first (Object: Expand Appearance), then scale the artwork.
- Scale the artwork after placing it into a page layout program.

Note: *When you apply a scale transformation to brushed paths, enabling Scale Strokes & Effects (Edit: Preferences: General) will also scale the brush art.*

More about brushes

- Pasting paths containing brushes will add the brush to the Brushes palette.
- Convert an applied brush into editable artwork, select the path and choose Object: Expand Appearance.
- Drag a brush out of the Brushes palette to edit the brush art.
- To create a brush from an applied brush path, blend, gradient, or gradient mesh expand it first (Object: Expand).

last-drawn path. If left enabled, the Edit Selected Paths slider is used to determine how close you have to be in order to redraw the selected path, as opposed to drawing a new path. The lower the number, the closer you have to be to the selected path to redraw it.

There are several ways to edit a brush: double-click it in the Brushes palette to change Brush options, or drag it out of the Brushes palette to edit the brush and then drag the new art into the Brushes palette. To replace a brush, press the Option (Mac)/Alt (Win) key and drag the new brush over the original brush slot in the Brushes palette. This will also replace all instances of the applied brush used in the document with the newly created brush.

Each of the brush types (Art, Scatter, Pattern and Calligraphy) provide a myriad of options to experiment with. Spend some time going over the lessons in this chapter to help you understand many of these options. For example, the Art, Scatter and Pattern brush art can adopt a stroke color or tint. To view Adobe's Colorization Tips in the dialog boxes for the individual brushes, click on the Tips button. To change the key color and shift the hue of the brush art, sample the preview art (in the dialog) with the Eyedropper tool.

When drawing with a pressure-sensitive stylus (pen) and tablet, the Calligraphy and Scatter brushes give you the ability to vary the scatter and the stroke thickness according to the pressure you apply to the tablet. In addition, the scatter brushes have settings to vary size, spacing and scatter of the brush art.

One last note about Sandee Cohen's "Special Brushes Supplement" —each of the brushes in the supplement (as well as some of the other art in the chapter), can be found in the "Brushes" folder on the *Wow!* disk

Closing a brush path

To close a path using the Brush tool, hold down the Option (Mac)/ Alt (Win) key *after* you begin creating the path, then let go of the mouse button just before you're ready to close the path. Border brushes work best on closed paths.

Where are the brushes?

Unlike the Swatches palette, which has convenient icons to switch between viewing all swatches, solid swatches, gradient swatches and patterns—with Brushes you have to individually select each type of brush that you want to appear in the palette from the Brushes palette pop-up menu.

Brushes to layers

Scatter brushed artwork can be easily separated onto individual layers for use in animations, etc. For details about working with layers, see the *Layers* chapter, specifically the Tip "Release artwork to layers."

Brush Strokes

Making Naturalistic Pen and Ink Drawings

Overview: *Adjust the Paintbrush Tool settings; customize a Calligraphic Brush; trace or draw your composition; make final adjustments.*

It's easy to create spontaneous painterly and calligraphic marks in Illustrator—perhaps easier than in any other graphics program. Creating highly variable, responsive strokes (using a graphics tablet and a pressure-sensitive, pen-like stylus), you can now edit those strokes as *paths,* or experiment with applying different brushes to the strokes *after* the path has been made. This illustration, one of 150 figures Sharon Steuer drew for Christina Sillari's teaching manual on Chakra Yoga, was created using one custom Calligraphy Brush and a Wacom tablet.

The digital photo saved as TIFF and placed as an Illustrator template

Maintaining your pressure

Only brush strokes *initially* drawn with pressure-sensitive settings can take advantage of pressure-sensitivity. Also be aware that re-applying a brush after trying another may alter the stroke shape.

1 If you'll be working from a source, prepare your template. Although you can draw directly into the computer, if you want to trace a sketch or a scan you'll need to prepare your template. For this series of illustrations, since the charcoal drawings were between 11" x 17" and 18" x 24", Steuer took digital snapshots of the drawings instead of scanning. The grayscale TIFF version of this posture "Easy Pose" was then placed as a template into Illustrator (see the *Layers* chapter for template help). Toggle between hiding and showing the template with View: Hide/Show Template.

2 Setting your Paintbrush tool preferences and customizing a calligraphy brush. Choose the Paintbrush tool and select one of the Calligraphy brushes in the Brushes Palette. In order to sketch freely and with accurate detail, the default Paintbrush Tool settings must be adjusted. Double-click on the Paintbrush tool to open Paintbrush Tool Preferences. Drag the Fidelity slider all the way to the left (.5 pixels), the Smoothness all the way to the right (100%), and disable all Options.

To create a custom brush, select a Calligraphic Brush, click the New Brush icon and click OK to New Calligraphic Brush. Experiment with various settings, name your brush and click OK. For this series of yoga illustrations, Steuer named the Calligraphic brush "6 pt oval" with settings of: Angle 60°, Random 180°, Roundness 60%, Pressure 40%, Diameter 6pt, Pressure 6pt. The Paintbrush is now set to use your current stroke color— if there is no stroke color, it will use the fill color. Now draw. If you don't like a mark, either choose Undo or use the Direct-selection tool to edit the path. (If you don't have a pressure-sensitive tablet, you may want to try Random as a variable in Brush Options, since Pressure won't have any effect.) To edit a brush, double-click it in the Brushes palette, or, drag a brush to the New Brush icon to duplicate it, then edit the copy.

3 Experimenting with your image. First, save any versions of your image that you are pleased with. Now try applying different brushes to specific strokes and to the entire image (to hide or show selection outlines, choose View: Hide/Show Edges). To access more Adobe-made Calligraphic Brushes, choose Windows: Brush Libraries: Calligraphic (at right, see two of Adobe's brushes applied to the same strokes).

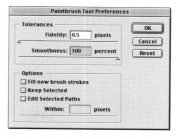

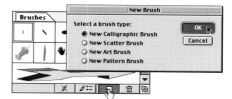

Customizing the Paintbrush Tool Preferences

Creating a new Calligraphic Brush

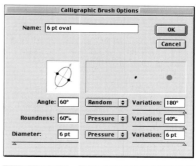

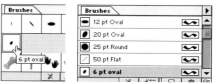

Customizing a Calligraphic Brush; the brush in the palette viewed with Tooltips and By Name

Strokes made with customized brush (left); applying default 3pt Oval, then 1pt Oval

STEUER

Sharon Steuer

Using the same Calligraphic Brush as in her preceding lesson, Sharon Steuer drew the seashells in black. On layers below (for help see the *Layers* chapter), she created a background gradient (see the *Blends and Gradients* chapter), and then used the Pencil tool to draw enclosed areas of flat color (shown alone below right). On a layer above, she drew a few details in color with the Calligraphic Brush. To create the textured background, she made two copies of the gradient layer, then transformed the first gradient copy into a Gradient Mesh (Object: Expand: Gradient Mesh) so she could select a few interior points and add highlights (see the *Blends and Gradients* chapter for more details about mesh). To the other gradient copy, Steuer

applied Filter: Pen and Ink: Hatch Effects, then chose "Stipple light" and "Match Object's Color" (for more on Hatches see the *Advanced Techniques* chapter). She applied this effect to a copy of the shadows as well.

JACKMORE

Lisa Jackmore

Lisa Jackmore often begins her Illustrator paintings by making smaller versions of the default Calligraphic Brushes. Although she often prefers more rounded brushes and draws in black for the initial sketch, sometimes she just makes a variety of brushes, then "doodles until the shape of a line inspires" her. Occasionally Jackmore will even save a doodle and figure out later how to incorporate it into the image.

She constructs her illustration, then colors the brush strokes toward the end of the project. To make a custom charcoal Art Brush, Jackmore used Adobe Streamline to turn a scanned charcoal mark into an Illustrator object. Jackmore opened the object in Illustrator and dragged it into the Brushes palette, then used the new brush to create the marks under the notepaper and in the framed painting.

ALSPACH

Jen Alspach

Jen Alspach started with a digital photograph of her cat Static, which she placed into a template layer (see the *Layers* chapter). In a new layer above, she traced over the photo, using brushes, with a Wacom "Pen Partner" 4" x 5" tablet. Alspach used darker, heavier brushes to draw the basic outline and the important interior lines like the eyes, ears and neck (all attributes set to Pressure with a 2–pt Diameter and a 2-pt variation). In another pressure-sensitive brush, she set a Fixed Angle and Roundness (diameter of 6-pt), while in a third brush she set all attributes to Random. Using the Wacom tablet with the pressure-sensitive Calligraphic Brushes, she was able to use very light hand pressure to draw the fine lines around the eyes and the whiskers.

Ellen Papciak-Rose

In this "Dance With The Stars" design for a Sun Theater T-shirt, Ellen Papciak-Rose created a "dashed line" pattern using the Pen tool (see above). She then selected the pattern and dragged it into the Brushes palette to make a New Art Brush, and then applied that dashed Art Brush to black strokes throughout the image. She then created two additional dashed brushes, one with irregular dashes, and one with more dashes, and applied these brushes to strokes as well.

Dance With The Stars

Ellen Papciak-Rose

Ellen Papciak-Rose wanted to give the musical T-shirt design for The Sun Theatre a slight "scratchboard" look, so she applied one of the default Art Brushes called "Charcoal-Rough" (Window: Brush Libraries: Artistic Sample) to the strokes of her filled objects. When she matched the stroke color to the background behind each object (e.g. objects on the yellow background were given yellow strokes), the fill sometimes extended beyond the charcoal brush's irregular and asymmetrical stroke. (See the "Scratchboard Art" lesson in the *Transparency* chapter for a more advanced scratchboard technique.)

Preparing Art

Adding Brushes to Existing Artwork

Overview: *Modify existing artwork; change closed paths to open paths; apply Art Brushes to modified artwork*

Red outlines indicate the type of closed paths to change in the original clip art

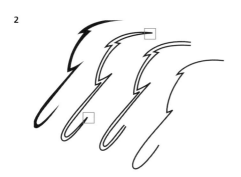

Use the Scissors tool to cut a closed path into two paths, swap the fill and stroke, then delete one path

Sandee Cohen, a vector expert and *Illustrator Wow!* consultant, enjoys working with Illustrator's brushes to modify existing art. This technique shows how Cohen changed ordinary clip art into more sophisticated artwork. Her technique can be used to give both commercial clip art, and any of your own existing artwork, a bit more pizzaz.

1 Examine the clip art shapes. First, Cohen examines the artwork in the Outline mode in order to plot her steps. She typically ignores open paths because they take brush strokes very well. She also does not worry about closed paths if they have large areas. She is most interested in finding thin closed paths that mimic the look of brush strokes. These paths are often found in artwork created by previous versions of Illustrator.

2 Split closed paths and delete segments. So they will accept the brush strokes, Cohen splits thin closed paths with the Scissors tool. She swaps the fill and stroke colors of selected paths by pressing Shift-X to make it easier to see each path. (You can also change from Preview to Outline View to see paths without fills.) After cutting a path, she deletes one of the cut paths, usually the smaller one.

3 Apply natural-looking brush strokes to simplified paths. Once the artwork is cleaned up, the simplified paths are ready to have brushes applied to them. Many different types of looks can be created without moving or deleting any more of the paths in the illustration. Cohen applies her choice of brushes to the simplified, open paths. Among Cohen's favorite brushes is Charcoal, one of the natural-looking brushes found in Illustrator's default set. She also uses brushes found in the Artistic library under Window: Brush Libraries: Artistic Sample.

Once the artwork has been cleaned up, you are ready to apply brushes

3

The Charcoal brush (shown in black) gives the art more of a hand-rendered appearance

4 Apply brushes to large closed paths. In most cases, Cohen leaves large, closed paths filled with solid color. Some of the large, closed paths could be made to look more organic by applying Art brushes to their strokes. For instance, Cohen applies natural-media brushes, such as Chalk Scribbler and Fire Ash to the large, closed shapes. Warning: These natural brush forms contain hundreds of points in each brush stroke. While there may be few points in each path, use of these brushes can add dramatically to the file size—a consideration if your computer is slow, or if you need a small file size for storage or to transfer by email.

4

The Chalk Scribbler (top left) and Fire Ash (bottom right) brushes applied to large closed shapes create a more organic look

5 Experiment with Calligraphic brushes. Cohen also uses Calligraphic brushes set to thin roundness and various angles to replicate the feeling of the original artwork. She creates several Calligraphic brushes, each set at a different angle, to apply various appearances to the paths. Cohen accesses the Brush Options in the Brushes palette fly-out menu and chooses the Random setting for the Angle, Roundness and Diameter options. She then experiments with the numeric settings of each option.

5

A Calligraphic brush set to an angle of 90 degrees, roundness of 10%, and diameter of 9 points brings back the look of the original art

If you alternate between applying a Calligraphic brush with Random settings and another brush, each time you return to the randomized Calligraphic brush the results will be different. Cohen often applies the same brush several times to the same object until she achieves the appearance she likes.

Pattern Brushes
Creating Details with the Pattern Brush

Overview: *Create interlocking chain links by drawing and cutting duplicate curve sections; select the link artwork and create a new Pattern brush; draw a path and paint it with the new brush.*

1

At the left, the ring drawn with the Ellipse tool and given a thick stroke; in the middle, the ellipse cut into four curve sections shown in Outline view (sections are separated to show them better); on the right, the four curve sections shown in Outline view, after using the Object: Path: Outline Stroke command

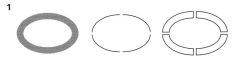

On the left, the two left curve sections copied and pasted, and colors changed to light brown in the middle; on the right, the two sections are slid to the right to form the right half link

*On the left, the half-link selected and reflected using the Reflect tool (the **X** in the middle of the guide ellipse served as the axis); on the right, both half-links in position*

One look at a Bert Monroy image and you will immediately recognize the intricacy and rich realism of his style of illustration. When crafting an image like the Rendez-vous Cafe (see the Gallery image that follows for the complete image), Monroy travels between Illustrator and Photoshop, stopping long enough in Illustrator to construct the intricate shapes and details that turn his scenes into slices of life in Photoshop. The easel chain is one such detail that Monroy created in Illustrator using a custom-made Pattern brush.

1 Drawing, cutting, copying and reflecting curves. To build a chain-link Pattern brush, Monroy first created one link that was interconnected with half-links on either side (the half-links would connect with other half-links to form the chain once the Pattern brush was applied to a path). To create the pattern unit with the Ellipse tool, begin the center link by drawing an ellipse with a thick stroke. Copy the ellipse, Paste in Back; then turn the ellipse into a guide (View: Guides: Make Guides). You'll use this guide later when making the half-links. Now select the original ellipse and use the Scissors tool to cut the ellipse near each of the four control points (choose

View: Outline to better see the points). Shift-select the four curved paths with the Direct-selection tool and select Object: Path: Outline Stroke. Illustrator automatically constructs four closed-curve objects.

   To make the right half-link, select the left two curve objects and duplicate them to make the right half-link by dragging the two objects to the right while holding down the Opt/Alt key; then change the color of the copies. For the left half-link, select the two curves you just dragged and colored, choose the Reflect tool, hold down the Opt/Alt key and click in the center of the ellipse guide (the center point is an **X**). In the pop-up dialog box, click the vertical axis button and click Copy to create a mirror-image of the right half-link for the left half-link. (**Note:** *The center link must be aligned exactly in-between the two half-links, so that the half-links join when applied to a path as a Pattern brush.*)

2 Finishing the link. The two adjoining half-links should look like they're entwined with the link. Monroy selected the top objects of both the left and right half-links and moved them behind the center link (Object: Arrange: Send to Back). You can create a different look by selecting the top of the left half-link, and the bottom of the right half-link, then move these two curve objects to the back.

3 Making and using a Pattern brush. To make the brush, select the artwork and drag it into the Brushes palette. Choose New Pattern Brush in the pop-up dialog box; in the next dialog box, name the brush and click OK (leave the default settings as you find them). You can now apply the chain pattern to a path by selecting the path and clicking on the brush in the Brushes palette.

   Depending on the size of your original links artwork, you may need to reduce the size of the brush artwork to fit the path better. You can do this by reducing the original artwork with the Scale tool and making a new brush, or by double-clicking the brush in the Brushes palette and editing the value in the Scale field of the dialog box.

Finished link artwork; at the left, the links as Monroy created them; at the right, an alternative version of the interconnected links

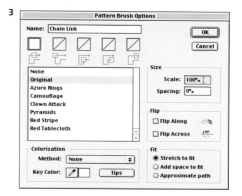

The Pattern Brush Options dialog box showing default settings

Original path on top; below, path painted with Chain Link Pattern brush

Drop Shadows

Even if your artwork is destined for Photoshop, you can make a drop shadow for it in Illustrator. Select the artwork, then choose Effect: Stylize: Drop Shadow. Copy the object (which automatically copies all of its appearances) and paste in Photoshop (Edit: Paste: Paste as Pixels). (See *Transparency, Styles & Effects* for more on appearances, and *Illustrator & Other Programs* for more on using Photoshop with Illustrator.)

MONROY

© Bert Monroy 1999

Bert Monroy

Artist Bert Monroy incorporates elements he draws in Illustrator into the detailed realism he paints in Photoshop. In this cafe scene, Monroy used Illustrator Pattern brushes for the sign post and the easel chain. For the leaves in the foreground, Monroy first drew one leaf object and made it into a Scatter brush (he used Random settings for the brush parameters). He brought resulting foliage into Photoshop where he detailed it further. (See the *Illustrator & Other Programs* chapter to learn more techniques for using Illustrator with Photoshop.)

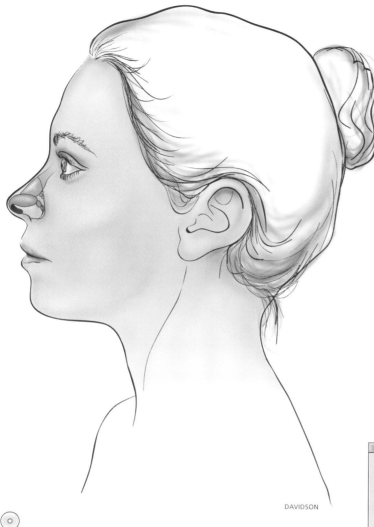

DAVIDSON

Calligraphic Brush Options

Name: 4 pt Calligraphic

OK

Cancel

☐ Preview

Angle: 0° Fixed ⇕ Variation:

Roundness: 100% Fixed ⇕ Variation:

Diameter: 4 pt Pressure ⇕ Variation: 4 pt

Shayne Davidson

Shayne Davidson used custom-made Calligraphic brushes to draw this profile. To create a brush, she opened the Brushes palette, selected New Brush from the palette's menu and picked New Calligraphic Brush from the New Brush dialog. This brought up the Calligraphic Brush Options dialog, where she left the brush Angle at 0° (Fixed), Roundness at 100% (Fixed), and specified a Diameter (she used diameters between 0.8 and 4 points). She also set Diameter to Pressure, and Variation to the same point size as the Diameter (this establishes the maximum width of the stroke on either side of the path), and clicked OK. She repeated this process to create brushes with different diameters.

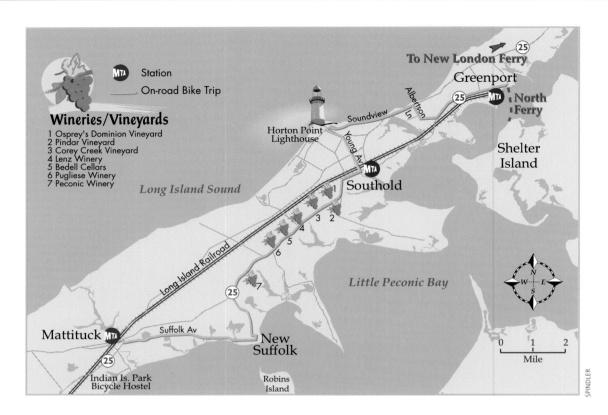

SPINDLER

Steve Spindler / Bike Maps

When cartographer Steve Spindler begins using a new version of Illustrator, he quickly adopts its new features to his method of making maps. In this bike map of part of Long Island, New York, Spindler created Art brushes for the bike route and railroad track. He placed scanned photographs on a template layer to draw the vineyard grapes and lighthouse. For the grapes symbol, he used the Tapered Stroke brush for the outlines of the leaves and the Marker brush to draw the stems (both brushes are found on the Illustrator 9 CD-ROM, in Illustrator Extras: Brush Libraries: Artistic: Ink). To

create a Scatter brush from this symbol, Spindler first expanded the artwork (because Illustrator cannot build a brush from artwork that already contains a brush), then dragged the artwork into the Brushes palette. For the compass rose symbol, Spindler imported a custom brush library (Window: Brush Libraries: Other Libraries) containing a collection of his own cartographic Art and Scatter brushes.

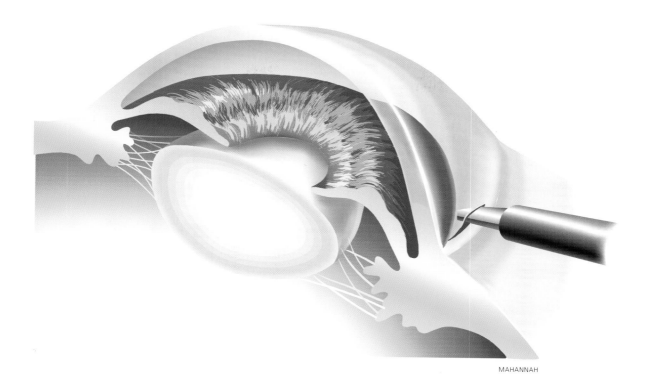

MAHANNAH

Jacqueline Mahannah

Drawing the delicate structure of the iris of the human eye to illustrate glaucoma surgery, artist Jacqueline Mahannah combined Illustrator brushes with the pressure-sensitivity of a Wacom tablet. For the iris structure, Mahannah used the Marker brush from the Ink Brushes library (found on the Adobe Illustrator Application CD, in Illustrator Extras: Brush Libraries: Artistic). She adjusted the width setting of this brush by double-clicking the brush in the palette, then editing the Width field in the Art Brush Options dialog. Mahannah chose a light blue color for the brush and drew the innermost strokes. Then she chose a darker color and drew the next set of strokes, letting them overlap the first strokes. She continued working outward, sometimes overlapping dark brush strokes with lighter ones to suggest highlights and texture.

Building Brushes

Building brushes for lettering

Overview: *Draw and shape letterforms; create and vectorize brush strokes in Photoshop; bring brush paths into Illustrator and edit them; add brushes to the Brushes palette; adjust color and layering, and apply Effects and transparency*

DONALDSON

1

Hand-drawn letterform paths using Pen and Pencil tools

Donaldson hand-drew two different sets of letterforms and positioned them on two different layers; each was then painted with a different brush (see Step 4 at right)

2

Brush stroke created in Photoshop using the Paintbrush tool; below, brush stroke edited with Eraser and Airbrush tools

Timothy Donaldson's style of abstract calligraphy challenges the lettering artist to look beyond Illustrator's default brushes (like the brushes sets found under Window: Brush Libraries) to paint programs like Photoshop and Painter, where he develops brush strokes with the look of traditional art tools.

1 Drawing, smoothing and shaping letterform paths.
Donaldson began the composition "abcxyz" by drawing letterform paths with the Pen and Pencil tools, going back over the paths with the Pencil to smooth them. (Use the Pencil Tool Preferences menu's Smoothness Tolerance to control how the Pencil will simplify and smooth a line you've drawn.) Once you draw the letterforms, refine them further with the Shear and Scale tools until you are satisfied with their shapes.

2 Creating brush strokes in a paint program. To build a custom brush, open any paint program that offers paintbrushes (Donaldson works in Painter and Photoshop). Start a new file in the paint program, specifying a resolution of 72 ppi and a transparent background. Set the foreground and background colors to black and white (this will make it easier when vectorizing the brush stroke in the paint program later). Next, select the Paint brush tool and edit the brush settings or preferences (opacity, blending mode, textures, pressure-sensitivity and others). (See the *Photoshop 5.5 Wow! Book* by Linnea Dayton and Jack Davis, or the *Painter 6 Wow! Book* by Cher Threinen-Pendarvis for more about painting with brushes.)

Now you're ready to paint a brush stroke. Hold down the Shift key (to constrain the cursor to straight movements) and make a stroke with the brush tool. Modify the look of the brush stroke with the eraser or other painting tools, or with filters (avoid filters that blur or otherwise antialias the brush stroke edge). If your paint program can export vector paths as an EPS or Illustrator file, then select the pixels of the brush stroke with the Magic Wand, or other selection tool, and convert the pixels to paths. Otherwise, save the image as a TIFF.

3

Top, work path based on selection made in Photoshop before being saved as an Illustrator file; bottom, path in Illustrator after editing and being filled with black

3 Opening, then editing brush strokes in Illustrator.

Bring your brush stroke into Illustrator by opening the EPS or placing the TIFF image. Use Illustrator's Auto Trace tool to automatically vectorize the raster brush stroke, or manually trace it using the Pen and Pencil tools. You can reshape the brush artwork using the selection tools or the Pencil tool. (See *Lines, Fills & Colors* for more on modifying paths.) Convert your brush stroke artwork into an Illustrator brush by selecting the artwork and dragging it into the Brushes palette. Select New Art Brush from the New Brush dialog and set various brush parameters in the Art Brush Options dialog box.

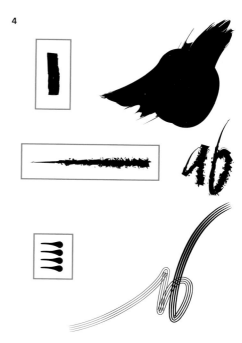

4

Three different brushes (outlined here in red) applied to the hand-drawn letterforms "ab"

4 Applying different brushes.

Donaldson created multiple brushed letterforms by first duplicating the layer with the paths (drag the layer to the New Layer icon in the Layers palette). For each layer with letterforms, select the paths and click on one of your custom brushes in the Brushes palette. Alter the look of your composition by changing colors or brushes, adjusting the stacking order of layers in the Layers palette, or applying Effects and modifying transparency and blending (see *Transparency, Styles & Effects* for more on Effects and transparency).

In the background, Feather Effect applied to gray letterforms; in the middle, an 80% transparency and Multiply blending mode assigned to greenish letterforms; in foreground, red letters given a Screen blending mode with 65% transparency

Map Techniques
Simplifying the creation of complex images

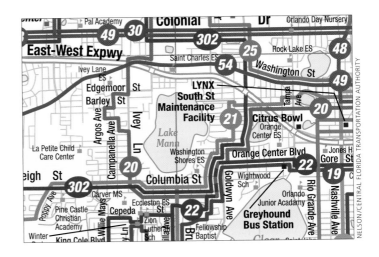

Advanced Techniques

Overview: *Use Simplify to reduce points in paths; create and select Scatter Brushes; create multicolored dashes, tapered lines and self-adjusting scales; import brushes from another document.*

1

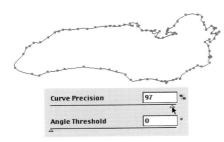

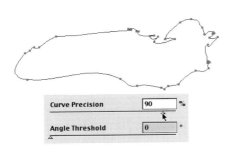

Top, the original lake shape, created from imported geographical data (195 points); middle, using Simplify reduces the lake to 89 points without noticeable distortion of shape; bottom, Simplify reduces the lake to 38 points but with some distortion of shape

From line simplification to brushes that solve many problems, Illustrator now offers professional illustrators and mapmakers many tools and features that help streamline the creation and updating of complex images. In creating a city bus map for Orlando, Florida, cartographer David Nelson was able to take advantage of dozens of recently added Illustrator features.

1 Simplifying paths. When you trace detailed lines such as rivers and roads, or bring clip-art or geographical data into Illustrator, you will likely have paths with too many points. To remove unnecessary points while preserving an accurate path shape, first select a line and choose Object: Path: Simplify. In the Simplify dialog, click to enable Preview and use the Curve Precision control to reduce points (a lower percentage results in fewer points but more distortion to the shape of the path). Use the Angle Threshold setting to make minute changes to some of the curves in the path by smoothing the curve at corner points with angles larger than those specified in the setting.

2 Making, placing and selecting Scatter brush "symbols." Scatter brushes are an ideal way to help manage map symbols. Create symbols for such features as schools, airports, parks, museums, golf courses and the like. When you've finished making a symbol, drag it into the Brushes palette. In the New Brush dialog, choose New Scatter Brush, then in the Scatter Brush Options dialog, specify 0% Fixed in the Scatter field and select None for the Colorization Method. To place symbols on the map, click once with the Pen tool and select a Scatter brush you made.

While Illustrator doesn't provide a way for you to select all strokes made with a particular Scatter brush, it can locate and select objects by color, so you can "cheat." Simply set a unique color as a Stroke or Fill, then click with the Pen tool to create the points to which you'll apply a particular Scatter brush. If you need to select all of the points you painted with a brush, click on a brush stroke on the map and choose Edit: Select: Same Fill Color. Illustrator will select all brushes whose points have the same Fill or Stroke color as the brush you chose.

3 Creating complex dashed lines. In Illustrator 9, you can make custom styles for applying complex multicolored dashed lines to paths. Draw stroked paths and color each stroke with a different color. Arrange the paths end-to-end: One way to accomplish this is to make sure you've enabled View: Snap To Point, then position the cursor over the endpoint of one segment and drag it so it snaps on the endpoint of another segment. After you've arranged the colored paths, select and drag them into the Brushes palette. In the New Brush dialog, choose New Pattern Brush. Then in the Pattern Brush Options dialog, choose the "Stretch to fit" option. (See "Pattern Brushes" earlier in this chapter for more about Pattern brushes.)

If your dashes are uneven or gapped when applied to a path, select the path and use the Smooth tool (from the Pencil tool pop-out palette) to "iron out" the problems (see Nelson's "Zooming more means smoothing less" Tip in the *Layers* chapter).

4 Creating tapered brushes. You can use custom brushes to create elements that taper, like creeks. Draw a color-filled rectangle; Nelson's was about 4 inches long and

On the top and the bottom-left, Scatter brushes representing map symbols and north arrow; on the bottom-right, the New Brush dialog

Selecting a Fill color on the left; in the middle, the points created with the Pen tool; on the right, the points after applying a Scatter brush

End-to-end strokes (shown enlarged) are made into a Pattern brush

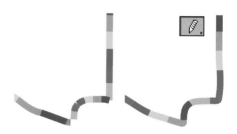

Pattern brush dashes on a path shown before (left) and after being adjusted with the Smooth tool

Two of the objects made into tapered brushes

Auto-replacing brush objects

To replace all applications of a brush, hold Option/Alt and drag one brush over another in the Brushes palette (you may wish to duplicate the brush being re-placed first!). —*David Nelson*

5

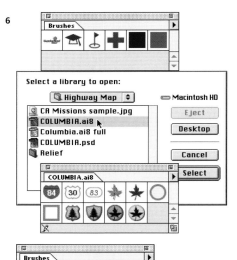

Three "self-adjusting scale" brushes and a map legend that includes a scale drawn with one of the brushes

6

The active document's Brushes palette (top); Window: Brush Libraries: Other Library dialog and the selected document's Brushes palette (middle); the active document's default Brushes palette after importing four new Scatter Brushes

2–3 pts wide. Select the right pair of anchor points and Average (Object: Path: Average), creating a triangle. Drag this path into the Brushes palette and define it as an Art brush, using the point-width in the name of the brush. Select the path that you wish to make into a tapered object and choose your new brush (if the path tapers the wrong way, see "Reversing Brush strokes," at the left). To create a brush that tapers at a different rate, adjust the shape of the triangular object (adding or editing points) and create a new brush with that version.

5 Making a "self-adjusting" scale. Create a scale, using evenly-spaced divisions to represent miles, kilometers or another unit of measure. (One way of creating evenly spaced tick marks is by creating a blend between the two end marks on the scale; see the *Blends & Gradients* chapter for more on setting up a blend with the Specified Steps option.) Because you are making a multi-purpose brush that you'll use on different maps, don't add text or numbers to your scale artwork. Now, select your artwork and drag it to the Brushes palette. In the New Brush dialog, choose New Art Brush. On your map, draw a horizontal line whose length represents X units of measure in your document (miles, kilometers, etc.) and apply your new brush—which will adjust proportionately to the length of the line. Add numbers for the units and other necessary text.

6 Sharing custom brushes between documents. You can bring custom brushes into a document by choosing Window: Brush Libraries: Other Library. In the dialog, select a document that contains brushes you'd like to import into your active document. After you select the document and click Open, a palette containing that document's brushes appears with the name of the document in the palette tab. To move brushes, drag from this document palette to your active document's Brushes palette, or apply brushes from the document palette to objects in your active document.

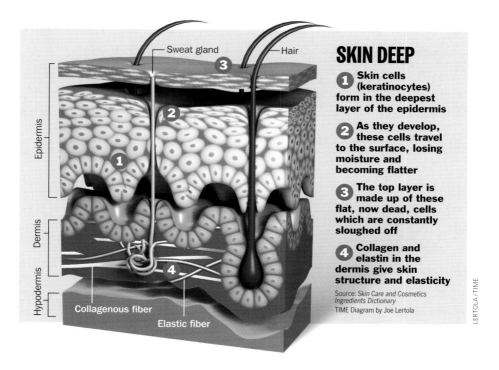

SKIN DEEP

1 Skin cells (keratinocytes) form in the deepest layer of the epidermis

2 As they develop, these cells travel to the surface, losing moisture and becoming flatter

3 The top layer is made up of these flat, now dead, cells which are constantly sloughed off

4 Collagen and elastin in the dermis give skin structure and elasticity

Source: *Skin Care and Cosmetics Ingredients Dictionary*
TIME Diagram by Joe Lertola

LERTOLA/TIME

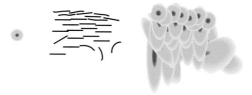

Joe Lertola / TIME

For this medical infographic, artist Joe Lertola relied on the suppleness of Illustrator's Art brushes to show closely packed skin cells. To begin the top layer of cells (**1** and **2** in the illustration above), Lertola built a single cell from two blends, stacking the smaller brown blend on top of the lighter skin-colored blend. Selecting both blends, Lertola chose Object: Expand. Then he dragged the expanded artwork into the Brushes palette and selected New Art Brush from the New Brush dialog. Next, Lertola developed three more cells, varying the oval shape of each cell before turning it into an Art brush.

To make the cells, Lertola drew short paths and painted each with one of the four cell brushes. Lertola finished the illustration by rasterizing the skin cells in Photoshop and exporting a color and grayscale version of the cells. He imported the grayscale cells into the Lightwave 3D modeler software, where he built a model of the cells and applied the color version of the cells as a color map. (To learn more about using Illustrator artwork with other software, see the *Illustrator & Other Programs* chapter.)

Organic Creation

Painting with Brushes, Hatches and Mesh

Advanced Technique

Overview: *Create Scatter brushes of stars; draw with a "hue-tinted" Art brush; create bark textures with Art brushes; automate drawing of grass with Pattern brushes; add Hatches and Gradient Mesh.*

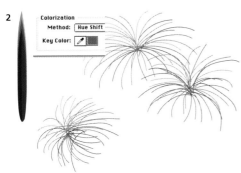

Dragging the star objects into the brushes palette to specify Scatter Brush; the settings for one of the four stars; three selected paths with different star Scatter brushes applied

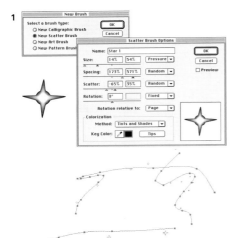

The leaf Art brush (left) with the Hue Shift Colorization option; the final color strokes for the leaves shown without the Art brush applied

Sharon Steuer painted these stars, trees and grasses using a variety of brushes, with gradients, hatches and mesh. Please see the *Blends & Gradients* chapter if you need help with the blend, gradient or mesh portions of this lesson.

1 Defining a star Scatter brush. Create a star. Steuer created her stars using Guilbert Gates's "Glowing Starshine" instructions (*Advanced* chapter), then expanded those blends (Object:Expand). Drag your star to the Brushes palette, and choose Scatter Brush. In Options, name the star and play with various settings, but keep "Rotation relative to" Page. Set Colorization to Tints and Shades. With the Brush tool and new star brush selected, draw some paths—your stroke color will tint the star. For brush variations, drag your brush to the New Brush icon, then double-click that brush to rename and edit it.

2 Drawing leaves. Make a straight leaf. Drag it into the Brushes palette, choose Art Brush, then name the brush and choose Hue Shift for Colorization. With the Brush tool and this brush loaded, choose a stroke color (hue) that this brush will be based on, and draw. Steuer first mixed and stored about a dozen colors, then drew leaves with a Wacom tablet. Though she chose stroke colors as she worked, she also edited the paths (with Direct-selection) and changed stroke colors as the image developed.

3 Creating tree trunks. Create objects to use as a trunk. In order to make a brush of blends or gradients, choose Object: Expand. Drag the trunk into the Brushes palette and choose Art Brush. Apply this trunk brush to a path. If it's too thin or thick for the path, double-click the brush and change the Size %. Steuer made a second trunk brush—slightly narrower and paler—and gave it a different scaling percentage. She applied the thinner trunk to a slightly offset copy of the first trunk path. For texture, draw some strokes and make an Art brush of the strokes with Hue Shift colorization. Selecting a path styled as you want sets the default for the next path.

4 Creating a Pattern brush to generate grass. Design a pattern tile with 20–30 blades of grass. Drag the grouping of grass into the Brushes palette and choose Pattern Brush. Set the direction to be perpendicular to the grass and Tints and Shades Colorization. Draw a curvy path and select the grass Pattern brush to apply it.

5 Creating water, sand and moon effects. To create the water, make an unstroked gradient-filled object on one layer and drag this layer to the New Layer icon to duplicate it (see the *Layers* chapter). Select the top gradient and choose Filter: Pen and Ink: Hatch Effects, choose "Wood grain Light" and enable "Match Object's Color" (see the *Advanced* chapter for Hatches tips). For added texture, offset a copy of the hatches (Option/Alt-drag).

For the sand, Steuer converted a linear gradient into a gradient mesh (Object: Expand). For the moon, she used a gradient mesh circle over the moon-glow gradient.

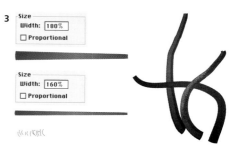
3

The three Art brushes used in the trunks (the top two with size scaled in Options); the trunks shown (from left to right) with one, two, and all three brushes applied

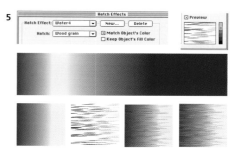
4

The Grass objects that make up the Pattern brush; then the brush applied to a path

5

The full two-piece gradient; then the left gradient, turned into Hatches, combined with the original gradient, then Hatches Option-dragged

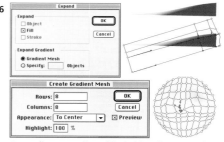
6

Expanding a gradient-filled object into a mesh (which was then adjusted to curve around the slope of the hill); for the moon, choosing Object: Create Gradient Mesh to convert a circle into a mesh (which was then manipulated using the Direct-selection tool and colored)

Calligraphic brushes allow you to create strokes that resemble those drawn with traditional pen and ink. You can control the angle, roundness and diameter of the brush, and brushes can be set to vary from the pressure of a drawing tablet or "randomly." Multiple calligraphic brushes allow you to create more sophisticated effects. In each of these illustrations, the hair has been changed only by applying different calligraphic brushes. (See the "Brushes Supplement" folder on the *Wow!* disk!)

Calligraphic brush: *0° angle; 100% roundness; 1 pt diameter.*

Calligraphic brush: *0° angle; 100% roundness; 1 pt diameter, 1 pt variation.*

Calligraphic brush: *0° angle, 101° variation; 26% roundness, 14% variation; 3 pt diameter.*

Dark brown calligraphic brush: *-136° angle, 180° variation; 26% roundness 26% variation; 12 pt diameter, 3 pt variation.*
Light brown calligraphic brush: *65° angle; 13% roundness, 3% variation; 2 pt diameter, 2 pt variation.*

Dark calligraphic brush: *0° angle; 100% roundness; 1 pt diameter, 1 pt variation.*
Light calligraphic brush: *0° angle; 100% roundness; .5 pt diameter.*

Dark calligraphic brush: *-90° angle, 180° variation; 10% roundness, 10% variation; 1.5 pt diameter.*
Medium calligraphic brush: *60° angle, 180° variation; 60% roundness, 40% variation; 1.5 pt diameter.*
Light calligraphic brush: *120° angle, 180° variation; 10% roundness, 10% variation; .5 pt diameter.*

Art Brushes can create distortions that can be used in animation. Each original silhouette (the left column) was defined as an art brush. The shape and direction of the brush stroke (gray line) then created different positions of the athlete. (See the "Brushes Supplement" folder on the *Wow!* disk!)

You can start with simple objects and then turn them into natural looking brushes. By applying these brushes to simple artwork, you can give it the feel of art drawn by hand, instead of art created using a computer. (See the "Brushes Supplement" folder on the *Wow!* disk!)

Wispy Brush: *Start with a rectangle and fill it with Pen and Ink Filter Hatch Effects. Use the vertical lines hatch. Release the masking element to see all the lines.*

Use the Scale tool or Bounding Box to make the lines much longer and compact them into a more dense area. Then change the strokes to .25 point and define this as a brush.

The result is a very thin, wispy brush which can be stroked even thinner by changing the Stroke weight after you've applied the brush.

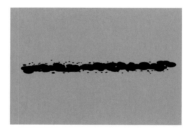

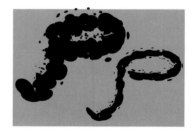

Leaky Pen: *Use the Pen and Ink Hatch Effects with the "Dots" hatch, in the "Scale" pop-up. Choose reflect to create small dots on either side of larger ones.*

Release the mask and apply Unite from the Pathfinder palette. Define this as your brush.

Variation: *Use the Scale tool or the Bounding Box to vertically scale the stroke into a thinner stroke.*
Advantage: *You can't get this ink on your fingers!*

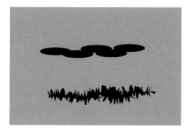

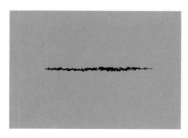

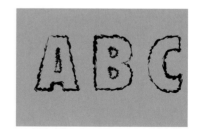

Sketchy line: *Start with a few ellipses. Use Unite from the Pathfinder palette and then apply Filter: Distort: Roughen. Use the bounding box to vertically compress the line into a thinner brush.*

Apply it to all sorts of objects to make a more natural, sketchy look.

Brushes can be used to create textures. The brush strokes (shown in the right corner of each figure), were applied to the outline and stripes of the sweater (original by Lisa Jackmore). None of the art-work was moved or otherwise altered. (See the "Brushes Supplement" folder on the *Wow!* disk!)

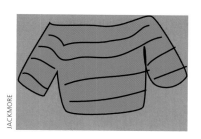

The original shirt. *Plain green with a black outline and black stripes.*

Sketched shirt. *Art brush of crossed lines was applied to the outline and stripes. Notice that the brush is distorted along the outside path.*

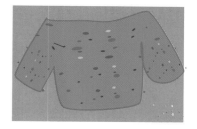

Funky t-shirt. *Art brush of small circles was applied to the stripes.*

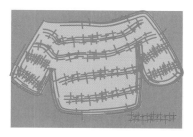

Sketched shirt 3. *An art brush of crossed lines was applied to the out-line. This brush was scaled up 150%. The same brush objects, but scaled down 75% with a tighter spacing was applied to the stripes.*

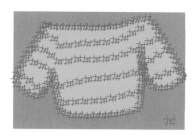

Sketched shirt 2. *Art brush of crosses was applied to the outline and strokes. Notice the distortion along the outside.*

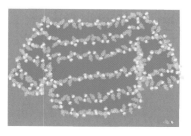

Fuzzy sweater. *Small circles, set with different opacities, were defined as a scatter brush. This brush was then applied to the outline and stripes with varying rotations and spacings.*

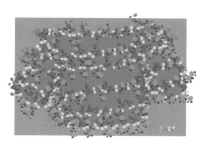

Fuzzy sweater 2. *Small circles were defined as a scatter brush and then applied to the outline and stripes with varying rotations and spacings.*

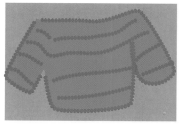

Knitted sweater. *One small circle was defined as a pattern brush, then applied to the outline and stripes.*

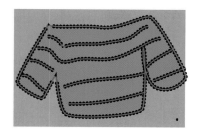

Knitted sweater 2. *One small circle was defined as a pattern brush. Using multi-ple strokes (see the Transparency chapter), the brush was applied first in black, then in green at a smaller size.*

Layers

5

Layers

Used wisely, layers can dramatically improve organization of complicated artwork, thereby easing your workflow. Think of layers as sheets of clear acetate, stacked one on top of the other, allowing you to separate dozens of objects and groups of objects. You can re-arrange the stacking order of the layers; lock, hide or copy layers; and move or copy objects from one layer to another.

By default, the Layers palette (Window: Show Layers) opens with one layer, though you can add as many layers and sublayers as you wish. Unlike previous versions of Illustrator, in which adding layers had a minimal affect on file size, layers now containing transparency or effects *will* increase your file size.

A few shortcuts will help when you're adding layers to the Layers palette. Click the New Layer icon to add a layer in numeric sequence above the current layer. Option (Mac)/Alt (Win)-click this icon to open Layer Options as you add the layer. To add a layer to the top of the Layers palette, ⌘ (Mac)/Ctrl (Win)-click the New Layer icon. To make a new layer below the current layer and open the Layer Options, ⌘-Option (Mac)/Ctrl-Alt (Win)-click the New Layer icon. Finally, you can easily duplicate a layer, sublayer, group or path by dragging it to the New Layer icon at the bottom of the Layers palette. To delete selected layers, click on the Trash icon or drag the layers to the Trash.

Note: *To bypass the warning that you're about to delete a layer containing artwork, drag the layer to the Trash or Option (Mac)/Alt (Win)-click the Trash. If you're not sure whether a layer has artwork or guides you may need, select the layer and click the Trash so you'll only get the warning if there is something on the layer.*

Sublayers are new to this version and, within limits, can be very useful. Keep in mind that the sublayers are contained within the layer directly above it. If you delete a container layer, all of the sublayers are deleted.

Layers palette navigation

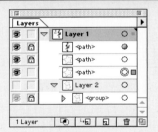

- To hide a layer, click the Eye icon. Click again to show it.
- To lock a layer, click in the column to right of the eye (a lock displays). Click again to unlock.
- To toggle between locking or showing the selected layer and all other layers, Option (Mac)/Alt (Win)-click on the appropriate icon.
- To duplicate a layer, drag it to either the *New Layer* or *New Sublayer* icon.
- To select contiguous layers, click one layer then Shift-click the other. To select (or deselect) *any* layer, ⌘ (Mac)/Ctrl (Win)-click a layer in any order.
- Double-click on a layer to open Layer Options.

Layer Options (double-click a layer name)

Maximizing Layer Options

Double-click a layer name to access these Layer Options:

- **Name the layer.** In complicated artwork, naming layers keeps your job, and your brain, organized.

- **Change the layer's color.** A layer's color determines the selection color for paths, anchor points, bounding boxes and Smart Guides. Adjust the layer color so selections stand out against artwork (see Tip "Color-coding groups of layers" to the right).

- **Template Layer.** There are three ways to create a Template: You can double-click a layer to open the Layer Options and then check Template, select Template from the Layers pop-up menu, or check Template when placing an image in Illustrator. By default, Template layers are locked. To unlock a Template in order to adjust or edit objects, click the lock icon to the left of the layer name.
  Hint: Template layers won't print or export. Make any layer into a Template to ensure that it won't print.

- **Show / Hide layer.** This option functions the same way as the Show/Hide toggle, which you access by clicking the Eye icon (see Tip "Layer palette navigation" on the opposite page). By default, hiding a layer sets that layer *not* to print.

- **Preview / Outline mode.** Controlling which layers are set to Preview or Outline is essential to working with layers. If you have objects that are easier to edit in Outline mode, or objects that are slow to redraw (such as complicated patterns, live blends or gradients), you may want to set only those layers to Outline mode. Uncheck Preview to set selected layers to Outline mode in Layer Options, or toggle this option on and off directly by ⌘ (Mac)/Ctrl (Win) - clicking the Eye icon in the view column.

- **Lock / Unlock layer.** This option functions the same way

Color-coding groups of layers

Select a set of layers and double-click any one of the layers to open the Layer Options dialog. Then set the layer color for all selected layers (see lessons later in this chapter). You can also use this technique to adjust other options globally on a set of selected layers.

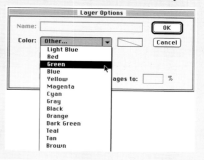

Reordering objects

To change the stacking order of several objects:
- Reorder the layers they are on.
- Move grouped objects from one layer to another.
- Cut the bottom objects, select the topmost object and Paste In Front with Paste Remembers Layers *off*.
- Drag the selection indicator (large square) from one layer to another, or collapse the disclosure arrow for a container layer and drag the small square.
- If all of the objects are not on the same layer, choose Collect in New Layer (Layers palette menu) and then drag the layer or contents of the layer to the desired location in the layer list.

Layer palette pop-up menu

as the Lock/Unlock toggle, which you access by clicking the lock column of the layer (see Tip "Layer palette navigation" in this chapter).

- **Print/Suppress printing.** When you print from within Illustrator you can use this feature to override the default, which sets visible layers to print. If you need to ensure that a layer will *never* print in *any* circumstances (for instance, when placed into a page layout program) make the layer into a Template layer.

- **Dim Images.** You can only dim raster images (not vector Illustrator objects) from 1% to 99% opacity.

Double-click any group, path, compound path, clipping path, blend, mesh, object, placed or raster layer to set Options such as the Name, Show and/or Lock status. If you prefer knowing what the items are once you've renamed them, retain the name of the subcomponent. For example, rename a group to help organize your layer list, but keep the bracket description: *floral <group>*.

The Layers pop-up menu

You can perform the first six functions in the Layers pop-up via the layer palette icons, or Layer Options (see above). With the ability to nest sublayers within other layers and create group objects, comes the confusion of how to find objects when they become buried in the layer list. Use Locate Object, or Locate Layer when Show Only Layers is checked in Palette Options, to find selected objects. Merge Selected is available when two or more layers are selected, and will place *visible* objects in the topmost layer. An alternative to Flatten Artwork is Select All, Copy and Paste, with Paste Remembers Layers unchecked.

Paste Remembers Layers is a great feature: when enabled, objects retain their layer order (see "Layer Registration" later in this chapter for a lesson using this feature); when unchecked, pasted objects go into the selected layer. If the layers don't exist, Paste Remembers Layers will make them for you! This feature can be turned on and off even after the objects have been copied—so if you paste, and wish that the toggle were reversed, you can Undo, toggle the Paste Remembers Layers option, then paste again. Important: *There is one significant problem with this feature. If you target a top-level layer and apply strokes, fills, effects or transparency and then copy/paste that layer into a new document, all appearance attributes that were applied to that layer will be lost in the new document, even when Paste Remembers Layers is enabled.*

Try this workaround by Jean-Claude Tremblay: Since the attributes of a top-level layer are not retained and you get no warning when pasting into the new document, you need to nest the top-layer into another layer, making it a sublayer. Then copy/paste this sublayer into the new document to retain the appearance attributes.

Collect in New Layer moves all of the selected objects, groups or layers into a new layer. Release to Layers allows you to make individual object layers from a group of objects, a layer or art created by using a brush. (For more on exporting to SWF see the *Web* chapter.)

Note: *When you're working with blend objects and want to place each object in the blend on a separate layer, you'll need to make sure your blend object is on a top-level layer and target the <Blend> layer before you can successfully use Release to Layers.*

Reverse Order reverses the stacking order of selected layers within a container layer. Hide All Layers/Others, Outline All Layers/Others and Lock All Layers/Others all perform actions on unselected layers or objects.

Lastly, Palette Options customizes the layer display. This is a great help to artists who have complicated files with many layers. Show Layers Only hides the disclosure arrow so you only see the container layer thumbnail. Adding sublayers reveals the arrow, but you still can't target groups or individual paths in this mode. Row Size defines the size of the thumbnail for a layer. You can specify a thumbnail size from Small (no thumbnail) to

If you can't select an object...

If you have trouble selecting an object, check the following:
- Is the object's layer locked?
- Is the object locked?
- Are the edges hidden?
- Is the Use Area Select box disabled (Edit: Preferences: General)?
- Locate the thumbnail in the layer list and click on the target indicator.

If you keep selecting the wrong object, try again after you:
- Switch to Outline mode.
- Zoom in.
- Hide the selected object; repeat if necessary.
- Lock the selected object; repeat if necessary.
- Put the object on top in another layer and hide that layer, or select Outline for the layer.
- Use the Move command: Option (Mac)/Alt (Win)-click the Selection tool in the Toolbox to move selected objects a set distance (you can move them back later).
- Check for objects with transparency. Overlapping transparency inhibits selection.
- Check if Type Area Select is *on* (Edit: Preferences: Type and Auto Tracing).

In certain situations, hidden selections will print:

- Objects on hidden layers do not print, but hidden objects on visible layers do print once the file is reopened.
- Hidden objects on layers with the print option disabled *will* print if saved as an .eps file and exported into QuarkXPress. There must also be visible art in the file to cause this to occur. To prevent this, save a version of the file without the art you wish to hide and re-export.

Exporting Layers to Photoshop

Export layered Illustrator files as Photoshop 5. Select options that allow you to maintain the layer integrity, such as *Point*-type. You can then edit the layers and the type in Photoshop. However, you can't "round trip" text back to Illustrator. (For more on exporting layered files to Photoshop see the *Other Programs* chapter.)

To select *all* objects

First, unlock and show everything in the Layers palette. Click-drag through the Eye and Lock icons or make sure Unlock All and Show All are unavailable in the Object menu). Then choose Edit: Select All (⌘-A for Mac/Ctrl-A for Win).

Large, or use Other to customize a size up to 100 pixels. Thumbnail lets you individually set thumbnail visibility for the Layers, Top Level Only (when Layers is checked), Group and Object.

CONTROLLING THE STACKING ORDER OF OBJECTS

Layers are crucial for organizing your images, but controlling the stacking order of objects *within* a layer is just as essential. The new intuitive layers and sublayers disclose their hierarchical contents when you open the disclosure arrow. Following is a summary of the functions that will help you control the stacking order of objects within layers and sublayers.

Sublayers and the hierarchical layer structure

In addition to regular layers, there are sublayers and groups, both of which act as containers for objects or images. When you click on the sublayer icon, a new sublayer is added inside the current layer. Artwork that you add to the sublayer will be below or underneath the art contained on the main layer. Clicking the New Layer icon with a sublayer selected adds a new sublayer above the current one. Adding subsequent layers adds the contents at the top of the stacking order or puts the artwork above the current layer. Clicking the New Sublayer icon creates a new sublayer level nested within the first one.

Grouping objects together automatically creates a container "layer" named *<group>*. Double-click the *<group>* layer to open its options. Group layers are much like sublayers. You can target them to apply appearances that affect all the objects within the group. In some cases, such as when Pathfinder effects are applied, objects have to be grouped and the group layer must be targeted in order to apply the effect. However, group layers cannot be moved in the same way as layers (see Note below).

Note: *If you rename your <group> layer you might get confused when it doesn't behave like a regular layer. Instead of removing <group> from the name appended to it, leave <group> as part of the renaming of the layer.*

PasteInFront, PasteInBack (Edit menu)

Illustrator doesn't merely reposition an object in front of or behind all other objects when you choose PasteIn Front/Back; it aligns the object *exactly* on top of or behind the object you copied. A second, and equally important, aspect is that the two functions paste objects that are Cut or Copied into the exact same location—in relation to the *ruler origin*. This capability transfers from one document to another, ensuring perfect registration and alignment when you copy and use Edit: PasteIn Front/Back. (See the lesson "Layer Registration" later in this chapter for practical applications of this option, and the *Wow!* disk for exercises in reordering objects using paste commands.)

Lock/Unlock All (Object menu)

When you're trying to select an object and you accidentally select an object on top of it, try locking the selected object and clicking again. Repeat as necessary until you reach the correct object. When you've finished the task, choose Unlock All to release all the locked objects.
Note: *Use the Direct-selection tool to select and lock objects that are part of a group (see the section "Selecting within groups" in the* Basics *chapter)—but if you select an unlocked object in the group with the Group-selection or other selection tools, the locked objects can become selected. Hidden objects stay hidden even if you select other objects in the same group.*

Hide/Show All (Object menu)

Another approach for handling objects that get in the way is to select them and choose Hide Selection. To view all hidden objects, choose Object: Show All.
Note: *Hidden objects may print if they're on visible layers and will reappear when you reopen the file.*

Bring Forward/Bring To Front, and more

These commands work on objects within a layer, Bring

○   *Target icon for any layer or subcomponent*

◎   *Selection is also currently targeted*

■   *Selection indicator for a container layer*

■   *Selection indicator when all objects are selected*

Selecting vs targeting

There are now several ways to make a selection and several other ways to target an object. The main difference between the two is selections don't always target, but targeting always makes a selection. In this example, "Layer 1" contains the selected object but is not currently the target. The circled "<path>" is the current target.

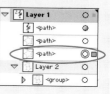

When opening a file created by an older version of Illustrator, it can take a long time for the layers palette to draw all the thumbnails for each path. Before you attempt to open layers to view their contents, you'll save a lot of time if you choose Palette Options from the Layers palette pop-up menu, and uncheck the Object option in the Thumbnails grouping. Once you've reorganized your paths in the Layers palette, be sure to re-enable the Object checkbox in the Palette Options in order to view the thumbnails for your paths.

There are unpredictable situations when using sublayers and New Views in which the view doesn't save the state of the sublayer.
Note: *You should think of views as a way to control top-level layers only.*

Forward (Object: Arrange) stacks an object on top of the object directly above it. Bring To Front moves an object in front of all other objects on its layer. Logically, Send To Back sends an object as far back as it can go in its stacking order. Send Backward sends an object behind its closest neighbor.

Note: *Bring Forward and Send Backward may not work on large files. In cases where they do not work, use the layer list to reorder items by moving the selection indicator to the right of the layer name up or down in the layer list.*

MAKING SELECTIONS USING THE LAYERS PALETTE

There are several ways to make selections in this version. Click on the layer's target icon or Option (Mac)/Alt (Win)-click the layer name, to select all unlocked and visible objects on the layer, including any sublayers and groups. Click on the sublayer's target icon to select everything on the sublayer, including other sublayers or groups. Clicking on the *group's* target icon will also select all grouped objects. Shift-click on the target icons to select multiple objects on different layers, including sublayers and groups. Always use the *target* icon to make a selection when applying an appearance to a layer, sublayer or group.

If you have selected artwork on the artboard, click on the small square to select all of the objects on the layer or in the group. A larger square means that all of the objects on that layer or group are already selected. Clicking in the small space to the right of the target indicator will also make a selection of all objects on the layer, sublayer or group.

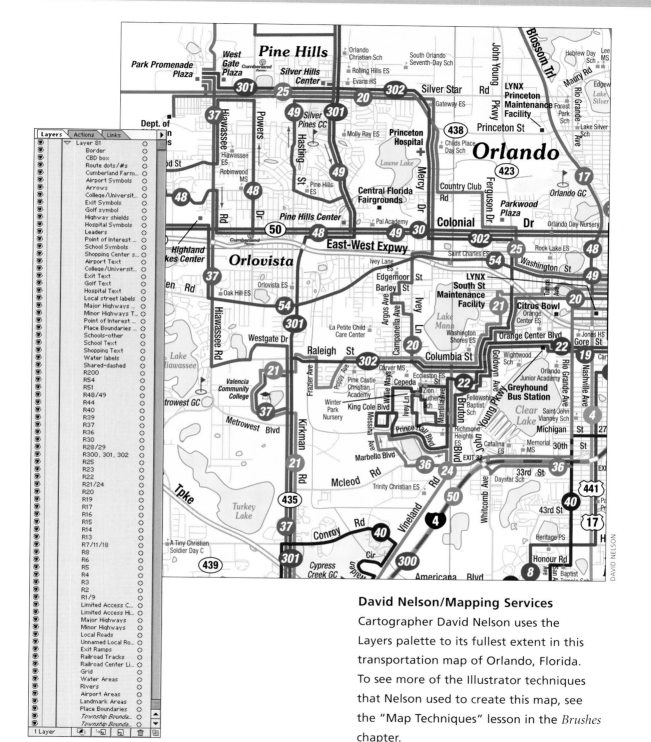

David Nelson/Mapping Services

David Nelson/Mapping Services
Cartographer David Nelson uses the
Layers palette to its fullest extent in this
transportation map of Orlando, Florida.
To see more of the Illustrator techniques
that Nelson used to create this map, see
the "Map Techniques" lesson in the *Brushes*
chapter.

Digitizing a Logo

Controlling Your Illustrator Template

Overview: *Scan a clean version of your artwork; place the art as a template in Illustrator; trace the template; modify the curve of drawn lines to better fit the template image by manipulating points and by using the Pencil tool.*

1

A large, clean scan of the artwork

Creating the template and a drawing layer

YIP (SAILOR JACK, BINGO & CRACKER JACK Designs are TMs of Recot, Inc., © Recot 1999.)

You can easily use Illustrator's Template layer to re-create traditional line art with the computer—easily, that is, if you know the tricks. San Francisco artist Filip Yip was commissioned to modernize the classic Cracker Jack sailor boy and dog logo, and to digitize the logo for use in a variety of media. Yip scanned the original logo artwork and several sketches he drew and used the scans as sources in developing the new logo.

1 Placing a scanned image as a template and using Filters to modify the image. Select a high-contrast copy of the original artwork that is free of folds, tears or stains. Scan the image at the highest resolution that will provide the detail you need for tracing. Open a new file in Illustrator (File: New), select File: Place, click the Template option, then choose your scan, thus placing it into a new template layer. Template layers are automatically set to be nonprinting and dimmed layers.

If you need to improve the quality of your scanned image to better discern details, you can edit the image with a program like Photoshop prior to placing it in Illustrator. Alternatively, if you've already brought the image into Illustrator, use the Filter menu to change focus or color. (If you placed the image on a Template layer, you'll need to double-click the layer name in the Layers palette and uncheck Template, which allows the image to be edited.) Select the image and select Filter: Sharpen to make the image more crisp. Choose the Filter: Colors menu and select options like Convert to Grayscale, Saturate, or Adjust Colors to modify image properties.

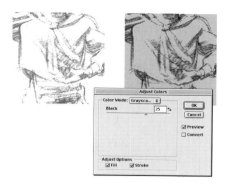

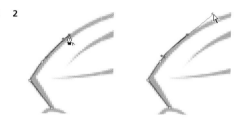

Darkening a scanned grayscale image using the Filter: Colors: Adjust Colors dialog

2 Tracing the template. With the template as an on-screen tracing guide (and the original scanned artwork handy as an off-screen reference), select the Pen or Pencil tool and begin tracing over the scanned image. To reduce visual clutter in small areas of the drawing, try viewing your active layer in Outline mode (while pressing ⌘-D on Mac or Ctrl-D on Win, click on the visibility icon next to the layer's name in the Layers palette). Don't worry too much about how closely you're matching the template as you draw. Next, zoom close (with the Zoom tool, drag to marquee the area you wish to inspect) and use the Direct-selection tool to adjust corner or curve points, curve segments, or direction lines until the Bézier curves properly fit the template. (See the *Lines, Fills & Colors* chapter for more on working with Bézier curves.)

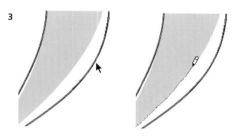

Modifying the fit of a drawn line using the Direct-selection tool to move a direction handle

3 Refining lines with the Pencil tool. To modify a line that doesn't follow the template, click the line to select it, then choose the Pencil tool and draw over the template with the Pencil. Illustrator automatically reshapes the selected line (instead of drawing a brand new line). You may need to edit the Pencil tool's settings (double-click the Pencil tool icon and edit the Pencil Tool Preferences dialog) to control the smoothness of the revised line or the pixel distance from the selected line in which the Pencil tool will operate. (Learn more about using the Pencil tool in *Tracing Details* in this chapter.)

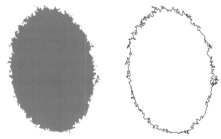

On the left, electing a previously drawn line, and on the right, redrawing the selected line with the Pencil tool

Manually tracing an intricate object may be more tedious and time-consuming than autotracing it; Yip drew the rough-edged parts of the sailor uniform with chalk on watercolor paper, which he then scanned, saved as a TIFF, and autotraced in Adobe Streamline

Tracing Details

Tracing Intricate Details with the Pencil

GRACE

Overview: *Scan a photo and place it into a Template layer in Illustrator; adjust Pencil Options; trace the photo with the Pencil; create new layers; adjust layer positions and modes.*

Saving images for tracing

While EPS is the preferred format for placed images (see the *Illustrator & Other Programs* chapter), saving images in TIFF format will display more detail for tracing.

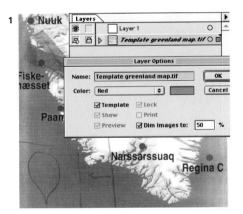

Double-clicking the Template layer to access Layer Options where "Dim Images" percentages can be customized

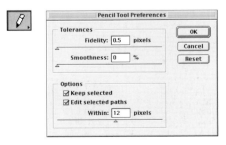

Double-clicking on the Pencil tool to set Options

Laurie Grace loves the way that the Pencil tool permits her to trace details with precision. Using the Pencil with custom settings and additional layers, she created this map of Greenland for a *Scientific American* article.

1 Scanning and placing the image into a Template layer. Scan the image you wish to use as a tracing template and save it in grayscale TIFF format. In a new Illustrator document, place your TIFF as a template (see "Digitizing A Logo" in this chapter). Your template will automatically be dimmed to 50%; to customize the percentage at which the template is dimmed, double-click the Template layer.

2 Setting up your Pencil Options for tracing. To draw with precision, you'll need to adjust the Pencil tool's default settings. Double-click the Pencil tool and drag the Fidelity slider all the way to the left, to 0.5 pixels, keeping Smoothness at 0% (higher numbers in Fidelity and Smoothness result in less accurate, smoother lines). For this lesson, keep "Keep Selected" enabled, so you can redraw lines and easily connect a new line to the last.

3 Drawing with the Pencil tool into Layer 1. It's very simple to attach one line to the next, so don't worry about tracing your entire template in one stroke. Zoom in on your work (see the *Basics* chapter for Zoom help) and trace one section. When you finish drawing that section (and it's still selected), move the Pencil tool aside until you see "×", indicating that the Pencil would be drawing a new path. Next, move the Pencil close to the selected path and notice that the "×" disappears, indicating that the new path will be connected to the currently selected one, then continue to draw your path. To attach a new path to an unselected path, simply select the path you wish to attach to first. To draw a closed path with the Pencil (like the islands in Grace's map), hold the Option/Alt key as you approach the first point in the path. **Note:** *With the Option/Alt key down, if you stop before you reach the first point, the path will close with a straight line.*

4 Creating and reordering new layers. To add the background water and the coastline terrain details, Grace had to create additional layers. To create additional layers, click on the New Layer icon in the Layers palette. Clicking on a layer name activates that layer so the next object you create will be on that layer. To reorder layers, grab a layer by its name and drag it above or below another layer. Click in the Lock column to Lock/Unlock specific layers.

5 Hiding and Previewing layers. Toggle Hide/Show Template layers from the View menu. To toggle any layer between Hide and Show, click on the Eye icon in the Visibility column for that layer to remove or show the Eye. To toggle a non-template layer between Preview and Outline mode, ⌘-click/Ctrl-click the Eye icon. (To move objects between layers, see Tip "Moving an object from one layer to another" in this chapter.)

Zooming more means smoothing less...

You can control the amount of smoothing applied with the Smooth tool by adjusting screen magnification. When you're zoomed-out, the Smooth tool deletes more points; zoomed-in, the tool produces more subtle results.—*David Nelson*

3

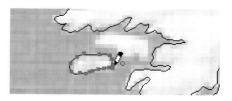

After drawing part of the coastline it remains selected. Moving the Pencil close to the selected path then allows the next path to be connected; continuing the path with the Pencil tool

Drawing with the Pencil tool and holding the Option key to close the path

4
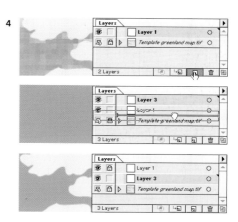

Making a New Layer; a blue object created in the new Layer 3 which is moved below Layer 1; Layer 1 locked with Layer 3 activated

5
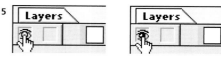

Toggling between Outline and Preview mode for a specific layer by ⌘-clicking the Eye

Layering Colors

Coloring Black-and-White Images with Layers

Overview: *Create your black out-lines; set up layers in Illustrator for the colors inside the lines and other layers for background elements; place black-and-white art into the upper layer; color the image; group outlines with their colors.*

KLINE / ACME DESIGN

1

The background for the illustration, created in the bottom two layers

2

An outline sketch

Choosing the "Transparent Whites" option when saving in a 1-bit (black-and-white) EPS format

While the most obvious way to trace placed images in Illustrator is to put the image to be traced into a locked lower layer and use an upper layer to trace the new Illustrator objects, in some cases you'll want your tracing layer to be *below* a placed image. When illustrating a three-ringed circus for a Ringling Brothers Barnum & Bailey International Program, Michael Kline placed his sketches with the whites transparent into a locked upper layer. This way, he could add color using Illustrator while maintaining a hand-sketched look.

1 Setting up your Illustrator layers. In Illustrator, create enough layers for the background elements of your image. (For help making layers, see "Digitizing a Logo" and "Tracing Details" in this chapter.) Each layer is assigned a different color—this help keeps track of the objects in each layer (selected paths and anchor points will be color-coded to match their layer). Create the background of your illustration in these layers, then lock the layers (in the Lock column of the palette). When the background is done, create at least two additional layers for the figures you will be coloring. For his circus illustration, Kline established four layers—using the bottom layer (Layer 1) to create the background itself and Layer 2 to create the objects directly on top of the background.

2 Sketching or scanning a black-and-white drawing.
Scan a hand-drawn sketch as a 1-bit Bitmap format
(black and white only), or draw directly into a painting
program set to a black-and-white mode. Save your image
as an EPS file with a 1-bit preview and enable "Transparent Whites" (if your painting program doesn't have this
option, you may have to open it in, and save it from,
Photoshop). Kline drew figure sketches with a soft pencil
on rough paper, scanned them, then saved them individually as transparent, 1-bit, black-and-white EPS files.

3 Placing your drawings into the top layer. From the
Layers palette, make the top layer active (click on the
layer name) and use the Place command (from the File
menu) to place one of your drawings into the top layer.

4 Coloring your drawings. To make coloring your drawings easier, it helps to lock all but the layer in which you
will be drawing. You must tell Illustrator which layer you
will be drawing in by activating the second layer (to the
left of the layer you should see the Eye icon but no Lock
icon). Then, lock the top layer. Now, using filled colored
objects without strokes, trace *under* your placed sketch.
To view the color alone, hide the top layer.

5 Grouping your drawing with its colors. When you're
finished coloring the first figure, select the placed EPS
with the objects that colorize that figure and group them
together. The grouped figure moves to the top layer, and
you can now easily reposition it within your composition.

The scanned drawing placed into Layer 4

The colorized drawing with the line drawing visi-
ble and the line drawing hidden

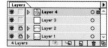
The drawing and the underlying color before
and after being grouped together; selected
objects that are on different layers, then
grouped, automatically move to layer where the
topmost selected object resided

Switching layers by selecting an object

You don't have to use the Layers palette to switch
your active layer. When you select an object from an
unlocked layer, the layer that the selected object is on
automatically becomes your new active layer. The next
object you create will use the same paint style as the
object you had selected and will be placed on that
new active layer.

Moving the grouped, colorized figure around the
composition

Organizing Layers
Managing Custom Layers and Sublayers

Overview: *Sketch and scan a composition; set up basic, named layers in Illustrator for the objects you will create; place art into temporary sublayers; trace the placed art; delete the temporary sublayers.*

Illustrator: STAHL/Designer: MITCH SHOSTAK

1

The initial concept for the illustration, used to set up a photo shoot; the assembled photographic collage

Hand-traced sketch scanned

Beginning your illustration with well-organized layers and sublayers can be a lifesaver when you're constructing complex illustrations. Using these layers to isolate or combine specific elements will save you an immense amount of production time by making it easy to hide, lock or select related objects within layers. When American Express commissioned Nancy Stahl to design a cover for their internal magazine *Context*, she saved time and frustration by creating layers and using sublayers for tracing and arranging various components of the cover illustration.

1 Collecting and assembling source materials. Prepare your own source materials to use as tracing templates in Illustrator. For the AmEx illustration, Stahl took

Polaroids of herself posed as each of the figures in her planned composition and scanned them into Adobe Photoshop, where she scaled them, composited some elements, and moved them into position. She then printed out the assembled "collage," roughly sketched in the other elements by hand and, with tracing paper, created a line drawing version of the full composition to use as an overall template. She then scanned it into the computer.

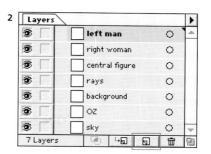

Setting up layers to isolate key elements

2 Setting up illustration layers. Before you begin to import any photos or drawings, take a few moments to set up layers to help you isolate the key elements in your illustration. For the cover illustration, before she actually started drawing in Illustrator, Stahl set up separate layers for the background, the sky, the rays of light and the building in the background, which she called "OZ," as well as a character layer for each of the figures. Name a layer while creating it by Option/Alt-clicking on the Create New Layer icon in the Layers palette. You can also name or rename an existing layer or sublayer by double-clicking on it in the Layers palette.

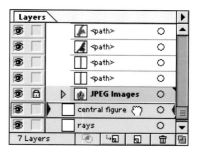

The temporary sublayer before placing the scan

3 Placing art to use as templates. Click on the layer in which you plan to trace your first object, then click on the Create New Sublayer icon in the Layers palette to create a sublayer for your template (Option/Alt-click on the icon to name your sublayer as you create it). Use File: Place to select the scan or artwork to be placed into this sublayer. The template sublayer should now be directly below the object layer upon which you will be tracing. Lock the template sublayer and draw into the layer above using the Pen, Pencil or other drawing tools.

Stahl activated a character layer by clicking on it in the Layers palette, then created a sublayer which she named "JPEG Images". She placed the hand-traced figures image into her sublayer, locked it, and traced her first character into the layer above. Using the Layers palette, she freely moved the locked JPEG Images template sublayer below each character's layer as she drew.

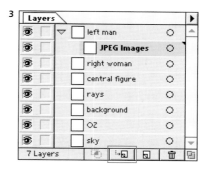

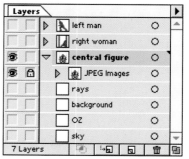

Moving the sublayer, and setting up the Lock and Show options for tracing

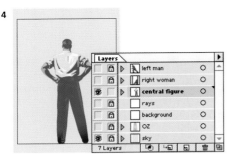

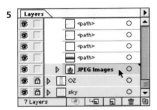

Isolating elements by viewing only the essential layers

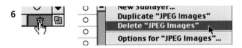

Clicking on a visible and unlocked sublayer to make it active for placing new art

Clicking on or dragging the sublayer to the Trash icon, or choosing Delete from the Layers palette pop-up menu

Changing placed art

Select the image you wish to replace. Next open the Links palette (Window menu) and click on the Replace Link icon (the bottom left icon) or choose Replace from the Links palette pop-up menu. In the dialog box, locate the replacement image and click Place.

4 Drawing into your layers. Now you can begin drawing and tracing elements into your compositional layers and sublayers. Activate the layer or sublayer in which you want to draw by clicking on the layer's name, make sure the layer or sublayer is unlocked and visible (there should be an Eye in the Visibility column and an empty box in the Lock column) and start to work. Use the Layers palette to lock, unlock or hide layers or sublayers, as well as to toggle between Preview and Outline modes, switch your active layer or add a new layer or sublayer. By maneuvering in this way, Stahl could easily trace a sketch of basic background elements, create rays against a locked background or develop one character at a time.

5 Adding new placed art to a layer or sublayer. If you need to import art into an existing layer or sublayer, first make sure the layer is visible and unlocked, then make it the active layer by clicking on it. For the AmEx cover, when Stahl needed additional references, she viewed and unlocked the JPEG Images template sublayer, clicked on it to make it active, and then used the Place command to bring the new scan or art into the template sublayer.

6 Deleting layers or sublayers when you are finished using them. Extra layers with placed art can take up quite a bit of disk space so you'll want to delete them when you are done with them. When you finish using a template, first save the illustration. Then, in the Layers palette, click on the layer or sublayer you are ready to remove and click on the trash icon in the Layers palette, choose the Delete option from the Layers palette pop-up menu, or drag the layer or sublayer to the trash icon in the Layers palette. Finally, use Save As to save this new version of the illustration with a meaningful new name and version number (such as "AmEx no JPEG v3.ai"). Stahl eventually deleted all the sublayers she created as templates so she could save her final cover illustration with all the illustration layers but none of the template sublayers or placed pictures.

STAHL

Nancy Stahl

Using the same techniques as in "Organizing Layers," Nancy Stahl created this image for the interior of American Express's internal magazine *Context*. When she wanted to move selected objects to another layer, she used the technique shown in the Tip below.

Moving an object from one layer to another

To move a selected object to another layer: open the Layers palette, grab the colored dot to the right of the object's layer and drag it to the desired layer (see near right). To move a copy of an object: hold down the Option/Alt key while you drag (see far right).

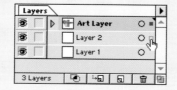

Nested Layers

Organizing with Layers and Sublayers

Overview: *Plan a layer structure; create layers and sublayers; refine the structure by rearranging layers and sublayers in the Layer palette's hierarchy; hide and lock layers; change the Layers palette display.*

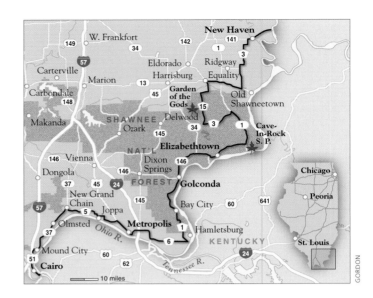

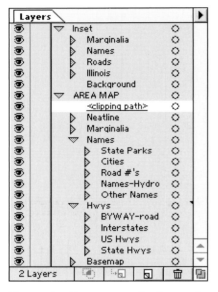

The completed layer structure for the map showing layers and two levels of sublayers

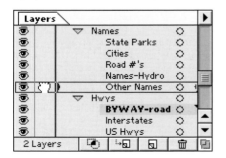

Selecting and dragging the BYWAY-road sublayer up and out of the Hwys sublayer, placing it on the same level in the hierarchy as Hwys

Layers have always been a great way of organizing your artwork. With Illustrator 9, you can organize your Layers palette as a nested hierarchy, making it easier to navigate and manipulate. For this map of the Great River Scenic Byway in Illinois, Steven Gordon relied on nested layers and sublayers to organize the artwork he developed.

1 Planning, then creating and moving layers and sublayers. Gordon began by planning a layer structure for the map in which layers with similar information would be nested within several "master" layers so that he could easily navigate the Layers palette and manipulate the layers and sublayers. After planning the organization of your layered artwork, open the Layers palette (Window: Show Layers) and begin creating layers and sublayers. (Illustrator automatically creates a Layer 1 every time a new document is created—you can use or rename this layer.) To create a new layer, click the Create New Layer icon at the bottom of the palette. To create a new sublayer that's nested within a currently selected layer, click on the palette's Create New Sublayer icon.

As you continue working, you may need to refine your organization by changing the nesting of a current layer or sublayer. To do this, drag the layer name in the

Layers palette and release it over a boundary between layers. To convert a sublayer to a layer, drag its name and release it above its master layer or below the last sublayer of the master layer (watch the sublayer's bar icon to ensure that it aligns with the left side of the names field in the Layers palette before releasing it). Don't forget that if you move a layer in the Layers palette, any sublayer, group or path it contains will move with it, affecting the hierarchy of artwork in your illustration.

2 Hiding and locking layers. As you draw, you can hide or lock sublayers of artwork by simply clicking on the visibility (eye) icon or edit (lock) icon of their master layer. Gordon organized his map so that related artwork, such as different kinds of names, were placed on separate sublayers nested within the Names layer, and thus could be hidden or locked by hiding or locking the Names layer.

If you click on the visibility or edit icon of a master layer, Illustrator remembers the visibility and edit status of each sublayer before locking or hiding the master layer. When Gordon clicked the visibility icon of the Names layer, sublayers that had been hidden before he hid the master layer remained hidden after he made the Names layer visible again. To quickly make the contents of all layers and sublayers visible, select Show All Layers from the Layers palette's pop-out menu. To unlock the content of all layers and sublayers, choose Unlock All Layers. (If these commands are not available, it's because all layers are already showing or unlocked.)

3 Changing the Layers palette display. As you utilize the Layers palette, change its display to make the palette easier to navigate. Display layers and sublayers (and hide groups and paths) in the palette by choosing Palette Options from the palette menu and in the Layers palette Options dialog, clicking Show Layers Only. To view tiny thumbnails of the artwork on each layer or sublayer, select a Row Size of Medium or Large, or select Other and set row size to 20 or more pixels in the dialog.

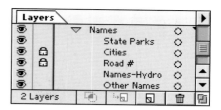

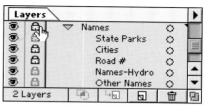

Top, a "master" layer with two sublayers locked; bottom, after the master layer is locked, the two sublayers' edit icons are not dimmed, indicating that they will remain locked when the layer is unlocked

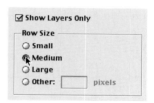

Selecting a row size in the Layers palette Options dialog

Another way to unlock layers

A quick way to unlock all the contents of a layer: Make sure the layer itself is unlocked (the lock icon is gone) and then choose Unlock All from the Object menu.

Let Illustrator do the walking

Illustrator can automatically expand the Layers palette and scroll to a sublayer that's hidden within a collapsed layer. Just click on an object in your artwork and choose Locate Layer or Locate Object from the Layers palette's menu.

Viewing Details

Using Layers and Views for Organization

Overview: *Establish your working layers; use layers to organize distinct categories of elements; save zoom levels and viewpoints using the New View command.*

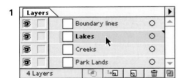

General organizational layers

Additional layers created to isolate categories of elements

CALIFORNIA STATE AUTOMOBILE ASSOCIATION

In addition to providing an ideal method for overlapping compositional elements, layers can help organize complex illustrations, even when many of the elements appear to exist on the same visual plane. When the California State Automobile Association (CSAA) creates road maps using Illustrator, the cartography department uses layers to delineate the different categories of labeling information. Even on the fastest computers, however, you can waste a lot of time zooming in and out, hiding and showing layers and toggling various layers between Preview and Outline modes. That's why the CSAA saves frequently used views to navigate quickly and easily around its large format maps.

1 Creating organizational layers. In addition to layers you create for compositional elements (such as background or figures), try creating separate layers for each category of labeling information you're including. If you construct your image with layers organized by the category of element, it becomes very simple to view and change all similar text or objects at once. For its Lake Tahoe map, the CSAA created individual layers for park lands, creeks, lakes and boundary lines, as well as layers for roads, type, symbols and the legend.

2 Saving frequently used views. To efficiently move around your image, you can preserve your current viewpoint for immediate return at another time. Along with "remembering" the specific section you zoomed to, saved views remember which of your layers were in Preview or Outline modes. To save your current view, simply choose View: New View, name your current view and click OK. Your view will then be added to the bottom of the View menu. Each successive view you save will appear at the bottom of the menu. The CSAA saved separate views for each area of the map requiring repeated attention, which included each of the four corners, the legend box and three additional locations.

3 Using views. To recall a saved view, choose the desired view from the list at the bottom of the View menu. Using Edit Views, you can rename or delete views, although you cannot change the viewpoints themselves. Another glitch is that Edit Views lists the most recently created or renamed view last, not alphabetically, so getting your views to list in a specific order takes a bit of organization. Finally, be aware if you add layers after creating views, the new layers will be visible in all previously created views.

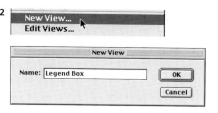

Saving and naming a viewpoint using New View

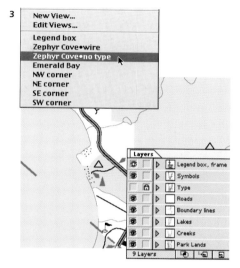

Recalling a view, which resets the zoom level, what portion of the image is visible, and which layers are visible or hidden, locked or unlocked

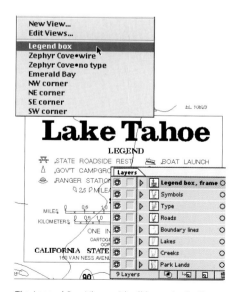

The Legend Box View, with all layers in Outline

Layer Registration

Paste Remembers Layers' Magic Alignment

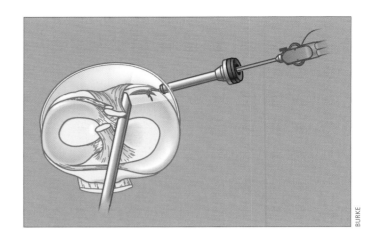

BURKE

Overview: *Create enough layers for all stages of your sequence; use New View to save settings for which layers are visible for each stage; control which layers print for proofing; set "Paste Remembers Layers" for separating stages for final printing.*

Organizing a series of interrelated illustrations in perfect registration with each other is simple using layers. This medical illustration shows three of the nine stages in a series that Christopher Burke created for Linvatec Corporation. It demonstrates the surgical procedure for repairing a knee injury once the fiber-optic light/camera is in place to illuminate the injury site.

1
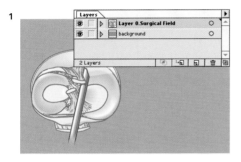

The background layer (the filled rectangle only) and main surgical layer, "Layer 0"

1 Creating layers to illustrate the unifying aspects of the series. Create the necessary layers into which you'll construct basic elements common to the whole series of illustrations (for layers help, see "Digitizing a Logo" and "Tracing Details" in this chapter.). Burke's basic layers for this surgical technique illustration were the surgical layer illustrating the knee, and the background.

2

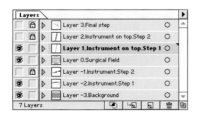

Choosing the View and Layers reset for "Step 1"

2 Simplifying the creation, viewing and proofing of the various stages of your illustration. Once the unifying aspects of your illustration are in place, use additional layers for creating variants. Use the Layers palette to hide and show various layers and thus isolate each of the different versions. Burke created all stages for the suturing technique in the same document. As he created a layer for a specific stage of the procedure, he would include that stage number in the layer name. For the numbering system, Burke named the main surgical layer "Layer 0"; this layer would appear in every stage. He numbered each progressive layer above it "1, 2, 3…" and then used "-1, -2, -3…" for each subsequent layer below.

When using layers to create a series of related illustrations, the New View command (View menu) can help track which layers need to be visible, hidden, locked or unlocked for each individual stage. Be aware, Views also remember Zoom level and location, and whether each layer is in Outline or Preview mode. After setting the Layers palette for a stage of your illustration, choose View: New View to name and save these settings. Repeat this procedure for each stage. To recall the Layers palette settings for any stage, select its view from the View menu.

When you're ready to print proofs, Illustrator will, by default, print only visible, non-template layers. To avoid having to make unnecessary changes to multiple documents, keep the file together as long as you can, using Views to help you keep track of which layers should be hidden or visible for each stage.

3 Preparing final versions for printing. In the Layers pop-up menu, enable "Paste Remembers Layers." This option ensures that your objects will stay in the correct layers, and that layers will be automatically replicated (or unlocked) as you move them into other files.

To print the final illustrations, you'll have to copy each completed stage into its own file. Select your saved views for the first stage, making sure all layers necessary to the illustration are visible and unlocked (all Eye icons should be visible and the Lock column should be empty). If you've hidden or locked any elements individually, choose from the Object menu: Unlock All and Show All. Then select and copy this version and, in a new document, use Edit: Paste In Front. When you use Paste In Front, all needed layers will miraculously appear in the Layers palette and the image will be in perfect registration, so you can still move objects back and forth between files. Repeat this step for each stage of the illustration. If you're printing from another application, save these in EPS format (see the *Basics* chapter for more on saving in EPS).

3

Setting "Paste Remembers Layers" in the Layers pop-up menu; the warning you'll get if you try to paste copied objects to locked or hidden layers (see "Organizing Layers" in this chapter for help with moving objects to other layers)

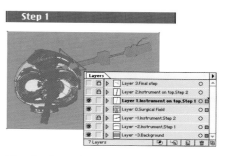

Choosing Step1 view, then selecting all needed layers for copying and pasting into a new file

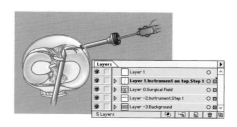

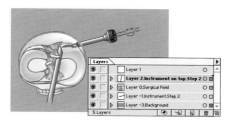

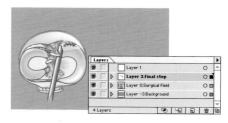

Each of the three stages pasted into its own document, with layers appearing automatically

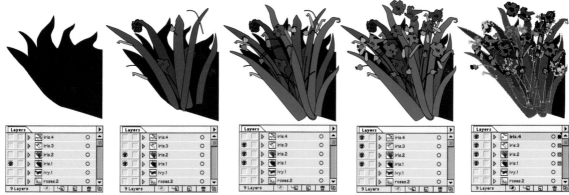

Jeffrey Barney / Barney McKay Design

For this image, serving as part of a five-tier pop-up promotion for *The Secret Garden*, Jeffrey Barney used dozens of layers to isolate various elements. Barney began by creating seven separate documents which, from front to back, were Ivy, Poppies, Roses, Irises, Mary, Sunflowers and Tree/Sky—each of the files containing four to twelve named layers. To properly arrange elements into the final five files for the pop-up, Barney kept the "Paste Remembers Layers" option enabled (see "Viewing Details" in this chapter). He was able to move objects between files while keeping them on the correct layers and in perfect registration. He

needed other arrangements of different layers for other materials, including the CD cover (shown with an "onionskin" overlay) and other print materials designed with Scott Franson.

Dorothea Taylor-Palmer

For this image, artist Dorothea Taylor-Palmer used the technique of placing one of her drawings on a top layer and painting the colored swaths in layers below (see "Layering Colors" in this chapter). She began with a traditional sketch and experimented with running it through a copier, while moving it slightly, until she captured an illusion of movement. After scanning the sketch into Photoshop, Taylor-Palmer saved it as a transparent, 1-bit EPS file, which she then placed into Illustrator. After locking the layer with the EPS, she created another layer and moved it below the first. Into the lower layer, Taylor-Palmer painted swaths of color to show through the white portions of the sketch.

TAYLOR-PALMER

PALMER

Charly Palmer

Although he's been a professional illustrator for many years, Charly Palmer has only recently begun using Illustrator, under the tutelage of his wife, Dorothea Taylor-Palmer. Even though his method of working is fairly similar to the one Taylor-Palmer used for the image above, his own vision and hand are strongly evident in this profile. After placing a scanned drawing that was saved as a transparent EPS onto an upper layer and locking it, Palmer used colors and blends to complete the composition.

Varied Perspective

Analyzing Different Views of Perspective

Advanced Technique

Overview: *Draw and scan a sketch; create working layers using your sketch as a template; in each "guides" layer, draw a series of lines to establish perspective; make the perspective lines into guides; draw elements of your image using the applicable perspective guides.*

Portion of the original pencil sketch placed on a template layer with a custom layer ready for creation of guides

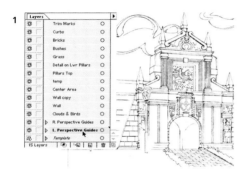

At the top, dragging a perspective line to the uppermost object from the vanishing point; below, paths blended to create in-between perspective lines

While any object can be made into a guide, converting lines into guides is indispensible when adding perspective to an image. To illustrate this McDonald's packaging design, Clarke Tate constructed several sets of vanishing point guides, enabling him to draw a background scene (Fort Santiago in the Philippines) that would contrast with the flat cartoon figures of Snoopy and Woodstock.

1 Setting up the layers. Sketch a detailed layout of the illustration on paper, shaping main elements like Tate's brick walk and wall with a perspective view. Scan your sketch and save the scan as a TIFF, then place the TIFF in Illustrator and choose Template from the Layers palette's pop-out menu. Analyze the image to determine the number of vanishing points in your illustration (points along the scene's horizon where parallel lines seem to converge). Create new layers (click the Create New Layer icon in the Layers palette) for compositional elements; add a layer for each vanishing point in the illustration.

2 **Establishing the location of vanishing points.** In the Layers palette, select the first layer you'll use for developing a set of perspective guides. Referring to your template, mark the first vanishing point and use the Pen tool to draw a path along the horizon and through the vanishing point. (Some or all of your vanishing points may need to extend beyond the picture border.) With the Direct-selection tool, select the anchor point from the end of the line that is away from the vanishing point. Grab the point, then hold down Opt/Alt and swing this copy of the line up so it encompasses the uppermost object that will be constructed using the vanishing point. You should now have a **V** that extends along your horizon line through your vanishing point, then to an upper or lower portion of your composition.

To create in-between lines through the same vanishing point, select both of the original lines, use the Blend tool to click first on the outer anchor point of one of the lines, and then on the outer anchor point of the other line. (If you need to specify more or fewer steps, you can select the blend and edit the number of steps in the Spacing: Specified Steps field of the Object: Blend: Blend Options dialog box.) For each different vanishing point, repeat the above procedure.

3 **Making and using the guides.** Because Illustrator cannot create guides from blended objects, you must first select each blend with the Selection tool and then expand it (Object: Blend: Expand). Next, transform the blends into guides by choosing View: Guides: Make Guides. Now pick an area of the illustration and begin drawing. You may want to lock the layers containing guides for other vanishing points so that you don't accidentally snap objects to the wrong perspective.

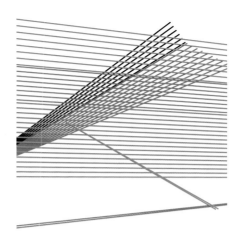

Perspective line blends before being transformed into guides

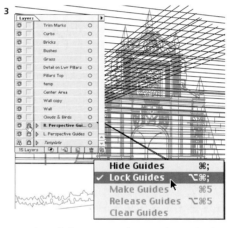

Turning off the "snap to" function for guides by locking the layer (left); locking guides in place by using the Lock/Unlock toggle in the View: Guides submenu

Locking and unlocking guides

- When guides are unlocked (disable View: Guides: Lock Guides), you can select any guide as an object and move or delete it.
- When a layer with guides is locked, the guides lose their "snap to" property—yet another good reason for you to keep guides on separate layers.

Type

6

Type

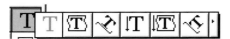

The Type tool, Area-type tool, Path-type tool, Vertical-type tool, Vertical Area-type tool, and Vertical Path-type tool. Select a Type tool and press Shift to toggle the tool between a horizontal and vertical orientation of the tool.

Illustrator is a powerful tool for graphically controlling type. Although you're likely to prefer a page layout program such as QuarkXPress, InDesign or PageMaker for multipage documents like catalogues and long magazine articles, and Dreamweaver or GoLive for web page layout, this chapter will show you many reasons to stay within Illustrator for single-page documents. The Type chapter of Adobe's *User Guide* covers the creation and manipulation of type in great detail, so this introduction will focus on essentials, what's new and production tips.

For creating and manipulating type, there are two palettes you can open from the Type menu: Character and Paragraph. When you first open these palettes, they may appear in a collapsed view. To cycle through display options for either palette, click the double arrow on the palette tab.

There are three type options in Illustrator that are accessible through the Type tool: *Point-type*, *Area-type* and *Path-type*. The flexible Type tool lets you click to create a Point-type object, click-drag to create an Area-type object or click within any existing type object to enter or edit text. You can gain access to type created in other applications by using the File: Open or File: Place commands.

Select letters, words or an entire block of text by dragging across the letters with the Type tool, or use a selection tool to select text as an *object* by clicking on or marqueeing the text baseline (the baseline is the line that the type sits on).

One option you may not want

If you keep accidentally selecting type when you're trying to select an object, disable Type Area Select (Edit: Preferences: Type & Auto Tracing). You can still select the type by clicking on it with the Direct-select tool or draw around the baseline with the Lasso tool.

Linking multiple blocks of text

Link multiple text objects so text flows from one to the next; select the desired objects and choose Type: Blocks: Link. Text does not have to be present to do this.

Typographic controls

Set keyboard-accessible typographic control defaults in Edit: Preferences: Type & Auto Tracing, but set units of measurement for type in Preferences: Units & Undo.

Selecting type

Use one of the Lasso tools to easily select type without first selecting the baseline and when Type Area Select is unchecked (Edit: Preferences: Type & Auto Tracing).

• **Point-type:** Click with the Horizontal-type or Vertical-type tool anywhere on the page to create Point-type. Once you click, a blinking text-insertion cursor called an "I-beam" indicates that you can now type text using your keyboard. To add another line of text, press the Return key. When you're finished typing into one text object, click on the Type tool in the toolbox to simultaneously select the current text as an object (the I-beam will disappear) and be poised to begin another text object. To just select the text as an object, click on a selection tool.

- **Area-type:** Click and drag with the Type tool to create a rectangle, into which you can type. Once you've defined your rectangle, the I-beam awaits your typing, and the text automatically wraps to the next line when you type in the confines of the rectangle. If you've typed more text than can fit in your text rectangle, you'll notice a plus sign along the bottom right side of the rectangle. To enlarge the rectangle to allow for more text, use the Direct-selection tool to deselect the text block, then grab one side of the rectangle and drag it out, holding down the Shift key to constrain the direction of the drag. To add a new text object that you will link to an existing text object, use the Group-selection tool to grab the rectangle only (not the text), hold down the Option (Mac)/Alt (Win) key and drag a copy of the rectangle. Text will automatically flow to the new rectangle.

Note: *You can't do this if you're accessing the Group-selection tool by temporarily holding down the Option/Alt key.*

Another way to create Area-type or Vertical Area-type is to construct a path (with any tools you wish) forming a shape with which to place the type. Click and hold on the Type tool to access other tools, or press the Shift key to toggle between horizontal and vertical orientations of *like* tools (see Tip "Type tool juggling" later in this chapter). Choose the Area-type or Vertical Area-type tool and click on the path itself to place text within the path. Distort the confining shape by grabbing an anchor point with the Direct-selection tool and dragging it to a new location, or reshape the path by adjusting direction lines. The text within will reflow.

Note: *If you use the Vertical Area-type tool, you'll see that your text will flow automatically, starting from the right edge of the area flowing toward the left! Those of you who use Roman fonts and typographic standards won't have much use for this tool since Roman type flows from left to*

It's Greek to me!

You can set type to be "greeked" on screen (it appears as a gray bar) by choosing File: Preferences: Type & Auto Tracing: Greeking. Greeked text prints normally.

Outlining type

Use this method to avoid distorting the characters. Select Type: Create Outlines. Use Paste In Back to make a copy behind. Give the *copy* a stroke value and make it a different color from the front text.

Selecting text or objects

Once you've entered your text, use the Type tool to select any text element by clicking and dragging across letters, words or lines, double-clicking to select a word, triple-clicking to select a paragraph or shift-clicking to extend a selection. If the text-insertion I-beam is activated, then Edit: Select All will select all type within that text object. If your text I-beam is not activated, then Select All selects *all unlocked objects* in your image.

Multinational font support

Illustrator supports Multinational fonts, including Chinese, Japanese, and Korean. Access the Multinational portion of the Character palette by clicking on the double arrows on the palette tab to fully expand it. To utilize the multinational font capabilities you must have the proper fonts and character sets loaded on your system, as well as special system software. Some of the multinational options will not work with Roman fonts, such as U.S. and U.K. English language fonts.

The quick-changing Type tool

When using the regular Type tool, look at your cursor very carefully in these situations:

- If you move the regular Type tool over a closed path, the cursor changes to the Area-type icon.
- If you move the Type tool over an open path, the cursor will change to the Path-type icon.

Making a new text object

Reselect the Type tool to end one text object; the next click will start a new text object. Or, deselect the current text by holding down the ⌘ (Mac)/Ctrl (Win) key (temporarily turning your cursor into a selection tool) and clicking outside the text block.

---

right, (see Tip "Multinational font support" to the left).

To set tabs for Area-type, select the text object and choose Type: Tab Ruler. The tab ruler will open aligned with the text box. As you pan or zoom, the Tab ruler does not move with the text box. If you lose your alignment, close the Tab ruler and reopen it. To wrap text around an object, select both the text box and the object and choose Type: Wrap: Make. After paths are wrapped to text objects, reshaping the paths causes text to reflow. To add a new path, Ungroup the current text and path objects, then reselect the text with the old and new paths and choose Type: Wrap: Make. (For more on tabs and wrapping text around objects, see the *User Guide*.)
Note: *You'll have to use Type: Wrap: Release or Ungroup before you can apply some of the filters to the text.*

- **Path-type:** The Path-type tool allows you to click on a path to flow text along the perimeter of the path (the path will then become unstroked or unfilled). To reposition the beginning of the text, use a Selection tool to grab the Path-type I-beam and drag left or right. Drag the I-beam up or down (or double-click it) to *flip* the text so it wraps along the inside or outside of the path.

As with Area-type, use the Direct-selection tool to reshape the confining path; the type on the path will automatically readjust to the new path shape.

ADDITIONAL TYPE FUNCTIONS (TYPE MENU)

- **Check Spelling**, **Find Font**, **Find/Change and Smart Punctuation** all work whether anything is selected or not, although some of these functions give you the option to work within a selected text block.

If you try to open a file and don't have the correct fonts loaded, Illustrator warns you, lists the missing fonts and asks if you still want to open the file. In addition, the warning dialog has an Obtain Fonts button. Clicking this button launches your web browser and takes you to the Adobe website to buy the missing fonts immediately. You do need the correct fonts to print properly; so if you don't have the missing fonts, choose Find Font to locate and replace them with ones you do have.

Find Font's dialog box displays the fonts used in the document in the top list; an asterisk indicates a missing font. The font type is represented by a symbol to the right of the font name. You can choose to replace fonts with ones on your system or used in the document. To display only the font types you want to use as replacements, uncheck those you don't want to include in the list. To replace a font used in the document, select it from the top list and choose a replacement font from the bottom list. You can individually replace each occurrence of the font by clicking Change and then Find Next. Otherwise, simply click Change All to replace all occurrences.
Note: *When you select a font in the top list, it becomes selected in the document.*

- **Type Orientation** lets you change orientation from horizontal to vertical, or vice versa, by choosing Type: Type Orientation: Horizontal or Vertical.

- **Change Case** lets you change the case of text selected with the Type tool to all upper, lower or mixed case.

- **Rows & Columns** can be used on Area-type or any selected rectangle. Use a selection tool (not the Type tool) to select the entire text object. You can enter your text first, or simply begin setting up your rows and columns with a rectangle. In the dialog box, specify the number and sizes of the rows and columns and whether you wish to use Add Guides. This creates grouped lines that you can make into Illustrator guides with View: Guides: Make Guides (see the *Illustrator Basics* chapter for more on guides). Keep Preview checked to see the results of your specifications while you work, and click one of the Text Flow options to choose whether text will flow horizontally or vertically from one block to another.

- **MM Design** stands for Multiple Master fonts. There's also

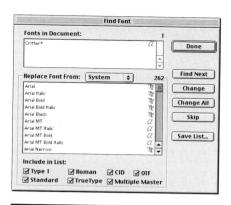

If you don't have the fonts...

Missing fonts? You can still open, edit and save the file, because Illustrator remembers the fonts you were using. However, the text will not flow accurately and the file won't print correctly until you load or replace the missing fonts.

Revert Path-type to path

Select the path with the Group-selection tool. Copy the path. Select the path with the Selection tool and delete it. Paste in Front to replace the path.—*Ted Alspach*

Type along the top and bottom

To create type along the top *and* bottom of a path, press the Option (Mac)/Alt (Win) key as you drag the I-beam to flip a *copy* of the type on the path.

Type tool juggling

To toggle a Type tool between its vertical and horizontal mode, first make sure nothing is selected. Hold the Shift key down to toggle the tool to the opposite mode.

Paint bucket and Eyedropper

To set what the Eyedropper picks up and the Paint bucket applies, double-click either tool to open the Eyedropper/Paint Bucket Options dialog box.

Eyedropper text

To restyle part of a text string or block, pick up a new sample with the Eyedropper tool, hold down the Option (Mac)/Alt (Win) key to select the Paint bucket tool and drag the cursor (as you would with the Text tool) over the text to be restyled. —*David Nelson*

Text different sizes?

To proportionally resize Area-type or Point-type of different sizes, select the text and use ⌘ (Mac)/Ctrl (Win)-Shift-> to increase all the font sizes or ⌘ (Mac)/Ctrl (Win)-Shift-< to decrease the sizes.

Bounding box resizing

If you resize a text block by its Bounding Box handles (see the *Basics* chapter), the text reflows (just as it does in page layout programs). —*Sandee Cohen*

a separate MM Design palette so you can customize Multiple Master fonts (see your font documentation for help).

- **Fit Headline** is a quick way to open up the letterspacing of a headline across a specific distance. First, create the headline within an area, not along a path. Next, set the type in the size you wish to use. Select the headline, then choose Type: Fit Headline, and the type will spread out to fill the area you've indicated. This works with both the Horizontal and Vertical-type tools.

- **Show Hidden Characters** reveals soft and hard returns, word spaces and an odd-shaped infinity symbol indicating the end of text flow. Toggle it on and off by choosing Type: Show Hidden Characters.

- **Glyph Options** can only be accessed if you have the appropriate Japanese Kanji font loaded. This option is only available for Macintosh users.

CONVERTING TYPE TO OUTLINES

As long as you've created text with fonts you have installed on your system (and can print), and you've finished experimenting with your type elements (e.g. adjusting size, leading, or kerning/tracking), you have the option to convert your text objects to Illustrator Bézier curves with compound paths. Compound paths form the "holes" in objects, such as the transparent center of an **O** or **P**. You can use the Direct-selection tool to select and manipulate parts of the compound paths separately. To convert a font to outlines, select the type with a selection tool and choose Type: Create Outlines. While the type is still selected, choose Object: Group, for easy reselection.
Note: *This is not recommended for small font sizes, see Tip "Don't outline small type" on next page.*

Why convert type to outlines?
- **So you can graphically transform or distort the individual curves and anchor points of letters or words.**

Everything from the minor stretching of a word to extreme distortion is possible. (For examples of this, see the lower right **M** on this page, and Galleries later in this chapter.)

- **So you can fill type with patterns/gradients, or use any brush to outline the type.** (For examples of this, see the top two **M** characters on this page, and the lesson "Brushed Type" later in this chapter.)

- **So you can make type into a masking object.** (For examples of this, on this page see the lower left **M**, and the lesson "Masking Letters" in this chapter.)

- **So you can work with vertically scaled type created in earlier versions of Illustrator.** Type is calculated differently in past versions of Illustrator, so opening a legacy document with a newer version of Illustrator may cause type to reflow. In lieu of editing, output the file from the original version, save as EPS or convert type to outlines.

- **So you don't have to supply the font to your client or service bureau.** Converting type can be especially useful when you're using foreign language fonts, or when your image will be printed when you're not around. (For an example of this, see the Model United Nations logo at right.)

- **If you don't want to convert to outlines, embed it and forget it.** Illustrator gives you the option to embed the fonts if you're saving the file for placement into another document. This text can't be edited, but you don't *need* to transport the fonts with the artwork.

Choose your words and letters carefully!

Having access to dozens of fonts doesn't make you a type expert, any more than having a handful of pens makes you an artist. Experiment all you want, but if you need professional typographic results, consult a professional. I did. Barbara Sudick designed this book.

Don't outline small type

If you're printing to a high-resolution imagesetter or using larger type sizes, you can successfully convert type objects to outlines. However, due to a font-enhancing printing technology (called "hinting"), a *small* type object converted to outlines won't look as good on the computer screen, or print as clearly to printers of 600 dots per inch or less, as it would have if it had remained a font.

Making one text block of many

To join separate Area-text boxes or Point-text objects, select all the text objects with any selection tool and copy. Then draw a new Area-text box and Paste. Text will flow into the new box in the original *stacking order* that it appeared on the page. (It doesn't matter if you select graphic elements with your text—these elements won't be pasted.)—*Sandee Cohen*

Transporting foreign or unusual fonts (artwork by Kathleen Tinkel)

Filling with patterns or gradients

Masking with type (artwork by Min Wang for Adobe Systems)

Transforming outlines (artwork by Javier Romero Design Group)

Custom Text Paths

Trickling Type with Variations of Type Style

Overview: *Prepare and Place text; create a set of evenly-spaced paths; copy and paste text into appropriate path lines; adjust text baseline paths and placement of text on the paths.*

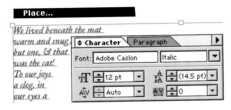

Placed text creates a new rectangle which contains the type; choose a font and size while the text is still selected

Opt/Alt-drag to create a second path below the first; use Object: Transform: Transform Again (or ⌘-D/Ctrl-D) to repeat this step

Grab the I-beam to move the text along the path

Adjust curved paths and text placement along those paths using the Direct-selection tool

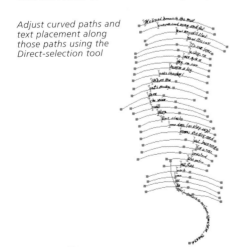

Laurie Szujewska placed type on curved Bézier paths to emulate the shaped lines of Lewis Carroll's original hand-lettered poem from *Alice's Adventures Underground* (an early version of *Alice in Wonderland*).

1 Preparing your type. Use a word processor to proofread and spell-check your text. In Illustrator, choose File: Place and select your text document; this creates a rectangle containing your text. Choose a typeface and size.

2 Creating your baselines and placing your type. Next to your type, draw a curved path with the Pen tool (see "Zen Lessons" in the *Wow!* disk "Tutorial" folder for Pen help). With the Path-Type tool, click on your Bézier path and type a few characters. To determine the spacing between lines, switch to the Selection tool, grab the path, holding the Opt/Alt key and drag the selected path downward, until the second path is spaced correctly (release the mouse button while still holding down the key). To duplicate the path and the spacing between paths, press ⌘-D/Ctrl-D (or Object: Transform: Transform Again), repeating until you've created the desired number of text paths.

Switch to the Type tool, select the text you want for the top path and Copy. Now click on the top path and Paste. Repeat with the remaining lines.

3 Adjusting the type. With all text placed, use the Direct-selection tool to adjust the curves. If you wish to see all of the text paths at once (whether selected or not), switch to Outline View. To move the starting point for lines of text, click on the path with the Selection tool and drag the I-beam along the path. For downward curving text in her image, Szujewska's adjusted the path, then individually selected the last words, progressively reducing them in size.

We lived beneath the mat
warm and snug and fat
but one, & that
was the cat!
To our joys
a clog, in
our eyes a
fog, on our
hearts a log,
was the dog!
When the
cat's away,
then
the mice
will
play.
But, alas!
one day, (so they say)
came the dog and
cat, hunting
for a rat,
crushed
the mice
all flat,
each
one
as
he
sat underneath the mat, warm, & snug and fat . . . Think of that!

SZUJEWSKA / ADOBE SYSTEMS, INC. / adapted from Lewis Carroll's *Alice's Adventures Underground*

Laurie Szujewska / Adobe Systems, Inc.

For Adobe's Poetica type specimen book, Laurie Szujewska was inspired by a "love knot" poem from the book *Pattern Poetry* by Dick Higgins, and created a similar spiral path with the Pen tool.

She used the Path-Type tool to place the text on the path. She then meticulously kerned and placed spaces along the type path to prevent text overlaps, and to get things just right.

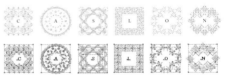

Laurie Szujewska / Adobe Systems, Inc.

For Adobe's Caslon type specimen book, Szujewska created these decorative orna-

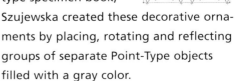

ments by placing, rotating and reflecting groups of separate Point-Type objects filled with a gray color.

WEINSTEIN

Ari M. Weinstein

Ari M. Weinstein developed techniques that allowed this Ketubah, a wedding present for a friend, to conform to traditional scribal standards and appearance. He began by entering text in a calligraphic Hebrew font, line by line, to avoid automatic text wrap. He re-created the traditional scribal method of crafting the length of each line by stretching letter cross-strokes instead of using paragraph justification (which would have created non-uniform word and letter spacing). To accomplish this, Weinstein converted the type to outlines (Type: Create Outlines) and then used the Direct-selection tool to select parts of letter outlines and move them in 1-point increments with the arrow keys.

PlanTea

BURNS

1 1 1 1   P P

John Burns

Lettering artist John Burns developed this logo for PlanTea, an organic fertilizer for plants that is brewed in water, like tea. He began by typing the name and then converted the letters to outlines (Type: Create Outlines). After drawing a leaf and placing it on the stem of each letter **a**, he selected and copied the artwork, pasted it in back (Edit: Paste In Back) to form the drop shadows, and offset them down and to the right. Burns then filled the copied letterforms with 40% black. To prevent the drop shadows from touching the black letterforms (creating a more stylized look), he selected the black art-work and again pasted it behind (but in front of the drop shadows) and then applied a white fill and thick white stroke to the pasted letter-forms. The stages of his process, here applied to the **l**, are shown above left. Finally, Burns used the Direct-selection tool to reshape some of the drop shadow shapes, adjusting the thick-ness of some of the shadow letter strokes and hiding slivers of shadows that stuck out a little behind the black letters (the **P** directly above shows the shadow before and after reshaping).

HORNALL ANDERSON DESIGN WORKS

Hornall Anderson Design Works / John Hornall (Art Director)

Designers at Hornall Anderson Design Works set the name "Yves" for this healthy, vegetarian line of foods in Gill Sans and then modified the letterforms to fit the logo design. First, they placed the text along a curve and then converted the font characters to outlines (Type: Create Outlines). To create the shadows on the left side of the name's characters, designers used the Scissors tool to cut the character paths, the Direct-selection tool to move cut pieces, and the Pen tool to connect points and close objects. Another way to accomplish a similar effect is to Copy the original letterforms and Paste in Back twice. Give the top copy a white Fill and a thick white Stroke; while still selected, choose Object: Path: Outline Path and set the new outline stroke to a small width.

Move the bottom copy of the letterforms to the left. Then select the two copies and choose the Minus Front command from the Pathfinder palette. Lastly, delete extraneous objects and use the Scissors and Direct-selection tools to reshape the remaining objects.

Masking Letters

Masking Images with Letter Forms

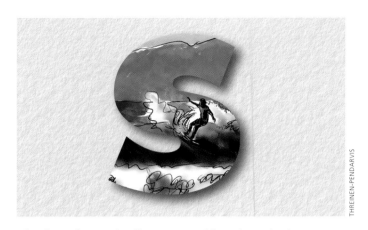

THREINEN-PENDARVIS

Overview: *Create a large letter on top of a placed TIF image; convert the letter to outlines; select all and make the letter form into a clipping mask for the placed image.*

Placing the TIF image; creating Point-Type letter

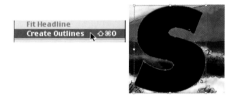

Converting the letter "S" to outlines

Selecting both the letter form and the image beneath; making a clipping mask

Selecting an object using the Layers palette, then moving it with the Direct-selection tool

This "**S** is for Surfing" was created by Cher Threinen-Pendarvis for an alphabet poster. Although you *can* mask with "live" type, convert text to outlines to avoid printing problems. For additional type and mask lessons, see the Gallery opposite and the *Advanced Techniques* chapter.

1 Positioning elements and converting a large letter to outlines. Place a TIF image into your Illustrator file by using File: Place. Using the Type tool, click on top of your image to create a Point-Type object and type one letter. Choose a typeface with enough weight and a point size large enough for the bottom image to show through the letter form itself. Select the letter with a Selection tool and choose Type: Create Outlines (⌘-Shift-O/Ctrl-Shift-O).

2 Creating the clipping mask and adjusting the image position. The topmost object in a selection becomes the mask when you make a clipping mask. If your letter isn't the top object, select it, Cut, then Edit: Paste In Front. To create the mask, select the outlined letter and the images to be masked and choose Object: Clipping Mask: Make; the mask and masked objects are automatically grouped. To adjust the position of an object within a mask, select it with the Layers palette or with the Direct-selection tool, then move it with the Direct-selection tool. Threinen-Pendarvis finished by applying Effect: Drop Shadow (default settings) to a filled copy of the **S** below the mask group, above a TIF background created in Corel Painter.

NEWMAN

Gary Newman

Artist Gary Newman combined a compound path and masking to create this title illustration. First, Newman typed the word "Careers" and converted the text to outlines (Type: Create Outlines). Next, he made a single compound path by choosing Object: Compound Path: Make. Newman masked a copy of his background artwork with this compound path. With the compound object on top and all elements selected, he chose Object: Clipping Mask: Make. He then selected the masked background objects and used Filter: Colors: Adjust Colors, increasing the black percentage. Newman added a drop shadow by layering a black-filled copy of the type behind the background-filled type. He set the words "Changing" and "at mid-life" in black type,

and added drop shadows behind them; drop shadows can also be made using the Transparency palette to adjust blending modes and Opacity (for help with blending modes and Opacity, see the *Transparency* chapter).

Bookcover Design

Illustrator as a Stand-alone Layout Tool

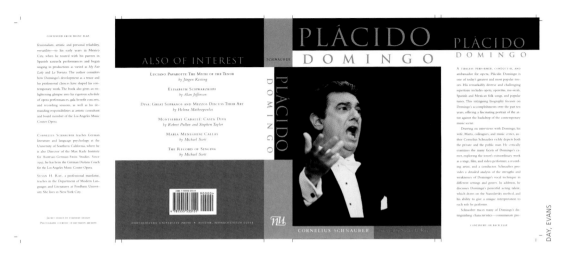

Overview: *Set your document size; place guides and cropmarks; place EPS files and make Area Type for columns and Point Type for graphic type; visually track type to fit.*

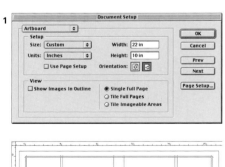

Setting up the Artboard and layout specs

Page layout programs such as QuarkXPress and Page-Maker are essential for producing multipage, complex documents. However, Rob Day and Virginia Evans often use Illustrator for single-page design projects such as book jackets.

1 Setting up your page. Choose File: Document Setup to set up the Artboard for your design. Click on landscape or portrait page orientation and enter your Artboard size, making sure it's large enough for crop and/or registration marks (the "Size" parameter will automatically switch to "Custom"). Choose View: Show Rulers and "re-zero" your ruler origin to the upper left corner of where your page will begin (see the *Basics* chapter for more on repositioning the ruler origin), and use View: Outline/Preview to toggle between Outline and Preview modes. Although you can generate uniform grids with Edit: Preferences: Guides & Grid, for columns of varying sizes, Day and Evans numerically created two sets of rectangles: one for bleeds, one for trims. With the Rectangle tool, click to make a box sized for a trim area (see the *Basics* chapter for Rectangle tool help), then immediately Option/Alt-click on the center of the trim area box to numerically specify a box .125" larger in each dimension in order to create a bleed area box. Day and Evans made trim and bleed boxes for the front, back, flaps and spine. To place an overall trim mark, select the boxes that define the entire trim area and choose Filter: Create: Trim Marks.

2 Customizing your guides. Select your trim and bleed boxes (not the trim marks) and create Guides by choosing View: Guides: Make Guides (see the "Varied Perspective" lesson in the *Layers* chapter for more on guides).

3 Placing and refining the elements. Choose File: Place to select an EPS image to import into your layout. Create rectangles or other objects which will define the area for columns of text. Click on the path of one of these objects with the Area Type tool. Once the text cursor is placed, you can type directly or paste text (see "Custom Text Paths" in this chapter). Area Type is used in this layout for columns of type on the flaps. Alternately, click with the Type tool to create Point Type, which is used to place lines of type for titles and headlines, and other individual type elements. To track type visually to fit a space, select a text object and use Option/Alt-←/→. For help with rotating or scaling objects (this applies to text objects as well), see the *Zen* chapter and the *Zen Lessons* on the *Wow!* disk.

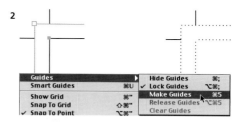
Converting trim and bleed boxes into Guides

All of the elements placed into the layout

Close-ups of an Area-Type object

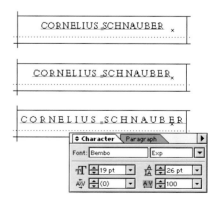
Close-ups of Point-Type objects

Creating "cropmarks," then "trim marks"

Create a rectangle that defines a cropping area, and choose Object: Cropmarks: Make. Cropmarks are visible in Illustrator but become invisible when placed into another program (such as QuarkXPress or PageMaker), except that they will reappear if you position objects beyond the cropmarks. To remove cropmarks, either choose Object: Cropmarks: Release, or make a new rectangle and again choose Object: Cropmarks: Make. Or create always-visible Trim Marks by selecting any object (a rectangle is not required) and choosing Filter: Create: Trim Marks. Files can contain multiple trim marks.

Tracking a line of Point Type with cursor-keys

JAVIER ROMERO DESIGN GROUP

Javier Romero Design Group

With a client as particular as Disney, Javier Romero needed the flexibility to create many design variations for children's clothing tags. And because the type needed to be fully integrated with the illustrations, Illustrator proved to be the most practical design tool. Of the dozens of designs that Romero presented, Disney selected as finals the designs shown in the photo above and to its right. Shown directly above are three of the comps, which include compositional elements contributing to the final design.

Javier Romero Design Group

Javier Romero Design Group converted the title in this illustration to outlines (Type: Create Outlines) and then manually distorted it. The resulting glowing effect, which the Design Group then applied to the type, can be used on any object—even regular, editable text objects. They filled the letters in a solid color, Copied and chose Edit: Paste In Back to place a copy of the letters behind the original, set the Fill for this copy to None, with a 5.5-pt, medium-colored stroke. They repeated the Copy and Paste In Back step, successively using different colored strokes of 7, 11 and 16 points.

JAVIER ROMERO DESIGN GROUP

GORSKA (design), BALDWIN (illustration) / MAX SEABAUGH ASSOCIATES

Caryl Gorska / Max Seabaugh Associates

After commissioning Scott Baldwin to create a nutcracker illustration (he used Macromedia FreeHand to re-create his linoleum cut), Caryl Gorska scanned a traditional, copyright-free Dover Publications typeface. She saved the scanned typeface to use as a template (see the *Blends* chapter) and used the Pen tool to carefully trace the letters she needed. She then created the frame into which the type would be placed and, using the Selection tool, she "hand-set" the type by copying and pasting letter forms. Lastly, she fine-tuned the letter spacing, checking herself by printing myriad proofs—both actual size and greatly enlarged. Although her typeface, Newport Condensed, was available as a PostScript commercial font, instead of spending time and money tracking down and purchasing the font, Gorska preferred to spend the time typesetting the letters herself. "It keeps me in touch with the real letter forms and how they fit together, in a way that we often miss, just doing typesetting on the computer."

Brushed Type

Applying Brushes to Letterforms

Overview: *Create centerlines for font characters; customize art brushes and apply brushes to the centerlines and outlines of the letterforms to simulate hand-rendered lettering.*

GORDON

Original font characters filled with 20% black

Black-stroked outlines of font characters on layer above original font characters

The letterform centerlines after drawing with the Pencil tool on a layer above the original font characters; the outline layer is not shown

2

Top, the default Splash brush; below, the edited brush with color fills

To convey the variety of museums in Boston, cartographer Steven Gordon wanted a map title that blended the "natural" artistry of pencil and brush with the classicism of serif font characters. Because Illustrator applies brushes as strokes along paths, Gordon drew centerlines for the font characters before painting the centerlines with customized brushes, giving them the look of hand-rendered letterforms.

1 Creating letter centerlines and outlines. To re-create Gordon's painted lettering, begin by typing text in a serif font (Gordon selected Type: Character and chose Garamond Bold Condensed Italic and 112 pt in the Character palette.) Select the text and give it a 20% black Fill. Copy the layer with the text by dragging it onto the Create New Layer icon at the bottom of the palette. To create the font outline, select the text on the copied layer and convert the characters to outlines (Type: Create Outlines), then change their Fill to None and Stroke to black. Now create a new layer (click the Create New Layer icon in the Layers palette) and drag this layer between the other two. On this new layer, draw centerlines for each font character with the Pen or Pencil tool. The paths don't have to be perfectly smooth or centered inside the letterforms because you will paint them with an irregularly shaped brush later.

2 Creating and applying custom brushes and effects. Gordon looked to Illustrator's brushes to give the letter centerlines the color and spontaneity of traditional brushwork. He opened the Artistic Sample brush palette (Window: Brush Libraries: Artistic Sample) and selected the Splash brush. To customize the brush, first drag the brush from the palette to the canvas. Select each brush object with the Direct-selection tool and replace the gray with a color you like. Next, drag the brush artwork into the Brushes palette and select New Art Brush from the New Brush dialog box. In the Art Brush Options dialog box, further customize the brush by changing Width to 50%, enabling the Proportional brush setting, and clicking OK. (You won't see the change in width displayed in the dialog's preview.) Make several brush variations by copying the brush and then editing brush Direction, Width and other parameters. Now individualize your letterforms by selecting the first centerline and clicking on a brush from the Brushes palette. Try several of the brushes you created to find the best "fit." Continue applying brushes to the remaining centerlines.

To create the look of loose pencil tracings for the font character outlines on the top layer, Gordon edited the Dry Ink brush from the Artistic Sample palette, changing its Width to 10% in the Art Brush Options dialog box. Gordon completed the look by selecting each character outline and applying the Roughen Effect (Size 1%, Distort 10%, Smooth). (See the *Transparency, Styles & Effects* chapter to learn more about applying Effects and using the Appearance palette.)

3 Finishing touches. Gordon selected all the centerlines and offset them up and left while moving the font outlines down and right from the original font characters on the bottom layer, suggesting a loose style. He also simulated the appearance of hand-rendering by adjusting the transparency and blending modes of the brushed letterforms: Gordon selected the centerline objects, and in the Transparency palette, chose Multiply mode and reduced transparency to 75%. This caused the colors of brushed centerline paths to darken where they overlapped, mimicking the effect of overlapping transparent inks.

Experimenting by applying different brushes to centerlines to lend individuality to the letter "s"

On top, the Dry Ink brush; left, the customized brush applied to the font outline; right, the Roughen Effect applied to the brushed outline

Artwork on three layers, from bottom layer (left) to top layer (right)

Left, the horizontal and vertical centerlines of the letter "t" with Normal blending mode and 100% opacity; right, strokes placed to form letter "t" and with Multiply blending mode and 70% opacity

Finished lettering on three layers, shown in composite view

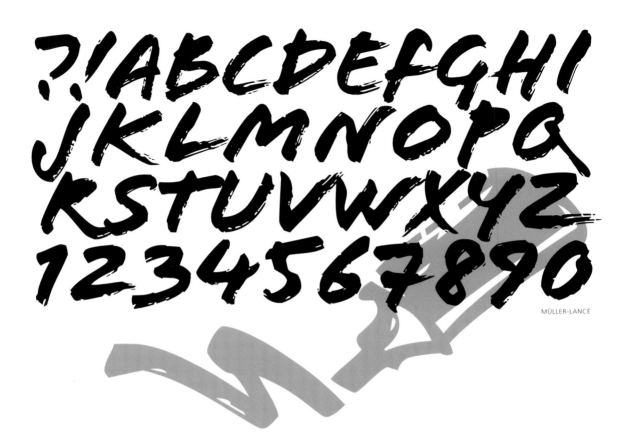

MÜLLER-LANCÉ

Joachim Müller-Lancé

The original characters of Joachim Müller-Lancé's Flood typeface were drawn with a worn felt marker during a type seminar hosted by Sumner Stone. Two years later Müller-Lancé rediscovered the drawings when Adobe asked him for new font ideas. Realizing that the original character traces were not of font quality, he redrew all of the characters using Illustrator's Pen and Pencil tools. He composed many of the characters as separate, black-filled objects, which he moved around while also adjusting width, slant and scale until he got the look he wanted. He used the Unite command from the

Pathfinder palette to join the overlapping objects of each character into a single shape. He also drew the holes and streaks as white-filled objects above the black-filled objects and used Minus Front (also from the Pathfinder palette) to knock out the holes and streaks in the characters. Then Müller-Lancé copied the artwork for each character and pasted it directly into the appropriate character slot in Fontographer, where he completed the font.

T H E MATRIX

Tim Girvin /
Tim Girvin Strategic Branding & Design

Designer Tim Girvin began the logo for this futuristic film by setting the title in Times New Roman and converting the type outlines to paths (Type: Create Outlines), He drew objects with the Rectangle and other tools that he used with the Divide command from the Pathfinder palette to break the letterforms into pieces. After modifying some of their shapes with the Direct-selection tool, Girvin repositioned the pieces to form the asymmetrical letterforms of the logo.

Jennifer Bartlett /
Tim Girvin Strategic Branding & Design

Jennifer Bartlett set this logo using a proprietary Girvin font. To keep the letters of the tagline upright but parallel to the wave of the background banner, Bartlett selected individual characters by dragging with the Text tool and adjusted their vertical positions by entering positive values (to move characters up) or negative values (to move characters down) in the Character palette's Baseline Shift field, accessed by choosing Type: Character and choosing Show Options from the Character palette's pop-out menu.

ICE HOUSE PRESS (AKSELSEN)

Bjørn Akselsen / Ice House Press

For this logo for Private Chef, a gourmet food and catering company, designer Bjørn Akselsen avoided the orderly appearance of calligraphic and script fonts by using Illustrator to distort letterforms. First Akselsen drew the letterforms with traditional brush and ink, then scanned the artwork and placed it in Illustrator, where he traced the letterforms. Next he reshaped their outlines and interiors with the Direct-selection tool to emphasize contrast in the strokes and applied three Distort filters from the top section of the Filter menu (Punk & Bloat, Roughen, and Scribble and Tweak) to further distort the letter shapes and enhance their individuality. Finally, Akselsen used the Pencil tool to smooth out rough edges.

Pattie Belle Hastings / Ice House Press
(Sharon Steuer illustration and production)

In redesigning the logos for The Traveling Radio Show, Pattie Belle Hastings wanted to convey activity in the title type treatment. Starting with characters from TheSans typeface, Hastings created the title in one line (as it appears on the business cards and brochures) and then outlined the characters (Type: Create Outlines). Zooming in on the characters, she pulled down four guidelines from the horizontal ruler (View: Show Rulers), so she could use them to align the letters. She then selected individual type characters and positioned each vertically, visually aligning it to one of the guidelines. The characters were also individually colored, and then horizontally positioned by Shift-selecting letters, and nudging them

ICE HOUSE PRESS (HASTINGS) / STEUER (illustration / production)

with the left and right arrow keys. For a sticker design (shown above), the title was split into two lines and enlarged.

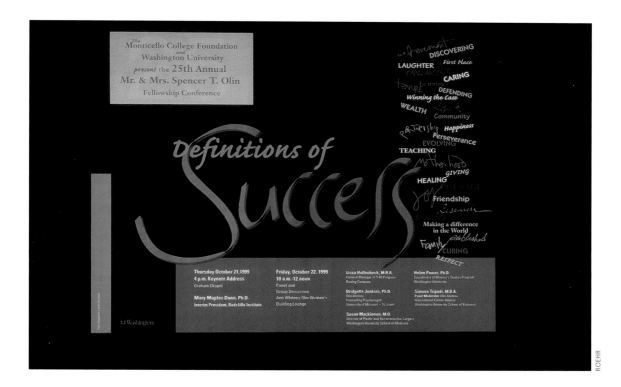

Karen Roehr

In this poster commemorating the 25th anniversary of a women's fellowship conference, artist Karen Roehr mixed computer fonts like Bodoni, Kabel and Univers with calligraphy she rendered by hand using a Wacom tablet and Illustrator's Pen, Pencil and Paintbrush tools. To use the Calligraphy brush, Roehr first double-clicked the Paintbrush tool and disabled the "Fill new brush strokes" option in the Paintbrush Tool Preferences. She chose a calligraphy brush (Angle 45°, Roundness 0%, Diameter 30 pt) from the Brushes palette and drew the word "Success." She copied the word and pasted it in back to form both a shadow and letterform gaps. For many of the poster's hand-drawn words, Roehr drew several variations of individual letters using different Illustrator tools, combining the letters that gave the word the appearance she wanted.

FISHAUF

Louis Fishauf / Reactor Art + Design

Asked to create the visual identity for a proposed news cafe and media tower, designer Louis Fishauf drew the letters for the name with the Pen tool, first assigning a thick stroke to the paths and then outlining the strokes (Object: Path: Outline Stroke). He moved points in the letter tips using the Direct-selection tool, angling the tips parallel to the black lines behind the name. To convey perspective, Fishauf pasted copies of the letters **t** and **H** behind the name, filled them with black, and manually offset each of these shadows to the left or right. For the letters **R** and **c**, Fishauf drew the shadows with the Pen tool, keeping the curves parallel to the white letterforms in front.

PAPCIAK-ROSE

Ellen Papciak-Rose inthestudio@gonet.co.za

Ellen Papciak-Rose / In The Studio

Ellen Papciak-Rose created the title "Zimbabwe" using geometric objects she drew with the Rectangle, Ellipse and other tools. She composited the objects and used Minus Front and other commands from the Pathfinder palette to knock out parts of the objects, forming the title letterforms. Papciak-Rose then painted the strokes of the objects with two custom-built variations of a rough charcoal brush found in

the Artistic Sample Brush library (Window: Brush Libraries: Artistic Sample). In the four panels of the poster, Papciak-Rose painted outlines of characters from the Sand font with the two custom-built rough charcoal brushes.

Blends & Gradients

7

Blends & Gradients

"W" Blend tool
"G" Gradient tool

BLENDS

Think of blends as a way to "morph" one object's shape and/or color into another. You can blend between multiple objects, and even gradients or compound paths, such as letters (see the *Advanced* chapter for more on compound paths). Blends are *live*, which means you can edit the key objects by altering their shape, color, size, location or rotation, and the resulting *in-between* objects will automatically update. You can also distribute a blend along a custom path (see details later in this chapter).

Note: *Complex blends require a lot of RAM when drawing to the screen, especially gradient-to-gradient blends.*

The simplest way to create a blend is to select the objects you wish to blend and choose Object: Blend: Make. The number of steps you'll have in between each object is based on either the default options for the tool, or the last settings of the Blend Options (details following). Adjust settings for a selected blend by double-clicking the Blend tool (or Objects: Blend: Blend Options).

A more reliable method of creating smooth blends in many circumstances is to *point map* between two objects using the Blend tool. First, select the two objects that you want to blend (with the Group-selection tool), then use the Blend tool to *point-map* by clicking first on a selected point on the first object, then on the correlating selected point on the second object.

When a blend first appears, it is selected and grouped. If you Undo immediately, the blend will be deleted, but your source objects remain selected so you can blend again. To modify a key object, Direct-select the key object first, then use any editing tool (including the Pencil, Smooth and Erase tools) to make your changes.

Blend Options

To specify Blend Options as you blend, use the Blend tool (see the *point map* directions above) and press the

The speed of the blend

To control the speed of the blend, create the blend and set the number of blend steps as you would normally do. This creates the blend spine, which is editable just like any other Illustrator object. Using the Convert-anchor-point tool, pull out control handles from the anchor point at each end of the blend spine. By extending or shortening these control handles along the spine, the speed of the blend is controlled. This is very similar to the way in which blend speeds are controlled in the gradient mesh.—*Derek Mah*

Recolor after expanding blends

If you've expanded a blend, you can use *filters* to recolor blended objects. Direct-select and recolor the fill for the start and/or end objects, then select the entire blend and choose Filter: Colors: Blend Front to Back. Your objects' fill colors will reblend using the new start and end colors (this won't affect strokes or compound paths). Also try Blend Horizontally or Vertically, Adjust and Saturate.

Note: *This doesn't work if your blend includes gradients.*

Option / Alt key as you click the second point. To adjust options on a completed blend, select it and double-click the Blend tool (or Object: Blend: Blend Options). Opening Blend Options, without any blend selected, sets the default for creating blends *in this work session*; these Options reset each time you restart.

- **Specified Steps** specifies the number of steps between each pair of key objects. Using fewer steps results in clearly distinguishable objects, while a larger number of steps results in an almost airbrushed effect.

- **Specified Distance** places a specified distance between the objects of the blend.

- **Smooth Color** allows Illustrator to automatically calculate the ideal number of steps between key objects in a blend, in order to achieve the smoothest color transition. If objects are the same color, or are gradients or patterns, the calculation will equally distribute the objects within the area of the blend, based on their size.

- **Orientation** determines whether blend objects rotate as the path curves. **Align to Path** (the default, first icon) allows the blend objects to rotate as they follow the path. **Align to Page** (the second icon) prevents objects from rotating as they are distributed along the curve of the path.

Blends along a Path

There are two ways to make blends follow a curved path. The first way is to Direct-select the "spine" of a blend (the path automatically created by the blend) and then use the Add / Delete-anchor-point tools, Direct-selection, Direct-selection Lasso, Convert-anchor, Pencil, Smooth—or even the Erase tool—to curve or edit the path; the blend will redraw to fit the new spine. The second way is to replace the spine with a customized path: select both the customized path and the blend, and choose Object: Blend: Replace Spine. This command moves the blend to its new spine.

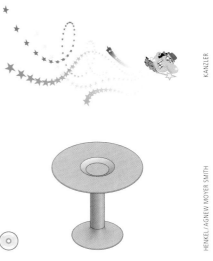

KANZLER

HENKEL / AGNEW MOYER SMITH

John Kanzler created the fairy (top) with multi-object blends and a replaced spine; Rick Henkel used gradient-to-gradient blends for the pedestal of his table (see his explanation, "Henkel-AMS flared effect," on the Wow! *disk for full details)*

STEUER (blend consultant: Eric Hess)

*Groups of objects blended into each other (pumpkins into pumpkins, shadows into shadows) using the Align to Path orientation, Specified Distance, and the "spines" edited into **S** curves (for more about blends see the "Blends folder" on the* Wow! *disk)*

A quick reverse Front to Back

One way to reverse the order of a blend that has only two key objects is to Direct-select one of the key objects and choose Object: Arrange: Bring to Front or Send to Back. This will reverse the order of the blend in the same way as using Object: Blend: Reverse Front to Back.

Expanding

Items such as gradients, gradient meshes, blends, patterns and brushes need to be expanded (Object: Expand) before you can use them for art defining a brush.

It's a bit tricky, but you can also blend between multiple objects. Create your first set of objects and Group them (⌘-G/Ctrl-G). Next, select this group and holding Opt/Alt, drag off a copy (making sure that you release your mouse button before releasing the keyboard—see "A Finger Dance" in the *Zen* chapter for help). Select both sets of grouped objects, and with the Blend tool, click on one anchor point on the first group, then hold Opt/Alt when you click on a correlating point on the second group to specify the number of steps. As long as you maintain the same number of points, you can rotate and scale the objects, and use the Direct-selection tool to edit the objects or the spine. (See "STEUER pumpkin blend.ai" in the "Blends" folder on the *Wow!* disk.)

Reversing, Releasing and Expanding Blends

Once you've created and selected a blend, you can:

• **Reverse** the order of objects on the spine by choosing Object: Blend: Reverse Spine.

• **Release** a Blend (Object: Blend: Release) if you wish to remove the blended objects between key objects and maintain the spine of the blend (be forewarned—you may lose grouping information!).

• **Expand** a Blend to turn it into a group of separate, editable objects. Choose Object: Expand.

GRADIENTS

Gradients are color transitions. To open the Gradient palette: double-click the Gradient tool icon on the toolbox, or choose Window: Show Gradient. Gradients can be either radial (circular from the center) or linear. To apply a gradient to an object, select the object and click on a gradient swatch in the Swatches palette. To view only gradient swatches, click on the gradient icon at the bottom of the Swatches palette.

To start adjusting or creating a new gradient, click on the gradient preview in the Gradient palette. Only after clicking on the preview will you see the color stops and midpoints. Make your own gradients by adding and/or adjusting the stops (pointers representing colors) along the lower edge of the gradient preview, and adjust the midpoint between the color stops by sliding the diamond shapes along the top of the preview.

You can adjust the length, direction and centerpoint location of a selected gradient. In addition, apply a gradient to multiple selected objects across a unified blend by clicking and dragging with the Gradient tool (see the "Unified Gradients" lesson later in this chapter).

To fill type with gradients, convert the type to an outline (see the *Type* chapter for more). To create the illusion of a gradient within a stroke, convert the stroke to a filled object (Object: Path: Outline Path). To turn a gradient into a grouped, masked blend, use Object: Expand (see the *Advanced* chapter for more on masks and masked blends).

GRADIENT MESH

You can apply a gradient mesh to a solid or gradient-filled object in order to create smooth color transitions from multiple points (but you can't use compound paths to create mesh objects). Once transformed, the object will always be a mesh object, so be certain that you work with a copy of the original if it's difficult to re-create.

Transform solid filled objects into gradient mesh either by choosing Object: Create Gradient Mesh (so you can specify details on the mesh construction) or by clicking on the object with the Gradient Mesh tool. To transform a gradient-filled object, select Object: Expand and enable the Gradient Mesh option. Use the Gradient Mesh tool to add mesh lines and mesh points to the mesh. Select individual points, or groups of points, within the mesh using the Direct-selection tool or the Gradient Mesh tool in order to move, color or delete them. For details on working with gradient meshes (including a warning tip about printing mesh objects, see Galleries and lessons later in this chapter).

Hint: Instead of applying a mesh to a complex path, try to create the mesh from a simpler path outline, then mask the mesh with the complex path.

Minimizing banding

Long blends and gradients may *band* when printed, appearing as hard-edged strips, not smooth color transitions. To avoid this:
- Keep blends shorter than 7.5"
- Try to avoid long blends made of dark colors or that change less than 50% between two or more process colors.

Super-size gradient palette

Even if the Gradient palette is docked with other palettes, you can make it both taller and wider.

Not enough warning!

Caution: Unlike previous versions, you aren't warned if you accidentally choose a masking object or a guide to use in a blend!

Don't lose that gradient!

Until gradients can be updated, you must take steps to ensure that you don't inadvertently lose the gradient you are creating:
- To design a gradient for only one object, keep your object selected and see your gradient develop within the object itself.
- To design a gradient for later use or for multiple objects, drag the initial gradient square from its palette to the Swatches palette to store it. Keep Option/Alt-dragging from your gradient square to that initial swatch to update the stored gradient.

Examining Blends

Learning When to Use Gradients or Blends

Overview: *Examine your objects; for linear or circular fills, create basic gradients; for contouring fills into complex objects, create blends.*

Adjusting the placement of colors, and then rate of color transition in the Gradient palette

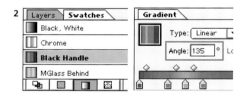

Selecting a gradient from the Swatches palette and setting the gradient Angle

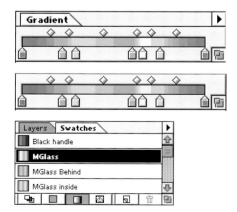

One gradient duplicated and altered for application to different related objects

You need to take a number of factors into consideration when you're deciding whether to create color transitions with blends or gradients. Steve Hart's magnifying glass, created for *Time* magazine, is a clear-cut example that demonstrates when to use gradients or blends.

1 Designing gradients. Select an object you'd like to fill with a linear gradient. Open the Gradient palette. Click on the gradient icon at the bottom of the Swatches palette. Choose Name from the Swatches pop-up menu and click on the "White, Black" gradient. This minimal gradient has two colors: white (at the left) and black (at the right). Click on the left gradient slider to display its position on the scale from 0–100% (in this case 0%). Move the slider to the right to increase the percentage displayed in the scale, and increase the black area of the gradient. Click on the bottom edge of the scale to add additional pointers. Click on a slider to access its numeric position, or to change its color or tint. Between every two pointers is a diamond icon indicating the midpoint of the color transition (from 0–100% between each color pair). Grab and drag a diamond to adjust the color transition rate, or type a new position into the percent field.

2 Storing and applying gradients and making adjustments. To store a new gradient you've made within a selected object, Option-click (Win: Alt-click) the New Swatch icon and name your gradient. Hart filled his magnifying glass handle with a gradient set at a 135° angle (in the Gradient palette). He created slightly different variants for gradients representing the metal rings around the outside, along the inside, and inside behind the glass. To create variants of a current gradient, make color adjustments first, then Option (Alt)-click the New Swatch icon to name your new gradient. Although you can experiment with changing the angle of a gradient, be forewarned that continued adjustments to a gradient in the Gradient palette will not update the gradient stored in the Swatches palette! (See the intro to this chapter.)

3

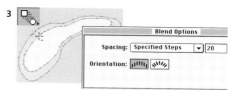

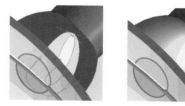

With the Blend tool, clicking first on a selected point of one path, then Option (Alt)-clicking on a selected point of the other to open Blend Options; choosing Specified Steps from the pop-up and entering 20; the blended objects

3 Using blends for irregular or contoured transitions.

A blend is often best for domed, kidney-shaped or contoured objects, such as shadows (for Gradient Mesh, see later in this chapter). Scale and copy one object to create another and set each to the desired color. With the Blend tool, click an anchor point on one, then Option-click (Win: Alt-click) a related point on the other. The default blend setting, "Smooth Color," often means many steps; however, the more similar the colors, the fewer steps you actually need. You can manually choose "Specified Steps" from the pop-up and experiment with fewer steps. Hart specified 20 steps for the glow in the glass, 22 for the handle knob and 12 for the shadow. To respecify steps of a selected blend, double-click the Blend tool (you may have to uncheck and recheck Preview to see the update). To blend selected objects using previous settings, click with the Blend tool without holding the Option/Alt key.

Selected paths before and after a 22-step blend

Before and after a 12-step blend to create a shadow

Automatically updating colors

Changing a spot-color definition (see the *Lines, Fills & Colors* chapter) automatically updates blends and gradients containing that color. Blends between tints of the *same* spot color (or a spot color and white) will update when changes are made to that spot color, even if the blend isn't "live." —Agnew Moyer Smith, Inc.

The final image as it appeared in Time

Shades of Blends

Creating Architectural Linear Shading

Overview: *Create an architectural form using rectangles; copy and paste one rectangle in front; delete the top and bottom paths and blend between the two sides.*

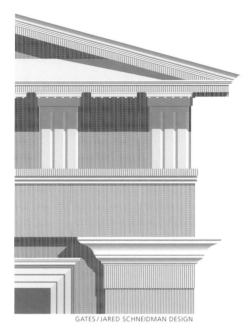

GATES / JARED SCHNEIDMAN DESIGN

1

A selected rectangle copied and pasted in front in full view, and in close-up

2

The top and bottom deleted with the sides selected

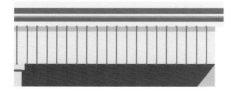

The full blend and a close-up detail

Without much difficulty, Illustrator can help simulate the traditional artistic conventions for rendering architectural details. Jared Schneidman Design developed a simple, but exacting, method to apply vertical line shading.

1 Creating an architectural structure. After establishing the overall form, color and tonality of your illustration, select and copy one rectangle. Choose Edit: Paste In Front to place the copy on top, then set the fill to None and the stroke to .1-pt Black. Choose Window: Show Info to note the line's width in points (to change your ruler units, see Tip, "Changing measurement units," in the *Illustrator Basics* chapter). Calculate the width of the rectangle, divided by the spacing you'd like between lines. Subtract 2 (for the sides you have) to find the proper number of steps for this blend.

2 Deleting the top and bottom and blending the sides. Deselect the copy, Shift-Direct-select the top and bottom paths and delete, leaving the sides selected. With the Blend tool, click on the top point of each side and specify the number of steps you determined above.

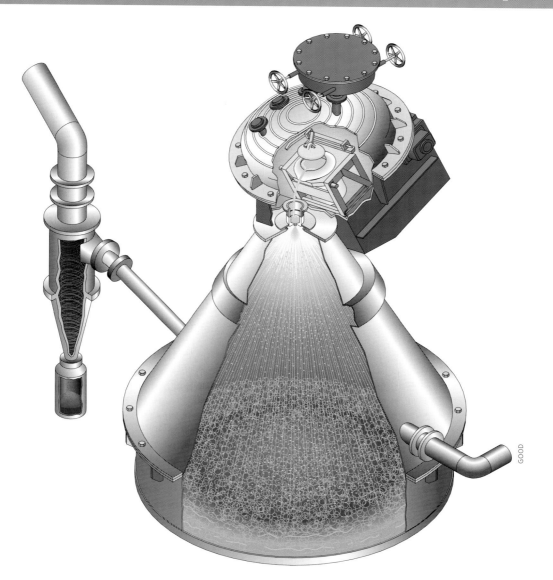

GOOD

Janet Good / Industrial Illustrators

Illustrator Janet Good's image of the white-hot glow of molten metal spraying inside a chamber of liquid nitrogen is based on a drawing by Crucible Research. For the fiery glow at the top of the chamber, she first drew yellow and orange objects and then blended them. (By making the edge of the orange object jagged,

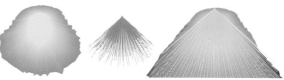

she created a blend that appears to have rays.) On a layer above the blend, Good drew several pairs of yellow and white lines, blending the pairs to form a fan of glowing light rays.

FERSTER

Gary Ferster

For his client Langeveld Bulb, Gary Ferster used blends to create the in-between layers in this flower bulb. He began by styling the outer peel with a .5-pt stroke in a dark brown custom color and filled the object with a lighter brown custom color. He then created the inner layer, filled it with white and gave it a .5-pt white stroke. Selecting both objects, Ferster specified a six-step blend that simultaneously "morphed" each progressive layer into the next while lightening the layers towards white. Blends were also used to create the leafy greens, yellow innards and all the other soft transitions between colors.

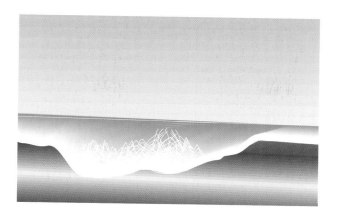

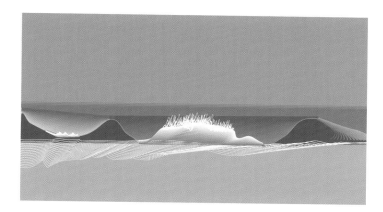

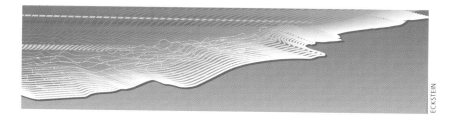

ECKSTEIN

Linda Eckstein

Linda Eckstein used blends in Illustrator to create these beautiful seascapes. In addition to controlling the regularity of blends to depict the ocean, Eckstein needed to control the irregularity of the blends as well. On the bottom layer of her image are blends that establish both the general composition and the broad color schemes. On top of these tonal-filled object blends are irregularly shaped linear blends that form the waves and surf. Using the Direct-selection tool, she isolated individual points and groups of points to stretch and distort the waves.

Popular San Francisco Buildings

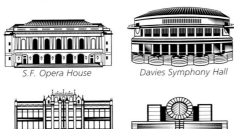
S.F. Opera House

Davies Symphony Hall

Orpheum Theatre

S.F. Museum of Modern Art

Palace of Legion of Honor

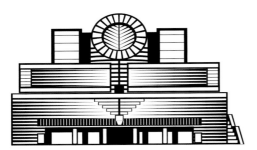
San Francisco Museum of Modern Art

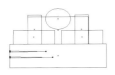
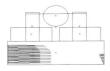

Fish in the San Francisco Bay

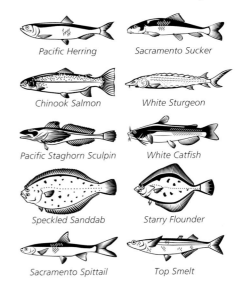
Pacific Herring   *Sacramento Sucker*

Chinook Salmon   *White Sturgeon*

Pacific Staghorn Sculpin   *White Catfish*

Speckled Sanddab   *Starry Flounder*

Sacramento Spittail   *Top Smelt*

Bluegill

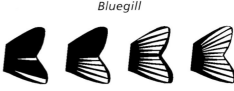

Joe Shoulak / *San Francisco Examiner*

Joe Shoulak frequently uses blends to create in-between repetitive shapes. Given the deadlines at a busy newspaper, the Blend tool has proved an essential production tool for generating the horizontal and vertical lines in buildings (for an article on "Retrofitting the Arts"), as well as sequences of organic shapes (the fins of fish for the series "Bay in Peril"). Shoulak also relies heavily on the use of Offset Path (Object: Path: Offset Path) to create white inset shapes that follow the contours of outlines, and Outline Stroke (Object: Path: Outline Stroke) to convert all stroked lines in final images to filled objects (so he doesn't accidentally resize without properly scaling the line weight).

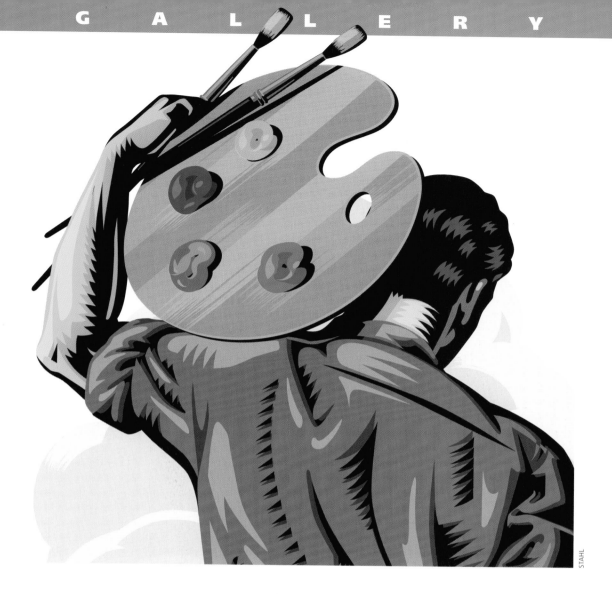

STAHL

Nancy Stahl

Nancy Stahl's cover illustration for the *Illustrator 8 Wow! Book* used blends to create the style of a block-printed poster. She created the jagged shirt wrinkles by drawing two triangular objects and blending them. Then she drew a curved path with the Pen tool and positioned it where she wanted a new spine for the blend. Shift-selecting the blend and the curved path,

Stahl replaced the straight spine of the bend with the curved path by choosing Object: Blend: Replace Spine.

Unlocking Realism

Creating Metallic Reflections with Blends

B. NEAL/THOMAS•BRADLEY ILLUSTRATION & DESIGN

Overview: *Form the basic shapes of objects; create tonal boundaries for future blends that follow the contours of the objects; copy, scale, recolor and adjust the anchor points of tonal boundaries; blend highlights and shadows.*

1

Designing the basic objects and choosing a base tone (Note: Gray strokes added to distinguish objects)

Creating tonal boundaries for future blends by following the contours of the objects

Achieving photorealism with Illustrator may appear pro-hibitively complex and intimidating, but with a few simple rules-of-thumb, some careful planning and the eye of an artist, it can be done. Brad Neal, of Thomas•Bradley Illustration & Design, demonstrates with this image that you don't need an airbrush to achieve metallic reflectivity, specular highlights or warm shadows.

1 Preparing a detailed sketch that incorporates a strong light source, and setting up your palette. Before you actually start your illustration, create a sketch that establishes the direction of your light source. Then, in Illustrator, set up your color palette (see the *Lines, Fills, & Colors* chapter). Choose one color as a "base tone," the initial tint from which all blends will be built, and fill the entire object with that value. After you create the basic outlines of your illustration, work in Outline mode to create separate paths—following the contours of your objects—for each of your major color transitions. After completing the initial line drawing of the lock set, Neal visually, and then physically, "mapped" out the areas that would contain the shading. He added a few highlights and reflections in the later stages of the project, but the majority of blends were mapped out in advance.

2 Using your color transition paths to create blends.
Next, use the contouring paths you've created to map out your tonal boundaries. Choose one of the objects and fill it with the same color and tonal value as its underlying shape. In the Neal locks, this initial color is always the same color and value selected for the base color. Then, copy the object and Paste In Front (Edit: Paste In Front). Next, fill this copy with a highlight or shadow value, scale it down and manipulate it into the correct position to form the highlight or shadow area. You can accomplish this step by one of two methods: by scaling the object using the Scale tool, or by selecting and pulling in individual anchor points with the Direct-selection tool. In order to ensure smooth blends without ripples or irregular transitions, the anchor points of the inner and outer objects must be as closely aligned as possible and should contain the same number of points. To then complete this highlight or shadow, use the Blend tool to *point map* (see the intro to this chapter for details). The blend in Figure 2 required eight in-between steps. If your blend isn't smooth enough, then use the Direct-selection tool to select anchor points on the key objects and adjust their position or Bézier handles until the blend smoothes.

3 Blending in smaller increments. Some blend situations may require more than two objects to achieve the desired look. For instance, to control the rate at which the tone changes or the way an object transforms throughout the blended area, you may wish to add an intermediate object and blend in two stages, instead of one.

4 Using blends to soften hard transitions. Always use blends when making tonal transitions, even when you need a stark contrast shadow or highlight. A close look at Neal's shadow reveals a very short but distinct blend.

2

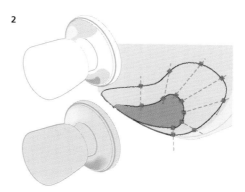

Pasting In Front a scaled down and adjusted copy with the same number of aligned points

3

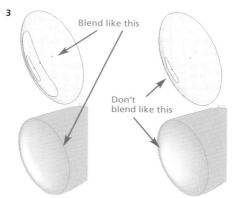

Adding an in-between contour to help control the rate and shape of blends; blending with too few contours flattens the image

4

Long, close-up, and Outline close-up views of highlight and shadow transitions

Blending Realism

Keeping Blends Clean and Accessible

Overview: *Delete the side of a rectangle; offset the top and bottom open ends horizontally; blend this open object with another smaller, darker object; place caps on top and bottom; create contouring blends on the sides.*

The final illustration in Outline mode

1

Two copies of a rectangle pasted on top with right side removed and points shifted left

Before and after blending offset objects

A quick look at an illustration in Outline mode usually reveals a lot about how an image is constructed. However, when you look at Andrea Kelley's Apple Computer product illustrations in Preview mode, you would probably mistakenly guess that she uses gradients to create her tonal changes. Actually, since her renderings are used on-screen as well as printed, Kelley often uses blends for more exacting control over her tones (gradients can look banded on the screen even if they print well). Her techniques can help you create a monitor screen with a soft, ambient lighting effect.

1 Creating an "offset" blend. Make a rectangle and fill it with a 35% tint of black. Copy the rectangle, choose Object: Hide Selection, then use Edit: Paste In Front to place the copy on top. Direct-select and delete the right side of the path. Since open objects remain filled in Illustrator, the object looks identical in Preview mode. With the Direct-selection tool, grab the top right point and slide it to the left slightly (about .25"), using the Shift key to constrain movement horizontally. Then grab the lower right point and slide it over to the halfway point on the rectangle (again, use your Shift key). Now select and copy the adjusted object, use Paste In Front to move the copy, and change the tint of this new object to 65%. Use the same technique you did before, but this time slide the bottom right point all the way to the left and the top right point over towards the left corner. (This polygon should look almost like a triangle.) Next, select the top right points of the two objects you just made, click on each point with the Blend tool and use the recommended number of steps. In Outline mode, instead of the expected sea of diagonally blended lines running across the screen, your monitor should appear "clean" and uncomplicated.

2 Creating the rounded top and bottom. Choose Object: Show All to reveal your hidden back rectangle. With the Pen tool, draw a bow-shaped "cap" filled with a 35% tint of black that overlaps the top of your blend with a long, almost horizontal curve. Have the points meet beyond the blend on either side, arcing into a bow shape above. To add shadow detail, copy the bottom path of the bow (the long, almost horizontal line) and Paste In Front to place a copy of the path. Change the Fill of this path to None, with a .25-pt stroke weight at a 40% tint of black. Lastly, copy and reflect the full filled cap along the horizontal axis, place it along the bottom of the blended monitor screen and set it to a 10% tint of black.

3 Contouring the sides. To create the illusion that the monitor is inset, create three long, overlapping rectangles on the left edge of your blended monitor screen, running from cap to cap. (Adjust the points as necessary so the objects run flush against the cap.) From left to right, make the rectangles 10%, 50% and 45% tints of black. Select the right two rectangles and blend between them, then lock the blend so you can easily blend the left two rectangles. Repeat from the right side of the monitor with rectangles of 5%, 10% and 25% (from left to right). You can make the monitor case the same way as the screen, but shade the case with 10% on the left, blending to 25% on the right. (See the *Advanced Techniques* chapter for blending and masking curved objects.)

2

Rounded "caps" put on top and bottom of the blended screen

3

Placing three rectangles of different shades on the left side of the screen (deleting the sides to reduce clutter), then blending the middle object first to the dark, then to the light

Placing three rectangles of different shades on the right side of the screen (again, deleting the sides to reduce clutter), then blending the middle object first to the light, then to the dark

The final monitor screen in Preview

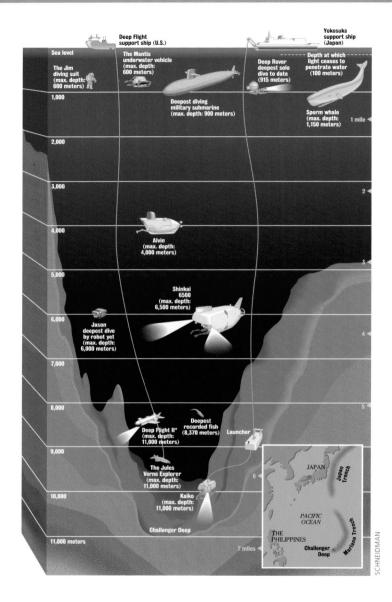

Jared Schneidman / JSD

Illustrator blends helped Jared Schneidman convey the murky depth and bright exploring lights in this *Newsweek* infographic about deep trenches in the Pacific Ocean. Schneidman created the subdued highlights and shadows of the subterranean trench using blended objects.

For the searchlights emanating from the explorer vehicles, Schneidman first made cone objects filled with a pale yellow. He then made companion objects using the dark colors of the ocean and trench. Finally, he made blends between each cone and its companion object.

KELLEY

Andrea Kelley

To illustrate this North Face camping equipment, designer Andrea Kelley carefully analyzed fabric folds, stitched seams, and the play of light and shadow. She began the sleeping bag by drawing the outline of the bag, creating a blend object and masking it with a copy of the sleeping bag outline. She drew each stitched seam as a solid line, and the fabric folds around the seams as jagged, filled shapes. Over the sleeping bag, Kelley drew light-gray-filled objects for the fabric highlights between the seams. Kelley created the tent by first drawing its outline, and then creating a multiple-object blend, which she masked with the tent outline. Kelley created additional masked blends to define other shapes that make up the tent. For the front flap, Kelley created a blend object and masked it with an oval, and then drew light and dark triangles on top of it to show wrinkles in the fabric.

Unified Gradients

Redirecting Fills with the Gradient Tool

Overview: *Fill objects with gradients; use the Gradient tool to adjust fill length, direction, center location and to unify fills across multiple objects.*

1

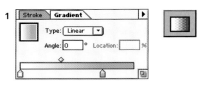

The Gradient palette, and the Gradient tool (This tool has the same name and icon as the one in Photoshop, but is completely different.)

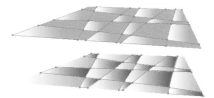

Filling the first group with the cyan gradient, then the other group with the purple gradient

2

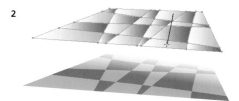

Clicking and dragging with the Gradient tool to unify the gradient fill across multiple objects, and to establish the gradient's rate and direction

How long can a gradient be?

Click and drag with the Gradient tool anywhere in your image window; you don't need to stay within the objects themselves. Also, see the *Wow!* disk for Eve Elberg's "Comet" Gradient tool exercise.

The Gradient tool allows you to customize the length and direction of gradient fills, and to stretch gradients across multiple objects. For this *Medical Economics* magazine illustration, Dave Joly used the Gradient tool to customize each gradient and unify the checkerboard floor.

1 Filling objects with the same gradient. Select multiple objects and fill them with the same gradient by clicking on a gradient fill in the Swatches palette. Keep your objects selected.

2 Unifying gradients with the Gradient tool. Using the Gradient tool from the Toolbox, click and drag from the point you want the gradient to begin to where you want it to end. Hold down the Shift key if you want to constrain the angle of the gradient. To relocate a radial gradient's center, just click with the Gradient tool. Experiment until you get the desired effect. To create his checkerboard, Joly used the Knife tool to segment the floor, grouped every other tile together and filled these with a cyan-to-white gradient fill. He then duplicated the gradient, changed the start color to purple and applied this purple gradient to the remaining tiles. With all tiles selected, he again applied the Gradient tool.

YIP

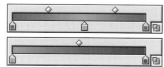

Filip Yip

Filip Yip prefers the simplicity of linear and radial gradients to the photo-realism of blends in creating the stylized look of many of his illustrations. The images above began as pencil sketches that Yip scanned, placed in Illustrator as templates and then traced over to create compositional elements. For the spoonful of vegetables, Yip developed gradients that share similar colors but differ in the number and location of intermediate colors and midpoints along the slider in the Gradient palette. The lobster is more stylized, conveying shadows with color-to-gray gradients. Both illustrations contrast the soft gradient effects with crisp highlights and shadows in strong, solid-filled colors.

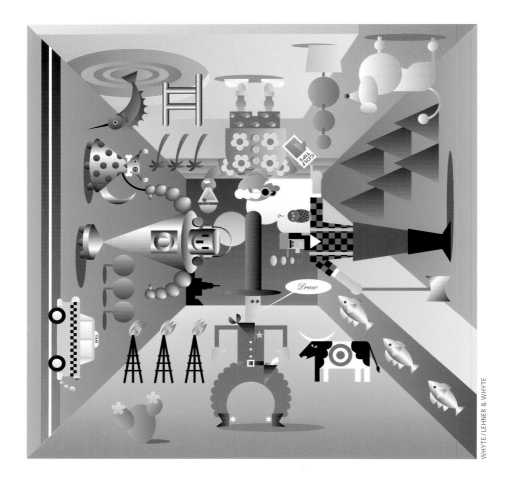

WHYTE / LEHNER & WHYTE

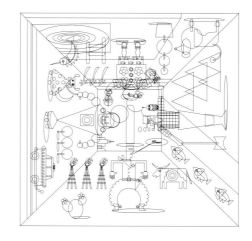

Hugh Whyte / Lehner & Whyte

In this image designed for a promotional poster, Hugh Whyte used gradients and the Gradient tool to create a colorful, cut-out look that is both flat and volumetric. The Outline view at right reveals that Whyte constructed the image entirely of gradients, with no blends.

GORSKA

Caryl Gorska

Caryl Gorska created "Bountiful Harvest" as a package design for Nunes Farms' dried fruits, nuts and chocolates. She used the Gradient tool to customize her radial blends (made of process colors). A scan of parchment paper, saved as an EPS file, is Placed on the bottom layer (see the *Layers* chapter).

Resetting gradients to the default settings

After you make angle adjustments with the Gradient tool, other objects that you fill with the same or other gradients will still have the altered angle. To "re-zero" gradient angles, Deselect All and fill with None by pressing the "/" key. When you next choose a gradient, angles will have the default setting. Or, for linear gradients, you can type a zero in the Angle field.

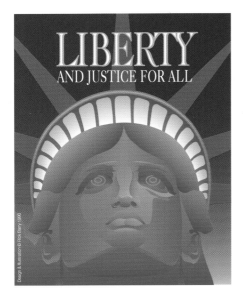

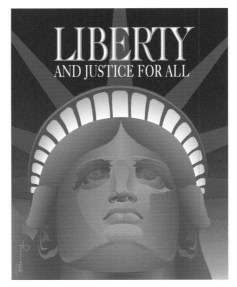

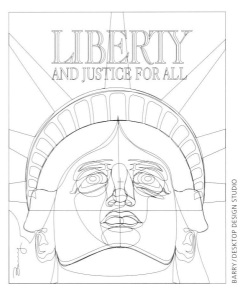

Rick Barry / DeskTop Design Studio

To demonstrate the difference between blends and gradients, Rick Barry took an image he created in Illustrator (upper left Preview mode, lower left Outline mode), selected the blends (by clicking twice with the Group-selection tool on one of the blend objects) and deleted them.

The objects used to create the blends remained, and Barry filled these objects with custom gradients and then adjusted the rate and range of the gradients with the Gradient tool (upper right Preview mode, lower right Outline mode).

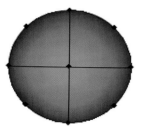

Ellen Papciak-Rose / In The Studio

Gabriella Catches a Star and Her Friends Find Some Stuff in the Sky is the first of four books featuring children who learn about real and abstract environmental topics in a fun way. In this two-page spread, artist Ellen Papciak-Rose filled shapes with soft bright glows she achieved using the Gradient Mesh tool (which gave her more control in placing mesh points, as compared with the uniform grid meshes that she would get from using the Object: Create Gradient Mesh command). To make Gabriella's

face, Papciak-Rose drew an oval with the Ellipse tool and then applied a Charcoal brush to it. After filling the oval with a dark brown color, she expanded the object (Object: Expand Appearance), which had to be done in order to fill the brushed object with a Gradient Mesh. She clicked with the Gradient Mesh tool to create the mesh points for the highlights. Then she Shift-selected the two cheek points with the Direct-selection tool and chose white from the Color palette.

Rolling Mesh

Converting Gradients to Mesh, then Editing

Overview: *Draw shapes and fill with linear gradients; expand gradient-filled objects into gradient meshes; use various tools to edit mesh points and colors*

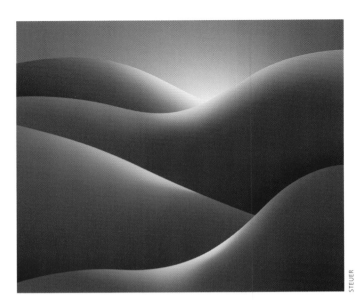

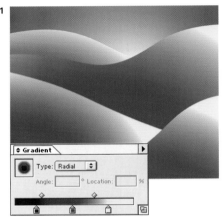

The hills shown filled with radial gradients—although there is some sense of light, it isn't possible to make the radial gradient follow the contours of the hills

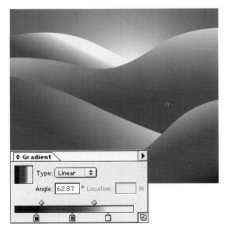

The hills shown filled with linear gradients, which are easier to edit than radial gradients when converted to gradient meshes

For many images, gradients can be useful for showing the gradual change of light to shadow (if you need to learn more about creating and applying gradient fills, first see "Unified Gradients" earlier in this chapter). For these rolling hills, artist Sharon Steuer expanded linear gradients into gradient mesh objects so she could better control the curves and contours of the color transitions.

1 Drawing shapes and then filling them with linear gradients. Begin your illustration by creating closed objects with any of the drawing tools. After completing the objects, select each object with the Selection tool and Fill it with a linear gradient fill. For each linear gradient, adjust the angle and length of the gradient transition with the Gradient tool until you can best approximate the desired lighting effect. Steuer created four hill-shaped objects with the Pen tool, filled them with the same linear gradient, then customized each with the Gradient tool. **Note:** *Although in some objects radial gradients might look better before you convert them, linear gradients create gradient mesh objects that are much easier to edit!*

2 Expanding linear gradients into gradient meshes. To create a more natural lighting of the hills, Steuer converted the linear gradients into mesh objects so the color transitions could follow the contours of the hills. To accomplish this, select all the gradient-filled objects that you wish to convert and choose Object: Expand. In the Expand dialog box, make sure Fill is checked and specify Expand Gradient to Gradient Mesh. Then click OK. Illustrator converts each linear gradient into a rectangle rotated to the angle matching the linear gradient's angle; each mesh rectangle is masked by the original object (see the *Advanced Techniques* chapter for help with masks).

3 Editing meshes. You can use several tools to edit gradient mesh objects (use the Object: Lock/Unlock All toggle to isolate objects as you work). The Gradient Mesh tool combines the functionality of the Direct-selection tool with the ability to add mesh lines. With the Gradient Mesh tool, click *exactly on* a mesh anchor point to select or move that point or its direction handles. Or, click *anywhere* within a mesh, except on an anchor point, to add a new mesh point and gridline. You can also use the Add-anchor-point tool (click and hold to choose it from the Pen tool pop-up) to add a point without a gridline. To delete a selected anchor point, press the Delete key; if that point is a mesh point, the gridlines will be deleted as well.

Select points within the mesh using either the Gradient Mesh tool or the Direct Select Lasso tool, using the Direct-selection tool to move multiple selected points. Move individual anchor points and adjust direction handles with the Gradient Mesh tool in order to reshape your gradient mesh gridlines. In this way, the color and tonal transitions of the gradient will match the contour of the mesh object. Recolor selected areas of the mesh by selecting points, then choosing a new color.

If you click in the area *between* mesh points with the Paint bucket tool (from the Eyedropper tool pop-out) you'll add the Fill color to the four nearest mesh points.

By using these tools and editing techniques, Steuer was able to create hills with color and light variations that suggest the subtlety of natural light upon organic forms.

2

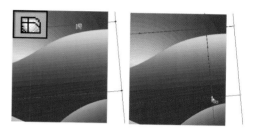

After Expanding the gradients into gradient mesh objects.

Using the Gradient mesh tool to add a mesh line, then moving the mesh point with the Direct-selection tool

Using the Add-anchor-point tool, using the Direct Select Lasso to select a point, moving selected point (or points) with the Direct-selection tool

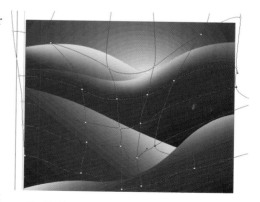

The final rearmost hill, shown after making mesh adjustments

Mastering Mesh

Painting with Areas of Color Using Mesh

Advanced Technique

Overview: *Create simple objects to make into gradient mesh; edit and color mesh objects; create compound-path masks for copies of mesh; make a mesh with no grid to reshape.*

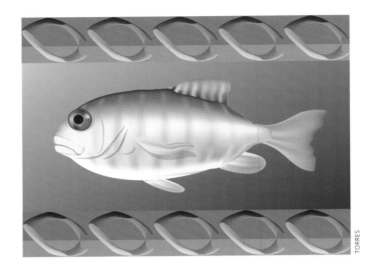

TORRES

1

The original oval; choosing Object: Create Gradient Mesh; setting the Mesh options

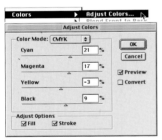

The mesh created; after selecting points and deleting to create a pattern in the mesh

Recoloring selected rows and columns using the Color palette and the Adjust Colors filter

With a background in painting, sculpture and 3D imaging, Ivan Torres knew that the Gradient-mesh tool would allow him to paint in a powerfully unique way. In creating this fish illustration, he demonstrates how, unlike *any* other medium, the mesh allows him to *move a stroke of color* without changing the relationship between colors.

1 Creating the fish's body. Create a solid-filled oval; while it's selected, choose Object: Create Gradient Mesh. Set fairly high numbers for rows and columns; for his fish (shown above at about 30% actual size) Torres set 17 rows, 35 columns. Set Flat for Appearance, 100% Highlight and click OK. Next, to make the base for the fish's stripes, you'll need to create an irregular pattern within the mesh. With the Direct-selection tool, select anchor points and delete—the connected rows and columns will be deleted along with the points. Torres deleted 8 columns and 10 rows. Marquee horizontal anchor points with the Direct-selection tool. For even more selection control, try working in Outline mode, uncheck Use Area Select in Preferences: General, or select points using the Direct-selection Lasso tool. With horizontal rows of points selected (make sure you are now in Preview mode), mix or choose new colors in the Colors palette (use View: Hide/Show Edges to hide/show selection edges). Torres horizontally selected sections of the mesh, changing colors to create a sense of volume. For more subtle color transitions, select an area and choose Filter: Colors: Adjust Colors to adjust the color cast of your selection. Carefully Direct-select points and reposition them to form the fish body.

2 Making the fish's tail and fins. Create several colored rectangles and ovals. Again, convert each object to a gradient mesh, but assign a *low* value for columns. Direct-select sections of each object and use the Adjust Color Filter to create gradual changes in tone (use ⌘-Option-E (Mac)/Ctrl-Alt-E (Win) to reopen the last-used filter). Direct-select points on the objects and adjust them to form tail and fin shapes. Move each object into a separate layer for easy editing (see the *Layers* chapter for help).

3 Creating the fish's eye and lips. Create three circles: one small, one medium and one large. Convert the medium-size circle to a gradient mesh this time by clicking on the circle with the Gradient-mesh tool. Add additional rows or columns by clicking again with the tool; delete by Direct-selecting points, rows or columns and deleting. Torres ended up with unevenly spaced rows and columns (five of each), which he colored to achieve a wet, reflective-looking surface. When you are pleased with the glossy part of the eye, combine all the circles and adjust the outlines of some to be less perfect.

To create the fish's mouth, begin with a rectangle on a layer above the fish. Convert the rectangle to a gradient mesh using Object: Create Gradient Mesh, and enter different low values for rows and columns, maintaining Flat for Appearance. Select areas of the object and use the Eyedropper to load colors from the fish to create smooth color transitions between the mouth and the body. Move this object into position and reshape it to form a mouth.

4 Creating shadows for the fish. Duplicate the layer containing the fish's body by dragging that layer to the

Creating the fish's tail

Creating the fish's eye and mouth

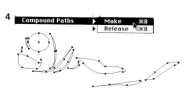

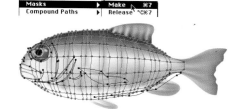

Drawing objects for shadow areas; making them into a compound path; masking a copy of the fish with the compound path; using Filter: Colors: Adjust Colors to darken a copy of the fish; the final fish shown with completed shadows

5

An oval

After applying a mesh with values of 1, deleting the original oval anchor points (in orange)

The remaining points moved and colored

After reshaping is complete, a copy is created, reflected and skewed, and colors are inverted

Adding to the mesh

To add new rows and columns to your mesh, click on the mesh object with the Gradient Mesh tool. To add a new mesh row, click on a column mesh line. To add a new mesh column, click on a row.

New Layer icon in the Layers palette. On a layer above this one, use the Pen tool to draw a contour defining each shadow as a closed object. Select all the shadow objects and choose Object: Compound Path: Make to unite them into one compound object. Use these shadow objects as a mask for the copy of the fish body. Select both the compound path and the copy of the fish body (in the Layers palette, Option-Shift/Alt-Shift-click the shadow and fish-copy layers to select all objects on those layers) and choose Object: Clipping Mask: Make. To simulate shadow colors, select the masked copy of the fish and use the Adjust Colors filter to darken the area and reduce the contrast. Torres created a shadow that contrasted the cyan color cast of the fish by decreasing cyan and increasing yellow and magenta—each in increments of 2 to 5%. After applying the filter, with selection edges hidden (View: Hide/Show Edges), he reapplied the filter (Mac: ⌘-E, Win: Ctrl-E) until he was satisfied.

5 **Creating the border "bone" shape.** Create an oval; while it's selected, choose Object: Create Gradient Mesh, assigning 1 for rows and columns and "Flat". Using the Delete-point tool, delete the four original points of the oval, leaving only mesh points. Reposition the remaining points to create an arcing effect, and assign colors to each point. Next, use the Reflect tool to flip a copy of this object horizontally. With the copy selected, Torres chose Filter: Colors: Invert Colors. Lastly, he used the Skew tool to adjust the copied image to touch the original border object (see the *Zen* chapter for reflect and skew help).

Printing gradient mesh objects

Gradient mesh objects rely on PostScript Level 3 (PS3) to print. Gradient mesh objects printed to older printers will convert to a 150-pixel-per-inch JPEG! If you can't print to a PS3 printer, you may wish to use Illustrator's Rasterize or Export commands, or open the file in Photoshop 5.02 or higher to rasterize it there. **Note:** *See also Tip "Grouping masks" in the* Advanced *chapter.*

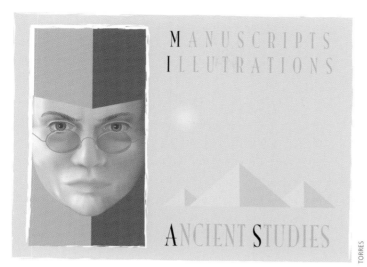

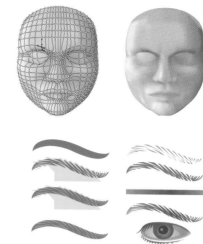

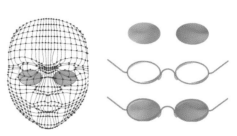

TORRES

Ivan Torres

Ivan Torres began this image by drawing an oval, then choosing Object: Create Gradient Mesh, entering approximately 30 rows, 15 columns and Flat appearance. Working in Out-line mode, Torres Direct-selected horizontal rows and moved them closer or farther from other rows to cluster more rows around the eyes, nose and lips (he wanted at least three rows around the lips, for instance). To form vertical structures such as the nose, he used the Direct-selection tool to select and move columns. To create more diagonal lines, he Direct-selected a section of the mesh and used the Shear tool (holding the Shift key). In some cases he used the Convert-anchor-point tool to reset direction handles. He Direct-selected and then colored points using the Color palette. Once he set base colors, he used the Eyedrop-per tool to transfer color from elsewhere to the selected anchor points. He used the Pen tool to draw the basic eyebrow shape and several over-lapping angular objects to represent hair. He

selected all eyebrow objects and cut the angles out of the brow with Effect: Pathfinder: Hard Mix (he selected one cut-out object and used Edit: Select: Same Fill Color to select all of the cut-out objects so he could move them aside). For the glasses he made two ellipses, chose Object: Compound Path: Make and then made this into a mask with a copy of the mesh face, to which he then applied the Filter: Colors: Adjust Colors filter to increase the cyan and yel-low (see the preceding technique for details). On layers above and below, Torres created details such as the eyeglass frames, and he used a Charcoal Art Brush (*Brushes* chapter) to add texture to the borders of his final illustration.

Transparency, Styles & Effects

8

Transparency, Styles & Effects

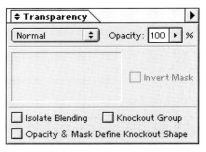

Transparency palette with all options shown (palette pop-up menu – Show Options)

Using transparency with

- **Fills**—apply an opacity, blending mode, transformation and/or distortion to the fill.
- **Strokes**—just as with fills, apply an opacity, blending mode, transformation and/or distortion.
- **Brush Strokes**—when you apply transparency attributes to brush strokes, they are not sticky for the next brush. When working with brush strokes, select all the strokes and then apply an opacity or blending mode.
- **Text**—apply transparency to selected text characters and/or the entire text block.
- **Patterns**—apply transparency to the objects that define a pattern or the objects that contain the pattern.
- **Charts**—apply transparency to the entire chart or the elements that make up the chart.
  —*Sandee Cohen.*

Transparency has been a top item on the wish list forever, and finally it's here! In fact, transparency is everywhere… not just in the new Transparency palette but also when you apply *Effects* (such as shadows, feathers, and glows) or *Styles*. As wonderful as it looks on screen, be aware that transparency can can turn your Illustrator file into a *raster file*—and without your even knowing it! Incorporating transparency and Effects will affect both your file size and how your file will look when printed (see Tips "Document Setup" and "The flattening process" in this chapter introduction, Tips "Settings for Export and Saving" and "Shortcuts Setting Resolution" at the end of the *Illustrator & Other Programs* chapter, and the Tech Notes appendix for the settings we used to print this book).

If the concepts of Transparency, Appearances, targeting, Opacity Masks or Styles are new to you, it's very important that you take the time to master the lessons in this chapter in order. Although this is not an Advanced Techniques chapter, we do assume that by now you have a basic knowledge of fills, strokes, and especially layers. If you're unable to keep up with this chapter, please see the *Lines, Fills & Colors* and *Layers* chapters first.

BASIC TRANSPARENCY

Although the artboard may look white, Illustrator treats it as transparent. To visually distinguish the transparent areas from the non-transparent ones, choose View: Show Transparency Grid. To set the size and colors of the transparency grid, select File: Document Setup: Transparency. Check Simulate Color Paper if you know you will be printing on a colored stock. Click on the top swatch to open the color picker and select a color close to that of the paper. Both of these options are non-printable file attributes and are only visible in the on-screen preview.

Transparency includes blending modes and opacity. To apply transparency to an object, group or layer, make a selection or click on the target indicator in the layers palette, then adjust the opacity slider in the Transparency palette. Completely opaque is equal to 100% opacity and 0% is completely see-through, or invisible. Be careful how you apply transparency because it is easy to get confused. Correctly targeting and applying transparency is very tricky (see the "Basic transparency" lesson in this chapter).

Blending modes control how the colors of objects, groups, or layers interact with one another. Since blending modes are color-mode specific, they yield different results in RGB and CMYK. Unlike Photoshop, most of the blending modes show no effect when they are over the *transparent* artboard. To see the effect of some blending modes, you need to add a color-filled or white element behind your artwork.

Opacity Masks

An opacity mask allows you to use the dark and light areas of one object or image as a mask to show or hide parts of another area. Where the mask is dark, you can see the objects below. Where the mask is light, those objects are less visible. (This is similar to the behavior of *layer masks* in Photoshop.)

The easiest way to create an opacity mask is similar to creating a clipping mask. Create the artwork you want masked. Place the object, group or raster image you want as the mask above it. Select the artwork and the masking element, and choose Make Opacity Mask from the Transparency palette pop-up menu. Illustrator automatically makes the topmost object the opacity mask.

You can also add an opacity mask to a selection. First choose Show Thumbnails from the pop-up menu in the Transparency palette. Next, select the artwork and choose Make Opacity Mask from the pop-up menu. Click on the mask thumbnail to target it. You will notice the Layers palette changes to show the opacity mask. You can now use the drawing and editing tools to create the mask. For instance, if you create an object filled with a gradient, you will see the artwork through the dark areas of the

Inverted opacity masks

New Opacity Masks are Inverted can be confusing. When it is *on*, some 100% black masks in your file may be completely transparent because they're inverted, as well as those with 100% white that are not inverted.

Editing opacity masks

- **Disable**—Shift click the mask thumbnail to turn it off. A red X will appear over the preview.
- **Enable**—Shift click again to reapply the mask.
- **Option (Mac) / Alt (Win) - click**— the mask thumbnail to view and edit only the masking objects on the artboard. This is also handy for viewing the grayscale values of the mask.
- **Release Opacity Mask (palette menu)**—releases the masking effect and reverts the *mask* back into objects.

Quick duotone

Creating a duotone is easy with an Opacity Mask. First, stack two copies of a grayscale image. Next fill a rectangle with a color (you can even use a spot color) and arrange it so it is between the two images. Select the top image and the rectangle and choose Make Opacity Mask (Transparency palette menu). To correct for the negative image, check Invert Mask.

Knockout checkbox

The knockout checkbox has a third or neutral state which is indicated by a dash. This neutral option indicates that the selection may have different knockout options for the group or layer (see lessons later in this chapter).

The flattening process

Transparency really only exists in the on-screen preview. Illustrator is constantly recalculating the transparent areas as objects are created or edited. Since the PostScript language used to print Illustrator files doesn't support transparency, transparent areas must be expressed as either vector objects or raster objects. The process of translating transparent regions into vector or raster objects is known as flattening.—*Sandee Cohen*

Overprint preview

In past versions of Illustrator you had the ability to set overprint attributes for fills and strokes in the Attributes palette, but were unable to preview on-screen the effects of these settings. This is no longer true; you can now preview these settings by selecting View: Overprint Preview. If you don't have any overprint attributes set, you won't see any changes on-screen. Illustrator is not capable of previewing patterns or brushes in this mode.

gradient. When the opacity mask thumbnail is selected, you will not be able to edit any other content in the document. Click on the artwork or the opacity mask thumbnail to toggle between the two.

A few hints can help you work with opacity masks. First, the masking objects may display in color, but behind the scenes they're being converted to grayscale. In addition, if you select Invert Mask, the dark and light values of the colors are reversed—not the colors themselves. You may find it difficult to identify which elements have an opacity mask. Look for the dashed underline in the Layers palette next to the name of the object or group that holds an opacity mask.

There is a special technique to display the opacity mask thumbnail in the Transparency palette when you are working with a group. It's not enough to simply select the artwork on the artboard. To display the opacity mask thumbnail for a group, you need to click the target indicator for the *underlined* <u>\<group\></u> in the Layers palette.

The link icon in the Transparency palette indicates that the position of the opacity mask stays associated with the position of the object, item or group of objects it is masking. Unlinked, it allows you to move the artwork without moving the mask and vice versa. The content of the mask can be selected and edited just like any other object. You can transform or apply a blending mode and/or an opacity percentage to each individual object within the mask.

Option (Mac)/Alt (Win)-click on an opacity mask thumbnail in the Transparency palette to hide the document's contents and display only the masking element in its true grayscale values. Shift-click the opacity mask thumbnail to disable the opacity mask from exerting its influence.

Knockout Controls

Choose Show Options from the pop-up menu of the Transparency palette to display the checkboxes that control how transparency is applied to groups and multiple objects.

With a group layer targeted, check the Knockout

Group option to keep individual objects of the *group* from applying their transparency settings to each other where they overlap. Use this option when you apply transparency to blends.

Check Isolate Blending to limit the effects of a blending mode to the bottom element of a targeted group or layer (see the "It's a Knockout" lesson later in this chapter).

The final checkbox, Opacity & Mask Defines Knock-out Shape, is used in very specific situations to limit the knockout of a color to the area defined by the opacity and the mask. To see any effect, you must have Knockout Group checked. However, we've yet to find an Illustrator user who can show us a practical example of this feature.

Document Setup

In order to reproduce (print) transparency accurately, transparent objects are flattened as they are processed for output. Two things can occur during flattening—images can be rasterized into bitmapped information or divided into smaller vector objects as the PostScript information is sent to the printing device. (See Tips "The flattening process" and "Preview flattening" for more.) The degree of rasterization versus the division into smaller vector shapes is defined by the Quality/Speed setting, File: Document Setup: Transparency. The lowest setting, of 1, is faster to process because it has fewer vector objects. Using this setting can greatly reduce the quality of the processed artwork. The highest setting of 5 has the greatest number of vector objects, requires the most time to process, and provides the best possible quality. When objects are rasterized, they are rasterized at the Rasterization Resolution. The Rasterization Resolution should be at least twice the linescreen of the final output device.

It's quite possible to see color shifts in documents that have been flattened. Objects are flattened to a white background. If you want to insure that an object is flattened to the desired background color, create a rectangle with the color and Send To Back. Then flatten the artwork and delete the extra colored rectangle.

Preview flattening

To see what your artwork will look like after the transparent areas have been flattened, select the appropriate objects, groups or layers, choose Object: Flatten Transparency. Check the Preview checkbox to see the effects without committing to the operation. If you click OK to apply the flattening process, the selected objects will be modified.

Note: *If you add more transparency, the already flattened artwork can be flattened again.*

Transparency is cumulative

The total effect of transparency is determined by the object, group, sublayers and container layer.

Note: *At the time of this writing, there wasn't any way to clear all effects for the multiple levels. For now, you have to target each level and click the Clear All icon (see "Appearances" later in the chapter).*

A known printing problem

Stitching is a visible transition between rasterized and vector data. It usually happens when transparency overlaps a filled object, but it's hard to predict. It occurs when part of the flattened artwork becomes rasterized while the rest remains as vector objects. Stitching is rare and can be completely avoided by using a Quality setting of either 1 or 5.

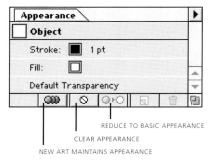

REDUCE TO BASIC APPEARANCE
CLEAR APPEARANCE
NEW ART MAINTAINS APPEARANCE

Default Basic Appearance

Appearance indicators

The appearance indica- 🗗🎨⊠
tors for Paint, Effects
and Transparency only show up in
the Appearance palette on layers
or groups that contain elements
with these attributes.

Target indicators

○ An object is said to have a
basic appearance as long as
it does not contain: multiple fills
or strokes, transparency, effects or
brush strokes. It is indicated by an
open circle in the Layers palette.

◉ More complex appearances
are indicated by a gradient
filled icon in the Layers palette.

Layer / Group overrides color

To force individual objects within
a *layer* or *group* to accept the fill
and stroke attributes of the targeted layer or group, make sure
Layer/Group Overrides Color is
checked in the Appearance
palette pop-up menu.

Note: *The flattening process is only applied when the file is sent to a PostScript printing device (see* Illustrator Basics *for more on PostScript printing).*

The last word on transparency

Always keep in mind when you're applying transparency attributes, that *every* object, group and/or layer adds another level of complexity to the document. At each level you can apply multiple strokes, fills, opacity percentage, blending mode, effect and/or a transforma-tion. As you are doing this, pay close attention to the doc-ument structure. Always try to rename your layers with descriptive names to reduce confusion and help locate specific objects in your artwork; make sure to maintain special characters such as in <path> or <group> layers, since object or group "layers" don't behave the same as actual layers. If you experience printing problems, you will find that named layers make it much easier to locate where you need to make an adjustment.

APPEARANCES

Within an appearance are a collection of strokes, fills, effects and transparency settings. An appearance can be applied to any path, object (including text), group, sub-layer or layer. The specific appearance attributes of a selection are shown in the Appearance palette. Attributes within the appearance are added to the palette in the order they are applied. Changing the order of the attrib-utes will change the appearance. An object, group or layer can all have different appearances.

   To apply an appearance, make a selection or click on a target indicator (Layers palette) and add transparency, effects, multiple fills and/or multiple strokes (see the "Adding Fills and Strokes" section). When a group, sub-layer or layer is targeted, strokes and fills will be applied to the individual objects within the selection, but any effects or transparency settings will be applied to the *tar-get* (see Tip "Target indicators" to the left). Drag the tar-get indicator (in the Layers palette) from one layer to another to move an appearance or Option (Mac)/Alt (Win)-drag the indicator to copy the appearance. To re-use an appearance, save it as a style in the Styles palette.

Appearance palette

When an item is selected or targeted, the Appearance palette displays all the attributes associated with the current selection. If there isn't a selection, the palette will display the attributes for the next object drawn. The minimum attributes always contain a single Fill, Stroke and Default Transparency (100% opacity). This default configuration is called the *Basic Appearance*. The basic appearance is not always a white fill and a black stroke (as suggested by the icon). A basic appearance is any single fill and stroke, even if it is a stroke or fill of *None*.

If the current selection has more than the *basic* attributes within the appearance, you can choose what attributes the next object will have. The first icon at the bottom of the palette is the New Art Maintains Appearance (when disabled) and New Art Has Basic Appearance (when selected). For example, if your last object had a drop shadow added to it but you don't want the next object to inherit this attribute, click on the icon and the new object will only inherit the basic attributes of the appearance. **Note:** *When the New Art Maintains Appearance icon is disabled, the palette pop-up menu item New Art Has Basic Appearance is unchecked. When the icon is enabled the menu item New Art Has Basic Appearance is checked.*

Click on the Clear Appearance icon to reduce all appearance attributes to no fill or stroke and the default transparency. Click on the Reduce to Basic Appearance icon to reduce the artwork's appearance to a single stroke and fill along with the default transparency. To delete a selected attribute, click on it or drag it to the Trash. **Note:** *Reduce to Basic Appearance removes all brush strokes!*

FINESSING THE FINER POINTS OF APPEARANCES
Adding fills & strokes

It's not until you start adding multiple fills and strokes

Expand appearance

Select Object: Expand Appearance to create multiple objects from the selected object. Each newly created object is treated as if it were flattened and consists of a single stroke and fill. Transparency is reduced to the default values and all effects are irreversible once the document is saved and closed.

Type objects

Text has attributes within the appearance and so does the Type Object. When you select text using the Type tool, you can modify the appearance, but you can also apply additional appearance attributes to the text by targeting the Type Object in the Appearance palette. Below is an example of how the two are different:

Text character selected

Type object selected

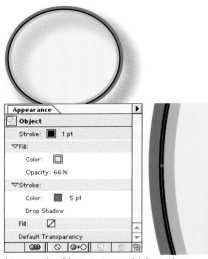

An example of how to use multiple strokes and fills.

Transform effects!

This one is a gem! Any transformation can now be applied as an *effect* (Effect: Distort & Transform: Transform). Know exactly how much you've rotated, skewed or scaled an object and completely undo or adjust it.

Why duplicate items?

Why are there duplicate items in both the Filter and Effects menus? If all of the filters had been removed from the application any legacy Action recorded with a *filter* would have no longer worked.

Rasterization resolution

The appearance of Effects like Drop Shadows and Blurs is affected by the resolution setting in Effects: Rasterize: Raster Effects Settings.— *Sandee Cohen*

to an appearance that you completely understand how useful the Appearance palette is. Line effects and text icons are great examples of how to use multiple strokes and/or fills in your artwork. (See lessons and Galleries later in this chapter for more examples.)

The Appearance palette has a stacking order similar to that of the Layers palette. Items at the top of the palette are at the top of the stacking order. You can click on items in the palette list to select them. Items in the palette list are rearranged by dragging them up and down.

Select Add New Fill or Add New Stroke from the palette pop-up menu to add these attributes to an appearance. You can also add Effects and transparency attributes to each fill or stroke.

There are several ways to duplicate or delete a fill, stroke or Effect. Select the attribute in the palette list and drag it to one of the icons at the bottom of the palette. Select the attribute and click on the appropriate icon at the bottom of the palette. Finally, you can choose the appropriate item from the palette pop-up menu.

Group, sublayer or layer appearances

Selecting objects on the artboard only displays the appearance for those individual objects. If the current selection contains objects with different appearances, the Appearance palette displays *Mixed Appearances*. To display attributes that have been applied to a group, sublayer or layer you will need to target the group, sublayer or layer in the Layers palette (see the *Layers* chapter) or click on the appropriate item in the Appearance palette list.

Multiple fills & strokes

Create multiple line effects by adding multiple strokes to a path. Select a path, group or layer and choose Add New Stroke from the Appearance palette pop-up menu. A new stroke is added on top of the current stroke and a stroke attribute is added to the Appearance palette. In order to see the additional stroke on the path, it has to have a different appearance from the initial stroke. Target the stroke attribute (in the Appearance palette) and alter the color, point size, shape and/or transparency settings of one of the strokes. If you are still having trouble with this technique, start with a wider stroke on the bottom (see the example to the left). To vary the results, try dashed lines and/or different end-caps.

To create multiple fills, target an object, group or layer and choose Add New Fill. In most cases, fills are identical to strokes, in that before you can see the effect of the additional fill, it needs to have a different appearance. To vary the results of additional fills, try applying an *Effect* or different transparency settings.

EFFECTS VS FILTERS

Prior to this version, Illustrator had a variety of methods for altering or enhancing a path. Filters were just one of the many ways in which you could achieve variation in your artwork. Effects are similar, and in some cases identical, to the filters with one exception—effects are dynamic. Effects alter the appearance without permanently changing the base art and they can be removed at any time. Filters permanently change the artwork. When an effect is applied to an object, group or layer, it will display as an attribute in the Appearance palette. The effect's position in the palette indicates which element it will modify.

The effects are organized in the same manner as the filters, with those that modify but retain the vector characteristic of the artwork at the top of the menu and those that require rasterization (the Photoshop-compatible filters) on the bottom. Like filters, most of the bottom effects must be applied to art created in the RGB color mode (space).

Most of the effects mirror the filters, but those that are completely new to this version are Convert to Shape: Rectangle, Rounded Rectangle and Ellipse (see Tip "Expandable text shapes" to the right), Path: Outline Object, Rasterize: Raster Effects Settings, and Stylize: Feather, Inner Glow and Outer Glow (see lessons and Galleries later in this chapter).

Expandable text shapes

Want to make a text button? Type a word, then select the text. Choose Add New Fill (Appearance palette menu) and choose a text color. Next select the second Fill (currently None) and choose a button color. With this Fill still selected, choose Effect: Convert to Shape and select one from the submenu. Make sure you check Relative.

Applying Pathfinder effects

Pathfinder effects can only be applied to a group or layer. To target the group, either click on "Group" in the Appearance palette or click on the target indicator for the *group* in the Layers palette. Then, select Effects: Pathfinder and choose an effect. You can do the same for a *layer*.

Replace styles

To replace a saved appearance in the Styles palette with a new set of attributes, option-drag the thumbnail from the Appearance palette, or artboard, to the Styles palette and drop it onto the highlighted style. To replace the currently selected style, make adjustments and choose Replace Style from the palette menu. The name of the style will not change and all objects or groups currently using the style will update to the new appearance.

Applying effects

Once an effect has been applied to an object, double-click the effect in the Appearance palette to change the values. If you reselect the effect from the Effect menu you will re-apply the effect to the object, not change it.

Merge styles

Select two or more styles in the Styles palette and choose Merge styles from the palette menu to combine appearance attributes and create a new *graphic* style.

Select all unused

When you're finished with your artwork, choose Select All Unused from the Styles palette menu and delete the highlighted swatches. Doing this will reduce your final file size.

Move or copy appearances

Drag an appearance target from one object, group or layer to another to move the appearance, or Option (Mac)/Alt (Win)-drag to copy the appearance.

Too many Stylize choices?

It seems like someone wasn't paying attention to how many times Stylize was used as a menu item (4 times). Both the Filter and Effect menus have the term listed twice. The bottom choices always require a RGB color space.

Multiple Pathfinders

Along with duplicate filters are duplicate Pathfinders. You can still access the Pathfinders via the palette, but you can also find them in the Effects menu. Which should you use? If you want to manipulate the final shapes or paths, use the Pathfinder palette. These Pathfinders actually perform the operation on the paths to create new shapes (see the *Lines, Fills & Colors* chapter for more about what the actual Path-finder filters do). The *effects* will only show you the result of the operation without actually creating new paths. Try them only if you don't need to manipulate the resulting shapes (see Tip "Applying Pathfinder effects" on the preceding page).

STYLES IN ILLUSTRATOR

If you plan on applying an appearance more than once, you might want to save it as a style in the Styles palette. Once saved, you can apply that style to objects, groups, text objects and layers. A Style provides a recipe, or formula, for producing a predictable appearance. The default style is a white fill and a 1 point black stroke.

To apply a style, simply select an object—or target a group, layer or text object—and click on a swatch in the Styles palette. You can also sample a style from another object using the Eyedropper tool. Next, drag a style from the Styles palette directly onto an object.

When creating a new style, apply the desired appearance attributes to an object, then either click the New Style icon on the bottom of the Styles palette or drag the *object* thumbnail from the Appearance palette to the Styles palette. Styles are saved with the color mode (space) in which they were originally created.

If you want to separate a style from an object, click on the Break Link to Style icon at the bottom of the palette, or select the item from the Styles palette pop-up menu. You might want to do this when you are replacing a style but you don't want to change all the objects using the current style to the updated or replaced version (see Tip "Replace styles" on the preceding page).

Sandra Alves

Sandra Alves created this interior using a variety of transparency and Effects features. The flowers in the vase were created using gradient meshes; each petal and bud are multi-colored gradient meshes (see the *Blends & Gradients* chapter for gradient and mesh help). Alves created a couple of flowers, then rotated, skewed, and scaled each of them (for transformation help see the *Zen* chapter). The stems were 2-pt strokes converted to outlined paths (Object: Path: Outline Stroke) so that they could be filled with gradients (gradients can't be applied to strokes). The vase itself was a gradient mesh with 50% opacity. She created the drapes with gradient mesh and gradient-filled objects set to various opacities. To add depth to the image, Alves applied the drop shadow effect to a number of objects (Effect: Stylize: Drop Shadow), including the drapes. The clouds outside the window were created in Photoshop and placed in Illustrator (File: Place). She created the floor and the room in this illustration using the default Wood grain light Hatch Effect setting (Filter: Pen and Ink: Hatch Effects) with Keep Object's Fill Color option checked (for more on hatches, see the *Advanced Techniques* chapter).

Basic Transparency
Blending Modes, Opacity & Isolate Blending

KANZLER

Overview: *Arrange elements; selectively apply blending modes to objects using Layers, Appearance and Transparency palettes; modify layer opacity; select objects, assign a blending mode, group objects and isolate the blending.*

1

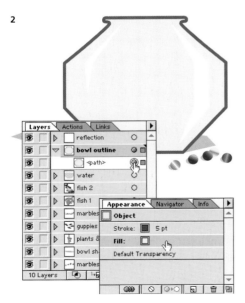

All elements of the final illustration, before transparency effects

2

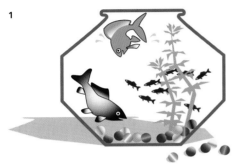

Use the Layers palette to target a path, and the Appearance palette to select the Fill attribute

Once you have mastered selecting and targeting in Illustrator, you can create cool effects using basic transparency effects. In this illustration, Diane Hinze Kanzler incorporated three aspects of the Transparency palette: opacity, blending modes and Isolate Blending.

1 Arrange elements of the final illustration on layers. The logical placement of groups and objects in layers will be helpful as you apply transparency effects to an illustration. In this illustration, for example, all parts of one fish are on one layer, the marbles in the bowl are on a separate layer from the marbles outside of the bowl, etc. (see the *Layers* chapter for help with organizing layers).

2 Selectively apply a blending mode to an object. Kanzler wanted the gray fill of her bowl to have a slight deepening color effect on the objects in the layers below. First, she selected the bowl and gave it a fill of light gray and a stroke of dark gray. Next, she targeted the bowl path in the Layers palette. In order to correctly apply a blending mode to the fill of the bowl, Kanzler selected Fill in the Appearance palette by clicking once on the Fill attribute. She chose Multiply from the list of blending modes in the Transparency palette. The light gray fill of the bowl has a blending mode applied to it, but the dark gray stroke of the bowl remains opaque, as intended.

To apply a blending mode to one of the paths in the water layer, Kanzler used the same targeting method. First, she targeted the larger water path (not the splash drops) and selected Fill in the Appearance palette. Then Kanzler chose Multiply as a blending mode in the Transparency palette.

3 Using the Opacity slider. For the reflection effect on the bowl, Kanzler simply reduced the opacity of the white objects. She targeted the "reflection" layer, and in the Transparency palette used the Opacity slider to reduce the opacity of the reflection objects to the desired amount. In this instance, the Appearance palette wasn't even used, as the effect was applied to the entire layer.

4 Isolate the blending. In order to prevent a blending mode from affecting objects *beneath*, the blending effect must be *isolated*. With Kanzler's illustration, she wanted the aquatic leaves and stems to be transparent with each other as they overlap, and those plants to show the fish behind them. But she also wanted to prevent the plants from interacting with the bowl shadow which is beneath the plants on a lower layer.

So that the individual paths in the plant group would interact with each other and with the fish, she first *selected* (rather than targeted) the plant paths by Opt/Alt-clicking on the plant group-layer. Then Kanzler chose the Hard Light blending mode in the Transparency palette. If she had *targeted* the plant layer instead, the blending mode would have applied to the plant group as a *whole*, and the overlapping leaves would not blend with each other. To prevent the bowl shadow from showing through the plants, Kanzler selected the plant group and rearmost fishes group and chose Object: Group, which placed all into one new group layer. She *targeted* that group in the Layers palette, and then enabled the Isolate Blending checkbox in the Transparency palette, which maintained the transparency within the group, but prevented the group from being transparent to layers below.

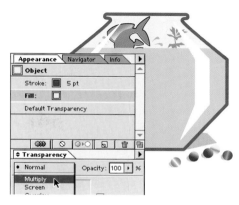

Docking the Transparency palette under the Appearance palette to keep both conveniently available

3

The Opacity slider in the Transparency palette was used to reduce opacity of the reflection highlight shapes

4

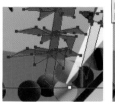

Apply a blending mode to multiple objects individually by selecting rather than targeting before applying the blending mode

Use the Layers palette to target a group of objects that have been assigned a blending mode, then enable "Isolate Blending" (in the Transparency palette) to prevent that blending mode from effecting objects outside the group

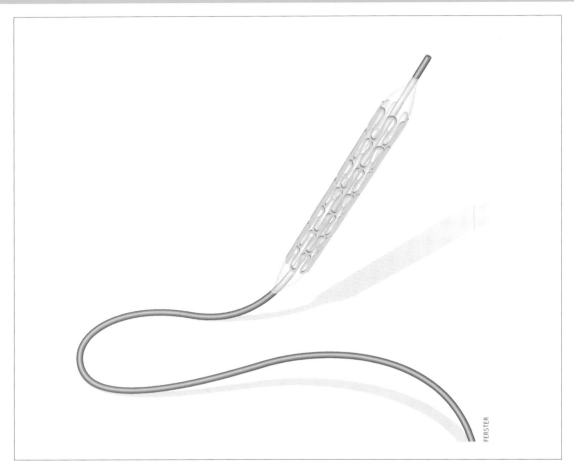

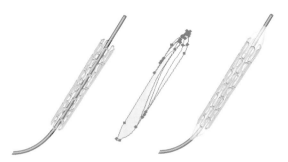

Gary Ferster

A product illustration for a catheter for Medtronic AVE challenged Gary Ferster to combine a subtle gradient mesh with transparency effects. To create a semi-transparent catheter balloon (positioned inside the lattice-like "stent" near the top of the catheter), Ferster drew a balloon object with the Pen tool and then created a mesh with the Gradient Mesh tool. After choosing subtle colors for the mesh intersection points, Ferster used the Transparency palette to specify a 65% Opacity value and Normal blending mode for the object.

WEIMER

Alan James Weimer

Alan Weimer's dragonfly, having broken out of the pattern in his *Advanced Techniques* chapter Gallery page and alighted on his wallflower pattern from the *Lines, Fills & Colors* chapter, demonstrates the play of shadows across background colors. To create the look of semi-trans-parent shadows in Illustrator 9, simply duplicate the objects that will serve as shadows, fill with black or another dark color, and then use the Transparency palette to assign Multiply mode and a low Opacity value. Add a Blur from the Effect menu to soften the shadows' edges.

HORNALL ANDERSON

Hornall Anderson Design Works / Jack Anderson (Art Director)

Designers at Hornall Anderson Design Works infused energy and balance into these covers for a GNA Power Annuities annual report by simulating the transparency of overlapping letter and number shapes. They converted the font characters to outlines (Type: Create Outlines) and then carefully considered tangency and negative space as they positioned the character shapes. Some of the visual blending effects seen here can be achieved with Illustrator 9's transparency and blending modes. Others require using the Divide command from the Pathfinder palette (Window: Show Pathfinders). Then select separate shapes and fill them with different colors or tints (for help with tints, see "Objective Colors" in the *Lines, Fills & Colors* chapter).

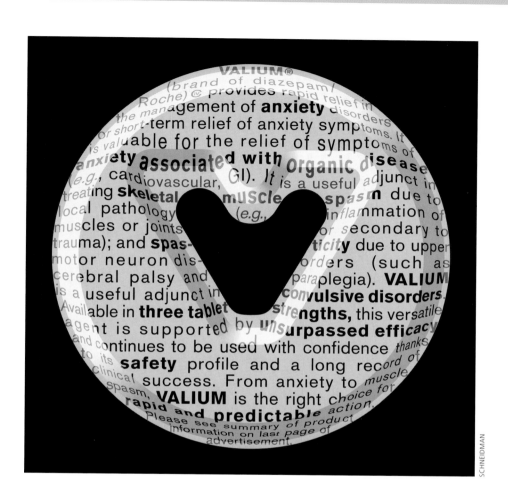

SCHNEIDMAN

Jared Schneidman / JSD

A painstaking process of scaling, shearing and distorting is how Jared Schneidman describes constructing this image. To simulate dimensionality, Schneidman manually distorted the outlines of type and then masked and colored the distorted outlines. To simulate a 3D surface, first draw a background object filled with a medium gray. Then create the shadowed and highlighted surfaces by drawing blend objects that define the contours of each surface (see "Contouring Masks" in the *Advanced Techniques* chapter for more on how to do this). Then Fill

the shadow objects with darker grays and the highlight objects with lighter grays. Next, move the highlight objects above the distorted type or other surface decoration by dragging them within the Layers palette (see the *Layers* chapter for more on moving items in the palette). Using the Transparency palette, reduce the Opacity value of the highlight objects (this lightens both the blend and type underneath it). For the shadow objects, apply the Multiply blending mode in the Transparency palette to allow the blends to darken the objects beneath.

Basic Highlights

Making Highlights with Transparent Blends

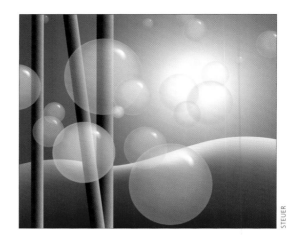

STEUER

Overview: *Create your basic objects and a light-colored highlight shape; use blends to make the highlights; scale the highlights to fit*

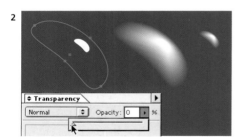

The original objects (locked in the layers palette) shown with the basic highlight shape

The highlight objects before blending (the outer object is set to 0% Opaque in the Transparency palette); after blending in 22 steps; the blend shown at actual size

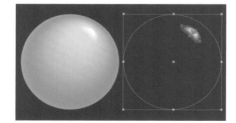

The final blend in place and shown in a "registration" circle for easy scaling on other bubbles

Using transparency, highlights are now as simple as creating a blend in the correct highlight shape. If you need help creating smooth contoured blends, see "Unlocking Realism" in the *Blends & Gradients* chapter.

1 **Creating your basic objects and determining your basic highlight shape and color.** Artist Sharon Steuer created this "Bubbles" image using overlaying transparent radial gradients (to see how she created the gradient mesh hill, see "Rolling Mesh Hills" in the *Blends* chapter). She modified an oval with the Direct-selection tool to create her basic highlight shape. After creating your main objects, make a light-colored highlight object on top. Use the Layers palette to lock everything except the highlighted object (see the *Layers* chapter for help).

2 **Creating the highlight.** Select the highlight shape and Copy, choose Edit: Paste In Back, then Object: Lock. Now, select and shrink the front copy (for scaling help see the *Zen* chapter). Choose Object: Unlock All, then set the Opacity of this selected outer object to 0% in the Transparency palette. Select both objects, then with the Blend tool, click on one anchor point of the outer object, then Option/Alt-click on the corresponding anchor point of the inner object and specify the number of blend steps (Steuer chose 22 steps). Steuer scaled copies of her highlight blend (with a "registration circle") for each bubble.

Nancy Stahl

Nancy Stahl created a soft, airbrushed look throughout her illustration for *The Illustrator 9 Wow! Book* cover by using opaque-to-transparent blends, as described in the "Basic Highlights" lesson opposite. Shown bottom left are the steps Stahl used in creating the hat band: the first two figures in the first diagram show her custom Pattern Brush and that brush applied to a path (see the *Brushes* chapter for brushes help), third down shows the opaque to transparent blends on top of the brushed path, next are the brush and blends masked, at bottom is that masked group on the hat colors, with the brushed path set to a Multiply mode with a 65% Opacity (Transparency palette). Bottom right show the gondolier with and without the opaque-to-transparent blends.

Basic Appearances

Making and Applying Appearances

Overview: *Create appearance attributes for an object; build a three-stroke appearance, save it as a style, and then draw paths and apply the style; target a layer with a drop shadow effect, create symbols on the layer, then edit layer appearance if needed.*

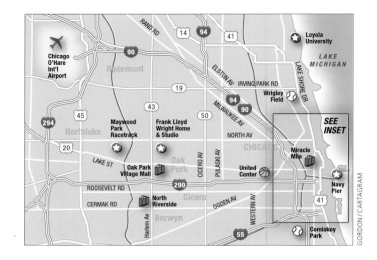

1

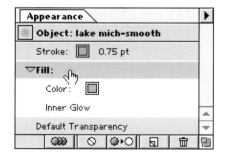

On the left, the lake with blue fill and stroke; on the right, the lake with the Inner Glow added to the appearance attribute set

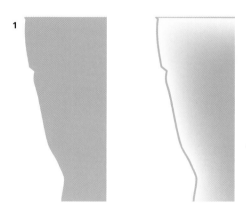

Appearance palette displaying the finished set of attributes (Gordon used the Appearance palette so that he could create a single path for the lake that contained a fill and the coastline stroke above it)

Complexity and simplicity come together when you use Illustrator 9's Appearance palette to design intricate effects, develop reusable styles and simplify production workflow. In this location map of Chicago, cartographer Steven Gordon relied on the Appearance palette to easily build appearances and apply them to objects, groups and layers.

1 Building an appearance for a single object. Gordon developed a set of appearance attributes that applied a coastline, vignette and blue fill to a path symbolizing Lake Michigan. To begin building appearance attributes, open the Appearance palette and other palettes you might need (Color, Swatches, Stroke and Transparency, for example). Gordon began by drawing the outline of the lake with the Pen tool and giving the path a 0.75 pt dark blue stroke. In the Appearance palette, he clicked on the Fill attribute and chose the same dark blue he had used for the stroke. To give the lake a light-colored vignette, he applied an inner glow to the Fill attribute (Effect: Stylize: Inner Glow). In the Inner Glow dialog box, Gordon set Mode to Normal, Opacity to 100%, Blur to 0.25 inches (for the width of the vignette edge), and enabled the Edge option. He clicked the dialog's color swatch and chose white for the glow color.

2 Creating a style. Until Illustrator 9, you created a "patterned" line like an interstate highway symbol by overlapping copies of a path, each copy with a different stroke width. Now you can use the Appearance palette to craft a multi-stroked line that you apply to a single path. First, deselect any objects that may still be selected and reset the Appearance palette by clicking the Clear Appearance icon at the bottom of the palette (this eliminates any attributes from the last selected style or object). Next, click the Stroke attribute (it will have the None color icon) and click the Duplicate Selected Item icon twice to make two copies. Now, to make Gordon's interstate symbol, select the top Stroke attribute and give it a dark color and a 0.5 pt width. Select the middle attribute and choose a light color and a 2 pt width. For the bottom attribute, choose a dark color and a 3 pt width. Because you'll use this set of appearance attributes later, save it as a style by dragging the Object icon at the top of the palette to the Styles palette. (Double-click the new style's default name in the palette and rename it in the dialog box if you want.)

3 Assigning a style to a group. Draw the paths you want to paint with the new style you created above. Then choose Select All and Group. To get the three levels of strokes to merge when paths on the map cross one another, click on Group in the Appearance palette and then apply the interstate style you just saved.

4 Assigning appearance attributes to an entire layer. By targeting a layer with appearance attributes, you can create a uniform look for all the objects you draw or place on that layer. Create a layer for the symbols and click the layer's target icon in the Layers palette. Then select Effect: Stylize: Drop Shadow. Each symbol you draw or paste on that layer will be automatically painted with the drop shadow. Later, you can modify the drop shadows by clicking the layer's targeting icon and then double-clicking the Drop Shadow attribute in the Appearance palette and changing values in the pop-up Drop Shadow dialog box.

2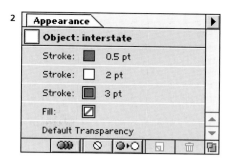

Appearance palette for Gordon's interstate highway symbol

3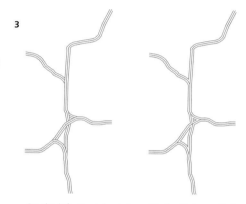

On the left, the interstates with the Style applied to the individual paths; on the right, the interstate paths were grouped before the Style was applied

4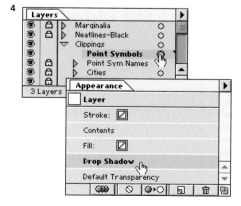

Top, targeting the layer in the Layers palette; bottom, the Appearance palette showing the Drop Shadow attribute (double-click the attribute to edit Drop Shadow values)

Scratchboard Art

Using Multiple Strokes, Effects and Styles

Overview: *Using simple objects, apply multiple strokes with brushes; apply effects to strokes; create and apply styles*

Seen in Outline View, the scratchboard art shows simple primitive shapes

PAPCIAK-ROSE / COHEN

Artist Ellen Papciak-Rose asked consultant Sandee Cohen if there was a way to simulate scratchboard art in Illustrator. Cohen devised a way to transform Papciak-Rose's artwork using Art Brushes, multiple strokes and stroke effects, which were then combined and saved as styles. Once a series of effects is saved as a style, you can easily apply that style to multiple objects to create a design theme. Art directors might find this method helpful for unifying and stylizing illustrations created by a number of different artists.

1 Applying Art Brushes and Fills. To create the look of a more natural stroke, Cohen applied Art Brushes to simple objects supplied by Papciak-Rose. Cohen chose from Charcoal, Fude, Dry Ink, Fire Ash and Pencil Art Brushes (found in the default Brushes palette or from Window: Brush Libraries: Artistic Sample). Select a simple object, then click on the Art Brush of your choice in the Brushes palette or in a Brush Library. (For more on Art Brushes, see the *Brushes* chapter.) Choose basic, solid fills for each object.

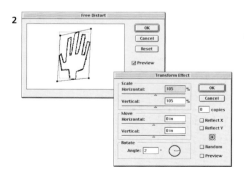

To offset a path's stroke from its fill, select the Stroke attribute in the Appearance palette and apply Free Distort and Transform Effect from the Effect menu

2 Offsetting a stroke. To develop a loose, sketchlike look, Cohen offset some of the strokes from their fills. First, select a Stroke attribute in the Appearance palette and apply Effect: Distort & Transform: Free Distort or Effect: Distort & Transform: Transform to manually or numerically adjust the position of the stroke so that it is not perfectly aligned with the fill. This gives the stroke a different shape than the fill without permanently changing the path. (You can further reshape the stroke by double-clicking the Transform attribute in the Appearance palette and manually or numerically adjusting the offset of the Stroke attribute.)

3 Adding more strokes to a single path. To add to the sketchlike look, Cohen applied additional strokes to each path. First, she selected a Stroke attribute in the Appearance palette and clicked the Duplicate Selected Item icon at the bottom of the palette. With the new Stroke copy selected, she changed the color, as well as the choice, of Art brush. She also double-clicked the stroke's Distort & Transform effect in the Appearance palette and changed the settings to move the Stroke copy's position. Cohen repeated this until she had as many strokes as she liked.

To make a stroke visible only outside its Fill, simply drag the stroke below the Fill in the Appearance palette.

4 Working with styles. To automate the styling of future illustrations, Cohen used the Appearance and Styles palettes to create a library of styles. Whenever you create a set of strokes and fills you like, click the New Style icon in the Styles palette to create a new style swatch.

Once Cohen had assembled a palette of style swatches, she could dramatically alter the look and feel of the artwork by simply applying a variety of styles to selected paths. This type of workflow allows an art director or designer to create a number of overall themes in a style library, and then apply them selectively to illustrations or design elements. This workflow can also help to keep a cohesive look throughout a design project or series.

3

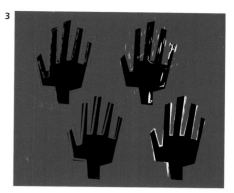

This graphic illustrates the individual strokes that Cohen combined to create the multiple strokes for the hand object in the final illustration

4

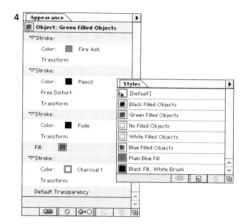

Multiple Strokes applied to an object shown in the Appearance palette; appearance attributes saved in the Styles palette by clicking the New Style icon

5

Applying different styles to objects can give the same artwork several different looks

Embossing Effects

Building 3D Appearances

Overview: *Apply object-level effects for highlights and shadows; build appearances, save as styles and apply to layers.*

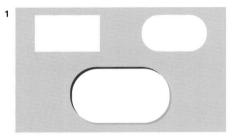

At the top, making the screw slots (on the left, the rectangle and on the right, the rectangle with Round Corners Effect): at the bottom, an enlarged view of the composite appearance

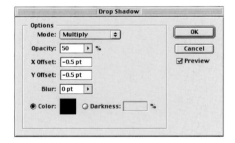

The Drop Shadow options pop-up dialog box; edit the X and Y Offset fields to adjust the position of the shadow and highlight (check the Preview box to see the effect as you work)

Resizing appearances

If you plan to resize an Illustration that contains appearances with stroke values, be sure to apply the appearances to objects, not to layers. Illustrator 9 may fail to rescale stroke values in layer-targeted appearances.

Ted Alspach, Senior Product Manager for Adobe Illustrator, choose the embossed letters, numbers and lines of a license plate to demonstrate the ease and flexibility of using Illustrator's effects and appearances. In this memorial to French mathematician Pierre Bézier, inventor of the original Bézier curve, Alspach simulated the look of embossing by applying a drop shadow effect and by building a sophisticated style.

1 Applying the drop shadow effect. Start the license plate by drawing the background shape, circles, curves and other linework. While technically not a raised surface, the four screw slots still require highlights and shadows to convey the impression of dimension. To create a slot, draw a rectangle and then Fill with White and Stroke with None. Use the Round Corners Effect (Effect: Stylize: Round Corners) to give the object a more oval shape. To cast the plate's shadow on the edge of the slot, select the slot rectangle and apply the Drop Shadow Effect (Effect: Stylize: Drop Shadow). In the Drop Shadow dialog box, choose black for color, Blur 0, and Offset up and to the left (using negative numbers for "X" and "Y" offsets). Then click OK. Repeat the drop shadow effect to make the highlight, except choose a light color and Offset down and to the right (using positive numbers). To further tweak the drop shadows (modifying their color or width, for example), simply double-click the attribute name "drop shadow" in the Appearance palette (Window: Show Appearance) and edit the values in the dialog box.

2 Building multiple appearances. Alspach took another approach to embossing by building a sophisticated style in which transparency and multiple offset strokes simulate highlights and shadows.

To make the license plate lettering, type the characters in a sans serif font and convert them to outlines (Type: Create Outlines). Ungroup the characters, select a character and set its Fill to orange. To make the first embossing highlight, select the orange Fill appearance attribute in the Appearance palette (Window: Show Appearance) and copy it by clicking the Duplicate Selected Item icon at the bottom of the palette. Now, select the lower Fill attribute in the palette, choose white from the Color palette and, in the Transparency palette, set Opacity to 25% and blending mode to Screen. Then, choose the Transform Effect (Effect: Transform: Distort & Transform) to offset it up and to the left by editing the Move fields (negative Horizontal and positive Vertical). Make two more copies of this white Fill attribute by once again clicking the Duplicate Selected Item icon. Offset each copy farther up and and to the left by double-clicking the Fill's Transform attribute and editing the Move values in the Transform dialog.

To start the shadows, first duplicate the lowest white Fill. Now select the bottom white Fill and set its color to black, Opacity to 50% and blending mode to Multiply. Double-click the Fill's Transform attribute and edit the Move values to offset it down and to the right. Copy this shadow and offset it farther down and to the right. When you have finished, the Appearance palette will display six Fill attributes for the object.

3 Creating and applying a Style. Alspach turned the appearance set into a style by dragging the Appearance palette's preview icon and dropping it in the Styles palette. He then applied the style to the layer with the number characters. You can achieve the same embossing look by applying the style to selected character outlines or to a group composed of the character outlines.

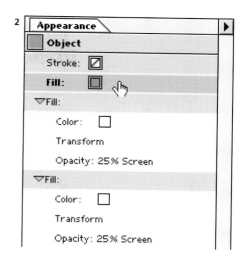

Appearance palette showing the appearance preview icon (top left), and the target of the appearance (Object)

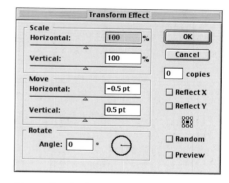

Move values in the Transform Effect dialog box to offset Fill attribute up and left

Close-up view of the embossed letter characters with the multiple highlight and shadow strokes that progressively hide the background artwork

Dramatic Effects

Applying Glows and Using Opacity Masks

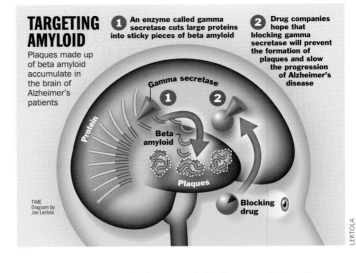

Overview: *Scan sketched artwork, place it as a template, and draw objects; apply Inner Glow; blend one object into another object using an opacity mask*

1

Pencil sketch layout of the illustration

2

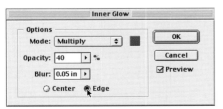

At top, head before and after applying Inner Glow; below, the Inner Glow dialog

Achieving contoured glows and shadows and blending complex shapes can be daunting tasks—unless you know how to use Illustrator's Transparency palette and Effect menu. Joe Lertola exploited glows and opacity masks in this *TIME* magazine illustration, enjoying the simplicity of staying in Illustrator while applying raster effects.

1 Sketching and scanning, then drawing. Draw the objects to which you want to add a glow. Lertola placed a scan of a rough pencil layout in Illustrator as a tracing template (File: Place, and check the Template box) and drew the brain, lobes, arrows and other elements.

2 Creating Inner Glows. Heighten the visual drama of the objects you've drawn by applying glows, shadows and other effects from the Effect menu. For example, Lertola selected the outline of the head and choose Effect: Stylize: Inner Glow. In the pop-up dialog, he selected Multiply for Mode, entered 40% for Opacity and set the Blur. Next, he clicked the color icon to bring up the Color Picker dialog and chose a dark color. To start the Inner Glow color at the edge so it fades inward to the object's center, Lertola selected Edge. To create the glow so the color you picked in the Color Picker dialog is at the center of the object and fades outward to the edges, you would select Center.

Similarly, you can add a drop shadow to a selected path by choosing Drop Shadow from the Effect: Stylize menu and specifying opacity, offset and blur in the Drop Shadow dialog.

3 Applying an opacity mask. Making an object appear to blend into another object may seem difficult. But by using an opacity mask, you can perform this trick easily. First, Lertola selected the brain lobe and moved it in front of the brain by dragging the lobe path above the brain path in the Layers palette.

To make the opacity mask, draw a rectangle (or other shape) in front of the object you want to fade. Fill with a black-to-white gradient, placing the black where you want to fully hide the top object and the white where you want that object fully revealed. (See the *Blends & Gradients* chapter to learn how to create and modify gradients.) Next, select both the rectangle and the object to be masked (Shift-click the outlines of both objects to select them). Make sure the Transparency palette is open (display the palette by selecting Window: Show Transparency) and choose Make Opacity Mask from the palette's pop-out menu.

Once you've made the opacity mask, the object and its mask are linked together. (Moving the object will move the mask with it.) To edit the object's path, click on the artwork thumbnail in the Transparency palette and use any of the path editing tools; to edit the mask, click on the mask thumbnail. Edit the gradient using the Gradient palette or the Gradient tool.

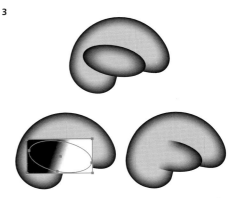

Brain object with overlying lobe (top); lobe and opacity masking object (black-to-white gradient fill) selected (bottom left); lobe following Make Opacity Mask (bottom right)

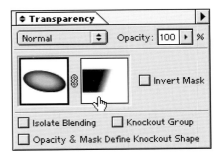

Entering mask-editing mode by clicking on the mask thumbnail in the Transparency palette

3

Four's company

"Stylize" makes the most appearances as a menu command: twice in the Filter menu and twice in the Effect menu. The Filter: Stylize commands change the paths of the object to which you apply them. The Effect: Stylize commands produce "live" effects, altering the appearance of objects but leaving the paths unchanged and available for editing.

Why can't I draw now?

You may be in mask-editing mode and not know it if:

- You draw an object, deselect it, and it seems to disappear
- You fill an object with a color, but the color doesn't display

If you are in mask-editing mode, the Layers palette tab will read "Layers (Opacity Mask)." To exit mask-editing mode, click on the artwork thumbnail in the Transparency palette.

Tinting a Scan

Using Transparency Effects & Simplify Path

KANZLER

Advanced Technique

Overview: *Place an EPS image and its clipping path; tint the image using the clipping path, Blending Modes and Opacity; reduce a path's anchor points using Simplify; use Isolate Blending to prevent double shadows*

1

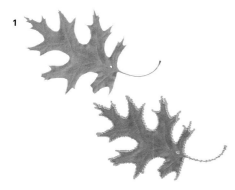

The grayscale leaf scan; the outline selection converted to a path in Photoshop and designated as a clipping path (the small hole in the leaf has been included in the path, making it a compound clipping group in Illustrator)

2

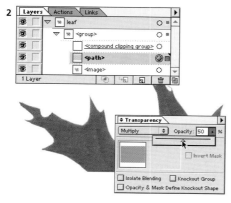

Drawing the russet-colored rectangle into the compound clipping path group; targeting the rectangle path and specifying a Multiply blending mode and opacity of 50%

Diane Hinze Kanzler enhanced her original salamander illustration using transparency effects and Simplify to make her image more unique and naturalistic.

1 Scanning and placing an image and its clipping path. If you don't have access to Photoshop, place a grayscale image with a simple outline shape and manually create your own clipping path (see the *Advanced Techniques* chapter for help). To add a bit of nature to her illustration, Kanzler scanned a real oak leaf in grayscale mode in Photoshop. To create a clipping path for the leaf, she used Photoshop's Magic Wand tool to select everything except the leaf (using the Shift key to add the hole to her selection) then chose Select: Inverse. To convert the leaf selection into a clipping path, Kanzler chose from the Path pop-up menu (in order): Make Work Path (with .5 Tolerance), Save Path, and Clipping Path (with a 4 Flatness). To preserve the clipping path, she used Save As and chose Photoshop EPS format, then in Illustrator she chose File: Place to place the EPS leaf, unchecking the Link option to embed the scan and its compound clipping path.

2 Tinting the scan in Illustrator. Kanzler used the leaf's compound clipping path in tinting her scan. First, she located the scan's <group> in the Layers palette, clicked on the scan <image>, and drew a russet-colored rectangle bigger than the leaf. She then *targeted* this object in the

Layers palette and, in the Transparency palette, chose a Multiply blending mode with 50% Opacity.

3 Adding a shadow. Kanzler moved a copy of the leaf's clipping path below the leaf scan image to create a shadow. Working in the Layers palette (see the *Layers* chapter for help), she clicked the New Layer icon, then moved this new layer below the leaf's layer. To move a copy of the leaf's clipping path to the new layer, she clicked to the right of the target circle to select <compound clipping group> and dragged the colored square to the new layer while holding Option/Alt. She chose a new fill color and used cursor keys to offset its position.

4 Creating a simpler shadow. Since the leaf required such a complex mask, Kanzler wanted a simplified shadow for her salamander in order to minimize the overall size of her file. She started by dragging a copy of her salamander outline object to a new layer *below* (see Step 3 above), then she used the Eyedropper tool to match the leaf's shadow color. To simplify the shadow (both reducing its anchor points and giving it a less-exact form) Kanzler selected the shadow object, chose Object: Path: Simplify, and set the Curve Precision to 82%, thus reducing the path from 655 to 121 path points while still maintaining the shape's integrity. She then offset the salamander's shadow.

Next, Kanzler selected all the objects in the leaf file, copied and pasted them into her salamander illustration (with Paste Remembers Layers enabled in the Layers pop-up). Using the Layers palette, she moved the leaf layers below the salamander layers, and *targeted* her salamander shadow object. In the Transparency palette, she chose a Multiply blending mode.

To prevent a "double-shadow" effect where shadows overlapped, Kanzler used Isolate Blending. She selected and grouped (⌘-G/Ctrl-G) the salamander shadow and the leaf group—but *not* the leaf shadow. She *targeted* this *new* group in the Layers palette, then clicked Isolate Blending in the Transparency palette until a ✔ appeared.

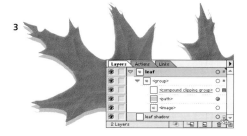

3

Using a copy of the leaf's clipping path to create an offset shadow on a layer below the leaf scan

4

Simplifying the salamander's shadow object path (left: before; right: after Simplify)

Assigning a blending mode to the salamander's shadow in the final, combined illustration

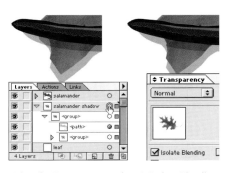

Using the Transparency palette's Isolate Blending feature to prevent an overlapping shadow effect

It's a Knockout!

See-through Objects With a Knockout Group

Advanced Technique

Overview: *Arrange elements in layers; apply a gradient fill and solid stroke to text; modify opacity and use a blending mode; create a Knockout Group; adjust transparency effects.*

1

All elements of the final illustration, before applying blending modes and Knockout Group

A copy of the gradient-filled "Organic" is pasted behind and given a 6-pt stroke of dark blue and a fill of None

2

Detail of the rainbow <group> after reducing opacity in the Transparency palette

For this sign, Diane Hinze Kanzler used Illustrator's Knockout Group feature to allow woodgrain to show through text while blocking out other elements.

The concept of the "knockout" comes from darkroom work and film prepress. A knockout film is typically used to "punch a hole" in an illustration or photograph, thus revealing images, text, or even the paper color below.

The Knockout Group feature in Illustrator (found in the Transparency palette) works according to the same principle as prepress knockout film, yet it is much more powerful because it also allows transparency effects to be applied with the knockout. The real trick to controlled use of the Knockout Group feature is the proper use of the Layers palette to correctly select or target objects.

1 Arrange elements of the final illustration on layers, convert text to outlines, and apply a gradient fill. It is important, particularly when you're planning to use a Knockout Group, that all of your illustration's elements are placed on layers in a logical fashion (see "Organizing Layers" in the *Layers* chapter) and grouped (Object: Group or ⌘-G/Ctrl-G) when appropriate. This will make selecting or targeting groups much easier.

Create some text using a font bold enough to fill with a gradient, and convert the text to outlines using Type: Create Outlines (converted text is automatically grouped). Next, *select* (rather than target) the group and click on a Gradient-fill swatch to apply the fill to each letter of the text. If you target the group using the Layers palette, the gradient will span the group as a whole rather than apply to each object in the group.

To add a stroke to her text without distorting it, Kanzler selected "Organic," copied it, deselected the text, created a new layer below the filled text layer and chose Edit: Paste In Back with the Paste Remembers Layers toggle off (see the Layers palette pop-up). She gave that copy a fill of None and a thick stroke of dark blue.

2 Apply transparency effects to chosen objects. Kanzler wanted her rainbow to be transparent, so she targeted the layer of her rainbow group and used the Transparency palette to adjust the Opacity slider to 75%. Depending on the specifics of your image, you can target a layer with a group of objects or the <group> itself. She also wanted the woodgrain of the background to show through "Organic" while still being affected by the gradient fill. Kanzler targeted the gradient-filled text group in the Layers palette, then chose a blending mode of Hard Light in the Transparency palette. Note that at this point, all the objects below the gradient-filled "Organic" show through, including the thick strokes from the copy of "Organic."

3 Grouping objects and creating a Knockout Group. Kanzler controlled which objects showed through the topmost "Organic" with the Knockout Group feature. First, she Opt/Alt-Shift-clicked the layers containing the filled "Organic" text, stroked "Organic" text, corn and rainbow to select them, and then Grouped them (Object: Group). Next, she targeted the group (in its new position in the Layers palette), and clicked on the Knockout Group box in the Transparency palette until a ✔ appeared (you may have to click more than once to get the ✔). All objects in the group beneath the topmost object were knocked out by the shape of that topmost object, allowing the woodgrain (which is not part of the Knockout Group) to show through and be affected by the blending mode of the filled "Organic" text.

A blending mode applied to the gradient-filled "Organic" allows all lower layers to show through and be affected by the blending mode (also shown enlarged)

Opt/Alt-click on layers to select multiple contiguous layers; after grouping, all selected objects are found within the topmost selected layer in a new group

Target the new group, now composed of all objects to be included in the Knockout Group

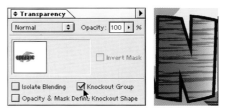

Knockout Group applied to selected objects; the topmost object's shape "punches a hole" through the rest of the objects in the group and reveal lower objects not included in the group

Masking Opacity

Making Transparency Irregular

Advanced Technique

Overview: *Draw an object outline and convert it to gradient mesh; duplicate the mesh and convert it to grayscale; make a copy of the grayscale object; rasterize, "reverse" and blur it; then add it to the grayscale mesh and create an opacity mask.*

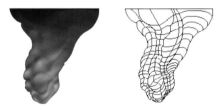

Original sketches of the movement of the flame

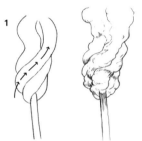

Flame mesh in Preview and Outline modes

TORRES

Rasterization resolution

If you're using live Effects and the screen redraw is too slow, set the Resolution in Effect: Rasterize: Raster Effects Settings to Screen (72ppi). But don't forget to reset this to the correct output (typically twice the line screen), and adjust each Effect setting, before saving for print!—*Ivan Torres*

Ivan Torres found that Illustrator's gradient mesh and opacity mask provided the perfect solutions for creating the light-and-dark, opaque-and-translucent character of a match flame, while allowing him to do all of his work within Illustrator rather than moving artwork between Illustrator and a bitmap program like Adobe Photoshop.

1 Drawing the gradient mesh. Torres began his flame by placing a scan of a sketch into Illustrator to use as a tracing template. He drew a filled outline of the flame and converted it to a gradient mesh (Object: Create Gradient Mesh). (See the *Blends & Gradients* chapter to find out more about creating and editing gradient meshes.) Torres edited the mesh to color the flame.

2 Making an opacity mask and modifying its opacity.
As Torres observed, a flame can contain transparent and opaque parts. To achieve irregular transparency, you can build and apply a customized opacity mask. First, select the gradient mesh object you made, Copy, and then Paste In Front. Next, convert the color mesh to grayscale by selecting Filter: Colors: Convert To Grayscale. Now use the Direct-selection tool to click on intersection points in the grayscale mesh and change their gray values in the Color palette. (The darker the point's gray value, the more transparent the object will be when the mesh is made into an opacity mask and applied to the object.)

3 Adding a blurred outline, then completing the opacity mask. Torres added a blurred outline to the grayscale mesh, so that when applied later as an opacity mask it would soften the edge of the flame. To create a blurred edge, begin by duplicating the grayscale mesh (Copy, then Paste In Front). In the Object menu, select Rasterize, and in the Rasterize dialog, click to enable Create Clipping Mask. Next, release the mask you just made (Object: Clipping Mask: Release) and Ungroup; select the square (which is the rasterized grayscale copy) and delete it. This leaves the mask object, an exact duplicate of the flame outline. Give this mask object a black stroke.

Next, create a "reverse" version of the mask using drawing tools or the Pathfinder functions (see the *Lines, Fills & Colors* chapter for more on creating and modifying paths). Fill this reverse object with black, and blur the object by selecting Effect: Blur: Gaussian Blur and assigning a blur radius that is wide enough to create the look you want.

To finish constructing the opacity mask, select the blurred object and the grayscale gradient mesh you created earlier and group them (Object: Group).

4 Applying the mask. Select the mask artwork and the original color gradient mesh and choose Make Opacity Mask from the Transparency palette's pop-out menu.

2

At the left, color mesh converted to grayscale; at the right, the edited version of the grayscale mesh made by changing the gray values of individual mesh intersection points

3

In Outline View, the rasterized grayscale gradient mesh (with the mask outline and the raster rectangle) on the left; on the right, the "reverse" object Torres created by cutting the top line with the Scissors tool, deleting the top segment, and then joining the remaining segments

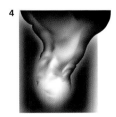

The filled "reverse" object of the rasterized mask on the left, and the same object on the right after blurring

4
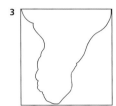

On the left, the composite artwork of the opacity mask (the grayscale gradient mesh and the blurred "reverse" object); on the right, the opacity mask applied to the flame

CROUSE

Scott Crouse

Although created in an older version of Illustrator, the transparency effects in the tan backdrop and red flag in Scott Crouse's memorial poster can be achieved using the Transparency palette's opacity slider and blending modes to control the opacity of objects and layers.

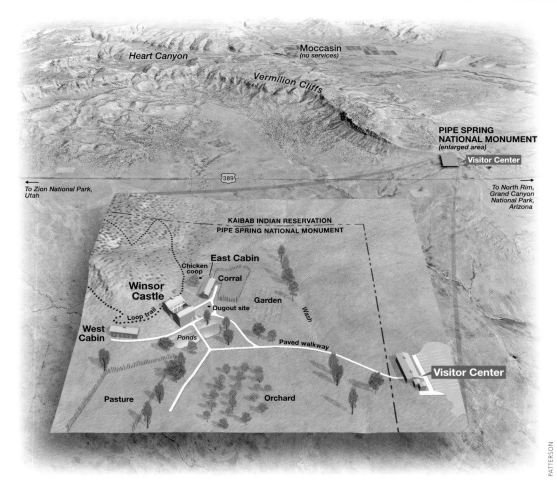

PATTERSON

Tom Patterson / U.S. National Park Service

After building the map background in Bryce and Photoshop, cartographer Tom Patterson applied Illustrator transparency to create special effects. He drew each tapered "zoom" line with the Pen tool, connecting the inset map with the background map. He filled the zoom lines with red-brown and applied 40% opacity using the Transparency palette. To make the lines appear more transparent as they zoomed down into the background, Patterson drew a large rectangle that overlapped them, and

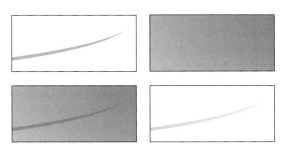

filled the rectangle with a black-to-white gradient. Then he selected the gradient-filled rectangle and the two zoom lines and chose Make Opacity Mask from the Transparency palette.

Advanced Techniques

Advanced Techniques

Choose Clipping Mask from the Object menu or use the Make Clipping Mask button on the Layers palette

Choosing Object: Clipping Mask: Make puts all of the masking objects into a group with the masking element at the top of the group

Clicking the Make Clipping Mask button at the bottom of the palette masks all of the objects on that layer. This is true even if the objects are moved above the clipping path

When you open a legacy file with layer-masks, the masked layers become sublayers of the masking layer, because all masking objects must be on the same container layer

Making masks

If you have problems activating the Make Clipping Mask button, the menu command can be much more reliable for making or releasing masks.

This chapter builds upon techniques and exercises covered in earlier chapters, and combines techniques found in different chapters. With masking effects in particular, the techniques will be easier to follow if you feel comfortable with layers and stacking order (*Layers* chapter), as well as blends and gradients (*Blends & Gradients* chapter), and are willing to try Pathfinder filters (*Lines, Fills & Colors* chapter).

Note: *You will be referred to the chapter name for more information on previously mentioned techniques.*

CLIPPING MASKS

Illustrator's masking feature operates like a stencil. It provides extraordinary control over the portions of objects, blends or images that are visible or hidden. Masks let you easily adjust both the contour of the masking object and the contents of objects being masked. Masking operates through the use of several tools: Direct-selection tool to edit paths, Group-selection tool to isolate objects within a group and the Lasso-selection tools to make selections.

Masking in this version of Illustrator is very different than in previous versions. Previously, you could apply what was known as a layer mask to the entire page. Everything beneath the layer that contained the mask would be included in the clipping path. This was a very helpful alternative to what many artists did, which was to cover unwanted image areas with white filled rectangles. However, the white rectangles were exported along with the image, creating false boundaries extending beyond the visible area. With a layer mask, any objects that extended beyond the mask's boundary would be masked as well. Alas, this created a bit differently.

In previous versions of Illustrator, if you selected objects on different layers and chose to Make Mask, you'd be creating a "layer-mask" that would mask all objects between the selected objects, with the topmost object becoming your mask. As of Illustrator 9, you can no longer mask across layers, so to achieve this effect, you'll have to first make your current layers into sublayers, and then mask. Although Illustrator does this automatically when you open a layer-mask created in a previous version, for new layer masks you'll now have to create a layer-mask: Select all the layers that you wish to mask (Shift-click on the first layer you want masked, then Shift on the bottom layer) and choose Collect in New Layer from the Layers pop-up menu—this places all of your layers within a new "master layer." Although any topmost object can now become your mask (including objects on sublayers), it's probably easiest to create or move a masking object in the "master layer" itself. Now, either select the top object or the master layer in the Layers palette and choose Make Clipping Mask from the Layers palette pop-up menu.

Note: *The following fact will either delight or alarm seasoned Illustrator users: once an object has been labeled "clipping path" in the Layers palette, you can move it around within the layer (for a layer mask) or group (for a clipping mask) and it will maintain its masking effect!*

Masking technique #1

To crop unwanted areas from an image or artwork, make a *layer mask*. Create a masking shape (or bounding shape) on top of the artwork or image you want to mask. Make sure the artwork and the masking shape are on the same top level layer. Select the mask and the backmost object in the stacking order that you want to mask, and click on the Make Clipping Mask button on the bottom of the Layers palette. The result is that the masking shape becomes the clipping path (always underlined even if renamed) and the clipped paths have a dashed divider line between them in the Layers palette. Move objects up or down within the layer or sublayers to change the stacking order. You can even move objects into or out of the layer (see the *Layers* chapter for more on layers). Moving a clipping path out of the layer releases the mask.

Inserting objects into a mask

To insert additional objects into a mask, make sure that Paste Remembers Layers (in the Layers pop-up menu) is off, then Cut or Copy the objects you wish to insert into the mask. Next, select an object within the mask (as long as it is not the first object in the group) and use Paste In Front or Back to place the copied object into the mask. An alternative method is to simply move the Selected Art indicator up or down. (see the *Layers* chapter for more).

Selecting within masks

Here are several methods of selecting individual masking objects.

- Click on the target icon in the Layers palette.
- Use the Lasso-selection tools.
- Use the Direct-selection tool when you want to edit individual masking objects.
- Use the Group-selection tool to select one object, and click again on the same object to select the rest of the objects in the mask group.

Selecting objects to mask

If you select objects on other layers in addition to the layer you want to mask, you'll not only mask all of those objects, but the artwork will become a sublayer of the current layer (technique #2).

If you're not sure whether a current selection contains a mask or is being masked, look for:

- The <u>clipping path</u> layer in the Layers palette. Even if the layer has been renamed, it will remain underlined if it is a mask. All clipped objects will be on the same layer or group as the mask.
- Object: Clipping Mask: Release also indicates that a mask is affecting your selection.
- An opacity mask is indicated with a *dashed* underline.

FABRICS

An example of how type can be used as a masking object

When a mask isn't a mask

Masks were once the only way to achieve certain effects that you can now accomplish in other ways. For example, you can now use both linear and radial gradients to make transitions within complex objects (see the *Blends & Gradients* chapter). Also, Pathfinder filters (see the *Lines, Fills & Color* chapter) can actually crop unwanted parts of objects that at one time required masking—a very useful example is the Trim filter (Window: Show Pathfinder: Trim). Remember, applying these filters irrevocably alters the shapes of objects, sometimes creating distortions (such as deleting strokes), and greatly limits your ability to make changes at a later time.

Note: *Masked objects or images can be in the sublayers or groups of the top level layer.*

Masking technique #2

Masks can do much more than simply create boundaries for printing and exporting. Masks can also directly affect objects or groups of objects. In a *clipping mask*, the mask and the objects are all in the same layer with the masking object on top. To *create* an object-mask, select all the objects, including the top object (which will become the mask) and choose Object: Clipping Mask: Make. When you use this method, all the objects, including the clipping path, become a group on the current layer. The masking effect is restricted to those objects within the group. Move objects up or down within the group to change the stacking order, or move objects into or out of the clipping group.

Note: *While clipping masks require all objects you want masked selected, layer masks only need the masking object selected when creating the mask.*

Type as a mask

When you use text as a mask it gives the appearance that the type is filled with the image or objects it is masking. You can create masked text in two slightly different ways. If you want the text to remain editable, select the type and the image/objects with which you want to fill the text. Then choose either Object: Clipping Mask: Make or click on the Make Clipping Mask button.

The second method requires that you convert the text to outlines (Type: Create Outlines). If you are using more than a single text character as your mask, you will need to make the entire text string a compound path (Object: Compound Path: Make). Then apply one of the two masking techniques described above. (See later in this chapter for a masking lesson with type.)

MASK PROBLEM-SOLVING STRATEGIES

There will be times when a mask doesn't work quite

right, or when Illustrator won't let you make an object into a mask. Here are some of the more common problems you may encounter when working with masks.

- **If a type character isn't turning into a mask, try converting it to outlines.** Select the character using a selection tool (not the Type tool) and choose Type: Create Outlines.

- **The text made into outlines and then into a mask hides everything including the text.** This occurs after you've converted text into outlines (see above) and tried to mask using multiple letters. Because only the topmost object can be the mask, the last letter of the text is the only one that acts as the mask. First, you must make a *compound path* of the entire text string (see the *Type* chapter for an example of masking with text).

- **You're trying to make a mask, but a dialog box says "selection cannot contain objects within different groups unless the entire group is selected."** This means that the objects you're selecting as a mask are only part of a group. Cut and Paste In Front (with Paste Remembers Layers checked *on*), then make the mask.

- **Moving a mask from one layer to another stops the masking effect.** Moving a *clipping path* (see earlier in this chapter) will release the masking effect. You'll need to select and reapply the masking command.

- **You're having trouble getting a masked object to print.** On a copy of your artwork, select the masking objects. As long as your masked objects don't contain strokes or raster images, apply Pathfinder: Trim to automatically trim hidden areas of the artwork (see the Pathfinder charts in the *Lines, Fills & Colors* chapter). This can make it easier for the file to print.
Note: *Trim deletes stroke styles and does not work on linked or embedded images!*

Finding masks

Deselecting all objects first and choosing Edit: Select: Masks should help you find most masks; this doesn't always work if you have placed or embedded images.

Memory intensive masks

Too many masks, or complex masking paths, may demand too much memory and prevent you from printing. To test whether a specific mask is the problem, select it and its masked objects, temporarily Hide them (Object: Hide) and then try to print. Hiding the mask will free up memory. **Note:** *Hiding only the mask will not alter the masking effect over the objects.*

If you want this vignette effect using an opacity mask made from a gradient mesh object, you'll need to do a little work with your opacity mask

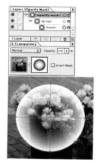

First, add your gradient mesh object to the opacity mask. Notice the Layers palette switches to the opacity mask

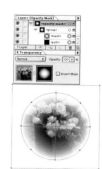

Finally, add a solid black shape behind the mesh object to hide the rest of the image or object you are trying to mask

Another handy tip: if you don't have the money for a large monitor (or better yet two monitors), buy a multi-button mouse and assign Shift+Tab to one of the mouse keys to easily hide all of the palettes.

Handy keyboard shortcuts

With the Keyboard Shortcut dialog (Edit: Keyboard Shortcuts), you can assign a shortcut to any tool or menu item. Unfortunately, you can't create keyboard shortcuts for palette options.

Stray points

Selecting a single point accidentally can prevent you from joining paths properly, or might even cause your objects to disappear if you choose Object: Clipping Mask: Make when a single point is the top-most object!

Transparent whites

You will only get the option to save a scanned image as an EPS with transparent whites if you have scanned your image as a Bitmap format, or converted it in Photoshop to Bitmap using Image: Mode: Bitmap (use 50% Threshold Method to get non-dithered black lines and solids). You may have to convert your image to Grayscale first before converting to Bitmap.

ADVANCED OPACITY MASKS

Using gradients, blends or gradient meshes in your opacity masks can create awesome transparent vignette effects (see the *Transparency* chapter introduction for more on basic opacity masks). Although worth the effort, the effect can cause some problems. First, Illustrator will become very slow. It will appear as if you haven't done anything, when you really have. Give the application plenty of time to think about the masking operation. Second, unlike Photoshop's layer masks, Illustrator's opacity mask does not automatically fill the outside area. Therefore, if you use an ellipse, oval or other non-rectangular shape you will need to create another shape that covers the image or object completely (like an additional rectangle filled with the masking color).

VECTOR BASED FILTERS
Hatch Effects

Hatch Effects allow you to apply textural effects to vector objects. Select a solid or gradient-filled object and choose Filter: Pen and Ink: Hatch Effects to open a complicated dialog box with endless possibilities. (See lessons and Galleries later in this chapter for examples of how to use this filter, as well as artist Victor von Salza's wonderful explanation "Victor V's Wow! Hatches.pdf" on the *Wow!* disk.)

Creating textural effects is just one way to use this filter. You can also create small illustrations that contain a few varying elements. For example, if you are drawing a tree, create a few simple leaves of different colors and shapes (avoid using groups or compound paths). Select the leaf art and make a new hatch pattern from the art (Filter: Pen and Ink: New Hatch) and click the New button. With the Pen tool, draw a shape to fill with the leaves. While the path is still selected, choose Filter: Pen and Ink: Hatch Effect. Choose the hatch you just added from the Hatch pop-up and then start making adjustments in the dialog. Once you've achieved the desired effect you can save it as a new setting. If you don't like the hatch effect you have created, immediately undo and try again (see the Tip at right, "Help with Hatch Effects" for where to go for more details and examples).

Photo Crosshatch

Photo Crosshatch (Filter: Pen and Ink: Photo Crosshatch) converts grayscale rasterized objects (such as photos) into vectors that simulate grayscale hatch effects with black lines. Use the histogram sliders to move the shadow and highlight points, and to adjust the density of hatches in specific tonal regions of your image. To get more detail from the filter, start with a larger sized image—but remember, the more detail, the more RAM you'll need. Since there are so many adjustments to choose from (and no preview!), work on a *copy* of your image, adjust the options one at a time to see how they'll affect your image, and undo immediately if you don't like the results. For examples of Photo Crosshatch artwork, see the final Gallery in this chapter for work by Adam Z Lein, and the *Web, Multimedia & Animation* chapter for work by Daniel Giordan.

Help with Hatch Effects

Hatch Effects are probably the most cryptic interface in illustrator (after graphs!), so if you want help deciphering the variables, see "Victor V's Hatches Explainer" in the Training folder on the *Wow!* disk. See the Galleries at the end of the chapter, and "Organic Creation" in the *Brushes* chapter for examples of applied Hatch Effects.

Colorful Masking

Fitting Blends into Custom Shapes

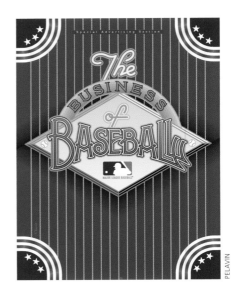

PELAVIN

Advanced Technique

Overview: *Create a complex blend; mask it with a custom masking object; create a second mask-and-blend combination; make a two-object mask using compound paths.*

GRACE

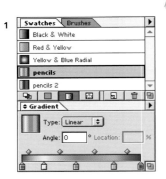

The gradient for a pencil body

Creating objects and blending them in pairs, then creating an object to use as a mask

Selecting the blends with an overlying object designed as a mask; the objects masked

The best way to learn how to mask is to make some masked blends. With Laurie Grace's pencils, you'll learn how to mask complex blends to fit into custom shapes. And with the patriotic corners of Danny Pelavin's baseball illustration, you'll learn how to mask one blend into two different objects by using compound paths.

1 Creating the basic elements not requiring masking. Create your basic objects. For her pencils, Grace created the long barrel of the pencil with a gradient fill.

2 Creating the first mask-and-blend combination. To prepare a mask for the pencils, create a closed object outlining the shaved wood and pencil tip, and Lock it (Object menu). To ensure that your blend will completely fill the mask, make sure that each created object extends beyond the mask. Then select and blend each pair of adjacent objects (see the *Blends & Gradients* chapter). Grace created the slanted outside objects first and the center object last so the blends would build from back to front towards the center. Unlock your pencil-tip object, choose Object: Arrange: Bring to Front, select the blends with the mask object and choose (Object: Clipping Mask: Make). Then Group the mask and blend together (Object menu).

3 Preparing the next masking objects and mask. Select and copy your mask, then select and lock the mask with the masked objects to keep from accidentally selecting any of them as you continue to work. Next, use Paste In Front to paste a copy of your previous mask on top, and make any adjustments necessary to prepare this object as the next mask. Grace cut and reshaped a copy of the full pencil-tip mask until it correctly fit the colored lead at the top. Hide this new mask-to-be (Object: Hide Selection) until you've completed a new set of blends.

4 Creating a new mask that overlays the first. Create and blend new pairs of objects as in Step 2. When your blends are complete, reveal (Object: Show All) your hidden masking object and Bring to Front to place the mask on top of these latest blends. Then select the colored-tip blends with this top object, make a mask as in Step 2 and, as before, Group them together for easy reselection. Finally, Unlock the first blends (Object: Unlock All), select the entire piece and Group it all together.

5 Making a mask from a compound path. Create a blend to be masked by two objects. As Pelavin did for his patriotic corners, start with a circle as a template. In Outline mode, use the Pen tool with the Shift key to draw a straight line from the circle's center point to its bottom edge. With the Rotate tool, Option-click/Alt-click on the circle center to specify an 11.25° rotation and click Copy. Then choose Object: Transform: Transform Again seven times to repeat the rotated copy a full quarter of a circle. Recolor every other line and blend from one to the next, as above. Next, create two paths for a mask (Pelavin cut and joined quarters of concentric circles) and choose Object: Compound Path: Make. Place the compound path on top of the blends, select them all and choose Object: Clipping Mask: Make to see your blend show through both compound paths. Pelavin recolored a copy of the red blend with a range of whites, masked the white blend with a larger arc and placed it behind the reds.

Completed objects selected and locked, then a copy of the last mask made into a new mask

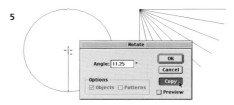

New objects before and after blending, and after being masked

Rotating a copy of a line about a circle's center 11.25°, then Transform Again 7 times

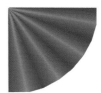

Coloring every other line and blending in pairs

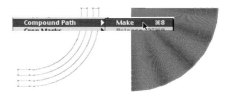

Compounding paths and getting ready to mask

Blends masked by compounds and a final corner (shown here also with a masked white blend)

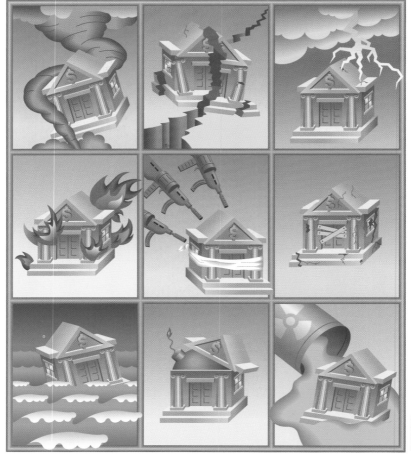

BATELMAN

Kenneth Batelman

Kenneth Batelman used masks to fit blends into contoured shapes all throughout this "Banking Disaster" illustration. Shown directly above are the stages of creating the flames, from making pure blends, to masking with a flame shape, to layering flames upon flames. Batelman used a similar technique to fit blends within a poured shape for the glowing,

radioactive slime, and to shape the tornado funnel. He also used masks to create splits in the earthquake

image (each split contains an entire bank, masked to show only the desired portion), and in the clouds and waves.

KANZLER

John Kanzler

In this illustration, John Kanzler's goal was to simulate the variable-width outlines that a cartoonist paints with a sable brush. To create the tentacles, Kanzler first drew a spiral with the Spiral tool, then copied it and used the Pen tool to join the original and the copy together. Then he moved points on each path with the Direct-selection tool, distorting their shapes. Next, Kanzler copied the tentacle object and pasted the copy behind the original. With the background object still selected, he used the Scale tool to enlarge the copy, and the Shear tool to skew it. He filled the bottom object with dark blue and the top object with light blue, leaving a variable-width "stroke" at the edges. To further shape the tentacle, Kanzler grouped the objects and then selected the Free Transform tool to slant and compress the tentacle. (See the *Lines, Fills and Colors* chapter for more on using the Free Transform tool.)

Contouring Masks
Using Masks to Control Realistic Tonality

Overview: *Create the full outline for your image; copy an object representing a surface; create a blend and mask it with the copy of the surface object; use simple lines as accenting details.*

KELLEY

Many of the shapes would serve as masks for blending

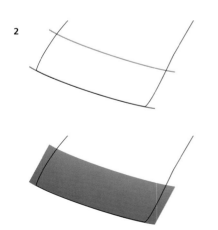

Two stroked paths (top) were blended (bottom) to create shading for part of the front surface of the PDA

For some purposes, gradients can make the smooth color transitions of light and shadow needed for a photo-realistic image. But many of the shapes you will model will have complex or curved surfaces that can best be modeled with masked blends. Andrea Kelley used masked blends to define the gentle curves, smooth edges and tapered sides of this Apple Computer PDA.

1 Creating outlines. Draw an outline version of your image, constructing each surface as a single closed object. You can draw all of the objects on a single layer, then use the Release to Layers option in the Layers palette menu to automatically distribute each object to its own separate layer. For each shape that requires a masked blend, select its layer and lock the others (see the *Layers* chapter if you need help with basic layer functions covered here).

2 Making blend objects. To create the blend, draw two objects whose shapes follow the contours of the surface object; alternatively, copy the object and use the Scissors or Knife tool to cut the copy into the pieces (open paths) you need as blending objects. Now, select the two paths and blend (Object: Blend: Make).

3 Masking and editing blends. To mask the blend inside the surface, select the surface object in the Layers palette and drag it above the blend object (but keep it on the same layer as the blend object). Select the layer in the Layers palette (it will highlight) and then click the Make/Release Clipping Mask icon at the bottom of the palette; Illustrator automatically masks the blend with the top object on the layer (in this case, the surface). If the blend doesn't fill the surface object, reshape the blend by Direct-selecting and adjusting points in one of the original blend objects.

When you create blends that lie in front of or next to other objects (for example, the highlight blend on the side of the stylus is positioned on the barrel), you can smooth the transition between the blended object and a neighboring object by matching the ending color of your blend with the color of the neighboring object. To do this, select the blend object and then click on the neighboring object with the Eyedropper tool.

When working on an illustration where many of the objects lie close together, use the Layers palette to lock and hide objects (by clicking on the palette's lock and eye icons) when you have finished masking their blends.

4 Accenting details. Carefully analyze the surfaces of your object to identify shape and lighting details. Kelley often uses thin lines in dark or light colors to create simple contrasting highlights and shadows.

Transform gradients into masked blends

To transform a gradient into a masked blend, expand the gradient (Object: Expand) and specify the number of steps; the gradient will be replaced by a masked blend.

3

The Layers palette showing the masking object (<path>) above the blend object

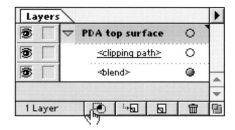

The Layers palette after clicking the Make/Release Clipping Mask icon

The masked blend

4

Before and after: light stroke added to show reflection on stylus tip and thin dark stroke added to show groove on stylus barrel

Dark and light strokes defining edges of the PDA's surfaces around the icon panel

Reflective Masks

Super-Realistic Reflection

Advanced Technique

Overview: *Move a copy of a blend area; if you're using type, convert it to outlines; skew and adjust it to the right shape; use filters to make an offset; recolor and remask blends; move blend back into position.*

1

A blended area selected and a copy moved off the image area 5" (using Shift-Option/Shift-Alt and cursor-keys set to .5" increments); and type converted to outlines

2

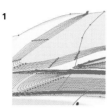

Skewing outlined type, then adjusting and coloring it to fit the blend contour

Creating reflections for an "outline" by copying the outlined type object, then stroking and choosing Object: Path: Outline Stroke and then Unite in the Pathfinder palette

Two techniques in earlier chapters demonstrated how Thomas•Bradley Illustration & Design (T•BI&D) used the Pathfinder palette to generate its basic objects for blending, and how the blends themselves are formed (see "Unlocking Realism" in the *Blends & Gradients* chapter). This technique focuses on replicating contouring blends to create reflectivity and surface variation.

1 Replicating an area of your image for placing new details. This process can be used to create color or surface variations, but we'll use the application of type detailing as a demonstration. After you've outlined your image and filled it with contouring blends, choose an area for detailing. With the Shift key down, use Selection and Group-selection tools to select all blends and originating objects for the blends that exist in that area. To move a copy of these blends out of the way, set the Cursor-key distance to .5" in Edit: Preferences: General. Now hold Shift-Option/Shift-Alt and press the → key to pull a copy of the selected blends 5" to the right (10 times the cursor-key distance). To move this copy further, use Shift → to move the selected blends in 5" increments, or use → alone to nudge in .5" increments. With the Type tool, place a letter or number on top of the moved blend (see the *Type* chapter for help). Click a Selection tool to select the type as an *object* and choose Type: Create Outlines.

2 Reshaping type to fit your blended contours and creating an offset. Working from templates, references or just your artistic eye, use the Rotate, Scale and Shear tools with Direct-selection to adjust various anchor points until the type fits the contour. For the type on the race car, T•BI&D skewed the letters (by clicking first in the center of a baseline, grabbing above right, and Shift-dragging to the right). Then they Direct-selected individual points and groups of points, moving them into the visually correct positions.

To create the outlining effect, first copy a solid-filled version, then set the stroke in the desired weight and color. While this object is still selected, choose Object: Path: Outline Stroke, then Unite in the Pathfinder palette.

3 **Pasting the original back on top, designing new colors for copies of the older blends and masking the new versions.** First, Paste In Front the original, unstroked type element. Next, select and Lock blends or objects that won't fall within the detail (Object: Lock), but that you want to keep for reference. Copy and Paste In Front each of the source (key) objects for new blends and recolor them for your detailing. To recolor a blend, Direct-select each key object you want to recolor and choose a new color—the blend will automatically update! As necessary, recolor each pair of key objects using the same procedure (bear in mind, blending between *Spot* colors results in *Process* in-between colors). T•BI&D recolored the car blends for the red **3**, then added a tear-shaped blend for more detail. Select and copy (in Outline mode if necessary) the original **3**, use Paste In Front, press the Shift key and click to add the new grouped blends to the selection, then choose Object: Clipping Mask: Make. Group and Hide these finished masked objects and repeat the recoloring of copied blends, masked by a top object for any additional highlights and shadows. Choose Object: Show All when these masks are complete, group all the masks together and use the cursor-keys to snap this group of reflective details into position. T•BI&D created one more version of the **3** for a dark offset. For areas requiring more reflections, they constructed even more masks upon masks, as well as occasionally applying compound-masks (see "Colorful Masking" earlier in this chapter).

3

Re-creating blends in new colors and preparing to mask them with a copy of the "3" on top

With the red, reflective blends masked, creating a darker, offset "3"

The dark "3" and the entire group of objects complete, before and after being moved back into position with cursor-keys

Other elements require more stages of blending (see "Colorful Masking" in this chapter for compounding multiple objects, like type elements, to apply as a single mask)

FERSTER

FERSTER

Gary Ferster

In creating a product illustration, Gary Ferster strives to combine realism with a dramatically appealing view of the product. For the Jeep and the sneaker, Ferster began by scanning photographs of the products and placing these grayscale TIFFs on template layers (see "Digitizing a Logo" in the *Layers* chapter). On layers above the templates, he drew the objects' outlines with the Pen tool and then drew blending objects, created blends, and masked them with copies of the outlines. For each sneaker lace, Ferster created several dark-colored blends overlaying a light background. Then he masked each of the blends and background with the lace outlines.

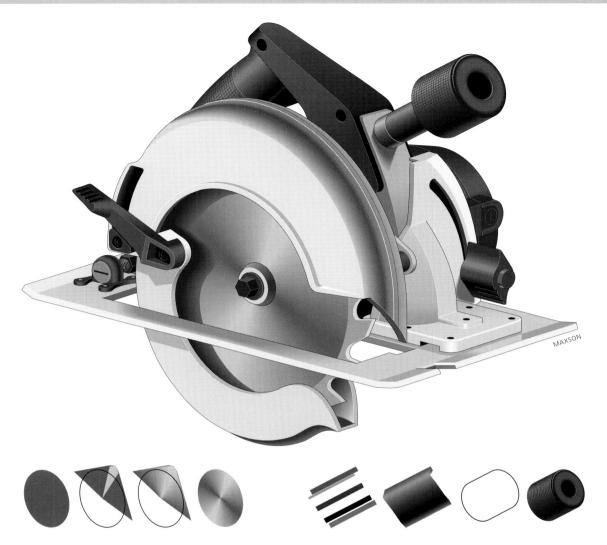

MAXSON

Greg Maxson / Precision Graphics

Illustrating the metal surfaces of this circular saw required Greg Maxson to create overlapping blends. For the blade, Maxson began with an ellipse filled with a dark gray. Next, he created two blending objects, one filled with the same dark gray as the ellipse and the other (on top) filled with a light gray. Maxson blended these to create the highlight and shadow. He used the Reflect tool to create a copy of the blend for the bottom half of the blade. He copied the dark gray ellipse and used the ellipse to mask both blends. For the round grip, Maxson created five blend objects, and blended between them to form the grip's surface. He masked these blends with an object built by connecting ellipse shapes (the cylinder and the circular face at the end of the cylinder) to form the grip.

Glowing Starshine

Blending Custom Colors to Form a Glow

Advanced Technique

Overview: *Create a custom color for the background and the basic object; scale a copy of the object; make object adjustments and blend a glow.*

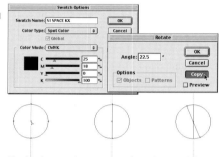

1

The background spot color; dragging a guide to the center of a circle, drawing a center line and rotating a copy of the line

After pressing ⌘/Ctrl-D six times, making guides and adding anchor points at guide intersections

2

After Shift-Option/Shift-Alt scaling the circle smaller and changing the center to 0% tint; Direct-selecting and moving top, bottom and side points outward

Before and after a 12-step blend

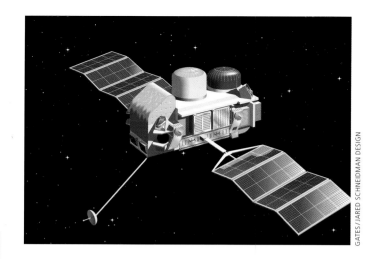

GATES / JARED SCHNEIDMAN DESIGN

Illumination is the key to creating a realistic nighttime sky. This variation on a technique by Guilbert Gates and Jared Schneidman Design (JSD) will help you create glowing lights, not just stars, simply and directly.

1 Creating a custom color and the basic object. Create a background rectangle filled with a dark, spot color. JSD's background was 25% C, 18% M and 100% K. In Outline mode, make a circle, then drag a guide from the ruler until it "snaps" to the circle's center (the arrow turns hollow). With the Pen tool, click on an edge of the circle where the guide intersects, hold Shift and click on the other edge. Select this line, double-click the Rotate tool, specify 22.5° and click Copy. Press ⌘/Ctrl-D to repeat the rotate/copy six times, then select only the lines and choose ⌘/Ctrl-5 to make the lines into guides. Use the Add-anchor-point tool to add eight points, one on each side of the circle's original points at guide intersections.

2 Creating the glow. With the circle selected, use the Scale tool to make a smaller copy of the circle (hold the Shift and Option/Alt keys) and specify a 0% tint fill in the Color palette. Direct-select the top point and Shift-drag it outward. Repeat with the bottom and two side points. With the Blend tool, click on corresponding selected points from each circle and specify 12 steps.

MORRIS / SAN FRANCISCO EXAMINER

Christopher Morris / *San Francisco Examiner*

Christopher Morris created "Mafia Chef" for a *San Francisco Examiner* story about a Mafia member who, after entering the Federal Witness Protection Program, wrote a cookbook and then went out on tour promoting it, only giving interviews in clandestine hotel rooms. To create this darkly satirical illustration, Morris constructed blends that fit roughly into compositional outlines that he had drawn with the Pen tool. He then used his compositional outlines as masks to fit the rough blends snugly into these contours. Shown directly above, (from left to right) is the chef, constructed only of blends (notice that the blends stick out in various places), next with the contouring masks in place, and then, after being masked. Also shown is the corner with the steaming pot, before and after masks were applied.

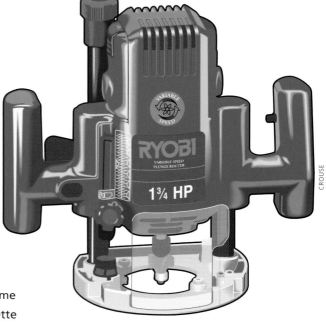

CROUSE

Scott Crouse

Scott Crouse finds masked objects cumbersome to work with, so he uses the Pathfinder palette to eliminate his masks. After completing the illustration of the router itself, he used the Pen tool to draw an object defining the Plexiglass shield. Then, with the Selection tool, he selected the lower third of the illustration (encompassing the base and the shield), created a new layer and placed a copy of this selection into the new layer by Option/Alt-dragging the colored square (at the right of the current layer) to the new layer. Crouse then locked the original layer, selected and copied the path drawn for the plastic shield, and applied Edit: Paste In Front and Object: Hide Selection to this pasted copy. Next he selected all (⌘-A) and chose Object: Clipping Mask: Make to turn the shield object (the topmost object) into the mask for the rest of the selected art. Crouse then grouped the entire selection, hid the selection edges (⌘-H), and chose Filter: Colors: Saturate

and desaturated the colors. With the objects still selected, he chose Crop (Pathfinder palette) to use the top object (in this case the mask) to cut away and delete everything outside the mask. Although using the Pathfinder tools reduces the number of objects in your illustration (which means smaller file size, easier selections and faster printing), you won't be able to reshape the mask—so make sure the shape of the mask is final and correct. (Also, Crop will delete strokes, so only perform this action on unstroked objects.) To finish this illustration, Crouse chose Object: Show All to reveal the hidden copy of the shield. This object was then cut in two places—the top part was stroked with white, and the bottom part was stroked with a dark gray to depict the lighting along the edges of the Plexiglass shield.

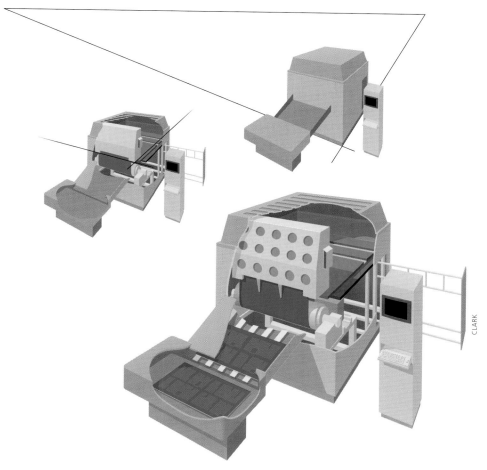

K. Daniel Clark

To create this "plate maker" for *Publish!* maga-zine, K. Daniel Clark began with a variation of the perspective guides covered in "Varied Per-spective" in the *Layers* chapter. With the Pen tool, Clark drew three lines: one horizontal line and two vanishing lines (one facing right, one facing left). Instead of converting these lines to guides, Clark kept the lines as paths so he could direct-select a free anchor point (not the van-ishing point on the horizon line), and swing that line to a new location. Using these lines as guides, Clark constructed the exterior on an upper layer, and the internal components on the layer below. To create the cut-away illusion, he set the upper "exterior" layer to Outline mode and locked it, then cut away the exterior objects with the Scissors tool in order to expose the objects below. For finishing touches, Clark connected the cut objects with the Pen tool, gave the walls some thickness, created shadows and highlights, and placed additional details within the plate maker and processing tray. He deleted the perspective lines in the version of the image that he sent to the client.

Painterly Effects

From Gradient Lighting to Painterly Trees

Advanced Technique

Overview: *Create an illustration in full outline; use filters and manual cut and join tools to separate sections and soften edges containing gradients.*

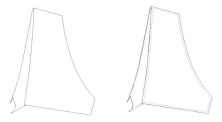

Outline view of original roof outline, and after choosing Offset Path (Object menu)

2

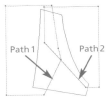

Path 1 and Path 2 objects before and after applying the Roughen filter

A copy of Path 1 selected with Path 2, then after choosing Minus Front in the Pathfinder palette

Copies of Path 1 and Path 2, and after the paths have been united, with a third path added

Some circumstances require more than just filling each object with a gradient fill (see the *Blends & Gradients* chapter for gradient help). Clarke Tate's night rendering of Mann's Chinese Theater for *USA Today* demonstrates using layered gradients upon gradients, and using filters to transform hard-edged objects into more painterly effects. Throughout this lesson, when you see a Pathfinder command, click on that icon in the Pathfinder palette.

1 Making inset subsections of architectural objects and filling them with different gradients. With the Pen tool, create detailed outlines of your image, using templates if desired (see the *Layers* chapter for detailed help with templates and layers). Since you'll be filling with gradients, make your outlines completely closed paths. Select a simple object, such as a roof, and create an inset copy of it. Choose Object: Path: Offset Path, and specify −6 pt (if you're working on a smaller scale, chose a smaller inset). With this path still selected, choose Pathfinder: Unite, deselect the inner part of the inset (hold Shift and click it with the Group-selection tool), then Delete any extraneous objects left by the filter.

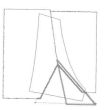

After the Minus Front filter, and before using Intersect on the last roughened shape

2 Creating roughened divisions to diminish contrast between gradients. Start by selecting the roof inset and hiding everything else (⌘-Shift-Option-3 for Mac, Ctrl-Shift-Alt-3 for Win). You're going to split the roof into four pie-shaped sections so you can vary the gradients within the roof. With the Pen tool, draw closed Path 1, which will surround the entire left side of the roof, bisecting two-thirds of the roof vertically and angling back toward the left so that it forms the left side of a "peace sign." For closed Path 2, surround the entire right side of the roof, creating the right side of the peace sign and overlapping Path 1.

Before and after the Crop filter

Select both paths, choose Filter: Distort: Roughen, and specify a 15% size and 30 segments with the Corner option. Make a new layer and place a copy of Path 1 on that layer by selecting Path 1 and Option/Alt-dragging its dot in the Layers palette into the new layer. Shift-select Path 2 as well and choose Pathfinder: Minus Front to cut the copy of Path 1 from Path 2.

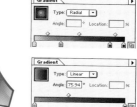

The roof after being cut into sections and filled with custom gradients, and customized with the Gradient tool

3 Creating the bottom of the roof sections. You'll be using the Pathfinder palette for this step. Make a new layer, select Paths 1 and 2 and place copies of these paths in the new layer. With the paths still selected, choose the Unite Pathfinder. Next, on a lower layer, create a triangle that extends beyond the bottom of the roof and overlaps Path 1 and Path 2. Then Shift-select the united path on top, and again choose Pathfinder: Minus Front to cut the united path from the triangle.

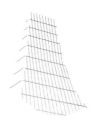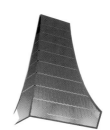

Outlining paths to fill them with gradients

Draw a last triangle surrounding the right half of the bottom section, choose Filter: Distort: Roughen using the

The final roof in Outline and Preview modes

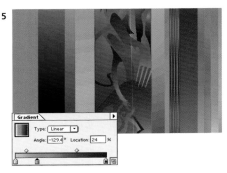

A detail of the tower and a gradient, shown in both the Gradient and Swatches palettes

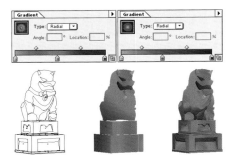

The main and "recessed" gradients for the lion, shown in Outline mode, then progressively filled with gradients

Progressive stages of theater detail and the taxi-cab gradient

previous settings. Now drag a copy of the bottom section to another layer, Shift-select the last triangle and choose the Pathfinder: Intersect. To fit all these objects within the original roof inset, drag a copy of the roof inset to the top layer. Shift-select all four sections of this copy, set a temporary fill style and choose Pathfinder: Crop.

4 Designing the roof lighting effects. To represent different lighting conditions that affect a roof surface, design some custom gradients (see the *Blends* chapter). Tate used two basic color ranges for the roof: a bright, wide-ranging, yellow-to-red radial, and a dark, linear gradient in a range of red-browns. Use the Gradient tool to customize each of the fills ("Unified Gradients" in the *Blends* chapter), then Group (⌘-G/Ctrl-G) the roof elements.

Next, with the Pen tool, create stroked lines following the vertical slope of the roof and Group them. Using a thicker stroke, create tiling lines that follow the horizontal slope of the roof and Group them. Finally, select both the horizontal and vertical lines (with the Selection tool) and choose Object: Path: Offset Path to convert these strokes to filled paths. Now fill each group of "lines" with gradients, unifying them with the Gradient tool.

5 Filling and customizing overlapping objects with multicolored gradients. More detail in an image requires the creation of more overlapping objects. Again, because you'll be filling these details with gradients, make sure to create closed objects. As you work, Group related objects together for easy reselection.

Design new gradients for different ranges of light and surface in other parts of the theater. Since you've grouped related objects together, Direct-select individual objects to fill each with a gradient. As with the roof, use the Gradient tool to customize each fill (again, see "Unified Gradients" in the *Blends* chapter). For his tower wall, Tate created elaborate multicolored gradients. For the lion, he used two radial gradients: one with a wide color and value range, while the shadow gradient is in dark tones.

6 Creating the front canopy for a painterly tree. Make the basic object for your tree canopy, copy it, and Lock it (Object menu). Paste In Front the copied canopy and apply these commands and filters, in this order: Object: Path: Add Anchor Points, twice; Filter: Distort: Roughen (specifying a 5% size, a detail of 10 segments, Corner option); and the default Filter: Stylize: Round Corners.

The original canopy, and after applying Add-anchor-points, and the Roughen and Round Corners filters

7 Creating the back canopy and "holes" for branches. Object: Unlock the original, undistorted canopy and, while it's selected, apply the Add Anchor Points filter three times (use Edit: Keyboard shortcuts to assign a shortcut!), then Filter: Distort: Roughen (specifying 5%, 10 segments, Rounded). Fill each shape with different solid colors so you can distinguish them. Make a new, irregularly shaped object to use as a hole in the front canopy. Select this new object and the front canopy and choose Pathfinder: Minus Front. Then create another object to use as a hole in the back canopy, of roughly the same size and location, but shaped differently enough so you can see parts of the back object while still seeing through to your background. Select this object with the back canopy and again apply Minus Front (⌘/Ctrl-4 applies the last used button in the Pathfinder palette).

Roughening the back and cutting holes

8 Creating the trunk and branches. Start with a 4-pt stroke weight and no fill, and draw a basic trunk with the Pen tool. For branches, create paths of progressively smaller stroke weights as you move up the tree, then group the branches with the trunk and transform these lines into filled objects with Object: Path: Outline Path. Now taper the objects of the trunk and branches, and fill each portion of the tree with custom radial gradients.

Adjusting outlined paths for trunk and branches

9 Creating the leaves. For the finishing foliage, Lock the tree and create random-sized, light-colored circles with the Ellipse tool. Select all the circles, group them and apply Filter: Distort: Roughen (specifying 60%, 10 segments, Rounded). Direct-select to refill individual leaves.

Making leaves from filtered circles

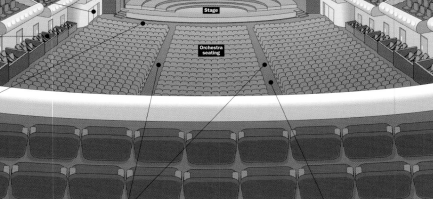

New side walls above stage and terrace consisting of 88 panels constructed of molded fiberglass and steel tubes filled with 66 tons of sand for acoustical density

New stage lighting above terrace level

Side and center terrace seating raised and angled

Side doors have been replaced by four wider doors on Orchestra level

New box seating on the sides and back orchestra level with private vestibules and new box-level bar

Increase of disabled seating from 34 to 64 seats (mostly in front 3 rows)

59-panel adjustable plexiglass canopy above the stage

Quadratic resonating diffusers around stage area and along back walls of orchestra section

New cherrywood grill-work stage walls raised and backed with sound diffusers and reflectors

Other improvements

▶ New sound and color video systems
▶ Orchestra and chorus risers
▶ Replacement of 'bullnose' projections in stage area with solid cherry-wood lips and caps surrounding the stage
▶ Upgrade of ventilation systems
▶ Modification of pit elevator to create new piano lift
▶ Refurbish-ment of orchestra lobby
▶ New burgundy-colored carpeting throughout the hall

Stage

Orchestra seating

SOURCE: San Francisco Symphony

EXAMINER/JOE SHOULAK

Addition of two aisles on Orchestra level reconfigured for better access and the elimination of 320 seats, reducing capacity from 3,063 to 2,743

New parquet floor on Orchestra level with new wood subfloor for acoustical purposes

Joe Shoulak / *San Francisco Examiner*

For this illustration detailing the renovation of Davies Symphony Hall, Joe Shoulak drew the first row of seats, then duplicated, moved, darkened, rotated and skewed it. He then blended the two rows using 18 steps. Shoulak then selected and grouped the left seats, and, with the Reflect tool, he Option-clicked (Alt-click for Win) to the right of the seats to specify a reflection along the vertical axis, and clicked Copy. For the panels that made up the Plexi-glass canopy, he skewed, scaled, and reflected rounded rectangles.

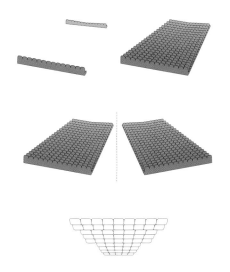

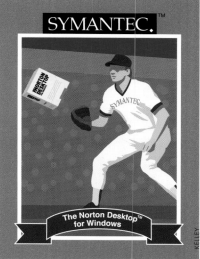

Andrea Kelley

For a series of promotional baseball cards produced for Symantec Corporation, Andrea Kelley developed a system to distort the dozens of logos and pictures that needed to be placed onto boxes in an identical turned-angle perspective. Kelley first drew a box using the Pen tool, then grouped (Object: Group) and scaled (using the Scale tool) her first logo to a rectangle the size of the angled placeholder on the box (see the *Zen of Illustrator* chapter for help with scaling objects). Because the turned face was thinner than a box front, she double-clicked on the Scale tool to specify 85% horizontal (100% vertical) scaling. She dragged the logo by its upper left corner until it snapped to the upper left corner of the turned face. With the Rotate tool, Kelley then clicked on the

upper left point of the logo again, grabbed the upper right corner and swung it up until it aligned with the top of the box. Next, with the Shear tool, she clicked once more on the upper left corner of the face, grabbed the lower right corner and, holding the Shift key, swung it down until that line aligned with the spine of the box. After moving the logo into alignment with the left corner of the spine and top of the box, she aligned the lower right corner to the box by clicking Reset, moving the lower right corner up the minimum amount and applying Filter: Distort: Free Distort twice. Finally, she held the Opt (Mac) or Alt (Win) key and chose Filter: Distort: Free Distort again to reset, then slid the right corner to the left a minimal amount.

WEIMER

Alan James Weimer

Alan James Weimer achieved the detailed symmetry in this design by using features of Illustrator's Rotate tool. He began by making a circle, which he divided into sections with guides. Then he created individual elements of the design, such as the smaller butterfly, by drawing half of the butterfly with the Pen tool and making a copy for the other side with the Reflect tool. Next, Weimer positioned the butterfly on one of the guides, selected the Rotate tool and Opt/Alt-clicked the cursor once on the centerpoint of the circle. In the dialog box he entered "360/8" (to have Illustrator calculate 360°÷8, the total number of butter-flies he wanted), and clicked Copy. He pressed ⌘-D (Ctrl-D for Win) to continue copying and rotating six more butterflies around the circle.

WEIMER

Alan James Weimer

To make the two medallions for a horizontal "tile" (right), Alan Weimer used the circle-and-guides technique described on the opposite page. After arranging the medallions and other elements to form the tile, he Opt/Alt-dragged the tile to the right to form the first row. To create the repeating pattern, Weimer diagonally Opt/Alt-dragged copies of the first tile row onto a grid of guidelines to form rows above and below the first row. To "crop" the design, he drew a rectangle on the same layer as the tiled design, and, at the bottom of the

Layers palette, clicked the Make/Release Clipping Mask icon. On a layer above the mask he added a border composed of blended, stroked rectangles.

Diane Hinze Kanzler & Sandee Cohen

Starting with Diane Hinze Kanzler's goldfish illustration (near right), Sandee Cohen used the Pen and Ink filter to add texture. The coral was given a plain pink fill. The Pen and Ink filter was then applied using the "Swash" hatch. The same hatch was also used on the top fin. The body of the fish was created using the "Dots" hatch. The two tail fins were filled with the "Wood grain" hatch. The pectoral fins were filled with the "Vertical lines" hatch, set for different angles. The ventral fins were filled with the "Worm" hatch. Finally, a hatch was defined for the bubble. Then a large rectangle was created over the entire illustration and filled with bubbles. (**Hint:** The bubble could also be a Scatter Brush; see "Organic Creation" in the *Brushes* chapter.)

KANZLER / COHEN

Kevin Barrack

Kevin Barrack began "Batik Dancer" by applying Streamline to his scanned drawing (see the *Illustrator & Other Programs* chapter). In Illustrator, he filled the body shapes with gradients (see the *Blends & Gradients* chapter), and on a separate layer, he created blob shapes for the background. In another layer, called "Ink Pen," he created a new blob object with a green fill. To this object he applied Filter: Pen and Ink: Hatch Effects, and set Hatch=Worm; Match Object's Color; Density=75%; Dispersion=Constant 180%; Thickness=Constant 70 pt; Scale=Linear 56–610%, 270°; Rotation=Random 10–180°; Fade=None; and the fourth color square in the indicator scale. Lastly, Barrack added thick strokes to the black solid-filled shapes outlining his figure.

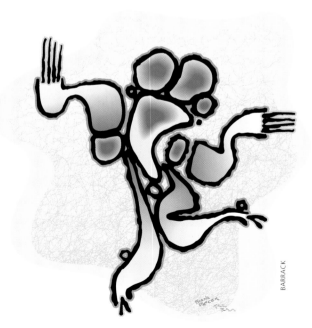

BARRACK

Adam Z Lein

Artist Adam Z Lein used Illustrator's Photo Crosshatch filter (Filter: Pen and Ink: Photo Crosshatch) to convert this grayscale TIFF image to a crosshatched illustration that is composed of black, 24-point long strokes.

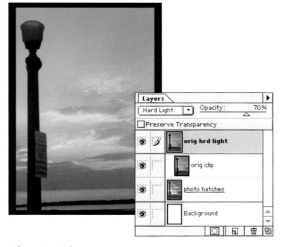

Adam Z Lein

After applying the Photo Crosshatch filter in Illustrator, Adam Z Lein rasterized the hatches by placing them in Photoshop and combining them with two copies of the original photo (see the *Illustrator & Other Programs* chapter for more on rasterizing Illustrator artwork).

Illustrator & Other Programs

10

Illustrator & Other Programs

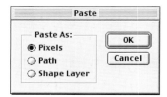

Paste dialog when you're pasting paths from Illustrator into Photoshop 6.0; a shape layer retains the vector characteristic of the path

This overview chapter demonstrates techniques for using Illustrator in conjunction with other frequently used programs. Examples of most of the topics presented in this introduction follow in the lessons and Galleries. One of this chapter's highlights is a step-by-step technique for bringing Illustrator images into Photoshop, as demonstrated by renowned artist and author Bert Monroy.

ILLUSTRATOR, PHOTOSHOP & RASTERIZATION

You can easily rasterize objects at any resolution from within Illustrator (see Tip "Rasterizing in Illustrator" to the left), though Photoshop is still the preferred way to rasterize high-resolution images. If you need to use Photoshop to rasterize an Illustrator document that includes linked images, you have two choices. The first option is to use the Links palette pop-up menu to embed the linked files, then save this file with a new name and open it with Photoshop to rasterize at the desired resolution. Alternatively, you can export your file to Photoshop 5 format. (See "Exporting Illustrator to Other Programs," later in this introduction.) When you export to Photoshop 5 format you can choose to save layers (nested and top-level) and editable text.

ILLUSTRATOR, DIMENSIONS & STREAMLINE

Two other Adobe programs that are popular with Illustrator users are Dimensions and Streamline. Dimensions allows you to create 3D-looking files that you can edit in Illustrator, or you can import Illustrator files to distort in 3D space. Streamline converts bitmapped images into vector art and is much more sophisticated at autotracing than Illustrator's Auto-trace tool. With Streamline, you can quickly create line art for comps. A number of artists are also using Streamline creatively to translate scanned drawings or photos into Illustrator art that looks very different from what the original looked like.

ILLUSTRATOR PATHS & OTHER PROGRAMS

In addition to being able to bring Illustrator *objects* into other programs, you can import and export Illustrator *paths*. Corel Painter lets you import Illustrator paths as "friskets" (stencils), which isolate regions of your image so you can apply painting and other effects selectively. **Note:** *Before importing paths as friskets, use the Pathfinder: Merge filter (not Effect) on a copy of the image to eliminate path overlaps.*

Photoshop allows you to create Illustrator-like paths and Layer Clipping Masks (which are vector shapes). Layer clipping masks are used to mask content-generated layers, or to create Shape Layers. By holding down the ⌘ / Ctrl key and dragging to a Photoshop window, you can import an Illustrator path into Photoshop, where it can become a Photoshop selection, a clipping path for masking image areas (see Tip "Illustrator and clipping paths" to the right), or a Layer Clipping Mask. In addition, any Photoshop path can be brought to Illustrator by either copy-and-pasting it in, or by exporting it as a path.

You can import Illustrator paths into 3D programs to use as either outlines or extrusion paths. Once you import the path, you can transform it into a 3D object. Strata's 3D StudioPro, Lightwave 3D and Ray Dream Designer are three of the many 3D programs you can use in combination with Illustrator.

DRAG & DROP OR COPY & PASTE

Any program that supports PostScript drag and drop behavior will accept Illustrator objects. Depending on the application you're dragging or pasting Illustrator objects into, you'll either paste in paths or raster objects. In the case of Strider Software's TypeStyler 3, you can freely drag and drop objects to and from both Illustrator and TypeStyler 3. With Photoshop, you're given the choice of pasting pixels, a path or shape layer.

When you are dragging and dropping, your Illustrator art will automatically be rasterized at the same physical size, or pixel-per-inch ratio you have specified in the

Illustrator and clipping paths

Just as you can use clipping masks in Illustrator to define irregularly shaped boundaries for your object, or for an entire image (see the *Advanced* chapter), a number of programs allow you to use Illustrator paths to create a clipping path. These paths define the boundary of an image when it's placed in other programs. Shown below is Photoshop's method of assigning a clipping path.

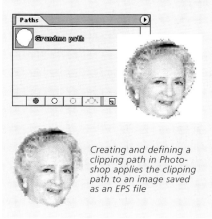

Creating and defining a clipping path in Photoshop applies the clipping path to an image saved as an EPS file

Extracting a clipping path

A raster EPS image with a clipping path displays as if it's cropped by the clipping path (see Tip "Illustrator and clipping paths" above) as long as it's *linked*. If you *open* the image, or *embed* it (using the Links palette), then the clipping path will convert to a clipping mask (see the *Advanced* chapter). **Note:** *The mask will have many more points than it did as a clipping path!*

raster-based program to which you are dragging the art. In addition to dragging and dropping paths from Illustrator to Photoshop, you can also do the reverse.

Note: *Print designers should be aware that dragging and dropping raster images from Photoshop to Illustrator results in only 72-ppi RGB files. Instead, save your Photoshop file as a TIFF or EPS and place it into Illustrator to preserve the desired resolution and color mode.*

You can also copy and paste paths between Illustrator and Adobe LiveMotion. Paste in an object from Illustrator, defined with RGB values of 0:0:0. With the object still selected in LiveMotion, open the Color palette and choose a color to colorize the black object. Colorizing your objects in LiveMotion allows you to change them without having to return to Illustrator and repaste.

When you are copying from Illustrator and pasting into Adobe InDesign, artwork that contains transparency settings or effects will be flattened and rasterized (see section "Exporting Illustrator to Other Programs" in this introduction.)

RASTER IMAGES IN ILLUSTRATOR

You can create image objects (raster images embedded in an Illustrator file) either by rasterizing Illustrator objects, or by placing a raster image such as a TIFF, EPS, PICT or JPEG file and choosing Embed Image from the Links palette pop-up menu. In contrast to *linked* images, embedded image objects can be permanently altered. The Links palette keeps track of both types of images in your document (see the *Basics* chapter).

Different file formats allow you to save different information with the file. For example, EPS format allows you to include Clipping Paths, which open as Clipping Masks when you embed them into Illustrator (see the Tip "Extracting a Clipping Path" on the preceding page, and the "Tinting a Scan" lesson in the *Transparency* chapter). EPS black and white images also allow you to save with "Transparent Whites" (see "Layering Colors" in the *Layers* chapter). With embedded black and white TIFF images, on the other hand, you can set a fill color to replace the black pixels (see Tip at right).

When deciding whether to use embedded image objects or linked image files, you'll need to consider a number of factors. First, since embedded images become part of your Illustrator file, your file size increases with each image you embed. An embedded image takes up almost twice as much disk space as a linked image.

Another argument in favor of linking instead of embedding files is that you can make changes to a linked file and re-send only that linked file to the service bureau or client. As long as it has exactly the same name it should auto-update without further editing of the Illustrator image itself.

Linking is not, however, a good choice if your file might have to be opened in a previous version of Illustrator. If you're transporting or color-separating files containing placed images and your client or service bureau doesn't have the most recent Illustrator version, all the linked images must be in EPS format. No matter which method you choose while your files are in process, to decrease the chance for errors you should replace embedded image objects with linked EPS files for final printing.

EXPORTING ILLUSTRATOR TO OTHER PROGRAMS

With Illustrator 9, Adobe has greatly improved the options for saving, importing and exporting to other formats. You can save directly in AI, EPS or PDF file format, and several other file formats can be selected through the Export command.

Note: *In EPS, unlike other formats, saving with the current program version compatibility will not sacrifice any editing capabilities.*

Now that many more formats are supported, you should make certain that you understand which format is most appropriate for the program into which you're exporting your Illustrator file. To place your Illustrator image into a page layout program such as QuarkXPress, you must save a copy of your image as EPS or export it as

Colorizing 1-bit TIFF images

If your image is a black and white 1-bit TIFF, you can change the color of the placed image in Illustrator. Select the placed TIFF file and set a color to replace the black pixels. The white pixels will be transparent. —*Sandee Cohen*

Photoshop filters in Illustrator

Most of the Photoshop-compatible filters aren't available to you unless your document is in RGB color space. Be aware that converting your document back and forth between RGB and CMYK will muddy the colors in your illustration. If you are primarily creating an illustration for print, work in CMYK. If you are primarily creating an illustration for Web or multimedia, work in RGB. To convert a copy of your file from one color space to the other, choose File: Document Color Mode and choose your color mode.

So you think it's linked?

If you apply a filter or an effect to a *linked image*, Illustrator will automatically *embed* the image. In addition to increasing the file size, you will no longer be able to update the link.

Resolution of placed images

Greatly reduce your printing time and ensure optimal image reproduction by properly setting the pixel-per-inch (ppi) resolution of raster images before placing them into Illustrator. The ppi of images should be 1.5 to 2 times the size of the line screen at which the final image will print. For example, if your illustration will be printed at 2" x 2" in a 150-line screen, then the resolution of your raster image would typically be 300 ppi at 2" x 2". Get print resolution specifications and recommendations from your printer *before* you begin your project!

The power of Adobe Acrobat

Acrobat's Portable Document Format (PDF) is platform and application independent—this means the format allows easy transfer of files between Mac and Windows.

Settings for Export and Saving

Illustrator 9 provides many exciting new features, but offers very little in the way of help for how to save your files for optimal output. Gone are the days when Illustrator EPS format images required merely a choice of whether or not to embed fonts. There are no fewer than 5 resolution settings that you have to be aware of. Please see the *Tech Notes* appendix for our settings for output.

TIFF. With Adobe PageMaker and InDesign you have the unique ability to place native Illustrator formatted files. However, when placing files with transparency settings, effects or a clipping mask, you should save the file as EPS and then place that file into InDesign.

To export an Illustrator file to Photoshop 5 format, choose File: Export, and then Format: Photoshop 5 as the file type. Select the desired color model, resolution, and whether or not you want to anti-alias the artwork. In addition, you can Write Layers (with or without maintaining their nested layer structure and/or editable text attributes) and Include Hidden Layers. Each layer will contain a rasterized version of the objects. These layers can be used not only in Photoshop, but along with Adobe's ImageReady, AfterEffects and Premiere (see the *Layers* chapter).

To save your file for use in Adobe Acrobat, simply choose Save As and select PDF format. If you want to edit the objects later in Illustrator, check Preserve Illustrator Editing Capabilities. PDF files created by other programs can be edited in Illustrator, however, text may be broken up and strokes will be converted to filled paths.

For details about the Save for Web features, please see the *Web, Multimedia & Animation* chapter.

© Bert Monroy 1999

MONROY

Bert Monroy
(Photoshop)

Bert Monroy capitalized on layered, resolution-independent artwork that he created in Illustrator and brought into Photoshop to create this image of a neon sign. In the image, Monroy used techniques similar to those detailed in his *Pic n Pac* image (see the lesson "Sketching Tools" on the next page) and in his Rendezvous Cafe image (see the *Brushes* chapter). Monroy's techniques for creating 3D images from 2D software are illustrated in his book, *Bert Monroy: Photorealistic Techniques with Photoshop & Illustrator* (New Riders Publishing).

Sketching Tools

Illustrator as a Primary Drawing Tool

Illustrator with Photoshop

Overview: Create your details in Illustrator; place Illustrator images into Photoshop at the right size; render and finish in Photoshop.

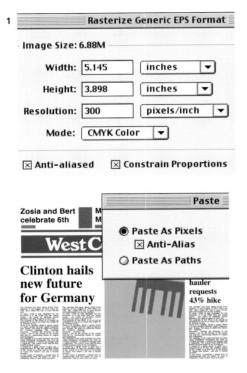

MONROY

© Bert Monroy 1995

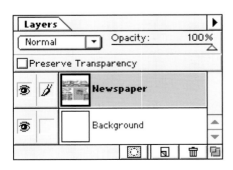

Three ways Illustrator images can be brought into Photoshop: opening, pasting and placing

When artist Bert Monroy paints one of his signature realistic scenes, he calls on Illustrator's resolution-independent precision and counts on Photoshop's high-resolution rasterization of Illustrator artwork. Monroy constructs his Illustrator images in flat colors and then brings them into Photoshop, where he can rework them into scenes rich in texture, light, shadow and volume.

1 Bringing detailed Illustrator images into Photoshop.
There are a number of ways to bring Illustrator images into Photoshop. First, from within Photoshop, choose File: Open and select an Illustrator or EPS file. Specify the size and resolution at which you plan to rasterize (turn

into a bitmap) the image. Second, copy the image in Illustrator, and paste directly into Photoshop, choosing to paste as Pixels. Pasting as Paths creates a working path, useful in defining a selection, or to serve as a clipping path for artwork masks. Third, if you have an image open in Photoshop, use the File: Place command, which lets you resize your Illustrator image visually before it is rendered into pixels. With the Place command, you can visually resize your Illustrator image before it is rendered. Fourth, with Illustrator 9 or later, Export as a Photoshop 5 file, which preserves the layer structure of the Illustrator file.

2 Measuring in Photoshop and resizing in Illustrator.

One of the greatest strengths of bringing Illustrator images into Photoshop is that you can render the maximum amount of detail at any resolution. If you resize (smaller or larger) a rendered Illustrator file, you'll sacrifice detail, so the key is to bring Illustrator files into Photoshop at exactly the right size. If simply using the Show Rulers command isn't exacting enough, in Photoshop, measure the space into which you'll place an Illustrator file. First open the Info Palette, then choose your Line tool, set the minimum opacity (1%) or line width to 0 pixels and, with the Shift key down, click and drag from the one side of the space to the other. While doing this, note the value in the Info palette representing the horizontal (ΔX) distance you just measured. In Illustrator, first make certain that "Scale Strokes & Effects" is enabled in General Preferences. Then, select the object you want to move into Photoshop and resize it to fit the space you just measured. In the Transform palette, enter the X value as the new width (W), making sure to hold ⌘ for Mac or Ctrl for Win as you press Return to maintain proportions (or, you could note the ΔY to enter as the height).

Monroy's preferred method is to prescale and copy his selection in Illustrator, switch to his Photoshop file, then select the area into which he wants to paste and then choose Edit: Paste Into.

2

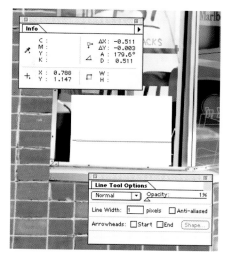

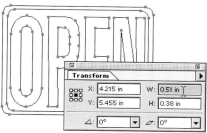

An Illustrator image; next measuring the space for pasting from within Photoshop; then scaling the image to the right size in Illustrator

After selecting an area, using Paste Into to place the copied Illustrator image within the selection (Monroy then moves the image around within the selected area, and deselects it to make it part of the main image, or places it onto its own layer)

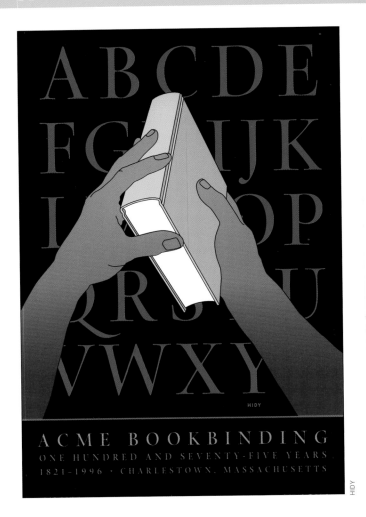

Lance Hidy
(Photoshop)

Illustrator Lance Hidy photographed hands holding a book several times until he had a "natural" pose. He scanned the photograph and, in Photoshop, lightened the shadows and other dark tones in the image before printing it. On this print, Hidy drew outlines of the hands directly using a fine-tipped pen. Then he scanned the marked print and placed the resulting TIFF file in Illustrator as a tracing template. He was able to clearly follow the contours and

details of the hands as he traced with Illustrator's Pencil tool.

Ron Chan
(Photoshop)

Illustrator Ron Chan began this illustration for the Catellus website by employing many of the same Illustrator techniques described in the "Cubist Construction" lesson (in the *Lines, Fills & Colors* chapter). After drawing and filling objects with color, Chan brought the artwork into Photoshop, where he selected individual elements and added textures to lend the illustration a more organic look. A similar look can be achieved using Effect menu commands, along with transparency and opacity masks (see the *Transparency, Styles & Effects* chapter for help with the Effects, the Transparency palette and opacity masks.)

MORRIS (illustration), STOREY (photography) / SAN FRANCISCO EXAMINER

Chris Morris / *San Francisco Examiner*
(Photoshop)

For an article discussing issues of copyright protection with the advent of digital imaging, Chris Morris created an illustration using black, closed objects in Illustrator. Where he wanted eventually to place photographs, Morris created black-stroked, white objects as placeholders. Morris opened the Illustrator image in Photoshop, then from another file, he selected and copied a scanned photo of Peter Gabriel, shot by *Examiner* photographer John Storey. In the main rasterized image, he used Photoshop's Magic-wand tool to select the first placeholder for the photo and chose Edit: Paste Into. While the selection was still active, Morris used Effects (Scale, Skew, Perspective and Distort) to fit the photo properly within the selected space before he "stamped it down." Morris repeated this procedure for each image he wished to place. (Hint: In Illustrator, try using colors not used anywhere in your image as placeholders, making it simple to pick up these colors with the Magic-wand tool within Photoshop.)

FISHAUF

Louis Fishauf / Louis Fishauf Design Limited (Photoshop)

For this image about e-commerce, Louis Fishauf brought Illustrator objects into Photoshop, where he created transparency and blurring effects. Fishauf filled the credit card and house front objects with white in Illustrator. Then he pasted them into the Photoshop file and built gradation layer masks to simulate progressive transparency in the objects. Besides using Illustrator-drawn objects as compositional elements in Photoshop, Fishauf also used the objects to create underlying glows (this can be done with Photoshop's layer effects). Some of the same effects can be created with Illustrator 9. (See the *Transparency, Styles & Effects* chapter for more on transparency and opacity masks, and on glow and blur Effects.)

DONALDSON

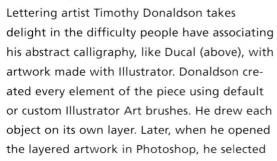

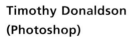

Timothy Donaldson
(Photoshop)

Lettering artist Timothy Donaldson takes delight in the difficulty people have associating his abstract calligraphy, like Ducal (above), with artwork made with Illustrator. Donaldson created every element of the piece using default or custom Illustrator Art brushes. He drew each object on its own layer. Later, when he opened the layered artwork in Photoshop, he selected objects, applied blurs and drop shadows and adjusted transparency. Beginning with Illustrator 9, some of these Photoshop treatments can now be achieved using the Effect menu and the Transparency palette. (See the *Transparency, Styles & Effects* chapter for more on the Appearance and Transparency palettes and the Effect menu.)

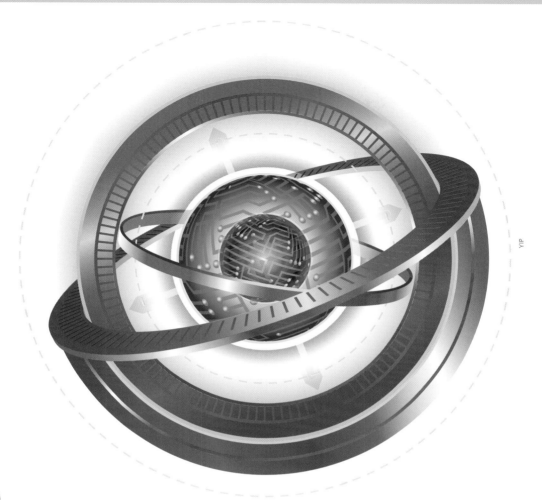

YIP

Filip Yip
(Adobe Dimensions)

Illustrating computer network hardware that encompasses worldwide service, artist Filip Yip converted flat artwork into 3D objects in Adobe Dimensions and then enhanced them with lighting effects he created with Illustrator gradients. Yip drew the compass tick marks and circular rings in Illustrator, copied and pasted them in Dimensions, and then extruded and angled them as 3D objects. He copied and pasted the objects back into Illustrator where he selected separate surfaces and filled them with gradients, adjusting gradient angles so that highlights fell where he wanted within the composition. Yip drew the transistors and wires of a computer chip in Illustrator and then mapped them to a sphere in Dimensions. He copied the spherized chip and pasted it in Illustrator, and then drew a radial gradient behind the chip to convey the image of a highlighted sphere.

JONES

Joe Jones/Art Works Studio (Photoshop)

To depict plowed fields in a logo for Irish Gold Potatoes, Joe Jones created a "corduroy" pattern using a variation of the default Scroll Pen Art brush. Starting by applying his Scroll Pen brush stroke to a simple line (above left), he expanded the brushed line into grouped and outlined objects (Object: Expand Appearance). While the group was still selected, he filled it with a custom gradient (see the *Blends &*

Gradients chapter). Jones duplicated the original brush group to create a line of objects. Using the Free Transform tool (see the "Distort Dynamics" lesson in the *Lines, Fills & Colors* chapter), he shaped the artwork to match the contour of each patch of farmland. Jones exported the finished Illustrator file (directly above) into Photoshop where he applied the final effects (main image).

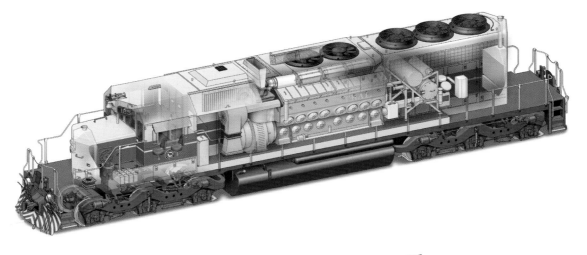

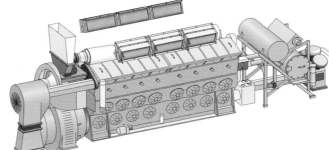

Rick Johnson / Kalmbach Publishing Co.
(Photoshop and Adobe Dimensions)

Rick Johnson illustrated this EMD diesel-electric locomotive for *Trains* magazine using engineering drawings, photographs and field notes. First he drew the front, top and side view objects in Illustrator as "flat" surfaces. Then he built a cube in Dimensions that conformed to an Off Axis view, copied and pasted it in Illustrator as a template. Next, he used the Scale, Shear and Rotate tools to distort the flat surfaces to the angles of the cube template. After distorting the surfaces, Johnson assembled the surfaces into 3D shapes and organized the illustration by placing interior and exterior shapes of the locomotive on their own layers. When he brought the layers into Photoshop, he selected the layer with the interior surfaces and airbrushed the cut-aways on its layer mask, exposing the locomotive's interior details. To increase or decrease the size of the cut-away, Johnson airbrushed or erased areas of the layer mask, preserving the layer's artwork in case it was needed later. (See the *Transparency* chapter for more on making opacity masks in Illustrator that you can use for cut-aways.)

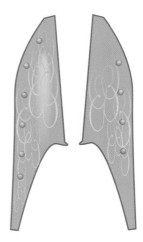

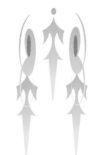

SPOLLEN

Christopher Spollen / MoonLighting Press
(Photoshop and Adobe Dimensions)

Chris Spollen developed Rocket Scientist as a lesson for a class he was teaching and later turned it into a signature piece for his website. To begin the piece, Spollen opened a scanned public domain image in Photoshop and then adjusted its brightness and contrast. Next, he cleaned up the image using Photoshop's Rubber Stamp tool and applied a tint. He saved the black-and-white image as a TIFF and placed it in Illustrator. Spollen drew most of the other elements in the image as simple objects in Illustrator. For the rocket, he drew flat artwork that he then copied and pasted directly into Adobe Dimensions. He used Dimensions to rotate the flat artwork 360° to create the cylindrical rocket object. Spollen copied the rocket and pasted it in Illustrator, where he decorated the fins and body with symbols from the Zapf Dingbats font that he converted to outlines (Type: Create Outlines).

GROSSMAN

Wendy Grossman
(Photoshop and Adobe Dimensions)

Wendy Grossman brought a Bird of Paradise flower and a bowl from Panama to this composition, titled "Mexico." She began by sketching the layout and then scanning the sketch and placing it in Illustrator as a template. To make the maracas, Grossman constructed the basic shapes and their decorations in Illustrator. Then she brought the artwork into Adobe Dimensions where she turned the flat shapes into 3D objects and mapped the decorations to the surfaces. Grossman copied the maracas and pasted them in Illustrator. Then she rasterized the layered Illustrator file in Photoshop, compositing it with scans of the Bird of Paradise and the bowl, and reworked the entire image using painting and retouching tools. Many of the effects Grossman achieved in Photoshop, like the drop shadows and blurs, can be duplicated using the Effect menu and the Transparency palette. (See the *Transparency, Styles & Effects* chapter to learn more on using Illustrator's Effects and transparency.)

STILLMAN

 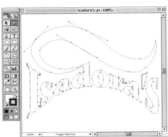 

David Stillman
(TypeStyler 3)

David Stillman needed to create a rich-looking logo for Isadora's Cafe but only had an hour to complete the job. To get the custom shaped look of cast gold, he used the shaping and styling power of TypeStyler 3 combined with the path editing tools in Illustrator. First, he made two text objects in TypeStyler. Using TypeStyler's Shape Library, Stillman selected a double-arched shape for Isadora's and a top-arched shape for Cafe, so that the two fit together. Next, he dragged the Isadora's object directly from the TypeStyler window into an open Illustrator window. This gave him the shaped headline already converted to outlines. He then used Illustrator's path editing tools to draw a simple flourish across the top of the headline and attached it to the top of the letter **d**. Stillman then dragged the entire graphic from Illustrator back into TypeStyler where he finished the logo by choosing Gold from the Style Menu and applying it to both Isadora's and Cafe objects. The whole process gave just the results he was looking for, yet took less than fifteen minutes to complete, including saving the final Isadora's Cafe logo as a 300 ppi Photoshop document from TypeStyler.

IVAN TORRES

Ivan Torres
(Virtual Mirror's Vector Studio Plug-in for Illustrator)

Torres used several gradient meshes to achieve the realistic translucency and perspective effects seen in this piece (see his lessons "Mastering Mesh" in the *Blends & Gradients* chapter, and "Masking Opacity" in the *Transparency* chapter for details about his mesh methods). To create the bottle, he combined two gradient mesh objects, one for the color and shape and the second as an opacity mask to allow a range of transparency levels. In Illustrator, Torres used Virtual Mirror's Vector Studio's Envelope Mesh plug-in to distort the type on the ribbon, label and shingle. The image at top right shows the original Vector Shoppe text, the envelope he created with Envelope Mesh matched to a series of concentric ovals, and the resulting letterforms. The image at bottom right shows the original and foreshortened versions of the bottle's label. See the *Wow!* disk for a demo version of Vector Studio.

FRIDBERG/MILES FRIDBERG MOLINAROLI (design), COSGROVE (illustration)

Dan Cosgrove *(illustration)*, **David Fridberg** *(design)*
(QuarkXPress / digital file transfer)

For a poster announcing the Smithsonian Institution's 1994 Jazz Orchestra Series, David Fridberg commissioned Dan Cosgrove to create the original illustration. The only problem was this: Fridberg lives in Washington, DC, and Cosgrove lives in Chicago, and the schedule was too tight to allow for even overnight courier, so the file had to be digitally transferred. Cosgrove created rough sketches directly in Illustrator, then digitally transferred them to Fridberg for comments. With quick feedback, Cosgrove was able to complete the illustration for the poster in record time. Cosgrove created each musician in his own layer, making it simple for Fridberg to select and copy any of them by hiding and showing the appropriate layers (see the *Layers*

chapter for help). With the final illustration received in DC, Fridberg used a combination of Illustrator and QuarkXPress to complete the design for this two-sided, fold-out poster. He created all graphic text (titles and the text on a curve) in Illustrator, although he decided to assemble the full poster from within QuarkXPress. (Hint: Since this *Wow!* book is produced in QuarkXPress, in order to fit the large (14" x 20") poster onto this page, I used the File: Save Page as EPS option, then resized the placed page in QuarkXPress.)

JACKSON / SAN FRANCISCO EXAMINER

Lance Jackson / *San Francisco Examiner* (Adobe Streamline)

To achieve the hard-edged, yet painterly look in this image, Lance Jackson sketched with traditional drawing media, then scanned the drawings into the computer at both high and low resolutions. In Streamline, Jackson translated both resolutions into Illustrator format. Opening both translated files in Illustrator, Jackson then combined them, mainly using the lower-resolution version while copying and pasting details from the higher-resolution version (the face and hands, for example). Finally, Jackson selected and recolored individual objects until he achieved the final effect in this illustration entitled "Doper."

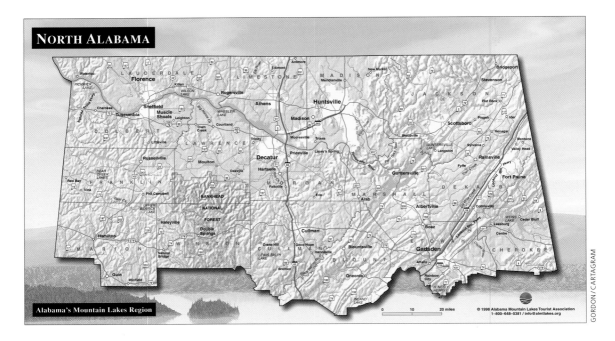

NORTH ALABAMA

Alabama's Mountain Lakes Region

0   10   20 miles

© 1998 Alabama Mountain Lakes Tourist Association
1–800–648–5381 / info@almtlakes.org

GORDON / CARTAGRAM

Steven Gordon
(Painter, Bryce, MAPublisher, Photoshop and FreeHand)

For this map of northern Alabama, cartographer Steven Gordon downloaded terrain data from the Internet, processed it in a data reader and imported the resulting PICT image into Painter. He built a color gradation and used the Apply Surface Texture command to create the color relief image. (This process is described in "Building a Terrain Map" in *The Painter 6 Wow! Book*.) Gordon couldn't find a photograph that flowed well around the map, so he instead developed the background landscape in Bryce by making an "artificial" terrain and adding surface texture, water and clouds (lower right). Gordon combined the relief and landscape images in Photoshop and then placed this new composite image in Illustrator. Using the MAPublisher suite of filters, he imported map data (roads, rivers, boundaries) into Illustrator,

colorized the linework, resized it to fit the relief, and added symbols and type. To register the Photoshop image with the map's Illustrator artwork, he drew a rectangle that matched the image and turned it into cropmarks with the Make Cropmarks command (see Tip "Creating cropmarks..." in the *Type* chapter). This enabled him to save the national forest shape (lower left on map) as a separate file, import it into Photoshop and use it as a registered selection for masking and darkening terrain in the forest area. (To reduce the number of points in your file, try using Object: Path: Simplify.)

BERGMAN

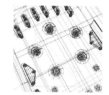

Eliot Bergman
(Photoshop and Alias Sketch!)

Bergman created this illustration for a trade magazine advertisement with a combination of 2D and 3D programs. He took advantage of the precision possible with Illustrator to draft sections, plans and profiles of objects before importing them into Silicon Graphic's Alias Sketch!, a 3D modeling program. He also made color and bump maps in Illustrator, then retouched them in Photoshop. For this illustration, the first step was to draft the the layout of the pinball machine in Illustrator. The elements in this design served both as a template for 3D objects and as a basis for a color map. Bergman used the gradient tool to create the background, and he used a combination of the Star tool (hidden within the Ellipse tool) and the Filter: Distort: Punk and Bloat filter to create the starbursts. Bergman imported the artwork into Sketch! where he created 3D objects by extruding and lathing individual items. After rendering a rough preview image, Bergman added the final maps, colors and lights. He brought the finished rendered image into Photoshop for retouching.

JONES

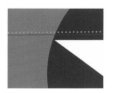

Joe Jones: Art Works Studio
(Ray Dream Studio, Bryce, Photoshop)

In this World War II tribute entitled "West Field Yardbird," Joe Jones used Illustrator artwork as components in building the 3D model in Ray Dream Studio, and as texture maps to cover the model in Bryce. To start the artwork that would serve as texture maps for the metal panel seams, window masks, rivets and other elements of the model, Jones drew objects on separate layers with the Pen tool. Then Jones brought the artwork into Photoshop where he applied edge treatments and simulated the effects of weathering by painting onto the art. Then he flattened and saved the files. In Bryce, Jones imported and mapped the images onto the modeled plane parts. In all, he filled the scene with nearly 3000 Illustrator-drawn objects.

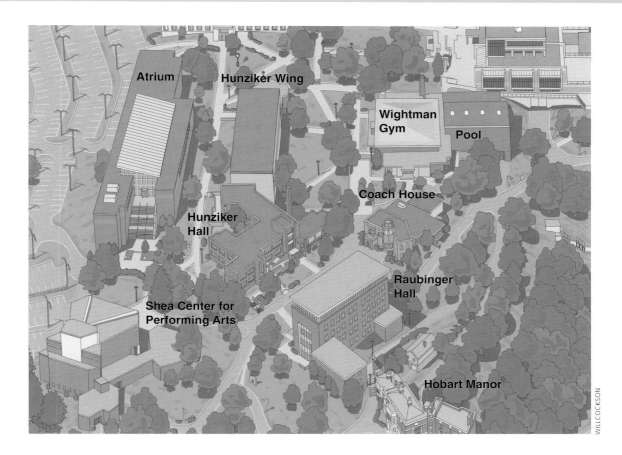

WILLCOCKSON

Tom Willcockson / Mapcraft
(Bryce)

Cartographer Tom Willcockson visited the campus of William Paterson University to acquire photographs, building floor plans and other materials. Then in Illustrator, he built a base map of the campus roads, rivers, vegetation areas, building outlines and other features. After scanning a contour map, Willcockson drew closed contour lines, filling them with gray shades based on elevation. He exported two JPEG images to serve as source images in Bryce: the grayscale contour layer and the base map artwork. In Bryce, Willcockson imported the contour JPEG and generated a 3D terrain image. Then he imported the base map JPEG and draped it across the terrain. He rendered the image and exported it as a JPEG, which he placed on a template layer in Illustrator. He traced the streets, building footprints and other features in Bryce-rendered perspective view. Willcockson drew the buildings, and then added trees and shrubs as Scatter brush objects from a brush library he had created for other maps. (See the *Brushes* chapter to learn about using scatter brushes for map symbols.)

Web, Multimedia & Animation

11

Web, Multimedia & Animation

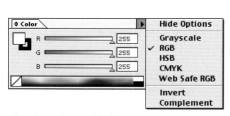

Choosing color models from the Color palette's pop-up menu; you can also cycle through color models by Shift-clicking on the Color Spectrum. Selecting a different color model to mix colors does not change the color mode of the file.

This chapter focuses on how you can use Illustrator to prepare artwork for on-screen display. Almost every aspect of the application has been enhanced to produce better web graphics. Although everything in this chapter relies heavily on Illustrator, some of the techniques also involve working with other applications (see the *Illustrator & Other Programs* chapter).

The actual assembly of animations and web graphics in this chapter was often produced using a number of other programs, including Macromedia Director; Adobe's Premiere, After Effects, and GoLive; Yves Piguet's GIF Builder; Thorsten Lemke's GraphicConverter and Bare Bones Software's BBEdit. Although not all of these are cross-platform, you'll find demos or light versions of some of these programs on the *Wow!* disk. Also, check the *Wow!* website for animations and links to related sites (http://www.peachpit.com/wow.html).

Web designers will not only find that Illustrator supports a wealth of file formats, but also that the workflow for creating web graphics has been simplified. The inclusion of Save for Web in the File menu makes it easy to visually compare compression settings and image quality side-by-side, in a multi-view dialog.

WORKING IN RGB IN ILLUSTRATOR

To create artwork in RGB, first start with a new RGB file (File: New: and Color Mode: RGB in the dialog), then select RGB from the Color palette pop-up menu to set RGB as the color model for the next colors you create. You can also choose a Web Safe RGB palette of colors if you want to create colors that are never dithered when viewed on 8-bit monitors.

A FEW THOUGHTS ON RGB AND CMYK COLOR

• **You can work in any color mode (space) if you're creating *on-screen* resolution graphics.** If you're designing for the web, it's particularly important to keep file sizes to a minimum, and the final files must be in RGB. (See "The Web Swatches Palette" section below.)

- **Don't convert the same artwork repeatedly between RGB and CMYK.** Converting RGB to CMYK forces one range of colors (a gamut) into an entirely different range of colors. This process involves either clipping or compressing certain colors, and can make the colors in your file appear muddy or muted. If you need both CMYK and RGB versions of your artwork, maintain two versions of your art—one in RGB and one in CMYK. To experiment with clipping or compressing colors between gamuts, see the *User Guide* on choosing the appropriate rendering intent in the Color Settings dialog.

- **If you are going to use your artwork for both print and on-screen viewing, create in RGB first and then convert a copy of the art to CMYK.** When you create your art in RGB first, you can choose from a wider range of colors. Then if you want to print your art, convert a copy to CMYK as one of your final output steps.

The Web Swatches palette

Illustrator includes a noneditable Web-safe Swatches palette. Its 216 RGB colors are common to both Mac and Windows platforms, and are the most reliable colors for creating web artwork. To access this palette, choose Window: Swatch Libraries: Web or open the file directly (Window: Swatch Libraries: Other). To create a smaller custom palette from the Web-safe palette, simply drag the desired color swatches to the Swatches palette for storage and save the file. (Remember to clear your palette before you build your custom palette—see "Setting up your palettes" in the *How to use this book* section.)

Note: *Know your target audience. How they will ultimately view your art should direct how you create your artwork. For example, don't choose a Mac system palette if you are creating artwork for a Windows-based intranet site. Your*

Converting CMYK to RGB

If you already have artwork prepared in CMYK and you need to change color mode for on-screen RGB viewing, make sure you first save a copy of your file, then choose File: Document Color Mode: RGB Colors.

Note: *Converting from CMYK to RGB will cause you to lose any association with stored swatches. This means editing swatches will no longer globally update objects filled with those colors.*

Rasterizing art for the screen

The process of turning vector art into a pixel-based image is called *rasterizing.* Anyone creating artwork for the web or for multimedia applications might, at some point, need to rasterize vector art, with the exception of SWF and SVG (see *"SVG"* later in the chapter). The Rasterize dialog (Object: Rasterize) makes it easy to control the rasterization of artwork. You can also rasterize artwork if you apply any of the Photoshop filters or effects.

Save as GIF if your art has large areas of solid color and/or is made up of "vector" graphics (such as Illustrator objects). Export or save as a JPEG if your image includes "raster" images (photos) with a wide range of colors or grays, or if your art contains gradients or gradient meshes. If your image includes a high-contrast photo, or has both large areas of solid colors and images, experiment with different optimizations in File: Save for Web to see which looks best at the smallest file size.

Web pages load faster if all the elements on them share the same palette. You can combine File: Save for Web with the Actions palette to batch optimize GIF files to a custom palette. Make a new file, then copy into it the group of Illustrator files that need to share a palette. Use Save for Web to find the optimum combination of colors and palette size, then choose Save Color Table from the pop-up menu. Close this file, and open one of the individual Illustrator files. Start recording a new Action, then open the file in Save for Web, load the color table and save the file. Now you can run this custom action to automatically process the rest of your GIF files.
—*Cynthia Baron*

art doesn't have to look perfect on every browser, provided you've satisfied the needs of your target audience.

THE ATTRIBUTES PALETTE & URLS

Illustrator's Attributes palette lets you create an image map area and assign a URL (Uniform Resource Locator) to any object, group or layer in your artwork. Creating image maps is an essential tool for web designers because it allows them to create links to other web pages by defining clickable parts of the artwork or image. Illustrator creates a separate text file containing the URL information, which can then be imported into an HTML (HyperText Markup Language) editor such as Adobe GoLive or BareBones Software's BBEdit.

To assign a URL to a selection, open the Attributes palette (Window: Show Attributes), select the type of image map from the Image Map pop-up, and type the URL address into the URL text field (see "Tabs for the Web" later in this chapter for a technique on applying URLs). You can verify whether your URL is correct by clicking the Browser icon in the Attributes palette, which will launch your default web browser and open the link. Finally, export the file using Save for Web with Save HTML selected.

RELEASE TO LAYERS

You now have the ability to take multiple objects or blended objects and distribute each onto its own layer. Having the objects on separate layers makes it easier, for example, to develop animations. *Target* a layer or a group by clicking on the target indicator in the Layers palette (see the *Transparency* chapter)—if you merely select the group this will not work. Next, choose Release to Layers from the palette pop-up menu. Each new layer is created within the current layer or group and consists of a single object. To perform an additive effect, ungroup the artwork and hold down the Shift key before you select Release to Layers. Instead of creating a layer with a single object, each new layer is generated with one less object. You end up with the same number of layers, but what is on those layers is very different.

Note: *If you don't ungroup the artwork, you can still use Release to Layers, but the cumulative effect doesn't happen.*

When releasing objects to separate layers, keep in mind that the order in which they were added to the artboard will determine their stacking order in the Layers palette, and can affect the final animation. The last object drawn is the first object in the stacking order of the new layers. With brush art, it is sometimes hard to predict the order in which each individual object will be released to the layers; the stacking order is dependent on the direction of the path. You can reverse the direction of a path by clicking on the end anchor point with the Pen tool. Blends can be reversed by choosing Object: Blend: Reverse Spine.

EXPORT FILE FORMATS
Save for Web

An important feature for web designers is the ability to export optimized files as GIF or JPEG from the Save for Web dialog. GIF is the most widely used image format on the web. GIF compression works well with vector-based images or files that have large areas of solid color (see the Tip "*GIF or JPEG (raster or vector)?*" in this chapter). GIF files support transparency and interlacing (whereas JPEG only supports interlacing).

JPEG provides a variable level of compression and works best for images with gradients or photos that have continuous tones. Although JPEG is considered a "lossy" format because when you optimize the file size you lose image detail, this trade-off still tends to result in good-quality images, making JPEG a particularly useful format for web designers. It can also be a useful alternative to a PDF file. For example, a JPEG file can be used to transfer a layout for client approval. JPEGs are much smaller than PDFs while sacrificing very little image detail, and smaller files transfer more easily (and sometimes more reliably) via the Internet. Other JPEG options include progressive

Save for Web

The Save for Web export plug-in provides many options for optimizing and saving Web graphics:

- **Tools:** A limited set of tools lets you zoom, pan and sample colors in the original artwork.
- **Views:** Multiple views are available for you to compare compression settings against the final image quality.
- **Settings:** Preset compression settings are easily accessed from the Settings pop-up menu. If you are new to web graphics you might want to start with one of these settings. You will notice that as you select different presets, the options for the specific file type are updated under the Setting grouping. Save your own settings by choosing Save Settings from the pop-up menu.
- **Color Table:** The color table updates the number of colors in the image for GIF and PNG file formats. You can lock colors or shift to a web-safe color by clicking on the icons at the bottom of the palette.
- **Image Size:** To change the dimensions of the final optimized file, but not the original artwork, click on the Image Size tab and enter a new size.
- **Browser button:** To preview the optimized image in a browser, click on the Browser button at the bottom of the dialog.

- **Color Table:** 8-Bit images have a maximum of 256 colors. The Perceptual table is more sensitive to colors that can be seen with the human eye. Selective gives more emphasis to the integrity of the colors and is the default setting.

- **Colors:** You can have up to 256 colors in a color table. However, the image might not need that many. Select a smaller number of colors when you optimize by adjusting the number of colors in the color table. The fewer colors, the smaller the file.

- **Dither:** Blends colors in a limited color palette. Diffusion dither is usually best. Vary the amount of dither to reduce banding of solid areas of color by adjusting the Dither slider. Leave it off for clean-edged vector graphics.

- **Transparency:** Choose this for artwork with irregular edges that you want to put over multicolored backgrounds. To reduce edge artifacts, choose a color to blend with the transparent edges from the Matte pop-up.

- **Interlacing:** Allows viewers to see a low resolution version of the image as it downloads, which continues to build until the image is at full resolution. A non-interlaced image draws one line at a time.

and optimized. A progressive JPEG is similar to an interlaced GIF—it first appears blurry, then builds up with increasing clarity until the image is fully displayed. An optimized JPEG is usually smaller in file size.

Note: *Optimized and Progressive are mutually exclusive. If you check Optimized with a Progressive JPEG, it doesn't do anything.*

To save a version of your artwork as either GIF or JPEG, choose File: Save for Web to adjust the various optimization settings, (see the Tip "Save for Web" in this chapter). First, select a setting or file type from the Optimized file format pop-up and click on the Optimized tab. If you want to compare the compression of two or more settings, click on one of the other views, either 2-up or 4-up. The final file format, size, download time and specifics about the compression are listed under each preview panel. Finally, click OK to save an optimized version of your file. If you have an image map area and URL associated with artwork, select Save HTML. Refer to the *User Guide* for a more complete description of all the format options.

Note: *PNG is an available file format in the Save for Web dialog, but is not yet completely supported by all browsers.*

Flash (SWF) export

Although many multimedia artists and designers use both Illustrator and Macromedia Flash to create web pages, there is no completely foolproof method for bringing artwork from one program to the other. Illustrator now comes with a Flash export module, but as of this writing it has some significant problems, ranging from poor rendering quality to the creation of extra frames and symbols. If you want to create Flash files from Illustrator artwork, your best bet is to import the Illustrator file into Macromedia Flash. You can then create animations there. If you have very simple artwork, you can also use the Flash Export dialog in Illustrator. Here are some strategies for maximizing the quality and usefulness of your Illustrator files in Flash:

- **Use Save As to convert the Illustrator file into the version 7 format.** This converts artwork, such as brushes (which Flash doesn't understand), into discrete objects (which it does). Artwork from later versions, particularly art with gradients, doesn't maintain all of its attributes. If you plan to alter the artwork after you've saved it, save the file as a version 7 file again before you export. Many people feel that this method produces the smallest SWF files.

- **Use flat colors rather than blends, gradients or gradient mesh objects.** You'll make smaller SWF files if you use Flash to add gradient colors. If you must use gradients or gradient mesh objects, recognize that you will be creating bitmapped images which create larger file sizes.

- **If you import or create rasterized art for the Internet,** rasterize at 72 dpi, not the default of 150 dpi, to keep file sizes small.

- **To import a file's layers or paths selectively,** lock and hide the ones you don't want before exporting. (This also works when using the Save for Web controls.

- **If the object you want to export to Flash contains a dashed stroke,** set the opacity of the object to 99.99% and then choose Flatten Transparency. This will convert the dashes into discrete objects that Flash will recognize. Or you can use the operating system clipboard to copy the stroke from Illustrator and paste it into Flash.

- **Choosing Export Layers as Separate Files makes each Illustrator layer into a separate Flash file,** which is the preferred method of exporting elements for animation. However, none of the export methods recognize sublayers, so objects in sublayers will be treated like grouped objects and all will export as part of their highest container layer.

SVG and alpha channels

Don't combine images with alpha channels with SVG. They are rendered as PNG files (not JPEG or GIF) and not all browsers completely support the PNG format!

—*Cynthia Baron*

Transparency and web colors

Even if you've been working in RGB mode with Web Safe Colors Only checked, if you've used Illustrator's transparency in your file you will end up with out-of-gamut shades when you flatten and save your file. Files with extensive transparency use should be saved as JPEG, not as GIF, to avoid excessive dithering.

Web-safe RGB

The new Web Safe RGB Color palette will not display the Out of Gamut warning for CMYK colors, but the RGB color model will.

SWF export

If you are familiar with Flash, you may be tempted to check the Auto-Create Symbols command in the Flash Export dialog box. Warning: Don't! Rather than intelligently creating one symbol that controls all the same objects, Illustrator makes individual symbols for all the objects—making the file terribly large.

—*Sandee Cohen*

SVG export

Illustrator supports the export of Scalable Vector Graphics (SVG). SVG is an emerging standard for saving web graphics that contains a combination of elements such as vectors, gradients, type, raster effects and JavaScript events. SVG is potentially a very exciting file format, because it combines very small file sizes with crisp artwork which, like Illustrator vector art, can be zoomed into and scaled up or down with no loss of quality. Like Flash, in order for exported SVG files to be viewed in a browser, a special SVG viewer (plug-in) is required. This plug-in is automatically installed in your browser when you install Illustrator.

The SVG format supports JavaScript interactivity as well as static image display. However, because of differing interpretations of JavaScript, some browsers (like Internet Explorer for Macintosh) can't yet take advantage of SVG's interactivity. To add a JavaScript event to your artwork you must know JavaScript! Open the SVG Interactivity palette (Window: Show SVG Interactivity); then, with an object selected, choose an event from the pop-up menu, and type a JavaScript command in the JavaScript text field. Select Add Event from the palette pop-up menu to have it added to the list in the lower section of the palette.

SVG files can be saved (File: Export: SVG or SVGZ) with several options which allow you to fine-tune the size and quality of the artwork you create. In almost every case, you should choose Only Glyphs Used for Font Subsetting. This limits embedded fonts to just the characters you used in the artwork. Embedded Font Location lets you choose whether to make your fonts part of the SVG file or to make them external, but linked. For only one or two SVG files, it makes more sense to embed the fonts to maximize the likelihood that they'll be seen as you intended. However, if you create a site full of SVG files that use the same fonts, it might be better to link them. This keeps the file sizes of all your SVG artwork smaller.

Raster Image Location is like Embedded Font Location, but for images rather than type. SVG files can contain JPEG images of placed art or gradient meshes that you can choose to make part of the file, or you can link them if they are used multiple times.

Decimal Places is a little like Illustrator's smoothing tool. You can use it to define how much information is used to display your artwork. Larger numbers provide better quality fidelity to the original artwork, but also result in bigger files. Adobe recommends a setting of 3.

Unless you are creating artwork in languages other than English, choose the ASCII character default. Most European languages can use either ASCII or UTF-8, while Asian languages will probably require UTF-16. Finally, CSS Property Location is an option for saving cascading style sheet attributes.

Choose the default, Style Attributes < Entity References >, which will generate a smaller file size and therefore render faster then the other two choices, Style Attributes and Style Element, both of which will result in larger (slower) files.

Like Flash, SVG requires a plug-in. Therefore, SVG files are not treated as regular image files by web page layout programs like Dreamweaver. Instead, use the < embed > or < object > tags to insert SVG images into your HTML.

Font Subsetting:	Only Glyphs Used
Embedded Font Location:	Embed Subsetted Font
Raster Image Location:	Embed Raster Images
Decimal Places:	3
Encoding:	ISO 8859-1 (ASCII)
CSS Property Location:	Style Attributes (Entity

SVG Options

Making Waves

Transforming and Blending for Animation

Advanced Technique

Illustrator with Photoshop

Overview: *Create "key" frames with transformation tools; blend to create steps; transform your steps; bring the steps into Photoshop.*

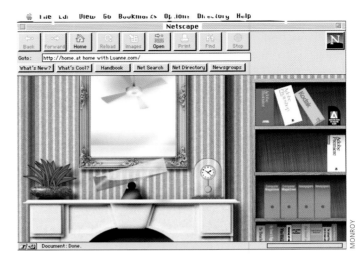

MONROY

1

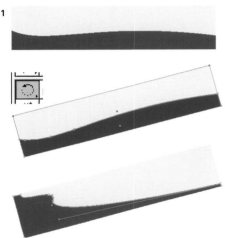

The first key frame; next, Rotating a copy; then using the Add-anchor-point and Direct-selection tools to transform the copy into the next frame

Making certain that the first and last frame have the same number of anchor points in similar alignment for smooth blending (see "Unlocking Realism" in the Blends & Gradients chapter for more on preparing objects for smooth blending)

Illustrator's transformation tools, used in combination with the Blend tool, are wonderful animation timesavers. Commissioned by Adobe Systems for a special promotion, Bert Monroy used these techniques to prepare many of the objects within a room for animation.

1 Establishing the "key" frames. To create an animation, you must first establish the "key" character positions. How many key frames you'll need will depend on the character, and how it will be animated. Create a character in a neutral position, and if you'll need help maintaining registration, draw an unstroked, unfilled bounding rectangle, amply surrounding the character. Select the objects making up the character and the bounding rectangle and Option/Alt-drag a copy to the side of the original. On the copy of the character (*not* the bounding box), use the transformation tools and Direct-selection editing to create the next extreme position (for more on transformations, see the *Basics* and *Zen* chapters). In Monroy's animation, the characters were: fan, clock second hand, clock pendulum, plant, and the "wave." He first drew the wave in horizontal position using a gray rectangle and a second object for the blue liquid. To create the left-tilted position, he rotated a copy of these two objects, then used the Add-anchor-point and Direct-selection tools to adjust the liquid anchor points manually.

2 Using the Blend tool to generate the in-between steps. Also called "tweening," the secret to smooth animation is to create the correct number of steps between the key frames. For video animations, smooth illusion of motion is achieved with 24 frames per second (fps) of animation; for film it's 30 fps; for on-screen animation it's simply as many frames as is needed for your animation to run smoothly. To make the steps between your first two key frames, select each pair of like objects and blend between them (for help with blends, see "Examining Blends" in the *Blends* chapter); you can only apply a blend reliably between two objects, so you'll have to apply the blend separately for each pair of like objects (including your bounding rectangle), making sure that each pair has the same number of anchor points, and that you select the correlating anchor point in each object when blending. For the wave, Monroy first blended in 12 steps from box to box, and then from liquid to liquid. Since the same number of steps was chosen for each transition, the liquid blends were perfectly registered within the box blends.

3 Transforming blends to extend the animation. Rather than continually starting from scratch, it's often easier to rotate, scale, skew or reflect your blends to extend your animation. Monroy selected the blended boxes and waves, and Reflected them vertically as copies (see the *Zen* chapter, Exercise #9) to create the right-side rocking motion.

4 Pasting it into Photoshop. With Illustrator still open, launch Photoshop and create an RGB document larger than your biggest key frame. In Illustrator, copy each character frame and bounding box, and then moving to the Photoshop file, paste "As Pixels" to create a new layer with that step. While that object is still in memory, *also* paste "As Paths" for easy reselection (see "Sketching Tools" in the *Illustrator & Other Programs* chapter). Monroy used his paths to make selections for applying special effects locally—using Alpha Channels to create effects such as the darkening and bubbles in the liquid.

2

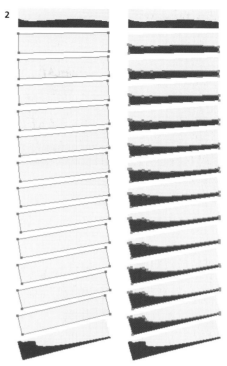

The outer objects after blending (left column), then blending the inner wave (right column)— **Note:** Selecting the upper right point on the wave gives the smoothest blend

3

4

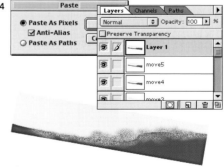

The option to "Paste As Pixels" or "Paste As Paths" when pasting from Illustrator to Photoshop; the frames after pasting into layers; the wave after effects using Alpha Channels

d'JAXN

d'JAXN

Artist d'JAXN began this teddy for the PrintPaks "KidGear" CD by taping his sketch to a Wacom tablet and tracing it with the Pencil tool. After converting those objects into Guides (View: Guides: Make Guides), in a new layer (see the *Layers* chapter) he outlined each of the shapes as separate closed objects with the Pen tool. The floor and the wall were filled with radial gradients (see the *Blends & Gradients* chapter) and overlaid with objects representing wallpaper pattern and floor texture. d'JAXN then separately rasterized (Object menu) at 72 ppi, then filtered each with various Photoshop filters to create texture. All background objects were then merged using Rasterize again, and then filtered together. Teddy was rasterized, filtered and then masked using a copy of the original

paths (for masking help see the *Advanced Techniques* chapter). d'JAXN created a plaid pattern for the footpads, which were rotated and scaled individually (see Tip "Controlling patterns" in the *Lines, Fills & Colors* chapter). To create Teddy's fuzz, he created a Pattern Brush using irregular hatch shapes, then applied it to copied sections of the outline (see the *Brushes* chapter for help). d'JAXN then exported the image as an anti-aliased JPEG (File: Export) at 180 ppi, as specified by the client (in the JPEG Options dialog box choose Custom from the Resolution: Depth pop-up to enter a custom resolution, and check Anti-Alias in the Options section). He used LemkeSoft's GraphicConverter (on the *Wow!* disk for Mac only) to Trim (crop) the image.

GIORDAN

Daniel Giordan / DigiRAMA Studios

Daniel Giordan began this illustration, and the subsequent animation, with a digitized photograph. He placed the image on a layer in Illustrator, and duplicated the layer three times (for a total of four aligned layers, each with the same image). Giordan applied the Photo Crosshatch filter (Filter: Pen and Ink: Photo Crosshatch) separately to each layer, adjusting the filter each time to emphasize a different part of the tonal range. By adjusting the midtone slider of the filter's histogram control, Giordan controlled what portions of the image were filtered. Together, the four layers were filtered to emphasize line distribution in the shadows, midtones, quartertones and highlights. In addi-

 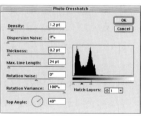

tion, Giordan varied the thickness of the lines on each layer to emphasize specific tonal areas. Once he achieved a balanced tonal range, Giordan selected the hatch lines on each layer and applied a stroke color. To animate the design, Giordan opened the file in Adobe Live Motion and selected Object: Convert Layers Into: Objects. This placed each layer as a separate object in the timeline. To finish the animation, he modified the layer's position and opacity.

Tabs for the Web

Preparing Navigational Web Maps

Overview: *Design your background tile; Create your tabs; design variations on the tabs for each web page; assign URLs; Save for Web as an interlaced GIF*

1

The background tile (yellow added for contrast)

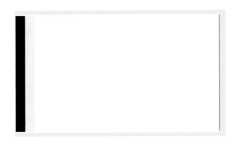

A detail of the background tile at actual size

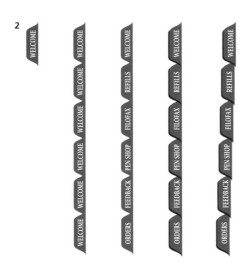

The background tiled to fill the entire screen

2

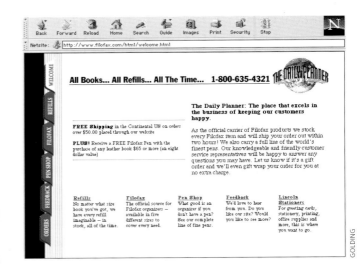

The process of creating one row of tabs

Since Filofax organizers rely heavily on tabs, designer Mordy Golding decided to use tabs as a navigation tool for one version of their Filofax product-ordering website. Illustrator's web-related features make it simple to design these web navigation objects.

1 Designing your background tile. To create a website background image, design a tile that will repeat to fill your visible screen. Almost anything that works as a simple pattern tile should work as a web tile (see the *User Guide* for tips on pattern making). To save download time, Golding created the "page edges" in the left part of the screen as part of the background image tile, which is wide enough so that it only repeats vertically in the browser window.

2 Creating your tabs. Design your first tab using the drawing tools (for help with drawing and tracing, see "Simply Realistic" in the *Lines, Fills & Colors* chapter, and "Digitizing a Logo" in the *Layers* chapter), and with the Type tool, create a center-aligned label for the tab (see the *Type* chapter for type help). Since his tabs were vertical, Golding rotated his text 90° (specified by double-clicking the Rotate tool). Next, Option /Alt-Shift-drag your first tab and label to make a duplicate, then repeat the transformation by pressing ⌘-D/Ctrl-D for a total of as many tabs as you have pages in your website. Correct the labels with the Type tool. Golding created six tabs, each representing a page on the website. He then added a drop shadow and staggered the tabs to give the illusion of depth.

3 Creating different versions of the tabs for each web page. To make it easier for viewers to tell which page they are on, create separate versions of your tabs, each highlighting the current page. Golding duplicated his line of tabs six times (one for each web page), then restyled one tab in each group to appear highlighted.

4 Assigning web addresses (URLs) to each tab. When users click on your tabs in the actual website, you want them to be taken to the correct web address, so you'll need to assign web addresses (URLs) to each non-highlighted tab (since highlights indicate your *current* address, these don't need URLs). With your first tab selected, open the Attributes palette, and in the text field labeled "URL," type in the appropriate web address (use the ← and → cursor-keys to scroll), and repeat this for all tabs in this first set. For the next set of tabs, you'll be able to choose the appropriate URL from the URL text field pop-up menu.

5 Saving the files for an HTML editor. Select, Copy and Paste each set of tabs into their own new document. Save each document separately. Next, to save a rasterized version of each file (for placement in your HTML editor) choose File: Save for Web and select "GIF" from the format pop-up. Golding set the following GIF options: Adaptive Palette (see Tip "Adapting to GIF palettes" earlier in this chapter for Golding's suggested approach for using this option), Interlace (allowing the image to load gradually), Anti-Alias (for smooth, non-jaggy edges) and Transparent (to allow the background image to show through where there are no fills). Since his images had embedded URLs, he enabled the Save HTML File checkbox in the Save Optimized As dialog box; this created a separate text file, which was later included in the final HTML document).

3
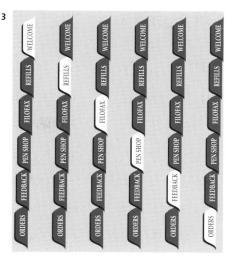

Creating versions of the tabs for each web page (grey added for contrast)

4

Using the Attributes palette to assign URLs to each non-highlighted tab

5
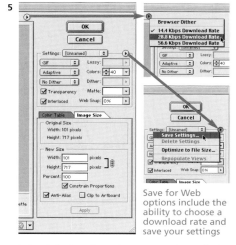

Save for Web options include the ability to choose a download rate and save your settings

Using Edit: Save for Web to save each set of tabs as an anti-aliased, interlaced, transparent GIF for use in an HTML editor; additional options and the ability to save your settings for easy re-use

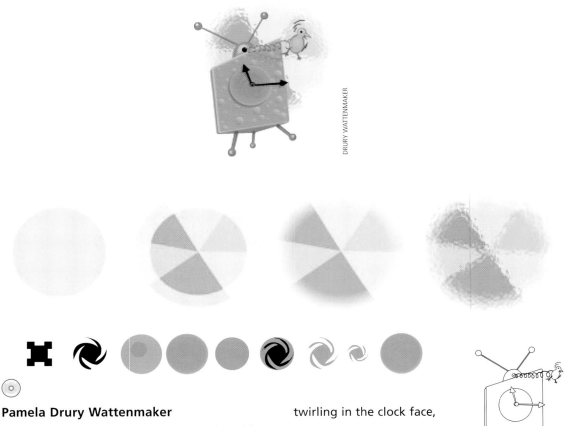

DRURY WATTENMAKER

Pamela Drury Wattenmaker

In this miniature illustration for an *Infoworld* calendar spot, Pamela Drury Wattenmaker re-created her initial sketch using the Pen tool to draw separate enclosed objects to be filled with different colors. For the background, she created two nested circles with intersecting lines drawn over the circles, and chose Divide in the Pathfinder palette. She recolored and then created blends for each pair of "pie-wedged" objects, selected all the shapes and chose Object: Rasterize at Other: 190 ppi. To this new embedded image object she applied Filter: Distort: Glass, with a Distortion of 5, Smoothness of 3 and a Frosted Texture. To create the twirling in the clock face, she created a checkerboard of rectangles, chose Unite from the Pathfinder palette, then experimented on the resulting object with the Twirl tool. Variations of this twirled shape were used as masks over nested sets of blends. The final illustration was converted to CMYK (see Note below), saved and sent to the client in EPS format.

Note: *Most of the Photoshop-compatible filters aren't available to you unless your document is in RGB color space. To convert a* copy *of your file to CMYK for printing, choose File: Document Color Mode: CMYK.*

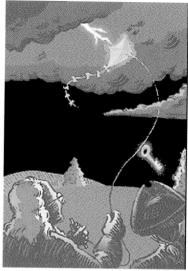

Dave Joly

Artist Dave Joly created this two-frame animation for the *National Geographic World* website for kids. Joly began this image as a traditional scratchboard illustration, then scanned the illustration and saved two versions: one scan of the full image, and one cropped detail of the key. Next he used Adobe Streamline (see the *Other* *Programs* chapter) to convert the image to Illustrator objects. In Illustrator, Joly placed the converted key objects into position on a layer above (see the *Layers* chapter for help). After saving this version as the first frame, he used the Rotate tool on the key object, created some sparkles with the Brush tool, and saved this version as the second frame.

Dave Joly

This moon is one of the Joly's animated holiday greetings characters. Mouth positioning was achieved by adjusting a few anchor points. Whenever possible, Joly uses masks in order to move objects easily—such as the eyeball. Joly made a mask the shape of the outer eye (see

the *Advanced Techniques* chapter for more on masks), then selected the blue eyeball and moved it into position for additional frames.

Web-safe Color

Special Supplement by Weinman/Heavin

To load exclusively browser-safe colors into Illustrator, directly open the Web Swatch Library file that ships with the program (and should be in your Illustrator folder). Choose File: Open, then locate the Web file in the "Swatch Libraries" folder (Web.ai for Windows)

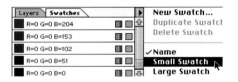

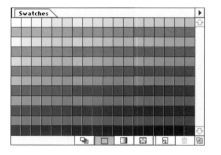

The Web library displayed by name, then shown in an expanded palette viewed by Small Swatch

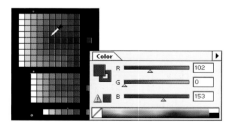

An aesthetically organized GIF format browser-safe palette for color picking, from Lynda Weinman and Bruce Heavin's book and CD-ROM Coloring Web Graphics.2 (see the Lines chapter for help storing colors as Swatches)

This section of *The Illustrator Wow! Book* was written by Lynda Weinman and Bruce Heavin, and was excerpted in part from their book *Coloring Web Graphics.2*. Their book and accompanying CD-ROM include invaluable information about screen-based color issues on the web, as well as hundreds of aesthetically organized, browser-safe color combinations and palettes for web graphics authoring. Be sure to check out Lynda Weinman's website for more information about web graphics and her book series on this subject: **www.lynda.com/books/**

RGB and web-safe colors

One of the best features of Illustrator for web graphics is its ability to work with RGB color. Like many other computer graphic programs, Illustrator was originally engineered to generate artwork for print projects, and only functioned in CMYK until Illustrator 7. With the popularity of the web, and so many Illustrator customers using this product for web graphics, Illustrator now supports the RGB color space. So, the next question is…how do you use Illustrator with "browser-safe" colors?

Browser-safe colors (also known as "web-safe" colors), for those of you not "in the know," are the 216 colors that will not dither unexpectedly (create unwanted arrangements of colored dots) within web browsers on systems with 8-bit video cards (256 colors). If you think your web audience doesn't have this color limitation, you may be wrong. Since you are a designer and work with graphics, it's likely that you have a high-end system that includes the ability to view graphics in 16-bit or 24-bit color. Most of the rest of the world use their computers for more mundane tasks, such as spreadsheets, word processing and database work. Many web surfers are using Wintel machines in 8-bit mode. If you want to create artwork with colors that will not dither on their machines, you will need to choose web-safe colors.

It would be great if you could load the web-safe colors from Photoshop, but unfortunately, the swatch interface in Illustrator is different, so you can't automatically load

Photoshop palettes into the Illustrator Swatches palette. If you want to make or use custom browser-safe color palettes, the workaround is to create browser-safe artwork in Photoshop and save it as a GIF. You can then Open or Place the GIF inside Illustrator, and use the Eyedropper tool to select any of the browser-safe RGB colors within the image. Once you've picked up a color with the Eyedropper tool, click on the New Swatch icon in the Swatches palette to store that browser-safe color as a swatch. Save the Illustrator document and the new swatch color will be stored permanently with that file. This is a useful technique if you have web artwork you've already made in Photoshop, and you want to create vector artwork that shares the same colors.

CMYK versus RGB color selection

If the values are CMYK, then change them to RGB (choose RGB from the Colors pop-up menu). The color readout will now be from 0–255, instead of in percentages. (To change colors you've already used, see the *Lines, Fills & Colors* chapter.)

The 216 browser-safe colors are constructed from combinations of six red, green and blue values: 0, 51, 102, 153, 204, 255 ($6^3 = 216$). If you use the Color palette to mix colors yourself, round off each color value to the nearest of these numbers to achieve a browser-safe color.

A few last things to keep in mind:

- You can rasterize your Illustrator images in RGB from within the program; however, the artwork may come out cleaner and crisper if rasterized in Photoshop using Place or Open (see the *Illustrator & Other Programs* chapter).
- Gradients between browser-safe colors *aren't* browser safe.
- If you are using the Eyedropper to pick colors from a GIF file, Illustrator will not let you recolor a stroke. You must transfer the color you've picked into the Illustrator Swatches palette first, using the methods described on this page, and then you can change the stroke color. This seems like a bug, or maybe it's a feature <grin>.

Make sure RGB is not CMYK!
Make sure the colors you pick with the Eyedropper tool are RGB! If the colors are CMYK, they will shift into non-browser-safe colors once the image is rasterized in RGB. Check your color palette to see if your values are in CMYK (see below). One clue that the colors are CMYK is that color values are in *percentages*. Also make sure to check both the Fill and Stroke, and check every object when changing colors so that your colors don't stray. (To update stored colors, see the *Lines* chapter)

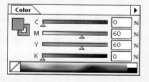

Hint: You can type browser-safe color values into the RGB palette.

Who's Who on the 9 Wow! Team

Sharon Steuer is the originator of *The Illustrator Wow! Books*, and is the managing author for this edition. She is a painter (with real paints!) and illustrator living in Connecticut with her wonderful husband Jeff, and soon to be famous cats Puma and Bear. Sharon is extremely grateful to her *Wow!* team members (past and present), Barbara Sudick (for the *Wow!* design), the *Wow!* artists, the *Wow!* testers, and all the members of the Peachpit *Wow!* team, for making this revision of the book possible.

Steven H. Gordon is the new primary co-author for Step-by-Steps and Galleries. He has too many boys to stay sane. If only they wouldn't fall off cliffs in Bryce—the National Park, not the software. Besides hiking, Steven runs Cartagram, a custom mapmaking company located at 34.7149429 N, 86.7582779 W. He thanks Sharon for this wonderful opportunity, and Monette and his mom for everything else.

Sandra Alves is the new primary co-author for the text-heavy portions of the book (the intros, *Illustrator Basics* and *Preface*). How the heck she can work at Adobe Systems AND do the *Wow!* Book is beyond us. She is a West coast (Bay Area) member of the team, where she lives with her best friend (and husband) Caleb and her two wonderful, bright and energetic daughters, Milada and Alina.

Sandee Cohen, in addition to being the one-and-only Vectorbabe, originated the role of the official *Illustrator Wow!* kibbitzer. For this edition, she expanded her role to include contributing writer and creative consultant. She is one of the three people in the world who uses brushes, hatch effects and multi strokes. Her New Year's Resolution for the year 2001 is to comprehend the Opacity & Mask Define Knockout Shape.

Diane Hinze Kanzler is the primary person in charge of retesting and updating all Step-by-Steps and Galleries from the previous edition. She also contributed transparency lessons for this edition. She has trained her Siamese cat Inkadink to say "Wow!" on command, and spends her non-digital hours hiking, kayaking, studying and drawing the natural world, and organic farming with her wacky husband, illustrator John Kanzler.

Mindi Englart is a writer, editor and designer who has has been a relief-pitcher at the last stage of this edition—editing, proofreading and doing final graphic production. She lives with her boyfriend Kiva, works as a personal coach and yoga therapist, and is yet another Libra on this project!

Cynthia Baron contributed her expertise to the Web chapter and was Sandra's editor for this edition. Besides holding down a full-time position at Northeastern University, she designs, and writes books, articles and the occasional grant proposal. While working on the *Wow!* book, she proved conclusively to her family and friends that there are more than 24 hours in a day and that cloning really is a practical technology.

Peg Maskell Korn has been Sharon Steuer's primary assistant since the first *Illustrator Wow! Book* in 1994. She is an expert in Quark production, puts up with more from Sharon than almost anyone, has a wonderful heart, and is a most dedicated *Wow!* worker.

Victor Gavenda in addition to being a tireless Peachpit employee, has been the masterer of the *Wow!* CDs, and for this edition became a *Wow!* editor and contributing writer. Victor is co-author, with Susan Kitchens, of the recently-released *Real World Bryce 4* (the software, not the park). In real life, he's also a harpsichordist and choral conductor.

Linnea Dayton is the *Wow!* series editor. She greatly enjoyed the opportunity to edit the Step-by-Step and Gallery portions of this edition. Linnea's thoroughness and patience were very much appreciated by Sharon and Steven.

Technical Notes

Book Design

Barbara Sudick is the artist behind the *Illustrator Wow!* design and typography. Using Jill Davis's layout of *The Photoshop Wow! Book* as a jumping-off point, she designed the pages in QuarkXPress, using Adobe fonts Frutiger and Minion.

Hardware and Software

With the exception of some of the testers, all of the *Wow!* staff use Macintosh computers. We use QuarkXPress 4, ALAP's XPert Tools II, Photoshop 4, 5 and 6 (depending on the user), SnapzPro2 for the screenshots (Sandee used Connectix's Virtual PC 3.0 to grab the Windows Startup Screen). Sharon is a QuicKeys (CE Software) and Action Files (Power On) addict.

Illustrator 9 Transparency, Gradient Mesh & Effects Settings for Output & Printing

Please, Adobe, make this easier next time! After running a series of tests (aided by Adobe), we came up with these settings for all five output variables in our Illustrator 9 files, based on the 150 line screen of our print output (**IMPORTANT:** Read the info and exceptions following the settings!):

① *Effect: Rasterize: Raster Effects Settings: Resolution:* **300 ppi**

② *Document Setup: Transparency: Quality/Speed:* the rightmost slider setting of **5**

③ & ④ *Document Setup: Printing & Export: Rasterization Resolution:* **300-600 ppi** / *Mesh:* **300 ppi**

⑤ *Save As: Illustrator EPS (EPS): Postscript®:* **Level 3**

The rule is: set the Transparency slider to 5, but if the image won't print at a setting of 5, try the slider at 1 (to the left)—most images print poorly with settings of 2, 3 (the default), or 4. *However*, in one case ("Bubbles" on page 230), in order to print the image correctly, the printer *had* to set the slider to 4. Make sure that all type with Effects applied is converted to outlines before final printing (see the *Type* chapter for details on how to do this). If your image includes type with Effects, or gradient mesh with Effects, the printer warns that it is possible your image *won't print correctly* no matter what the output settings! Lastly, when an image wouldn't scale properly in Illustrator (some brushed art, for instance), we scaled it in QuarkXPress instead; with such images, the Effects resolution was reduced accordingly (for example, if an image was to be scaled at 50%, we reduced the values for settings ①, ③ and ④ by 50%). We'll post new insights to: www.peachpit.com/wow

Pre-press (Color Separations, Proofs and Printing)

High Resolution, Inc. produced the films and final proofs for our first 4 editions. They scanned our photos on an Optronics ColorGetter, using Kodak Precision Color Management. Screen captures were separated in Photoshop using a GCR with maximum black generation. Our new printer, CDS Documentation Services, created film signatures and matchprints to use as proofs. Then, using the same PS3 RIP Prinergy, they generated the book using CTP (computer to plate) technology.

Acknowledgments

My most heartfelt gratitude goes to the more than 100 artists and Illustrator experts who generously allowed us to include their work and divulge their techniques.

Thanks to Adobe for letting us include the updater on the *Wow!* disk! And thanks to all at Adobe who answered our zillions of questions, with special thanks to: Ted Alspach, Leon Brown, Kim Large, Susan Gile, Dave Burkett, Marcus Chang, Jill Nakashima, and Cara Broglia.

This revision required a major team effort, and would not have happened but for an amazing group of people. Steven Gordon took on the impossible tasks of learning to write in *Wow!* style for most of the new Step-by-Steps and Galleries, finding new artists and managing the testing of the lessons. Sandy Alves did a great job working on the text-heavy portions of the introductions, the *Illustrator Basics* chapter and *What's New*. In addition to updating material from the previous edition, Diane Hinze Kanzler devised some of the essential Illustrator 9 transparency lessons, and helped with the *Wow!* disk. Peg Maskell Korn gave Sharon her unsurpassed loyalty. Victor Gavenda did a stupendous job of putting together the *Wow!* disk. Mordy Golding and Robin AF Olson were revisions co-authors for earlier editions. Gary Pfitzer edited the first two editions and prepared the stylesheet that we all lived by; Linnea Dayton, Cynthia Baron, Victor Gavenda, Whitney Walker, and Mindi Englart copyedited sections of this edition. Barbara Sudick expertly designed the layout of this book. As always, thanks also go to the stellar team of testers and consultants, especially Adam Z Lein, Lisa Jackmore and Jean-Claude Tremblay. Sandee Cohen was not only the *Wow!* creative consultant, but also our EVT (Emergency Vector Technician), and the one and only Vectorbabe.

Thanks also to Adobe, Aladdin Systems, ALAP, Aridi, Auto FX, Avenza, BareBones, Cartesia, CE Software, Chronchart, CValley, Design Tools Monthly, Dynamic Graphics, Hot Door, Image Club Graphics, LemkeSoft, Macromedia, Micro Fox Software, Photosphere, Sapphire Innovations, Strider Software, Ultimate Symbol, Vertigo Technology, and Virtual Mirror for their special *Wow!* offers.

High Resolution Inc. produced the PostScript color separations for the first four editions of this book and is now becoming a premier fine-art digital printmaking center (irisprints.com). So, for this edition, Roberta Great and Tom Mueller of CDS Documentation Services held our hands through the scary world of going direct to plate with Illustrator 9 files.

Thank you to Lynda Weinman and Bruce Heavin for adapting the Illustrator section of *Coloring Web Graphics.2*, and for allowing us to include this material.

And of course, thanks to Linnea Dayton as the *Wow!* series editor, and to everyone at Peachpit Press (especially Nancy Ruenzel, Connie Jeung-Mills, Cary Norsworthy, Mimi Heft, Kim Lombardi, Paula Baker, Jimbo Norrena, Gary-Paul Prince, and Victor Gavenda) for helping with this project.

How to contact the author…

Sharon Steuer, c/o Peachpit Press, 1249 Eighth Street, Berkeley, CA 94710, or via Internet e-mail: *wowartist@bigfoot.com*, or via the Web: *http://www.peachpit.com/meetus/authors/sharon.steuer.html*

Artists

Note: *E-mail and Web addresses will be posted on the* Wow! *website:* **www.peachpit.com/wow.html**

Acme Design Company
  see also Michael Kline
  215 North Saint Francis #4
  Wichita, KS 67201
  316-267-2263

Erik Adigard, *see* M.A.D.

Adobe Systems, Inc.
  345 Park Avenue
  San Jose, CA 95110-2704
  408-536-6000
  see also Laurie Szujewska, Ted
  Alspach, Min Wang

Agnew Moyer Smith, Inc.
  503 Martindale Street
  Pittsburgh, PA 15212
  412-322-6333

Bjørn Akselsen, *see* Ice House Press

Jen Alspach
  jen@bezier.com

Ted Alspach
  Illustrator Sr. Product Manager
  Adobe System, Incorporated
  345 Park Ave., Mailstop W11
  San Jose, CA 95110
  www.adobe.com/Illustrator

Sandra Alves
  254 Jackson Street
  Sunnyvale, CA 94086
  408-536-3044

Jack Anderson, *see* Hornall Anderson

Jeff Barney
  Barney McKay Design
  425 E. 1070 S.
  Orem, UT 84058
  801-225-9949

Kevin Barrack
  3908 Pasadena Drive
  San Mateo, CA 94403
  415-341-0115

Rick Barry
  DeskTop Design Studio
  1631 West 12th Street
  Brooklyn, NY 11223
  718-232-2484

Jennifer Bartlett
  Girvin Strategic Branding &
  Design
  1601 2nd Ave. The Fifth Floor
  Seattle, WA 98101
  206-674-7808

Kenneth Batelman
  407 Buckhorn Drive
  Belvidere, NJ 07823
  908-475-8124

Eliot Bergman
  362 West 20th Street
  New York, NY 10011

BlackDog
  Mark Fox
  239 Marin Street
  San Rafael, CA 94901
  415-258-9663

John Buchmann
  261 Tall Pines Drive
  West Chester, PA 19380
  610-324-5205

Christopher Burke
  4408 Chad Court
  Ann Arbor, MI 48103-9478
  313-996-1316

John Burns
  John Burns Lettering & Design
  1593 Parkway Drive
  Rohnert Park, CA 94928
  707 585-7604

California State Automobile
  Association
  Cartographic Department
  150 Van Ness Ave.
  San Francisco, CA 94102
  415-565-2468

Ron Chan
  24 Nelson Ave.
  Mill Valley, CA 94941
  415-389-6549

K. Daniel Clark
  3218 Steiner Street
  San Francisco, CA 94123
  415-922-7761

Sandee Cohen
  33 Fifth Avenue, #10B
  New York, NY 10003
  212-677-7763

Dan Cosgrove
  203 North Wabash Ave.
  Suite 1102
  Chicago, IL 60611
  312-527-0375

Scott Crouse
  755 W. Cummings St.
  Lake Alfred, FL 33850
  863-956-8891

Michael D'Abrosca, *see* California
  State Automobile Association

Linnea Dayton
  c/o Peachpit Press/1249 Eighth St.
  Berkeley, CA 94710
  800-283-9444

d'JAXN
  Portland, OR 97229-7609
  503-526-9573

Shayne Davidson
  Medical Illustration & Graphics
  1301 Granger Ave.
  Ann Arbor, MI 48104
  734-994-6223

Rob Day & Virginia Evans
  10 State Street, Suite 214
  Newburyport, MA 01950
  508-465-1386

Timothy Donaldson
  Domus Crossheads
  Colwich Staffordshire ST180UG
  England
  01889 88 20 43

Linda Eckstein
  201 W. 70th St. #6G
  New York, NY 10023
  212-721-0821

Eve Elberg
  60 Plaza Street East, Suite 6E
  Brooklyn, NY 11238
  718-398-0950

Mindi Englart
  145 Cottage Street
  New Haven, CT 06511
  203-752-1959

Virginia Evans, *see* Day & Evans

Gary Ferster
756 Marlin Ave., Suite 4
Foster City, CA 94404
800-953-3535

Louis Fishauf
47 Lorne Ave.
Kettleby, Ontario
Canada L0G1J0
905-726-1597

Mark Fox, *see* BlackDog

David Fridberg
Miles Fridberg Molinaroli
4401 Connecticut Ave., NW
Suite 701
Washington, DC 20008
202-966-7700

Guilbert Gates
145 West 12th/Apt 2-5
New York, NY 10011
212-243-7853
see also Jared Schneidman Design

Victor Gavenda
c/o Peachpit Press/1249 Eighth St.
Berkeley, CA 94710
800-283-9444

Kerry Gavin
154 East Canaan Road
East Canaan, CT 06024
203-824-4839

Daniel Giordan
Digi-RAMA Studios
542 Berkshire Rd
Southbury, CT 06488

Tim Girvin
Girvin Strategic Branding &
Design
1601 2nd Ave. The Fifth Floor
Seattle, WA 98101
206-674-7808

Mordy Golding
320 Leroy Avenue
Cedarhurst, NY 10001
516-239-2083

Janet Good
Industrial Illustrators, Inc.
P.O. Box 497
Harrison City, PA 15636-0497
800-683-9316

Steven H. Gordon
Cartagram, LLC
136 Mill Creek Crossing
Madison, AL 35758
256-772-0022

Caryl Gorska
414 Jackson Street/Suite 401
San Francisco, CA 94111
415-249-0139
see also MAX

Laurie Grace
New York, NY 10025
212-678-6535

Adele Droblas Greenberg
AD. Design & Consulting
202 Sixth Ave. Suite #2a
New York, NY 10013
212-431-9132

Wendy Grossman
Grossman Illustration
355 West 51st Street
New York, NY 10019
212-262-4497

Steve Hart
TIME/Editorial Art Dept
1271 Sixth Avenue/Rm 2440 D
New York, NY 10020
212-522-3677

Pattie Belle Hastings, *see* Ice House
Press & Design

Bruce Heavin
www.stink.com

Rick Henkel, *see* Agnew Moyer Smith

Eric Hess
all things illustrator…
14 Polton Bank
Lasswade, Scotland EH18 1J1

Kurt Hess, *see* Agnew Moyer Smith

Lance Hidy
2 Summer St.
Merrimac, MA 01860
978-346-0075

John Hornall, *see* Hornall Anderson

Hornall Anderson Design Works
1008 Western Ave., Suite 600
Seattle, WA 98104
206-467-5800

Ice House Press & Design
Pattie Belle Hastings
Bjørn Akselsen
266 West Rock Ave.
New Haven, CT 06515
203-389-7334

Lisa Jackmore
13603 Bluestone Court
Clifton, VA 20124
703-830-0985

Lance Jackson
LSD
1790 Fifth Street
Berkeley, CA 94710
415-777-8944

Jared Schneidman Design
16 Parkway
Katonah, NY 10536
914-232-1499
see also Guilbert Gates

Javier Romero Design Group
24 East 23rd Street, 3rd Floor
New York, NY 10010
212-420-0656

Rick Johnson
Kalmbach Publishing Co.
21027 Crossroads Circle
Waukesha, WI 53186
262-796-8776

Dave Joly
15 King St.
Putnam, CT 06260
860-928-1042

Joe Jones
Art Works Studio
802 Poplar St
Denver, CO 80220
303-377-7745

Eric Jungerman
4640 Edgewood Avenue,
Oakland, CA 94602

Diane Hinze Kanzler
15 Carrington Rd
Bethany, CT 06524

John Kanzler
15 Carrington Road
Bethany, CT 06524
203-393-1634

Andrea Kelley
451 Sherwood Way
Menlo Park, CA 94025
650-326-1083

Michael Kline
Michael Kline Illustration
1106 S. Dodge
Wichita, KS 67213
316-264-4112
see also Acme Design Company

Adam Z Lein
3 Woodlands Ave
Elmsford, NY 10523
(914) 347-1710

Joe Lertola
TIME / Editorial Art Dept
1271 Sixth Avenue / Rm 2434
New York, NY 10020
212-522-3721

Randy Livingston
Bona Fide Design
206 Ernest Street
Washington, IL 61571
309-745-1126

Patrick Lynch
Yale University C/AIM
47 College Street / Suite 224
New Haven, CT 06510
203-737-5033

M.A.D.
Patricia McShane & Erik Adigard
237 San Carlos Ave.
Sausalito, CA 94965
415-331-1023

Jacqueline Mahannah
Medical and Biological Illustration
Mahannahj@aol.com

Elizabeth Margolis-Pineo
margolispineo concept, copy &
design
138 Glenwood Avenue
Portland, ME 04103
207-773-8447

Richard Marchesseault
35 Locust St.
Naugatuck, CT 06770
203-432-3905

Rob Marquardt
Toast Design
300 First Ave North, Suite 150
Minneapolis, MN 55401
612-330-9863

MAX
246 1st Street / Suite 310
San Francisco, CA 94105
415-543-1333
see also Caryl Gorska

Greg Maxson
116 W. Florida Ave
Urbana, IL 61801
217-337-6069

Scott McCollom
808 N. Kaufman St.
Seagoville, TX 75159

Patricia McShane, *see* M.A.D.

Bert Monroy
11 Latham Lane
Berkeley, CA 94708
510-524-9412

Christopher Morris
9828 Smoke Feather Lane
Dallas, TX 75243
214-690-1328

Joachim Müller-Lancé
125 A Stillman St.
San Francisco, CA 94108

Bradley Neal, Thomas Neal
see Thomas • Bradley Illustration

David Nelson
Mapping Services
721 Grape St.
Denver, CO 80220
303-333-1060

Gary Newman Design
2447 Burnside Rd
Sebastapol, CA 95472

Charly Palmer
TP Design
7007 Eagle Watch Court
Stone Mountain, GA 30087
770-413-8276

Ellen Papciak-Rose
In The Studio
In Africa:
17 Cadoza St.
Westdene, Johannesburg
South Africa 2092
In America:
90 Westview Drive
Meriden, CT 06450

Tom Patterson
National Park Service
Division of Publications
Harpers Ferry, WV 25425-0050
304-535-6020

Daniel Pelavin
90 Varick Street, Suite 3B
New York, NY 10013-1925
212-941-7418

Cher Threinen-Pendarvis
4646 Narragansett Ave.
San Diego, CA 92107
619-226-6050

Dorothy Remington
Remington Design
632 Commercial Street
San Francisco, CA 94111
415-788-3340

Karen E. Roehr
93 Thorndike St.
Arlington, MA 02474
781-646-9933

Romero, Javier, *see* Javier

San Francisco Examiner
see Lance Jackson, Chris Morris,
Joe Shoulak

Ulrik Schoth
Brunnenhof 30
Bochum, 44866
GERMANY
+49-2327-939811

Max Seabaugh, *see* MAX

Jared Schneidman Design
155 Katonah Ave.
Katonah, NY 10536
914-232-1499

Charles Shields
Shields Design
415 East Olive Ave.
Fresno, CA 93728
209-497-8060

Mitch Shostak Studios
57 East 11th Street
New York City, NY 10003
212 979-7981

Joe Shoulak
5621 Ocean View Drive #2
Oakland, CA 94618
415-777-7974

Steve Spindler
Steve Spindler Cartography
1504 South St.
Philadelphia. PA 19146
215-985-2839

Christopher Spollen
Moonlightpress Studio
362 Cromwell Ave.
Ocean Breeze, NY 10305
718-979-9695

Nancy Stahl
470 West End Ave, #86
New York, NY 10024
212-362-8779

Sharon Steuer
c/o Peachpit Press/1249 Eighth St.
Berkeley, CA 94710
800-283-9444

David Stillman
Strider Design Studio
4841 Bay Shore Heights
Sturgeon Bay, WI 54235
906-863-7798

Barbara Sudick
California State University
Dept. of Communication Design
Chico, CA 95929
530-898-5028

Laurie Szujewska
shoe yév skä design
7045 Toma Lane
Penngrove, CA 94951
707 664 9966

Clarke W. Tate
Tate Studio
P.O. Box 339/301 Woodford St.
Gridley, IL 61744-0339
312-453-0694

Dorothea Taylor-Palmer
TP Design
7007 Eagle Watch Ct.
Stone Mountain, GA 30087
770-413-8276

Thomas • Bradley Illustration & Design
411 Center Street/P.O. Box 249
Gridley, IL 61744
309-747-3266

Threinen-Pendarvis *see* Pendarvis

Kathleen Tinkel
MacPrePress
12 Burr Road
Westport, CT 06880
203-227-2357

Ivan Torres
12933 Ternberry Ct.
Tustin, CA 92782
714-926-4356

Jean-Claude Tremblay
Illustrator Instructor & Prepress
Technician
7180 Des Erables
Montreal (Quebec)
H2E2R3

Jean Tuttle Illustration
145 Palisade Street, Suite 406
Dobbs Ferry, NY 10522
914-693-7681

Victor von Salza
Digital PhotoGraphic Arts
4918 SW 37th Ave.
Portland, OR 97221
503-246-2146

Min Wang, *see* Adobe Systems, Inc.

Pamela Drury Wattenmaker
17 South Plomar Drive
Redwood City, CA 94062
415-368-7878

Alan James Weimer
Bliss Street Illustration
67 Bliss St.
Rehoboth, MA 02769-1932
508-252-9236

Lynda Weinman
www.lynda.com

Ari M. Weinstein
ari@ariw.com
www.ariw.com

Hugh Whyte
Lehner & Whyte
8-10 South Fullerton Ave.
Montclair, NJ 07402
201-746-1335

Tom Willcockson
Mapcraft Cartography
731 Margaret Drive
Woodstock, Illinois 60098
815-337-7137

Filip Yip
P.O. Box 320177
San Francisco, CA 94132
877-463-4547

Resources

Adobe Systems, Inc.
345 Park Avenue
San Jose, CA 95110-2704
408-536-6000
www.adobe.com

AGFA
Agfa Corp.
100 Challenger Road
Ridgefield Park, NJ 07660
201-440-2500
www.agfa.com

Aladdin Systems, Inc.
Stuffit
165 Westridge Drive
Watsonville, CA 95076-4159
408-761-6200
www.aladdinsys.com

A Lowly Apprentice Production
XPert Tools
5963 La Place Court Suite 206
Carlsbad, CA 92008-8823
888-818-5790
www.alap.com

Apple Computer
800-767-2775
www.apple.com

APS Technologies
Hardware
22985 NW Evergreen Pkwy
Hillsboro, Oregon 97124
800-395-5871
www.apstech.com

Aridi Computer Graphics
Digital Art
P.O. Box 797702
Dallas, TX 75379
972-404-9171
www.aridi.com

Auto F/X
31 Inverness Center Pkwy
Suite 270
Birmingham, AL 35242
205.980.0056
www.autofx.com

Avenza
MAPublisher
6505-B Mississauga Road
Mississauga, Ontario L5N 1A6
905-567-2811
www.avenza.com

Bare Bones Software, Inc.
BBEdit
P.O. Box 1048
Bedford, MA 01730
781-778-3100
www.barebones.com

Cartesia Software
Digital Maps
PO Box 757
Lambertville, NJ 08530
800-334-4291 (x3)
www.mapresources.com

CE Software, Inc.
QuicKeys
P.O. Box 65580
West Des Moines, IA 50265
515-221-1801
www.cesosft.com

Chronchart
4640 Edgewood Ave.
Oakland, CA 94602
510-482-3576

CDS Documentation
Printer of this book
2661 South Pacific Highway
Medford, OR 97501
541-773-7575

Corel Corporation
Painter, KPT Vector Effects
1600 Carling Avenue
Ottawa, Ontario K1Z 8R7
800-772-6735
www.corel.com

Dantz
Retrospect
4 Orinda Way/Bldg C
Orinda, CA 94563
925-253-3000
www.dantz.com

DK&A PrePress
Trapper (formerly Island Trapper)
1010 Turquoise Street, Suite 300
San Diego, CA 92109 U.S.A
858-488-8118
www.dka.com/trapper.html

Dynamic Graphics Inc.
Clip art, etc.
6000 N. Forest Pk. Drive
Peoria, IL 61614
800-255-8800
www.dgusa.com

EyeWire, Inc.
(formerly ImageClub)
Fonts, Images
8 South Idaho Street
Seattle, WA 98134
www.eyewire.com

GifBuilder
Yves Piguet
Av. de la Chabliere 35
Lausanne, CH-1004
piguet@ai.epfl.ch

Graffix Plug-ins
Rick Johnson
(shareware & freeware)
2216 Allen Lane
Waukesha, WI 53186

High Resolution, Inc.
87 Elm Street
Camden, ME 04843-1941
207-236-3777

hot door
CADtools/ Transparency
101 W. McKnight Way, Suite B
Grass Valley, CA 95949
530-274-0626
www.hotdoor.com

Illom Development AB
LogoCorrector, Toolbox I
Box 838, Strandgatan 21
Ornskoldsvik, Sweden S-891 18
+46-660-786-57
www.illom.se

IRIS Graphics, Inc.
3 Federal Street
Billerica, MA 01821
978-313-4747
www.creoscitex.com/products/pro
ofing/iris/index.asp

LemkeSoft
GraphicConverter
Erics-Heckel-Ring 8a
31228 Peine, Germany
+495171 72200
www.lemkesoft.de

Letraset
www.letraset.com

Publications

Macromedia
FreeHand, Director, Flash
600 Townsend Street
San Francisco, CA 94103
800-989-3762
www.macromedia.com

Mainstay
Captivate
591-A Constitution Ave.
Camarillo, CA 93012
805-484-9400
www.mstay.com

Micro Fox Software
Screen Ruler
P.O. Box 14932
Columbus, OH 43214
614-267-8638
www.kagi.com/microfox

Pantone, Inc.
590 Commerce Blvd.
Carlstadt, NJ 07072
201-935-5500
www.pantone.com

PhotoSphere Images Ltd.
380 West First Avenue, Suite 310
Vancouver, BC V5Y 3T7
800-665-1496
www.photosphere.com

PrePRESS Solutions
Panther
29 Dunham Road
Billerica, MA 018212
978-262-8300
www.prepress.pps.com

Sapphire Innovations
PO Box 21870
Fulham, London, SW6 2FL,
United Kingdom
(0044) 020 7 795 271
www.sapphire-innovations.com

Strata, Inc.
StudioPro
567 South Valley View Drive
Suite 202
St. George, Utah 84770
435-628-5218
www.strata3d.com

Strider Software
Typestyler 3
1605 7th Street
Menominee, MI 49858
906-863-7798
www.typestyler.com

TruMatch, Inc.
50 East 72nd, Suite 15B
New York, NY 10021
800-TRU-9100
www.trumatch.com

Ultimate Symbol
Design Elements
31 Wilderness Drive
Stony Point, NY 10980
914-942-0003
www.ultimatesymbol.com

Vertigo Technology
3D Dizzy, 3D Words, 3D HotText
1255 Pender Street
Vancouver, BC V6H3Y8
888-483-7844
www.vertigo3d.com

Virtual Mirror Corporation
Vector Studio
P.O. Box 6727
San Rafael, CA 94903
866-386-7328
www.virtualmirror.com

Vision's Edge
TIFF Export
2709 Allen Road
Tallahassee, FL 32312
800-983-6337
www.visionsedge.com

WACOM
Graphics Tablets
1311 SE Cardinal Court
Vancouver, WA 98683
800-922-9348
www.wacom.com

Design Tools Monthly
400 Kiowa, Suite 100
Boulder, CO 80303-3633
303-543-8400
www.design-tools.com

John Wiley & Sons
New York, NY
www.wiley.com
Professional Photoshop 6
by Dan Margulis

Sams Books
201 W. 103rd Street
Indianapolis, IN
www.mcp.com/sams/
**Sam's Teach yourself Illustrator
9 in 24 hours** by Mordy Golding

New Riders Publishing
Indianapolis IN
800-545-5914
www.newriders.com
**Designing Web Graphics.3
Coloring Web Graphics.2**
by Lynda Weinman

Peachpit Press and Adobe Press
Berkeley, CA
800-283-9444
www.peachpit.com
Real World Adobe Illustrator 9
by Deke McClelland and Sandee
Cohen
Illustrator Illuminated, 2nd ed.
by Clay Andres
The Painter 6 Wow! Book
by Cher Threinen-Pendarvis
The Photoshop 6 Wow! Book
by Linnea Dayton & Jack Davis
The Web Design Wow! Book
by Jack Davis & Susan Merritt
**Interactivity By Design: Creating
and Communicating with New
Media**
by Ray Kristof and Amy Satran

Step-by-Step Publications
Peoria, IL
800-255-8800 / 309-688-8866
Step-by-Step Electronic Design

Yale University Press
New Haven, CT
www.yale.edu/yup/
Manual of Ornithology
by Patrick Lynch & Noble Proctor
The Shape of Time
by George Kubler

General Index

Note: *Find an expanded, searchable version of the index on the **Wow!** disk in PDF format!*

direction,
    lines, pulling out and
        collapsing; 8
    points, term description; 6
disappearing,
    paths, sources of, (Tip); 61
disclosure arrow,
    hierarchical layer contents
        revealed by; 128
Disney; 170
distance,
    determining, for a move; 19
distortion,
    3D simulation use; 229
    in box design; 275
    contour; 296
    creating brushes with; 120
    Free Transform tool use,
        (Tip); 18
    techniques; 84
    type; 171, 176
        outlining use for; 158
distribution,
    of objects along a blend,
        specification of; 183
    specified space, alignment use
        of; xxi
dithering,
    as a GIF option, (Tip); 314
Divide and Trim (Pathfinder
        filters); 64
documents,
    accessing colors from, (Tip); 63
    accessing styles, brushes, and
        swatches in; 30
    color profile, changing; xviii
    new, setting up; 1
    setup,
        File:Document Setup
            options; 3
        for transparency; 217
    sharing brushes between; 114
Donaldson, Timothy; 110, 294
doodling; 99
drag-and-drop,
    of colors, between palettes,
        (Tip); 60
dragonflies; 277
    as transparency illustration; 226
drawing(s),
    See also sketching;
    calligraphic; 100
        techniques for; 96
    curves, in creating Pattern
        brush; 104

difficulties, mask-editing mode
        role, (Tip); 239
ink, naturalistic, techniques
        for; 96
letterform paths; 110
medical; 109
    Layer Registration lesson; 146
pen, naturalistic, techniques
        for; 96
scale, coordinating preferences
        settings with; 70
drop shadows; 164, 165, 167, 223
    See also shadows;
    applying; 236
    (Tip); 105
    type art use; 294
drop-out,
    compound, avoiding, (Tip); 64
duotone,
    creating, (Tip); 215
duplicating,
    in Filters and Effects menus,
        reason for; 220
    layers; 124
        (Tip); 124
    objects, Bounding Box use; 18
dynamic(s),
    adding, Free Distort tool use
        for; 84
    blends; 182
    effects; xxii
    shapes; xxii
    styles; xxi, 15

E

e-commerce cartoon; 293
earthquakes,
    fitting masked blends to
        contoured shapes; 258
Easy Access,
    removing, importance for
        Illustrator use, (Tip); 51
Eckstein, Linda; 191
edges,
    Bounding Box and, (Tip); 25
    Photoshop vs. Illustrator
        handling, (Tip); 20
Edit Selected Paths slider
        (Paintbrush tool); 94
editable,
    text, exporting to Photoshop;
        xxiii

editing,
    See also Pathfinder filters;
    Bezier curves, tools for; 8
    brushes; 97, 110
    colors, from color libraries; 29
    gradient meshes; 206
    keyboard shortcuts; xvii
    opacity masks, (Tip); 215
    selected styles, for multiple
        objects; 14
effects,
    as appearance component; xxi
    as appearances; 15
    applying, (Tip); 222
    (chapter); 213
    as component of appearance;
        218
    designing, appearances use; 232
    filters vs.; 63, 221
    Pathfinder, applying, (Tip); 221
    printing speed cost of, (Tip); 33
Effects,
    Raster:Raster Effects Setting,
        impact on document;
        xxii
effects,
    scaling, with Transform
        palette; 19
    as style component; 15
    transparency use by; 214
Elberg, Eve; 17, 86, 200
elements,
    categories, organizing with
        layers; 144
    organization of, importance for
        transparency
        management; 24
    pattern, positioning; 82
Ellipse tool,
    creating geometric objects
        with; 10
    rendering mechanical devices
        with; 66
ellipses,
    mathematical description of; 6
embedding,
    linked images, printing
        advantages of; 32
    type; 159
    when to and when not to,
        (Tip); 284

embossing,
    effect, creating with
        appearances; 236
end caps,
    line endpoint tuning with,
        Stroke palette use; 62
    placing on blended objects; 197
endpoints,
    line, drawing options, Stroke
        palette use; 62
    path, drawing options; 62
energy,
    adding, Free Distort tool use
        for; 84
engineering drawings; 297
Englart, Mindi; 329
environment,
    working, preparing for
        exercises; 38
EPS (Encapsulated PostScript) file
        format,
    color management issues; 28
    images,
        embedding; 32
        placing; 169, 240
    importing into Illustrator; 30
Erase tool,
    functions of; 10
Evans, Virginia; 168
exercises,
    See also advanced techniques;
        lessons;
    in alternative options for same
        task; 36
    Illustrator mastery,
        (chapter); 36
    object construction; 39
    power key; 37
        rules and guidelines; 50
    Zen rotation; 48
expanding,
    appearances, (Tip); 219
    blends; 184
export,
    file formats for; 313
    SVG; 316
exporting,
    Illustrator files; 285
    to PostScript printers; 31
    settings for, (Tip); 286
extracting,
    a clipping path, (Tip); 283
Eyedropper tool,
    changing brushes with; 95
    copying type attributes with; 62

    customizing settings for; 61
    graphic style format copying;
        xxiii
    picking up color, fill, strokes,
        and text formatting with;
        61
    picking up text with, (Tip); 158
    *see*ing what it picks up, (Tip);
        158
    setting fill and stroke colors
        with; 15

F

faces,
    gradient mesh use; 211
felt marker,
    style lettering; 175
Ferster, Gary; 87, 190, 226, 264
file(s),
    size, Pathfinder palette
        reduction in; 268
fidelity,
    color, color management aids
        for handling; xvii
Fidelity option,
    Pencil, Brush, and Smooth
        tools, (Tip); 9
Fidelity (Paintbrush tool),
    customizing a calligraphic brush
        with; 97
    lower vs. higher numbers; 94
file(s),
    digital transfer of; 302
    exporting; 285
    formats,
        for export; 313
        for images to be traced,
            (Tip); 134
    palettes stored with; 327
    saving,
        for the Web; 310
        in PDF format; 286
        in PostScript for use in
            Illustrator; 282
    size,
        controlling; 32
        effects impact on; 214
        impact on Bring Forward
            and Send Backward; 130
        minimizing, (Tip); 31, 33
        natural brush form impact
            on; 103
        reducing, (Tip); 222

    transparency and effects
        impact on; 124
    transparency impact on; 214
Fill (Paintbrush tool); 94
Fill tool; 15
fill/filling,
    adding to appearances; 219
    as appearance component; xxi
    as component of
        appearance; 218
    depositing, Paint-bucket
        tool; 61
    gradient, applying, It's a
        Knockout! lesson; 242
    lines, colors and, (chapter); 60
    multiple, creating; 220
    objects; 15
    open objects, (Tip); 61
    path outline; 91
    pattern, manual trapping of,
        (Tip); 78
    picking up, Eyedropper tool; 61
    redirecting, with Gradient
        tool; 200
    in scratchboard art; 234
    setting; 60
    as style component; 15
    transparency use with; 214
    type, with patterns or
        gradients; 159
filter(s),
    Add Anchor Points,
        (exercise); 41, 43
    Adjust Colors; 61
    color modification; 61
    Edit: Select menu,
        as project organization
            tool; 74
        (Tip); 64
    effects vs.; 63, 221
    Illustrator menus and palettes
        that contain,
        See Edit: Select menu;
        See Filter menu;
        See Object: Path menu;
    Object: Path menu, (Tip); 64
    Pathfinder,
        Pathfinder Effects compared
            with; 63
        preparing for blends with; 88
        working with; 64
    Photoshop, in Illustrator,
        (Tip); 285
    requirements for application to
        text, (note); 156

opacity, masks *continued*
modeling match flames
with; 244
using; 238
as style component; 15
transparency,
control of; 246
use; 214
open/opening,
Color Picker; 60
Layer Options dialog, (Tip); 124
objects,
blending of; 196
filling, (Tip); 61
paths,
converting closed paths
to; 102
Type tool cursor, (Tip); 156
optimizing,
patterns, for printing; 83
Option key (Mac),
geometric shape manipulation,
(Tip); 10
Option (Opt) key,
how to use; 38
Options dialog,
viewing appearance attributes
with, for Eyedropper and
Paint-bucket tools; xxiii
ordering,
of objects, changing and
grouping, as benefit of
PostScript description; 6
significance in the application
of appearance
attributes; 218
organization,
See also composition; stacking;
of artist's palette of colors; 76
deleting unneeded layers and
sublayers; 140
of elements, importance for
transparency
management; 224
groups, naming conventions;
128
hierarchical layer
organization; 142
importance when working with
transparency; 218
of layers,
as information classification
tool; 145
color-coding groups of,
(Tip); 125

heterogeneous component
management with; 138
importance for effective
Knockout Group use; 242
naming strategies for; 126
of objects,
color name use for; 74
layers as a tool for; 124
reordering (Tip); 125
orientation,
paper, changing, with File: Page
Setup menu; 3
of type, selecting; 157
origin,
ruler; 24
Out of Gamut Warning,
handling, (Tip); 30
Outline mode,
Preview mode vs.; 22
setting layers to; 125
value of; 38
outlines/outlining,
blurring, modeling match
flames with; 245
converting text to, It's a
Knockout! lesson; 242
Cubist Constructs lesson use; 91
dashed strokes, (Tip); 64
letters, as mask; 166
type; 158, 163, 164, 165
(Tip); 155
Oval tool,
creating mechanical images
with; 66
overlapping,
letters and numbers,
transparency use; 228
objects, creating illustrations
using; 68
overprint,
preview, (Tip); 216

P

page,
layout programs, placing art
into; 28
setup; 1, 168
with File: Page Setup
menu; 3
Page Setup,
synchronizing Document Setup
with; 4
Use Page Setup (File: Document
Setup menu),

synchronizing Artboard
size to printer; 3
PageMaker,
creating art for placement
into; 28
Paint bucket tool,
gradient mesh creation use; 207
Paint Bucket tool,
*see*ing what it applies, (Tip); 158
Paint-bucket tool (K),
applying type attributes with; 62
depositing color, fill, strokes,
and text formatting ; 61
graphic style format
applying; xxiii
customizing settings for; 61
Paintbrush palette,
ink sketching with; 100
as Pressure alternative; 97
Random option as
alternative; 97
Paintbrush tool,
making naturalistic drawings
with; 96
setting brush preference ; 94
setting preferences for; 97
Painter; 304
developing brush strokes in; 110
Illustrator and; 283
painterly,
drawings, techniques for; 96
effects; 303
Painterly Effects lesson; 270
painting,
See also drawing; sketching;
nature scenes; 116
palette(s),
See also Action palette; Align
palette; Appearance
palette; Attributes palette;
Brushes palette;
Character palette; Color
palette; Gradient palette;
Info palette; Layers
palette; Links palette;
Navigator palette;
Paintbrush palette;
Paragraph palette;
Pathfinder palette; Stroke
palette; Styles palette;
Swatches palette;
Transform palette;
Transparency palette;
Web Swatches palette;
Windows menu;

pen,
drawings,
naturalistic; 100
naturalistic, techniques
for; 96
Pen tool,
Auto Add/Delete option impact
on; 9
Bezier curve creation with; 6
cursor feedback, (figure); 7
Direct-selection tool
interactions; 8
(figure); 8
P key selection of; 4
reflecting a profile made with,
(exercise); 43
Zen lessons, *Wow!* disk Tutorial
folder; 7, 160
pencil(s),
masked blends use; 256
sketches, as templates; 201
style lettering; 172
Pencil tool,
drawing letterform paths
with; 110
functions of; 9
Keep Selected option, as source
of disappearing paths,
(Tip); 61
manipulating traced curves
with; 132
option descriptions, (Tip); 9
tracing detailed photography
with; 134
Threinen-Pendarvis, Cher; 166
performance,
See also precautions and
warnings; size;
deleting unneeded layers and
sublayers; 140
Easy Access removal, (Tip); 51
layers slow to open, (Tips); 130
natural brush form impact
on; 103
Navigator palette impact on; 23
opacity mask issues; 254
rasterization and resolution
impact on, (Tip); 244
redraw speed, Outline view
preferred over
Preview; 22
scaling images, (Tip); 19
size; 182
Smart Guide impact on; 25

transparency and effects impact
on; 124
Web page loading; 312
perspective,
adding, Free Distort tool use
for; 85
effects; 301
Free Transform tool use,
(Tip); 18
guides; 269
maps; 307
turned-angle; 275
type design use; 178
varied, handling different views
of; 150
Photo Crosshatch filter; 255, 279
photographs,
detailed, tracing with template
layers; 134
photorealism,
See also realism;
blending techniques for; 196
Contouring Masks technique;
260
Pathfinder filter use; 88
Sketching Tools lesson; 288
Photoshop; 282, 283, 284, 287, 290,
291, 292, 293, 294, 296,
297, 298, 299, 304, 305,
306, 319
developing brush strokes in; 110
exporting layers to, (Tip); 128
file format, Illustrator support
of; 30
filters, in Illustrator, (Tip); 285
Sketching Tools lesson; 288
transparency features; xix
picking up,
color, Eyedropper tool; 61
fill, Eyedropper tool; 61
strokes, Eyedropper tool; 61
text formatting, Eyedropper
tool; 61
PICT file format,
Illustrator support of; 30
Pixar file format,
Illustrator support of; 30
pixel,
preview, (Tip); 317
units, (Tip); 316
pixel-per-inch (ppi) resolution,
printing considerations; 33
placed/placing,
art,
changing, (Tip); 140

into page layout
programs; 28
EPS images; 169
and clipping path; 240
images,
for use with letter mask; 166
printing preparation
considerations; 32
repeating patterns not able
to use; 82
type; 160
PlanTea; 164
plants; 190, 203
illustration, Tinting a Scan
lesson; 240
plugins,
SVG, required to view SVG
graphics; xix
PNG file format,
support issues; 314
point map,
creating blends with; 182
Point-type (Type tool); 154
outline type use; 166
points,
See also anchor points;
adding,
Add Anchor Points filter,
(exercise); 41, 43
Add-anchor-point tool,
(exercise); 39
(exercise); 39
aligning, with Object: Path:
Average; 13
anchor, direction point
relationship to; 6
averaging, (exercise); 41
equivalent to letter size, point
size equivalent to; 3
extraneous,
avoiding, (Tip); 8
removing, (Tip); 8
manipulating, to modify traced
curves; 132
stray, precautions on, (Tip); 254
political commentary; 292
polygon,
six-sided, creating,
(exercise); 40
three-sided, Add Anchor Points
filter use, (exercise); 41
Polygon tool,
creating geometric objects
with; 10
portraits,

Calligraphic brush use; 107
    complex layering; 149
positioning,
    pattern elements; 82
posters; 202, 246, 290, 302
    creation; 177
PostScript,
    exporting; 31
    file format, Illustrator support
        of; 31
    Level 3, required for printing
        gradient mesh objects;
        210
    new language features, (Tip); 30
    objects, working with; 6
    printing; 31
    saving files in, for use in
        Illustrator; 282
power keys,
    exercises; 37
        rules and guidelines; 50
ppi (pixel-per-inch) resolution,
    printing considerations; 33
precautions and warnings,
    back up strategies; 21
    brush strokes removed by
        Reduce to Basic
        Appearance; 219
    copying objects, before using
        filters; 89
    embedding, (Tip); 284
    file rasterization in
        Photoshop; xxiii
    graphs,
        formatting, (Tip); 16
        ungrouping, (Tip); 16
    high memory requirements,
        of complex blends; 182
        of complex masks,
            (Tips); 253
    linked images, when they are
        not, (Tip); 285
    numeric input, Transform
        palette idiosyncrasies; 19
    opacity mask issues; 254
    printing, handling Out of
        Gamut Warning,
        (Tip); 30
    RGB and CMYK; 310
    ruler origin resetting impact on
        pattern alignment; 25
    saving files, crucial importance
        of; 21
    stray points, (Tip); 254
    SWF export, (Tip); 315

transparency drawbacks; 214
transparency production of
    resolution-dependent
    artwork; xx
Precision Graphics; 265
Preferences,
    General (Edit menu), setting
        new document
        measurement units with,
        (Tip); 5
Premier; 310
preparing,
    a template; 96
    type; 160
pressure sensitive strokes,
    issues,, (Tip); 96
Preview mode,
    checking changes with; 63
    interrupting, (Tip); 22
    Outline mode vs.; 22
    setting layers to; 125
previewing,
    printer colors, soft-proofing use
        for; xviii
primitives,
    geometric, creating; 10
printer,
    color differences between
        monitor and, color
        management aids for
        handling; xvii
    synchronizing Artboard size
        to; 3
printing,
    accurate proofing
        techniques; 28
    color consistency, strategies for
        ensuring; 79
    controlling layers for; 146
    gradient mesh objects; 210
    handling layers, (Tip); 144
    handling Out of Gamut
        Warning, (Tip); 30
    hidden object issues; 129
        (Tip); 128
    layers as production tool for,
        (Tip); 126
    masks, troubleshooting
        problems with; 253
    optimizing patterns for; 83
    organizing a palette of colors
        for; 76
PostScript; 31
preparing file for; 32, 33

problems, correcting and
    avoiding; 31
proofing images for, (Tip); 30
registration, trapping as aid
    for; 78
speed, considerations
    affecting; 33
suppressing; 126
suppression, italic layer name as
    indication of, (Tip); 126
visibility and setting issues in a
    complex set of layers; 147
Private Chef; 176
process,
    colors, Soft Mix filter
        conversion of spot colors
        to, (Tip); 91
Process colors,
    accessing; 74
Proctor, Noble S.; 66
product illustrations; 199, 264
    contouring blends use; 196
production,
    workflow, appearances as
        facilitation tool; 232
profile,
    color,
        changing; xviii
        viewing, (Tip); xviii
Progress Software Company; 76
project management,
    changing the Layers palette
        display; 143
Projecting-cap end cap; 62
proofing,
    images, (Tip); 30
    requirements, for accurate
        printing; 28
proxy,
    rectangles,
        See also Bounding Box;
        moving complex images
        with, (Tip); 18
PS3 (PostScript 3) language,
    new language features, (Tip); 30
PSD format,
    export to Photoshop in; xxiii

Q

QuarkXPress; 302
    creating art for placement
        into; 28
    Illustrator and; 285

R

radial gradients; 201
  relocating center of; 200
  transparency use, in making
      highlights; 230
raised surface,
  effect, creating with
      appearances; 236
RAM (Random Access Memory),
  allocating, (Tip); 5
rasterization,
  of art, for the screen; 311
  as danger of transparency
      use; 214
  effects; 238
  of hatches; 279
  high-resolution, Sketching
      Tools lesson; 288
  Illustrator and; 282
  images,
      in Illustrator; 284
      printing speed
          considerations; 33
      registration not a problem
          for; 78
      repeating patterns not able
          to use; 82
      sampling, with Eyedropper
          tool; 61
  potential with transparency
      use; xx
  preview, (Tip); 317
  resolution,
      and, (Tip); 244
      interaction; 220
  vector to, preview of; xviii
Ray Dream Designer,
  Illustrator and; 283
Ray Dream Studio; 306
realism,
  See also photorealism;
  blending techniques for; 196
  controlling tonality, with
      contoured masks; 260
  detailed; 106
  geometry role in; 66
  translucency handling of; 301
recording,
  actions,
      creating a new set; 27
      object selection in, (Tip); 26
Rectangle tool,
  creating geometric objects
      with; 10

creating mechanical images
    with; 66
rectangles,
  mathematical description of; 6
refining,
  elements of a book cover
      design; 169
Reflect tool,
  (exercises); 49
  reflecting a Pen profile,
      (exercise); 43
  Shear tool hidden in; 21
reflection(s); 265, 274
  controlling the amount of
      opacity in; 225
  creating, with contouring
      blends and masks; 262
  curves, in creating Pattern
      brush; 104
  (exercises); 49
  geometry tool use in
      creating; 66
  handling; 21
  metallic, creating; 194
  of a Pen profile, (exercise); 43
  as transformation; 18
registration,
  impact of Paste In Front
      and Paste In Back
      alignment; 129
  of layers, for a series of
      drawings; 146
  marks, setting up the Artboard
      with; 168
  trapping,
      as aid for; 78
      issues and solutions,
          (Tip); 28
releasing,
  blends; 184
  guides; 25
Remington Designs; 79
Remington, Dorothy; 79
removing,
  anchor points, Pen tool cursor
      feedback, (figure); 7
  cropmarks; 169
  Easy Access, importance for
      Illustrator use, (Tip); 51
  overlaps, from combined
      objects; 68
renaming,
  views; 23, 145
rendering,

architectural details, with
    blends; 188
  illustrations, observation as key
      role in; 66
reordering,
  objects,
      paste command lessons,
          Wow! disk; 129
      (Tip); 125
repeating patterns,
  designing; 82
replacing,
  appearances, (Tip); 221
  brushes; 94
  missing fonts; 157
  styles; xxi
      (Tip); 221
requirements,
  computer and system; 1
resetting,
  Bounding Box; 18
  gradients, to the default settings,
      (Tip); 203
Reshape tool; 20
resizing,
  selections, (Tip); 4
  text, (Tip); 158
resolution,
  high-resolution rasterization,
      Sketching Tools
      lesson; 288
  independence,
      Sketching Tools lesson; 288
      transparency impact on; xx
      transparency impact on,
          (Tip); 33
  ppi, printing considerations; 33
  rasterization and, (Tip); 244
  rasterization interaction; 220
  scanning artwork for template
      use; 132
  settings, (Tip); 286
  specifying for a brush in
      Photoshop; 110
reversing,
  blends; 184
  brush strokes, (Tip); 114
RGB (Red Green Blue),
  CMYK color matching issues
      and partial solutions; 27
  color; xvii
      sliders, (Tip); 63
  converting CMYK to; 311
  converting to CMYK, (Tip); 27
  Web-safe; 326

(Tip); 315
  working in; 28, 310
Ringling Brothers Barnum &
    Bailey,
    Layering Colors lesson; 136
Rocket Scientist; 298
Roehr, Karen; 177
Rotate tool,
  Mark Fox use; 69
rotating,
  exercises on; 48
  Free Transform tool use,
      (Tip); 18
  objects,
    Bounding Box use; 18
    (exercise); 40
  as transformation; 18
  Zen lessons, *Wow!* disk Tutorial
      folder; 169
Round-caps; 62
  creating highlights with; 67
Rounded Rectangle tool,
  rendering mechanical devices
      with; 66
rows,
  text, setting up; 157
ruler(s); 24
  See also measurement units;
  changing measurement units
      with, (Tip); 5
  guides, creating; 25
  origin,
    Paste In Front and Paste In
        Back positioning with
        respect to; 129
    setting; 168
  recentering, (figure); 15

S

sable brush,
  simulation; 259
safety,
  See precautions and warnings;
sampling,
  Eyedropper tools use; 61
San Francisco Examiner;
        192, 267, 292, 303
sand,
  creating from a gradient
      mesh; 117
SandeeC's Mix Soft Chart,
  Wow! disk Plug-ins folder; 87
Saturate filter; 61
Save for Web export plug-in,

(Tip); 313
saving,
  files,
    crucial importance of; 21
    in PostScript for use in
        Illustrator; 282
  gradients, (Tips); 185
  images, for tracing, (Tip); 134
  settings for, (Tip); 286
  views; 23, 145
scalable,
  art, preparing for the Web; xix
Scale Strokes & Effects; 33
Scale Strokes & Effects checkbox,
  resizing selections with; 4
Scale tool,
  resizing selections with; 4
  scaling brushes with, (Special
      Brushes Supplement); 120
scaling,
  3D simulation use; 229
  brushes, (Tip); 94
  brushes impact on; 33
  design elements, as graph
      customization
      technique; 17
  drawing scale, coordinating
      preferences settings
      with; 70
  (exercises); 49
  Free Transform tool use,
      (Tip); 18
  objects,
    Bounding Box use; 18
    to an exact size, (Tip); 19
  performance considerations,
      (Tip); 19
  selections, (Tip); 4
  self-adjusting scales,
      creating; 112
  strokes, handling problems
      with; 236
  as transformation; 18
  Zen lessons, *Wow!* disk Tutorial
      folder; 169
Schneidman, Jared;
        73, 188, 198, 229, 266
Scientific American,
  map of Greenland; 134
Scissors tool,
  creating a Pattern brush
      with; 104
  functions of; 10
  splitting closed paths with; 102
scratchboard art; 101

techniques for creating; 234
screens,
  anti-aliasing benefits, (Tip); 7
searching,
  for hidden sublayers, (Tip); 143
seascapes; 191
seashells; 98
selecting,
  actions; 26
  all objects, (Tip); 128
  all strokes made with a Scatter
      brush; 113
  color space, for a new
      document; xvi
  difficult elements, Lasso tools
      use in, (Tip); 32
  empty text paths, (Tip); 64
  key object, for alignment, with
      Align palette; xxi
  layers, (Tip); 124
  objects; 11
    as layer-switching technique,
        (Tip); 137
    color name use for; 75
    difficulties with, (Tip); 64
    in a group, (Tip); 11
    Lock and Unlock All (Object
        menu) use; 129
    strategies for, (Tip); 127
    to mask; 251
    with Layers palette; 130
  singular points, (Tip); 64
  targeting vs.,
    in Basic Transparency
        lesson; 225
    (Tip); 129
  text,
    as object, (Tip); 155
    (Tip); 155
  tools, using keyboard; 4
  type,
    as an object; 154
    as text; 154
    objects, targeting vs.,
        (Tip); 219
  unpainted objects, (Tip); 64
  within masks; 251
Selection tools,
  grouping objects with; 12
  selecting objects with; 11
selective,
  editing, of multiple objects; 14
separating,
  objects, Pathfinder palette
      use; 63

separation,
    of colors, in an artist's
        palette; 77
sequence,
    of drawings, layer registration
        techniques; 146
series,
    of drawings, layer registration
        techniques; 146
service bureaus,
    strategies for obtaining color
        consistency from; 79
setting(s),
    default appearance, with
        Eyedropper tool; 61
    for exporting, (Tip); 286
    fill; 60
    resolution, (Tip); 286
    for saving, (Tip); 286
    stroke; 60
    type; 171
setting up,
    new document; 1
    page; 1
        with File: Page Setup
            menu; 3
shadows; 265
    See also drop shadows;
    blends use for; 187
    creating; 67, 241
    details, Soft Mix (Pathfinder
        palette) use; 89
    drop; 164, 165, 167
    embossed effect use; 237
    geometry tool use in
        creating; 66
    as mask; 209
    semitransparent; 227
    simplifying; 241
shapes,
    clip art, modifying; 102
    complex, opacity mask use in
        blending; 238
    conversion of; xxii
    creating objects, (exercises); 49
    geometric,
        creating manually; 10
        rendering mechanical
            equipment with; 66
    letterform paths; 110
    serious fun with, (Tip); 10
sharing,
    brushes between documents; 114
Shear tool; 21
shearing,

3D simulation use; 229
Free Transform tool use,
    (Tip); 18
as transformation; 18

Shields Design 86
shift key,
    geometric shape manipulation,
        (Tip); 10
Shoulak, Joe; 192, 274
Show Original option,
    checking changes with; 63
    Object: Path: Simplify menu;
        xxii
showing,
    layers; 125
Silicon Graphics' Alias Sketch; 305
Simplify (Object: Path menu),
    as filter; 63
    optimizing patterns for printing
        with; 83
    options, (Tip); 63
    path simplification with; xxii
    reducing points in paths
        with; 112
simplifying,
    shadows; 241
single-key,
    navigation and tool selection; 4
        disabled in text blocks; 5
size,
    file,
        controlling; 32
        effects impact on; 214
        impact on Bring Forward
            and Send Backward; 130
        minimizing, (Tip); 31
        natural brush form impact
            on; 103
        Pathfinder palette reduction
            in; 268
        reducing, (Tip); 222
        transparency and effects
            impact on; 124
        transparency impact on; 214
    paper, changing, with File: Page
        Setup menu; 3
    points equivalent to letter size; 3
sizing,
    object, controlling, in technical
        illustration; 70
sketching,
    See also drawing; Pencil tool;
    ink; 100
    multiple strokes use; 235

pencil, as templates; 201
sketchy line brush, (Special
    Brushes Supplement); 120
tools; 288
sketchy line brush,
    creating, (Special Brushes
        Supplement); 120
skewing,
    (exercises); 49
    perspective; 85
skills,
    Illustrator, mastery exercises,
        (chapter); 36
slicing,
    objects, (Tip); 12
sliders,
    color, (Tip); 63
    moving multiple, (Tips); 76
Sliding Design,
    of graph elements; 17
Smart Guides; 24
    components and use, (Tip); 25
Smithsonian Jazz Orchestra; 302
smoke,
    Masking Opacity lesson; 244
smooth shading,
    printing advantages of; 31
Smooth tool,
    functions of; 9
    Keep Selected option, as source
        of disappearing paths,
        (Tip); 61
    option descriptions, (Tip); 9
    Simplify (Object: Path menu)
        compared with; xxii
smoothing,
    letterform paths; 110
    paths, Simplify (Object: Path
        menu) use; xxii
    zooming as tool for
        controlling; 135
Smoothness option,
    Pencil, Brush, and Smooth
        tools, (Tip); 9
Smoothness (Paintbrush tool),
    customizing a calligraphic brush
        with; 97
    lower vs. higher numbers; 94
snap-aligning,
    geometric objects, centers use
        for; 10
Snoopy; 80, 150
soft-proofing,
    setting up, (Tips); xvii
    term description; xvii

space,
saving, (Tip); 31
spacebar key,
geometric shape manipulation,
(Tip); 10
spaces,
color, *See* color, spaces;
showing; 158
special,
characters, showing; 158
speed,
of blend, controlling, (Tip); 182
printing, considerations
affecting; 33
Spindler, Steve; 108
spine,
of a blend, path use; 183
blend, replacing; 193
Spiral tool,
creating geometric objects
with; 10
splitting,
closed paths; 102
Spollen, Christopher; 298
spot-color,
defining and organizing; 74
modification, impact on blends
and gradients containing
it, (Tip); 187
Soft Mix filter conversion to
process, (Tip); 91
stacking order,
appearances; 220
layers,
changing, (Tip); 125
controlling; 128
Stahl, Nancy; 138, 141, 193, 231
Standard Screen Mode tool (F); 23
Star tool,
creating geometric objects
with; 10
stars,
creating Scatter brushes for; 116
starshine,
creating; 266
starting,
object, Pen tool cursor
feedback, (figure); 7
startup,
documents, using and creating,
(Tip); 3
Startup page,
selecting, for a new
document; xvi
status line,

information on, (Tip); 21
stencils,
Illustrator paths as; 283
STEUER pumpkin blend.ai,
Wow! disk Blends folder; 184
Steuer, Sharon; 50, 81, 87, 96, 98,
116, 176, 206, 230, 328,
Wow! disk
Stillman, David; 300
stitching,
handling, (Tip); 217
Stroke palette; 62
strokes,
creating scratchboard art
with; 234
storing,
gradients; 186
straight line,
converting curved lines into,
with Simplify (Object:
Path menu); xxii
Straight Lines option,
Object: Path: Simplify menu;
xxii
Strata 3D Studio Pro,
Illustrator and; 283
Streamline; 303
converting scanned charcoal
mark into Illustrator
object; 99
Illustrator and; 282
streams,
creating, with tapered
brushes; 113
stretching,
letters; 163
Strider Software's TypeStyler 3,
Illustrator and; 283
Stroke palette; 60
changing line end caps with; 62
purpose, (Tip); 60
stroke(s),
color, applying to a brush; 95
Stroke tool; 15
strokes,
adding to appearances; 219
as appearance component; xxi
of color, gradient mesh use to
move; 208
as component of appearance;
218
depositing, Paint-bucket
tool; 61
multiple,

creating multiple lines
with; 220
sketching effect of; 235
objects; 15
offsetting, in scratchboard
art; 235
outlining dashed strokes,
(Tip); 64
path, deletion by some
Pathfinder filters; 64
picking up, Eyedropper tool; 61
pressure-sensitive, issues,
(Tip); 96
rescaling, handling problems
with; 236
reversing brush strokes,
(Tip); 114
scaling, with Transform
palette; 19
setting; 60
simulating gradients in; 185
as style component; 15
transparency use with; 214
weight, including, (Tip)
Preference: Use Preview
Bounds); 60
weights, scaling, (Tip); 4
structures,
nested hierarchical layer
organization; 142
stuffed animals; 320
Style palette,
relationships with Layers,
Appearance, and
Transparency palettes; xx
styles; 222
See also appearances;
as appearances; 15
applying; 222, 237
to objects; 15
assigning, to groups; 233
(chapter); 213
components of; 15
copying, with Eyedropper
tool; 61
creating; 222, 233, 237
scratchboard art with; 234
custom startup documents use,
(Tip); 3
graph, changing; 16
as group work unification
tool; 234
merging, (Tip); 222
in other documents,
accessing; 30

label hints, as Smart Guides, (Tip); 25
linking multiple blocks of, (Tip); 154
as mask, for images; 252
object, creating, (Tip); 156
palette fields, measurement unit changing; 13
picking up with Eyedropper tool, (Tip); 158
resizing, (Tip); 158
selecting,
    as object, (Tip); 155
    (Tip); 155
    type as; 154
Tab-delineated, as graph import format; 16
transparency use with; 214
type objects, (Tip); 219
wrapping, in Area-type; 156
textures; 116
applying to vector objects, hatches use for; 254
creating with brushes,
    (Special Brushes Supplement); 121
    Wow! disk Brushes Supplement folder; 121
The Matrix; 174
The Secret Garden; 148
The Traveling Radio Show; 176
themes,
styles as implementation tool for; 235
Thomas • Bradley Illustration & Design,
Practical Path-cuts lesson; 88
Reflective Masks technique; 262
Unlocking Realism lesson; 194
Threinen-Pendarvis, Cher; 166
thumbnails,
border, changing color of, (Tip); 23
layer, managing; 127
tick marks,
creating evenly spaced; 114
TIFF file format,
Illustrator support of; 30
placing images, for use with letter mask; 166
tiles; 277
pattern, creating; 81
Tim Girvin Strategic Branding & Design; 174

time,
printing, file size impact on, (Tip); 31, 33
Tinkel, Kathleen; 7, 159
tints/tinting,
colors, with an artist's palette; 77
creating; 67
filling objects with; 67
scanned images; 240
stroke, applying to a brush; 95
tolerance,
options for Pencil, Brush, and Smooth tools, (Tip); 9
tool(s),
Add-anchor-point, (exercise); 39
Auto Trace, cleaning up after using, with Simplify filter; 63
Bezier-editing; 8
Direct-select Lasso, properties of; xxiii
Direct-selection, path editing with; 6
Ellipse, rendering mechanical devices with; 66
Eyedropper,
    copying type attributes with; 62
    customizing settings for; 61
    graphic style format copying; xxiii
    picking up color, fill, strokes, and text formatting with; 61
Free Transform, Free Distort use; 64
keyboard selection of; 4
keyboard shortcuts, changing; 5
Lasso,
    Photoshop compared with Illustrator; xxii
    properties of; xxiii
options, Eyedropper and Paint-bucket; xxiii
Oval, creating mechanical images with; 66
Paint-bucket,
    applying type attributes with; 62
    customizing settings for; 61
    depositing color, fill, strokes, and text formatting with; 61

graphic style format applying; xxiii
Pen, Bezier curve creation with; 6
Rectangle, creating mechanical images with; 66
Rounded Rectangle, rendering mechanical devices with; 66
for sketching; 288
Smooth, Simplify (Object: Path menu) compared with; xxii
tips,
as valuable learning tool; xvi
enabling/disabling; xvi
finding keyboard equivalents for tools with; 4
use, (Tip); 1
tolerance options, (Tip); 9
tornados,
fitting masked blends to contoured shapes; 258
Torres, Ivan; 211, 244, 301
Toyo library,
selecting colors from; 29
toys; 320
tracing,
from beneath a placed image; 136
detailed photographs; 134
templates; 132
trains; 297
Transform palette; 19
modifying transformations, (Tip); 19
as transformation tool; 18
transformations; 18
for animation; 318
applying as an effect, (Tip); 220
gradients, into masked blends, (Tip); 261
isometric, *Wow!* disk, (Tip); 71
multiple, Transform Each (Object: Transform menu) handling of; 21
numeric specification, Transform palette use; 19
of objects, with isometric formulas; 70
of outline type, (figure); 159
repeating, (Tip); 18
temporary, Distort & Transform (Effect menu); 21

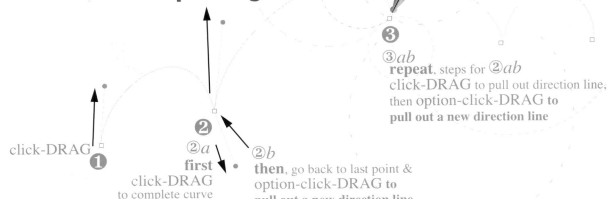

Windows Finger Dance Summary *from "The Zen of Illustrator"*

Object Creation — *Hold down keys until AFTER mouse button is released.*

⇧ Shift	Constrains objects horizontally, vertically or proportionally.
Alt	Objects will be drawn from centers.
Alt click	Opens dialog boxes with transformation tools.
	Spacebar turns into the grabber Hand.
Ctrl	Turns cursor into the Zoom-in tool. Click or marquee around an area to Zoom in.
Ctrl Alt	Turns cursor into the Zoom-out tool. Click to Zoom out.
Caps lock	Turns your cursor into a cross-hair.

Object Selection — *Watch your cursor to see that you've pressed the correct keys.*

Ctrl	The current tool becomes the last chosen Selection tool.
Ctrl Alt	Current tool becomes Group-selection to select entire object. Click again to select next level of grouping. To move selection release Alt key, then Grab.
Ctrl Tab	Toggles whether Direct-selection or regular Selection tool is accessed by the Ctrl key.
⇧ Shift click	Toggles whether an object, path or point is selected or deselected.
⇧ Shift click	With Direct-selection tool, click on or marquee around an object, path or point to toggle selection/deselection. **Note:** *Clicking inside a filled object may select the entire object.*
⇧ Shift click	Clicking on, or marqueeing over objects with Selection or Group-selection, toggles selection/deselection (Group-selection chooses objects within a group).

Object Transformation — *Hold down keys until AFTER mouse button is released.*

⇧ Shift	Constrains transformation proportionally, vertically and horizontally.
Alt	Leaves the original object and transforms a copy.
Ctrl Z	Undo. Use Shift-Ctrl-Z for Redo.

To move or transform a selection predictably from within dialog boxes, use this diagram to determine if you need a positive or negative number and which angle is required. (*Diagram from Kurt Hess/Agnew Moyer Smith*)

Windows Wow! Glossary of Terms

Ctrl **Alt**	**Ctrl** will always refer to the Ctrl (Control) key. **Alt** will always refer to the Alt key, and is used to modify many of the tools.
← ↑ → ↓	The keyboard Cursor-keys: Left, Up, Right, Down.
Toggle	Menu selection acts as a switch: choosing once turns on, again turns it off.
Marquee	With any Selection tool, click-drag from your page over object(s) to select.
Hinged curve	A Bézier curve that meets a line or another curve at a point.
Direct-selection **Group-selection** **Selection**	*Direct-selection* tool selects points and paths. *Group-selection* tool. The first click always selects the entire object, subsequent clicks select "next group-up" in the grouping order. *Selection* tool (selects the biggest grouping which includes that object— if an object is ungrouped, then only that object is selected). **Note:** *See the* Basics *chapter for help with selection tools.*
Select object(s)	Click on or marquee with Group-selection tool to select entire object. Click on or marquee with the regular Selection tool to select grouped objects.
Deselect object(s)	To Deselect *one* object, Shift-click (or Shift-marquee) with Group-selection tool. To Deselect *all* selected objects, with any selection tool, click outside of all objects (but within your document), or press Shift-Ctrl-A.
Select a path	Click on a path with the Direct-selection tool to select it. **Note:** *If objects are selected, Deselect first,* then *click with Direct-selection tool.*
Select anchor points	Click on path with Direct-selection tool to see anchor points. Then, Direct-select marquee around the points you want selected. Or, with Direct-selection tool, Shift-click on points you want selected. **Note***: Clicking on a selected point with Shift key down deselects that point.*
Grab an object or point	After selecting objects or points, use Direct-selection tool to click and hold down mouse button and drag to transform entire selection. **Note:** *If you click by mistake (instead of click-and-hold),* Undo *and try again.*
Delete an object	Group-select the object and press the Delete (or Backspace) key. To delete grouped objects, use the Selection tool, then Delete.
Delete a path	Direct-select a path and press the Delete (or Backspace) key. If you delete an anchor point, both paths attached to that anchor point will be deleted. **Note:** *After deleting part of an object the entire remaining object will become selected; therefore, deleting twice will always delete the entire object!*
Copy or Cut a path	Click on a path with Direct-selection tool, then Copy (Ctrl-C) or Cut (Ctrl-X). **Note:** *See the* Windows Finger Dance *Summary for more ways to copy paths.*
Copy or Cut an object	Click on an object with Group-selection tool, then Copy (Ctrl-C) or Cut (Ctrl-X). For grouped objects, Click on one of the objects with the Selection tool, then Copy (Ctrl-C) or Cut (Ctrl-X).